ISBN 978-1-331-15041-1
PIBN 10150957

This book is a reproduction of an important historical work. Forgotten Books uses
state-of-the-art technology to digitally reconstruct the work, preserving the original format
whilst repairing imperfections present in the aged copy. In rare cases, an imperfection in
the original, such as a blemish or missing page, may be replicated in our edition. We do,
however, repair the vast majority of imperfections successfully; any imperfections that
remain are intentionally left to preserve the state of such historical works.

1 MONTH OF
FREE
READING

at
www.ForgottenBooks.com

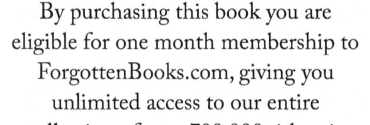

By purchasing this book you are eligible for one month membership to ForgottenBooks.com, giving you unlimited access to our entire collection of over 700,000 titles via our web site and mobile apps.

To claim your free month visit:
www.forgottenbooks.com/free150957

English
Français
Deutsche
Italiano
Español
Português

www.forgottenbooks.com

Mythology Photography **Fiction**
Fishing Christianity **Art** Cooking
Essays Buddhism Freemasonry
Medicine **Biology** Music **Ancient**
Egypt Evolution Carpentry Physics
Dance Geology **Mathematics** Fitness
Shakespeare **Folklore** Yoga Marketing
Confidence Immortality Biographies
Poetry **Psychology** Witchcraft
Electronics Chemistry History **Law**
Accounting **Philosophy** Anthropology
Alchemy Drama Quantum Mechanics
Atheism Sexual Health **Ancient History**
Entrepreneurship Languages Sport
Paleontology Needlework Islam
Metaphysics Investment Archaeology
Parenting Statistics Criminology
Motivational

THE

SHÁHNÁMA OF FIRDAUSÍ

DONE INTO ENGLISH BY

ARTHUR GEORGE WARNER, M.A.

AND

EDMOND WARNER, B.A.

"The homes that are the dwellings of to-day
Will sink 'neath shower and sunshine to decay,
But storm and rain shall never mar what I
Have built—the palace of my poetry."

FIRDAUSÍ

VOL. VII

LONDON
KEGAN PAUL, TRENCH, TRÜBNER & CO. L^{TD}
BROADWAY HOUSE, CARTER LANE, E.C.
1915

Printed by BALLANTYNE, HANSON & Co.
at the Ballantyne Press, Edinburgh

PREFATORY NOTE

The publication of this translation has advanced sufficiently to enable me to state that it will be completed in nine volumes, the last of which will include a General Index to the whole work.

E. W.

CONTENTS

THE SASÁNIAN DYNASTY (*continued*)

BAHRÁM GÚR—

vii

BAHRÁM GÚR (*continued*)

SECT.   PAGE

13. How Bahrám went to the Chase and espoused the Daughters of the Thane Barzin . . . 48

14. How Bahrám slew Lions, went to the House of a Jeweller, and married his Daughter . . . 55

15. How Bahrám went to the Chase and passed the Night in the House of Farshídward . . . 67

16. How a Bramble-grubber revealed the Case of Farshídward, and how Bahrám bestowed that Householder's Wealth upon the Poor . . 70

17. How Bahrám went to the Chase and slew Lions . 74

18. How Bahrám went to hunt the Onager, showed his Skill before the Princes, and returned to Baghdád and Istakhr 80

19. How the Khán of Chin led forth a Host to war with Bahrám, and how the Íránians asked Quarter of the Khán and submitted to him . 84

20. How Bahrám attacked the Host of the Khán and took him 89

21. How Bahrám took a Pledge from the Túránians, how he set up a Pillar to delimit the Realm, and placed Shahra upon the Throne of Túrán . 90

22. How Bahrám wrote to announce his Victory to his Brother Narsí and returned to Írán. . . 92

23. How Bahrám wrote a Letter of Directions to his Officials 96

24. How Bahrám called before him the Envoy of Cæsar, and how the Envoy questioned and answered the Archmages 101

25. How Bahrám dismissed Cæsar's Envoy and charged his own Officials 106

26. How Bahrám went with his own Letter to Shangul King of Hind 109

27. How Shangul received the Letter from Bahrám and made Reply 114

28. How Shangul prepared a Feast for Bahrám, and how Bahrám displayed his Prowess . . . 116

29. How Shangul suspected Bahrám and kept him from Írán 118

30. How Bahrám fought with the Wolf at the Bidding of Shangul and slew it 121

PART I. NÚSHÍRWÁN'S ADMINISTRATION, *etc.* (*continued*)

THE SHÁHNÁMA

b

ABBREVIATIONS

C.—Macan's edition of the Sháhnáma
L.—Lumsden's   do.
P.—Mohl's   do.
T.—Tihrán   do.
V.—Vullers'   do.

BLRE. History of the Lower Roman Empire.   By J. B. Bury.

DZA.   Professor Darmesteter's Trans. of the Zandavasta in the
       Sacred Books of the East.   Reference to Parts[1] and
       pages.

EHI.   The History of India as told by its own Historians.   By
       Sir H. M. Elliot, K.C.B.

EP.   Eastern Persia, an Account of the Journeys of the
       Persian Boundary Commission, 1870–71–72.

GDF.   The History of the Decline and Fall of the Roman
       Empire.   By Edward Gibbon, Esq.   With Notes by
       Dean Milman and M. Guizot.   Edited, with additional
       Notes, by William Smith, LL.D.

GIP.   Grundriss der Iranischen Philologie . . . von Wilh.
       Geiger und Ernst Kuhn.

HS.   Syntagma Dissertationum quas olim auctor doctissimus
       Thomas Hyde S.T.P. separatim edidit.

JFB.   The earliest English version of the Fables of Bidpai . . .
       now again edited and induced by Joseph Jacobs.

MHP.   History of Persia.   By Sir John Malcolm, G.C.B

MM.   Maçoudi: Les Prairies d'Or.   Texte et Traduction par
       C. Barbier de Meynard et Pavet de Courteille.

NIN.   Das Iranische Nationalepos von Theodor Noldeke.

---

[1] The second edition of Part I is referred to unless otherwise
specified.

NPS.   Nöldeke : Persische Studien. II. Sitzungsberichte der Kaiserlichen Akademie der Wissenschaften. CXXVI. Band.

NT.   Geschichte der Perser und Araber zur Zeit der Sasaniden . . . von Th. Nöldeke.

RM.   The Rauzat-us-safa ; or, Garden of Purity . . . By . . . Mirkhond . . . Translated . . . by E. Rehatsek.

RSM.   The Seventh Great Oriental Monarchy. By George Rawlinson, M.A.

WPT.   Dr. E. W. West's Translation of the Pahlavi Texts in the Sacred Books of the East. Reference to Parts and pages.

ZT.   Chronique de Abou-Djafar-Mo'hammed-Ben-Djarir-Ben-Yezid Tabari, traduite . . . Par M Hermann Zotenburg.

NOTE ON PRONUNCIATION

á   as in "water."

í   as in "pique."

ú   as in "rude."

a   as in "servant."

i   as in "sin."

u   as in "foot."

ai as in "time."

au as in *ou* in "cloud."

g   is always hard as in "give."

kh as *ch* in the German "buch."

zh as *z* in "azure."

IV

THE SÁSÁNIAN DYNASTY

(Continued)

XXXV

BAHRÁM GÚR

HE REIGNED SIXTY-THREE YEARS

ARGUMENT

Bahrám's accession and inaugural measures. His adventures, amorous and otherwise, among his subjects. His relations with foreign potentates. His instructions to his officials, and remission of taxation. His introduction of the Gipsies into Írán, and his death.

NOTE

Bahrám Gúr (Varahran V., A.D. 420–438) is said by Tabarí and Mas'údi to have been twenty years old at the time of his accession.[1] According to Tabarí he reigned either eighteen or twenty-three years.[2] Mas'údí says the latter.[3] On the other hand Mír Khánd, who tells us that he followed the most generally received account, perhaps Firdausí's own, states that Bahrám reigned sixty-three years.[4] No doubt popular tradition lovingly prolonged to the utmost the reign of this Sháh who, like James V. of Scotland, was a "King of the Commons." The poet was at no loss for material in this part of his work, and the reign is the most diverting in the Sháhnáma. Its interest with regard to the question of the provenance of the *Arabian Nights* has been noted already.[5] As is to be expected in the circumstances the subject-matter is largely legendary, though some authentic features have been preserved, and there can be little doubt but that Bahrám's own character as depicted by Firdausí is in the main historically correct. He fulfilled the promises made by him when a candidate for the throne,

---

[1] NT, p. 98; MM, ii. 190.   [2] NT, p. 112.   [3] MM, *id.*
[4] RM, Pt. I., Vol. ii. p. 362.   [5] See Vol. vi. p. 250.

but gave himself up largely to pleasure, though this does not seem
to have impaired his activities at critical moments. He appears, too,
to have been fortunate in his administrators. His chief minister,
Mihr Narsí, who is not to be confounded with Narsí, the Sháh's
brother, and three of his sons were at the head of affairs. One
was the principal, or nearly so, of the official hierarchy, another
was chief superintendent of the taxes, and the third was com-
mander-in-chief.[1] Mihr Narsí and his father Buráza are stated to
have held office under Yazdagird, Bahrám's father, and the former
was reappointed chief minister when Yazdagird, Bahrám's son,
came to the throne.[2] He was himself a prince and an Arsacid, so
it would seem that the supplanted family had regained a great
position for itself under the new dispensation, and that the state of
things fully justified the pronouncement put by later legend into
the mouth of Kaid.[3] Bahrám Gúr began his reign with a persecu-
tion of the Christians, which led to war with the Eastern Roman
Empire. There is a slight allusion to such a war in the poem,[4] but
the chief incident recorded to have taken place is a pacific one.[5]

§§ 1 and 2. Bahrám devotes the first days of his reign to
carrying out his promises of reform made before his accession,[6]
and to the relief of taxation.

§§ 3–16. We have here a series of popular legends of Bahrám's
adventures when going about unrecognised among various classes
of his subjects.[7] The story of the miser occurs twice.[8]

§§ 19–22. We have here the story of Bahrám's most famous
exploit, which is historical, though as much cannot be said of the
various details with which popular appreciation has embellished it.
Historically, the foes over whom Bahrám won his great triumph
were the Haitálians, or White *Huns*.[9] This is clear on Firdausí's
own showing when he comes to the reign of Pírúz.[10] Later on
again, in the reign of Núshírwán, ample distinction is made
between the subjects of the Khán of Chín and the Haitálians.[11]
In substituting the former for the latter on this occasion Firdausí
errs in good company. Tabari, Mas'údi, and Mír Khánd all name
the Turks as the enemy,[12] and since they did not come upon the
scene for another century and more,[13] we learn approximately the

[1] NT, pp. 106, 108 *seq.*   [2] ZT, ii. pp. 122, 127 ; NT, pp. 113.
[3] See Vol. vi. pp. 256, 267.   [4] See p. 84.   [5] See p. 100 *seq.*
[6] See Vol. vi. p. 406.   [7] *Cf.* Vol. vi. p. 250.
[8] §§ 4 and 15 *seq.*   [9] See Vol. i. p. 19.
[10] See p. 164 *seq.*   [11] See p. 328 *seq.*
[12] NT, p. 99 ; MM, ii. 190 ; RM, Pt. I., Vol. ii. p. 357.
[13] See Vol. i. p. 20.

earliest date at which the story of Bahrám's exploit could have
been edited in its existing form. According to the Persian Tabarí[1]
—the version adapted from the original Arabic by Bal'amí, the
minister of the Sámánid prince Mansúr, son of Núh (A.D. 961–976),
about A.D. 963—the Khán was put to flight, according to the Arabic[3]
slain in the battle by Bahrám's own hand. Both agree that the
Khátún, or wife of the Khán, was taken prisoner and sent to serve
in the famous Fire-temple at Shíz, whither Bahrám had gone to
pray for success in his expedition.[3] According to the Arabic
Tabarí, Bahrám, as an act of thanksgiving for his victory, relieved
his subjects of taxation for three years.[4] This probably is the
popular version of the fact that great reforms in that connexion
were effected during his reign, but they could not have been
justified, one would think, to the extent stated by the amount of
plunder taken from the Haitálians, and still less to the extent
described in the Sháhnáma, which affirms that he almost reformed
taxation away altogether. It may be added that the various
accounts of Bahrám's expedition against the Haitálians are in
substantial accord though they differ in detail, e.g. as to how far
the enemy had advanced at the time of the battle, the route that
Bahrám followed in his march, and the number of troops that he
took with him.

§ 24. Bahrám's war with the Eastern Roman Empire, in which
he was not very successful, came to an end in A.D. 422, but Firdausí
(§ 19) makes it synchronise with that against the Haitálians which,
according to the Persian Tabarí,[5] took place five years later. Next
we hear of an envoy sent by Cæsar (§§ 19, 23), and then of his be-
lated audience with the Sháh. The points discussed are not the
terms of peace, but certain " hard questions,"[6] and it is only inci-
dentally that the envoy mentions that Rúm is ready to pay tribute
to Írán. We have a similar case in the reign of Núshírwán when
the Rája of Hind sends the game of chess to that Sháh, who
returns the compliment with the game of nard,[7] while in the next
volume we shall find the disgraced counsellor Búzurjmihr regaining
the favour of the same Sháh by his success in solving another
problem set by Cæsar.

§§ 26–38. For instances in the Sháhnáma of kings going
incognito to visit foreign courts, see Vol. vi. pp. 325, 335. In the
Arabic Tabarí, Bahrám's motive for visiting Hind is to see whether
by annexing a portion of it he could lighten the taxes of his own

[1] ZT, ii. 120.   [2] NT, p. 101.
[3] See p. 86; ZT, ii. 121; NT, 104.   [4] NT, 105.
[5] ZT, ii. 119.   [6] As to which see p. 102 seq.   [7] See p. 384 seq.

subjects.[1] Unlike his expedition against the Khán of Chin, as Firdausí puts it, and historically against the Haitálians, the one to Hind appears to be wholly fabulous. It is given, however, at length by Tabarí and Mír Khánd, and mentioned by Mas'údí.[2]

It will be seen that Bahrám in the course of his well meant efforts to promote the welfare of his subjects does not find it quite so easy as he expected to make everybody happy by legislation.

§ 39. Professor Noldeke is inclined to consider Bahrám's importation of Gipsies from Hind to Írán historical.[3] The details of course belong to the province of popular legend, but are delightfully characteristic of both parties concerned. The Gipsy language appears to be a debased form of Hindústáni. According to Mír Khánd the Gipsies intermarried with the Persians, and the Jats were said to be their offspring. Consequently nearly every Jat is a musician.[4]

§ 40. Firdausí is almost alone in his statement that Bahrám Gúr died in his bed. The common account is that he was killed when out hunting by falling into one of the underground watercourses, so common in Persia, and that his body never was recovered. Popular tradition places the scene of his death in a valley between Shíráz and Ispahán and known as the "Vale of Heroes," where there are numerous springs supposed to be intercommunicating and of great depth. Sir John Malcolm states that one of his escort was drowned in 1810 when bathing in the identical spring in which Bahrám is said to have perished.[5] Tabarí lays the scene of the accident in Media, and it took place, if it took place at all, probably not far from Hamadán at a spot called, according to Dínawarí, Dái Marj. Nóldeke, however, considers that the whole story was made up to account for the nickname "Gúr" bestowed upon Bahrám. The word in question means both "onager" and "tomb."[6] The same collocation of letters also means a "Fire-worshipper," and it is possible that some Muhammadan translator from the Pahlaví may have thought fit to dispatch the guebre to the grave.

[1] NT, p. 106.
[2] *Id.* RM, I, ii. 360 ; MM, ii. 191.
[3] NT, p. 99 *note.*
[4] RM, I, ii. 357.
[5] MHP, i. 94 and *note.*
[6] NT, 103 and *note.*

§ 1

*How Bahrám ascended the Throne, charged the Officers,
and wrote Letters to all the Chiefs*

Whenas Bahrám Gúr sat upon the throne
The sun acclaimed him while the Sháh adored
The Maker—the all-seeing, watchful World-lord,
The Lord of victory and majesty,   C. 1488
The Lord of increase and of loss—then said :—
" From Him have I received the throne and crown,
For He hath fashioned fortune, and my hopes
And fears are all in Him.   I give Him thanks
For all His benefits ; do ye too praise Him,
And strive to keep His covenant unbroken."
    The Íránians answered : " We are girt for service.
May this crown prove right glorious to the Sháh,
And may his heart and fortune live for ever."
    Their praises done, all scattered gems before him.
Thus said Bahrám : " O chiefs experienced
In daily good and ill ! we all are slaves,
And God is One, sole-worthy to be worshipped.
From fear of evil days we will secure you,
And not expose you to malignant Need."
    He spake.   They rose and homaged him anew.
They spent the night in converse, and at sun-rise
The Sháh sat peacefully upon his throne,
The Íránians came to audience, and he said :—
" Ye chieftains famed and favoured by the stars !
Put we our trust in God and joy in Him,
Boast not and root out of the world our hearts."
    He spake and then those Glories of his court—
His chiefs—called for their steeds. The Sháh, the
        third day,
Sat on the throne, and said : " Religious usage

Must be observed.   We witness to God's being,
And make our souls familiar with the Faith.
There is a Resurrection, Heaven, and Hell,
And we can not escape from good and ill.
Ascribe not Faith or knowledge to the man
That doubteth of the Day of Reckoning."
   The fourth day, donning on the ivory throne
The   well-loved   crown,   he   said :   " Men,   not   my
      treasures,
Are my delight.   This Wayside Inn I ask not,
And grudge not going, for the other world
Is everlasting and this transitory.[1]
Abstain from greed and trouble not thyself."
   The fifth day he said thus : " I have no joy
In others' toils for mine aggrandisement ;
We toil in quest of jocund Paradise ;
He that hath sown but seed of good is blest."
   The sixth day said he to his subjects : " Never
May we ensue defeat ; we will protect
Our troops from foes and make malignants tremble."
. 1489   The seventh day, when he took his seat, he said :—
" Ye chiefs wise, wary, and experienced !
Since with the vile we practise villainy
We will have conversation with the wise.
Ye that are cold to me shall fare still worse
Than with my sire, but ye that do my will
Must not experience sorrow, pain, and toil."
   The eighth day, when he took his seat, he bade
Call Jawánwí of those about the court,
And said to him : " To every mighty man,
To every chief and clime, indite for me
A letter couched in just and loving terms,
And say : ' Bahrám hath mounted on the throne
With joy—a lord of bounty and of right,
A shunner of all fraud and knavery—

------

[1] Reading with P.

For he hath Grace and stature, love and justice :
The Judge all-holy is in all his thoughts.
" I will accept," he saith, " the obedient,
But fault-condoning maketh faults increase.
I sit upon my glorious father's throne,
I keep the customs of just Tahmúras,[1]
And treat all justly howsoe'er perverse.
I will be juster than mine ancestors,
And guide you to the Faith—that of Zarduhsht,
The prophet—quitting not my fathers' path.
I put the Faith of old Zarduhsht before me ;
The way of that true prophet is mine own.
Be ye all sovereign in your own affairs,
And guard your marches and your loyalty,
Kings of your children and your women-folk :
Blest is the man that is both wise and pure.
If God accord us life and favouring stars
We will not fill our treasury with gold ;
Such treasures keep the poor in travail. Read
This joyful letter which assureth you
Of lasting wealth and honour. To all kings
Our greeting, most to those whose warp and woof
Are love." ' "
     They sealed the letters and made choice
Of glorious envoys. Archmage, man of lore,
And wary cavalier, those letters bore.

§ 2

How Bahrám pardoned the Fault of the Íránians, farewelled
* Munzir and Nu'mán, and remitted the Íránians' Arrears*
* of Taxes*

Next day when Sol rose, when the hills bulked large,
And sleep was broken, to Munzir there came

   [1] For Tahmúras see Vol. i. p. 125.

A panic-stricken throng and said to him :—

C. 1490

" Make intercession for us with the Shâh
To pardon our offences, for the crimes
Of Yazdagird so wrought us that the blood
Froze in the nobles' hearts ! So much of foul
In word and deed, iniquity, distress,
And anguish chilled our hearts toward Bahrám .
Because we suffered so beneath his sire."
  Munzir's warm pleadings mollified the Shâh,
Who being just and noble pardoned all,
Whate'er the fault. He decked the imperial palace,
And all the good and great resorted thither.
When they had got the place of majesty
In readiness they seated there the worthy,
In every place they spread the board and called
For wine and harp and minstrelsy. Next day
Another crowd assembled, yet the chief
Was wearied not of giving. On the third
There were both revels and festivities,
And grief was banished from the world-king's palace.
He told the offices done by Nu'mán
And by Munzir—those men of stainless birth—
On his behalf, and all the chiefs acclaimed
Those desert dwellings and those men of war.
The Shâh next oped his treasury and filled
His palace with brocade and gold, steeds, trappings,
Mail-coats and scents [1] and gems of every hue.
He gave all to Nu'mán and to Munzir,
And Jawánwí told o'er to them the gifts.
None matched the Shâh in bounty and in travail.
He gave the other Arabs many presents,
So that they left the royal halls, rejoicing.
He then had brought a royal robe of honour,
A steed, and raiment of a paladin ;
These gave they to Khusrau, made much of him,

    [1] Reading with P.

And seated him upon the glorious throne.
Then, turning from Khusrau,[1] the king of kings,
Descending from his throne, approached the seat
Where sat Narsi—a prince, his younger brother,
And one with him in heart and tongue. He made
Narsi the captain of the host to set
The land in order, gave up to his keeping
The host at large, and ravished all the realm
With bounty, oped the treasury, and paid
The troops who gladdened with dinárs. The Sháh,
That man of lore, then bade Gushasp, the scribe,
With prudent Jawánwí, the chief accountant,
Approach, and ordered them to cancel all
Arrears of taxes for the Íránians.
These two wise scribes went to their registers,   C. 1491
And in this matter called in aid Kaiwán
Because he was the expert of the day,
And kept the world's statistics in his breast.
They added up the sum of the arrears,
And found it ninety and a hundred times
Three hundred thousand drachms.[2] These he forgave,
And burnt the registers, and all Írán
Rejoiced thereat. Whenas all folk were ware
Of that event they praised him mightily.
They all flocked to the Fire-fanes, to the halls
Where New Year's Day and Sada feast were kept,
Flung musk upon the Fire and blessed Bahrám,
The Sháh. Thereafter he dispatched officials
To go about the world. He sought and gathered
Within a certain city all the exiles
Of Yazdagird that thus the monarch's letter
Might reach those noble Persians, and inquire
Their wishes, sent each chief a robe of honour,
And gave to each a province that befitted
His station. Noble, archimage, and marchlord,

---

[1] *Id.*   [2] *Cf.* p. 215, *note.*

Whoever heard Bahrám's deliverance,
All visited his court with open hearts,
And blithe of countenance. He bade each suitor
Repair to the high priest and, when the world
Had recognised his bidding, he let stand
A herald at his gate thus to proclaim :—
" Ye subjects of the watchful Sháh ! abstain
From sorrow and from sin, and praise henceforth
Him through whose justice earth is prosperous.
Take refuge from the world with God alone,
For He possesseth all and helpeth all.
The man that giveth heed to our command,
Not turning from our path and fealty,
To him will we increase our benefits,
And clear our mind of hate and covetise ;
But whosoever shunneth what is just
Shall suffer retribution at our hands.
If God hereafter shall vouchsafe us strength,
And matters turn out to our heart's content,
We will add benefit to benefit,
And ye shall utter praise on our account."
    At these words all the people of Írán
Went full of joy and bright of countenance,
And, as the sovereignty became secure,
Joy waxed and sorrow minished, while the Sháh
In feasting, horsemanship upon the Ground,
In sport and polo, full employment found.

§ 3

How Bahrám went to the House of Lambak, the Water-
carrier, and became his Guest

C. 1492   It happened that Bahrám Gúr went one day
With certain warriors to hunt the lion.

An old man, staff in hand, drew near to him,
And said : " God-fearing Sháh ! within our city
There are two men, one rich, the other poor.
Now Baráhám, the Jew, a miscreant knave,
Is rich in silver and in gold.   Lambak,
The water-carrier, is of noble nature,
Fair-spoken, hospitable."
                              So Bahrám
Inquired about the two, their words and ways.
A worthy said : " Lambak, the water-carrier,
O great, famed, noble king l is generous,
Doth keep a table, and is well disposed.
He passeth half the day in water-carrying,
The other half in entertaining guests,
And leaveth nothing over for the morrow,
While Baráhám is but a barren Jew,
And grasping, and his greed should be exposed.
He hath drachms, treasure, and dínárs, brocades,
And goods of all kinds, but none seeth his bread,
And he is ever wrathful at a guest." [1]
    The Sháh then bade a herald : " Go, proclaim
Before the court : ' To every one concerned :
The water of the water-carrier,
Lambak, is bad to drink.' "
                              He stayed till Sol
Grew pale, then mounted a fleet steed and came,
Like wind, toward the dwelling of Lambak,
Knocked with the ring against the door, and cried :—
" A captain of the Íránian host am I,
The night is dark, and I have far to go.
Let me lodge here to-night.   I will behave
With honour and discretion."
                              Then Lambak,
Pleased with the voice of one that spake so fairly,
Made answer straight : " Come in, O cavalier !

----

[1] This line is inserted from P.

And may the king approve thee. If ten others
Were with thee it were better : each had been
A moon above my head."

     Then Sháh Bahrám
Dismounted, and Lambak saw to the steed.
He gladly rubbed it down and haltered it,
Then, when Bahrám was seated, ran and brought
A chess-board [1] and made shift to furnish food,
And all things needful, saying : " Noble sir !
Put by the chess-men and begin thy meal." [2]

 The eating done, the host in high delight
Brought out a cup of wine. The Sháh was all
Amazement at that feast of his, kind speech,
And cheery mien, passed night there, and at dawn
Woke at the salutation of Lambak,
Who said : " Thy steed, good sooth, fared ill last
  night.
Stay just this one day with me, and if thou
Wouldst have a comrade we will summon one,
And find the needful. Joy with me one day."

 The king made answer to the water-carrier :—
" I have not much on hand to-day."

       Lambak
Departed, taking divers water-skins,
But nobody appeared to buy his water.
In dudgeon he put off his vest and, taking
His porter's knot and bucket in his arms,
Went and procured instead at the bázár
Meat and dried curds, and in due course put on
The pot. His guest took note of all his trouble.
Lambak prepared the meal ; they ate and drank,
And had another sitting. All that night
Bahrám had wine in hand ; Lambak too loved it.

· 1493

---

[1] According to the poet's own showing later on, chess was not intro-
duced into Persia till the reign of Núshírwán. See p. 384 *seq.*
[2] Couplet omitted.

When it was day he hurried to Bahrám,
And said : " Be merry night and day, and franked
From trouble, grief, and toil.   Consort with me
For yet another day, for, know, thy presence
Is life and goods to me."

                    " Now God forbid
That we should not be happy for a third day,"
Bahrám said, while the water-carrier blessed him :—
" Be merry in thy heart and mate with fortune."
    He took to the bázár his water-skins
And tackle, which he pledged to some rich man,
Bought what he needed and returned in haste
Rejoicing to Bahrám, and said to him :—
" Help with the food, for man must eat."

                                Bahrám
Took the meat promptly from him, cut it up,
And then proceeded with the cookery.
When they had eaten they took wine and goblet,
And first of all drank to the king of kings.
Lambak, when they had drunk, prepared for sleep,
And set a candle by Bahrám Gúr's couch.
The fourth day, when the sun shone and Bahrám Gúr
Awoke, his host approached and said : " Famed sir !
Thou hast resided in this small, dark house,
And doubtless in discomfort ; still if thou   C. 1494
Fear'st not the Shah stay in my mean abode
Two se'nights more if so thou hast a mind."
    Then Shah Bahrám blessed him and said : " Live
       thou
Thy years and months in mirth and happiness.
We have been jolly in this house three days,
While quaffing to the monarchs of the world,
And elsewhere I will speak a word for thee
That shall make bright thy heart and plans, for why
Thy hospitality shall yield thee fruit,
And, if thou perseverest, thrones and crowns."

Dust-swift he put the saddle on his steed,
Departed merrily and sought the chase.
He hunted on till night the hills 'gan ride,
Then lightly from his meiny turned aside.

§ 4

How Bahrám went to the House of Baráhám, the Jew,
who treated him scurvily

He stole away and made toward the house
Of barren Baráhám, knocked at the door,
And said : "The Sháh hath come back from the
    chase,
But I was left behind. 'Tis night and I
Know not the way, can find not Sháh and escort.
If I may sojourn in this house to-night
I will not trouble any one."
                   A slave
Went and reported this to Baráhám,
Who answered : "Trouble not thyself hereat,
But say : 'Thou wilt not get a lodging here.' "
    The messenger departed to Bahrám Gúr,
And said : "There is no shelter here for thee."
    Bahrám replied : "Return to him and say :
'I mean to stop. I ask thee for a lodging
To-night and I will trouble thee no further.' "
    The servant, hearing this, ran back and said :—
"This horseman will not budge to-night and saith
As much in many words."
                  Said Baráhám :—
"Go instantly and say : 'This house is small.
The Jew is very poor and every night
Reposeth, bare and hungry, on the ground.' "
    They gave the message, and Bahrám Gúr said :—

" If here my lodging will prove troublesome
I will not enter but will sleep outside
The door, 'tis all I want."

     Said Baráhám :—

" Brave horseman ! thoughtlessly [1] thou troublest me.
Were any one to rob thee in thy sleep
I should be plagued enough on thine account.
Come in if thou art in distress and want,   C. 1495
But on condition that thou askest naught.
I have not e'en a napkin wherewithal
To wipe my body when 'tis washed at death,
Or shroud wherein to wind it."

        " My good sir ! "
Bahrám rejoined, " I will not trouble thee
In any way. Thy portal will suffice.
I will be watchman, barring bell and cry.'

 Then Baráhám was troubled, and his soul
A brake of cares. He thought : " This saucy fellow
Will not depart. How can I cause him trouble
About his steed ? " then said again : " Great sir !
Thy many words afflict me. If thy steed
Shall leave its droppings here and stale or break
The tiles, thou shalt remove its dung at dawn,
Sweep up, bear off its refuse to the plain,
And pay for any breakages at once."

 Bahrám replied : " I pledge my head to this."
Dismounting from his steed he tethered it
With its own bridle and unsheathed his sword.
He spread his saddle-cloth, used as his pillow
The saddle, and reposed upon the floor.
The Jew secured the door, brought victuals forth,
And sat him down to eat.   " O cavalier l "
He said, " remember, having heard, this saw :—
' Who hath may eat and who hath not look on.' "

 He answered : " I have heard so from of old,

     [1] Or " grievously."

And now I have beheld made manifest
What thou hast quoted from a sage's words."
    The Jew brought wine forth and, when satiate
With food and blither for the drinking, bawled :—
" O toilful horseman ! list this ancient saw :—
' He that hath food and purposeth to eat
Will offer his thanksgiving for the meat,
For one of substance hath a happy mind,
And in his wealth a coat of mail will find ;
But Empty Pockets is a dry-lipped wight,
And, like thee, ravenous at mid of night.' "
    Bahrám replied : " 'Tis passing wonderful
What I have seen, and must not be forgotten,
And if thy goblet give thee good at last
Then heigh for drinker, wine, and genial cup ! "
    When o'er the mountains Sol displayed its sword
Bahrám Gúr shunned more sleep and put the saddle
On his fleet grey. His saddle ! Nay, hard pillow.
Came Baráhám and said : " O cavalier !
Thou art not faithful to thy word. Thou saidst :—

C. 1496

' I will sweep up the droppings of the steed
At once.'   Away with them as thou didst promise.
I am annoyed by a dishonest guest."
    Bahrám Gúr answered : " Go and fetch a slave.
He will remove the droppings fast enough,[1]
And I will give him gold for sweeping up,
And bearing off, the refuse to the plain."
    " No one have I," he said, " to sweep up refuse,
Take it away, and fling it in the ditch.
Break not thy promises deceitfully ;
Let me not say that thou hast played the knave."
    Bahrám Gúr, hearing, took another course.
He had a dainty handkerchief of silk
Inside his boot, all musk and spicery ;
He took it out and put therein the droppings,

[1] Reading with P.

Then flung them all together in the ditch.
Away went Baráhám and snatched it up
While Sháh Bahrám stood dazed. " Oho ! " said he,
" Thou scrupulous ! If the great king shall hear
Of all thy nobleness he will secure thee
From want in this world, and will set thee high
Among the chiefs."
                                    He went back to his palace,
And all night long was planning what to do.
Within his halls thought banished all repose,
He laughed himself but kept the matter close.

§ 5

How Bahrám bestowed the Wealth of Baráhám upon Lambak

Next morn he donned his crown and held an audience,
Then called to him Lambak, the water-carrier,
Who came before him with enfolded arms.
They brought withal and quickly Baráhám,
That curst, malicious Jew. When he arrived
They made him sit and called an honest man,
To whom the Sháh said : " Take some baggage-beasts
And, acting with the utmost honesty,
Go to the house of Baráhám forthwith,
And look thou bring what thou find'st hoarded there."
    That honest man went to the Jew's abode.
The house was all brocade, dínárs, and raiment,
All carpetings, and draperies, and hoards.
There was a caravanserai attached,
And no room too on earth for all the goods—
Gold, silver, every gem, and, on the top
Of every bag, a lofty diadem.
The archmage's reckoning failed. He called for camels,

A thousand from the desert of Jahram,

1497 And packed the baggage but much still remained.[1]
That good man drove apace the caravans,
And, when the bells resounded from the court-gate,
Went and informed the Sháh : " As many gems
Are here as in thy treasury, yet are left
Two hundred ass-loads ! "
                          Thought the Sháh, amazed :—
" The Jew hath greatly toiled, but to what profit
Since food hath failed him ? "
                          Then the Sháh, the world-lord,
Bestowed a hundred camel-loads of gold,
Of drachms, of carpets, and things great and small
Upon the water-carrier.   Lambak
Departed with his treasures.   Then the Sháh
Called Baráhám and said to him : " O thou
Consorting in thy meanness with the dust !
Dost tell me that thy prophet was long-lived,
And yet bewail life's superfluities ?[2]
A horseman came and quoted me this saw,
Out of the sayings of the past, which saith :—
' Hath will enjoy and Hath not withereth.'
So now withdraw thy grasping hand and watch
Henceforth the enjoyment of the water-carrier."
   Then to that vile Jew of the synagogue
He spake at large of droppings, handkerchief
Gold-woven, and tiles, bestowed upon the knave
Four drachms, and said : " Take this as capital ;
No more befitteth thee.   To mendicants
Thy wealth, to thee thy head."
                          He gave the poor
All that there was.   The Jew departed wailing.
The Sháh gave up the house to plundering ;
'Twas well that other folk should have their fling.

[1] Reading with P.
[2] If your prophet managed to live long on little so can you.

§ 6

How Bahrám slew Lions and forbade Wine-drinking

He found employment for the hunting cheetah,
Bestirred him and was minded for the chase.
He mounted him upon a speedy steed,
And pricked forth to the plain with hawk on hand.
He found a wood that was a rich man's seat.
It was as verdurous as Paradise,
And there was neither man nor beast in sight.
He said : "Here lions should be found. No man
Of prudence would sleep here."

                     He entered in,
And rode about surveying it. He saw
A lion there and that he must employ
The scimitar. He shouted at the beast
And, when it bravely charged him, rode outside
The forest, blazed forth like Ázargashasp,   C. 1498
And, when the lion followed, strung his bow,
A hero he, shot and transfixed the creature
Through side and heart ; that of the lioness
Grew all a-flame, and she too charged Bahrám,
Roared out and clawed at him. The cavalier
Smote with his sword her loins, and that brave beast
Gave up the fight. Now in the wood there dwelt
A country magnate, a God-fearing man,
Whose name was Mihr Bidád. That sword-stroke
    charmed him.
With sweet words on his tongue that old man left
The wood, drew near the Sháh, blessed him, did
    reverence,
And said : " O famous chief ! may fortune's star
Be at thy beck. A rural chief am I,
O holy one ! and owner of this march,

This tilth, and mansion, ox and ass and sheep.
Those lions caused me sorrow and despair ;
Now by thy hand, thy thumb-ring, and thy hilt
God hath removed them.   Tarry in our wood,[1]
And I will bring thee milk and wine and honey.
I have as many lambs as thou canst want
With trees fruit-laden that will furnish shade."

The Shâh alighted and surveyed the forest ;
He found it verdurous, supplied with streams,
And fitted for a young man's dwelling-place.
Then Mihr Bidád went and fetched minstrelsy
As well as divers of the village-chiefs.
He slaughtered numbers of fat sheep and came,
Gold cup in hand.   When they had eaten bread
The servants set on cups of wine with roses
And fenugreek.   The host quaffed one and gave
Another to Bahrám and took all pains
To set him at his ease.   When Mihr Bidád
Grew blithe with wine he said : " Fair-fortuned hero !
Thou favourest the Shâh or the full moon
At midnight."

Said Bahrám : " Yea, that is so ;
The King of kings designed this face of mine.
He maketh as He willeth, waxing not
Nor waning, but if I am like the Shâh
Then I have given thee this seat and forest."

This said, he mounted, sought his pleasure-palace,
Bemused, but sleepless in the garth all night
Romanced about the lips of the beloved.

. 1499   Next morn he took his seat and called for wine.
The captains of the host approached rejoicing,
And with the others came a noble man
Who from his village brought a gift of fruit—
Pomegranate, apple, quince, in camel-loads,
And posies fashioned for imperial use.

----

[1] Reading with P.

The world-lord, seeing him, saluted him,
And seated him among the paladins.
The lord that brought the posies and the fruit
Bore in the olden tongue the name Kírwí.
While he was joying to behold the Sháh,
The nobles, and the banquet-hall, he spied
A crystal goblet filled with wine which proved
His ruin.   Reaching out among the lords
He grasped it, rose, and drank " The king of kings ! "
Then cried : " A toper I, my name Kírwí.
Since in the presence of the king of kings
I drain the goblet I will drain again."
    This said, he drained the goblet seven times,
And distanced all the other revellers.
Then by the Sháh's permission he departed
To learn if he could bear off all that wine.
He left the jovial city for the plain,
And when the wine was warm within his breast
He galloped from among his retinue
Toward the hills, dismounted, chose him out
A quiet, shady spot, and slumbered.   Came
A black crow from the mountains and pecked out
His eyes !   His escort following found him dead
And eyeless with his roadster by his side,
And wailed o'er him and at such revelry.
    Now when Bahrám had wakened in his chamber
A courtier came to him, and said : " A crow
Hath pecked out both Kírwí's bright eyes while he
Was lying drunk among the hills."
                                    The world-lord
Grew pale of cheek thereat and sorrowful,
And from the palace proclamation issued :—
" Ye men of name endowed with Grace and sense !
Wine is a thing forbidden in the world
Alike to paladin and artisan."
    Thus passed a year while all held wine forbidden

E'en when the Sháh himself held revelry,
Or called for tales from old time legendry.

§ 7

*The Story of the young Shoemaker, and how Bahrám
allowed Wine again*

C. 1500 Now at that time a young shoemaker wedded
A virtuous wife, rich and of good repute,
But failed in nuptial duty, and his mother
Lamented bitterly his grievous case.
Howbeit she had some wine in store. She took
Her son to her own house and bade the youth :—
"Drink seven cups to hearten thee. Perchance
Thou mayest break this stubborn seal to-night.
How can a woollen mattock mine in stone ?"
   He quaffed cups seven or eight, and verily
His feet and hide waxed strong. The cups had made
The young man confident ; he came, achieved
His purpose, and then went back to his mother
In high delight thereat, and thus it chanced :
A lion of the Sháh's had broken loose,
And came along the road. Now at the time
The shoemaker was still in drink—a sea
That made his fingers thumbs. He ran, bestrode
The roaring lion, and then reaching out
He clutched its ears. The lion had been fed ;
The youth maintained his seat. Post-haste the keeper
Came running after them, a chain in one hand,
A lasso in the other. He beheld
A shoemaker upon the lion's back,
Perched there like some bold rider on an ass,
Ran to the palace-gate, came unabashed
Before the Sháh, and told about the wonder

That he had seen, with his own eyes, and none
Beside had heard.   The world-lord all amazed
Called the high priest and chiefs, and bade the former:—
" See what the stock of this shoemaker is.
If he shall prove a paladin by birth
'Tis well, for courage fitteth paladins."
   They sought and asked his mother : " Is his rank
Above his station ? "
              When the talk grew long
She hurried to the Sháh and told him all,
First doing her obeisance and exclaiming :—
" Live happily till time shall be no more.
This youth, who had not come to man's estate,
Must take himself a partner and keep house,
And then prove impotent !   His wife, she said :—
' This weakling was self-sown ! '   All privily
I gave to him three cups of wine, and none
In all the world was ware thereof.   Forthwith
It flushed his cheeks and made a man of him.   C. 1501
Three cups of wine are his nobility ;
Who could imagine that the Sháh would wish
To hear thereof ?   Shoemaker was his granddad,
And so is he, and not by birth above
His trade."
          The Sháh smiled on the crone, and said :—
" This is no tale to hide."
             He thus addressed
The archmage : " Wine is now permissible,
And we should drink thereof to his extent
Who in his cups still can bestride a lion,
And not be overthrown, but not to his
Who lieth all dead-drunk upon the road
What while some black crow pecketh out his eyes."
   A proclamation went up from the gate :—
" O paladins who wear the golden girdle !
Drink wine in moderation, all of you !

Considering the end when ye begin,
And when the wine hath led you to delight
Then go to sleep but not in helpless plight."

§ 8

How Rúzbih, Bahrám's High Priest, ruined a Village
by a Stratagem and restored it

The third day at the dawn the Sháh went forth,
He and his men, to hunt upon the plain ;
Hurmuz, his minister, was on his left,
And on his right the holy archimage.
They told him tales, discoursing of Jamshíd
And Farídún.[1]   Before them were the hounds,
The cheetahs, hawks, and falcons.   Thus they shortened
The tedious day.   Bright Sol was high, but still
They saw no trace of deer or onager,
And so Bahrám Gúr, troubled by the heat,
Turned back in dudgeon from the hunting-field.
He came upon a verdurous spot fulfilled
With houses, men, and cattle.   Many folk
Came from the settlement to see the troops,
But no man did obeisance !   Thou hadst said :—
" The earth hath tethered every ass of them ! "
The monarch, vexed and overcome by heat,
Had fixed upon that village for a halt.
Its folk disgusted him, he viewed them not
With favour, and in anger thus addressed
The high priest : " What an ill-starred spot is this !
Be it a lair for wild beasts and for game,
And may its streams run pitch."
                                    The archimage,
Who took this for an order, turned aside

─────────
[1] See Vol. i. pp. 129 *seq*, 147 *seq*.

Toward the village and informed the folk :—
" This verdant spot—all fruitage, men, and cattle—
Hath greatly pleased Bahrám, the king of kings,
Who hath a new design respecting it.
He raiseth all of you to noble rank
To turn this pleasant village to a city.
Here, lord and hireling, ye shall be all equal.
Men, women, children, ye shall be all chiefs,
Each of you be the master of the village."
    Glad shouts rose from that prosperous settlement
Because the people were all lords alike.
Thenceforth, man's rede or woman's, 'twas all one,
And slave and hireling were their master's peers.
The village-youths, no longer checked by awe,
Cut off their elders' heads, then fell upon
Each other and, where roads were not, shed blood.
At that to-do folk fled incontinent.
The helpless aged remained, but there remained not
The implements of culture, goods, and crops.
The settlement had ruin in its face,
The trees were withered and the streams ran dry,
The land and houses were all desolate,
And shunned of man and beast.   Now when a year
Had passed and spring returned the monarch went
A-hunting in those parts and reached that spot
Erst populous and blithe, and saw the place
O'erturned, trees withered, habitations waste,
And not a man or beast throughout the march.
Thereat the Sháh turned pale, the fear of God
Came on him, he was grievously distressed,
And thus addressed the archmage : " O Rúzbih !
Alack ! this place so jocund once is ruined !
Go to now and restore it with my treasures,
And take such order that the folk henceforth
Be scathless."
                Going from the royal presence

The archmage sped forth to that scene of ruin.
From street to street he hurried and at last
Came on an old man unemployed.   Dismounting
He spake the elder fair, made him sit down
Near by, and said to him : " Old, honoured sir !
Who wrecked this district once so populous ? "
    The old man answered thus : " Our monarch once
Was passing through our parts, and thereupon
There came to us a witless archimage,
One of those useless people with big names,
And said to us : ' Ye all are chieftains here :
See that ye pay respect to nobody.
Be masters, all of you, both men and women,
And great among the great.'   Such were his words,
· 1503   And all the township was convulsed thereat,
All rapine, murder, stick !   May God befriend him
In like proportion, may grief, death, and hardship
Ne'er stale with him.   Our case is growing worse,
And such that folk must weep for us."
                                    Rúzbih,
Grieved for that old man, asked : " Who is your
    chief ? "
    The other answered : " Who will have a place
Where there is naught excepting seed and grass ? "
    Rúzbih replied : " Be thou the governor,
Be as the crown upon the head in all things,
Make requisition from the world-lord's treasures
For money, oxen, asses, grain, and produce ;
Bring to the village all the unemployed ;
They all are subjects, thou alone art chief,
And curse no more the ancient archimage,
Who spake not as he would in what he said.
If thou wilt have assistants from the court
I will dispatch them.   Ask for what thou wilt."
    The elder joyed to hear this and was freed
From longsome grief.   He hied him home forthwith,

Brought others to his Cistern and began
To people and apportion out the lands.
They borrowed from their neighbours ox and ass,
And furnished all the plain.   He and his settlers
Worked hard and planted many trees on all sides,
And, when his labour had restored one piece,
The hearts of those that dwelt therein rejoiced.
Those that had fled, their heart's blood in their eyes,
Flocked back on hearing of that restoration,
And of the toils of that white-headed chief,
And reinstated street and water-course,
While fowl, ox, ass, and sheep all multiplied
Upon the cultured parts, and everywhere
Folk planted trees till that waste spot became
Like Paradise.   The third year he restored
The town : the chief was blessed in all his labours.
When jocund spring came round the Sháh went forth
Upon the plain a-hunting with Rúzbih,
The high priest.   When the pair drew near the hamlet
Bahrám Gúr suddenly beheld the world
All crops and cattle, lofty mansions rose,
And all the township thronged with sheep and oxen.
'Twas all streams, pleasances, and growing crops,
And fenugreek and tulips filled the hills,
Whereon roamed sheep and lambs, for hill and dale
Had grown to be a paradise.   The Sháh
Said to the high priest : " O Rúzbih ! what didst thou c. 1504
To make this verdant village waste and scatter
Its men and beasts, and what hast thou dispensed
In thus restoring it ? "
                              The high priest answered :—
" This ancient seat was ruined by a word,
And by a word restored, to please the Sháh.
He bade me : ' Take thou treasure and dinárs,
And make this verdant spot a wilderness,'
But I feared God and blame from great and small.

When friends, though one in heart, are two in aim
'Tis ruin, as I have perceived, to both ;
So when there are two rulers in a state
Their land will be o'erturned.   I went and said
Thus to the elders of this settlement :—
' O men ! there is no ruler over you
From this time forth, but women, children, slaves,
Hirelings and husbandmen, are lords alike.'
When those who had been underlings became
Lords too the nobles' heads were all brought low,
And all the place was ruined by a word.
Thus was I far removed from all reproach,
And apprehension of God's chastisement.
Thereafter, when the Sháh had ruth on them,
I went and pointed out another course ;
I made a wise, old man and eloquent,
A man of leading and informed, the ruler.
He laboured and restored the waste, rejoicing
His subjects' hearts.   When one man ruled, the counsel
Was good, prosperity increased, ill waned.
I, unobserved, had shown them what was bad,
And opened afterward the way of God.
Discourse is better than fine-watered gems
When 'tis employed aright.   Let wisdom be
The Sháh, the tongue the paladin, if thou
Wouldst have thy spirit easy.   May thy heart
Be glad for aye and free from wile and waste."
    The Sháh, on hearing, cried : " Well done, Rúzbih !
Thou'rt worthy of a crown ! "
                            Bahrám Gúr gave
That old man worshipful and prescient
A purse all filled with gold dinárs.   For him
A robe of honour too they fashionéd
Of royal stuffs, and cloud-ward raised his head.

§ 9

How Bahrám married a Country-miller's Daughters

Another week the monarch of the world
Went forth to hunt with lords and archimages,
Prepared to spend a month upon the chase,
To revel with his meiny, and to take
Illimitable game on waste and mountain.   C. 1505
He and his escort reached in merry pin
A town. The night came on, and all was dark.
The chiefs dismissed the escort and recited
Tales of the Sháhs. He saw afar a fire,
Such as Sháhs kindle on Bahman's high day.[1]
The king of kings gazed at the light and spied
A pleasant village with a mill before it,
Where sat the village-chiefs, while all the maidens,
Each with a crown of roses on her head,
Were feasting by themselves beside the fire.
The minstrels sat about, the maidens sang
Tales of the royal wars, and every one
Began to tell a story in her turn.
They all were moon-faced, all had locks a-curl,
All were sweet-spoken, and all savoured musk.
They sat ranked on the grass and close before
The mill-door, singing, with a posy each,
And half bemused with wine and merriment.
Then from that scene of revel rose a cry,
And one exclaimed : " The toast of Sháh Bahrám !
He hath Grace, stature, mien, and love. Before him
The rolling sphere upstandeth. Thou wouldst say :—
' His face distilleth wine, the scent of musk
Proceedeth from his hair.' He only hunteth
The lion and the onager, and so
Folk title him ' Bahrám Gúr.' "
                              This he heard,

----
[1] The day Bahman of the month Bahman was a time of festivity.

And rode toward them.   Drawing near the girls
He scanned the plain, beheld it filled with Moons,
And saw that he should stop short of the city.
He bade, and from the road cup-bearers came,
Provided wine and boon-companions,
And handed him a crystal cup.   Meanwhile
Four of the girls, those chief in rank, came forth—
One Mushkináb,[1] the others Mushkinak,
Náztáb, and Súsanak.   With cheeks like spring,
With stately mien, and hand in hand, they went
Before the Sháh and sang about Bahrám,
The king of kings, the wise and prosperous.
Bahrám Gúr asked, for they perturbed his heart :—
" Who are ye,[2] rose-cheeked ?   Wherefore is this fire? "
      One said : " O cavalier of cypress-height,
So like a king in everything ! our father
. 1506   Is an old miller who is shooting game
Upon this mountain and will come anon
Since it is night, and he can see no longer."
      With that the miller and his men came bringing
Their quarry.   When his eyes fell on Bahrám Gúr
He rubbed his face upon the dust and bare him
With awe and reverence.   The Sháh bade give
That old man just arrived a golden cup,
And said to him : " Why keepest thou these four
With sunny faces thus ?   Is it not time
For them to wed ? "
                        The old man offered praise,
And said : " There is no husband for them ; they
Are maidens still and pure in chastity,
But that is all the property they have,
And this is all that I can say for them."

---

[1] Mushkináz in C. and P.   Mushkináb means " Pure Musk "; Mush-
kinak is a species of bird ; Náztáb is " Charmer," and Súsanak " Little
Lily."
      [2] Reading with P.

Bahrám said : "Give me all the four, and henceforth
Regard them not as daughters."

Quoth the ancient :—
" Do not as thou hast said, O cavalier !
No cups have we, no land, no crops, no silver,
No mansion, ox, and ass."

Bahrám Gúr said :—
" 'Tis well, for I would have them portionless."
The miller said : " The four shall be thy wives,
The handmaids of the dust within thy chambers.
Thine eye hath seen their good points and their ill,
And, seeing, hath approved."

Bahrám Gúr said :—
" From holy God, the All-giver, I accept them."
He spake and rose. Steeds neighed upon the plain.
He bade the eunuchs of his escort bear
Those Idols to the royal women's house,
And through the night the troops filed o'er the waste.
The miller marvelled, mused all night, and said
Thus to his wife : " This moon-like lord so tall
And masterful, how came he here by night ? "
She answered : " He perceived the fire from far,
The noise the girls were making, and the sound
Of minstrels, harp, and revelry."

The miller
Said to his wife : " Advise me, O my spouse !
If this affair will turn out well or ill ? "
She answered : " It is all God's providence.
The man, on seeing them, asked not their race,
Thought not of dowry. On earth's face he sought
For Moons and not for money or kings' daughters.
If idol-worshippers saw these in Chin
There would be no more idol-worshipping ! "
Thus till above the Raven's back the sun   C. 1507
Rose, and the world grew like a shining lamp,
They talked at large of base and upright men,

But with the day the village-chief arrived,
And said to that old man : " O brave of luck ! [1]
Good fortune visited thy couch last night !
The verdant branches of thy tree bear fruit.
One looked, beheld the merriment and fire,
And, having turned his horse about, drew near ;
So now thy daughters have become his wives,
And rest securely in his women's house.
By giving them such faces, hair, and carriage
Thou didst prepare them for the Sháh !   Bahrám,
The king of kings, is now thy son-in-law !
Henceforth thou wilt be famous through the realm.
He hath bestowed upon thee all this province
And march, so sorrow not, for thou hast 'scaped
From cares and fears.   Command.   'Tis thine to bid.
We all of us are thralls and bound to thee ;
We all of us are subject to thee now,
Are subject !   Rather we are all thy slaves."
    The miller and his wife in their amaze
Invoked God's name.   The village-chieftain said :—
" Such locks as those and countenances too
Would bring the sun from his fourth heaven to woo."

§ 10

How Bahrám found the Treasures of Jamshíd and
bestowed them upon the Poor

Another week he went forth to the chase
With favourites from the host and archimages.
Swift as the wind there came a loyal liege
With spade in hand and asking of the troops
Where was Bahrám, the Sháh, amid the throng ?
An archimage replied : " What wilt thou ?   Speak.

[1] " O vaillant Rouzbeh."   Mohl.

Thou canst not see the monarch of the world." [1]
  The man said : " Since I may see not his face
I will speak not before his followers."
  They brought before the Sháh that seeker—one
Both learned and eloquent—who seeing him
Said : " I have words to speak to thee in private."
  Bahrám Gúr turned his horse's head aside,
And rode some distance from his followers' sight.
Then said the man : " O world-possessing Sháh !
Thou must observe my words. A countryman
Am I, and landlord here. I own the soil,
The homestead, and the crops. I was engaged
In making water-courses on my land
To benefit my property, and when
There was much water, and the stream ran strong,
In one place there was formed an orifice,
A wondrous clamour reached mine ears, and I   C. 1508
Came crying out in terror of my life.
The clash of cymbals issued from the stream—
A sound denoting treasure." [2]
                              Hearing this
Bahrám Gúr went and saw a plain all verdure,
And watered, bade bring labourers with spades
From far, and lighted from his steed. They pitched
His tent among the crops. Night came. The warriors
Lit lamps and everywhere enkindled fires.
  Now when the sun set up above the deep
Its banner, burnishing the violet air,
The workmen mustered from all sides, as though
A mighty army, and began to dig.
That portion of the plain was excavate,
And, as the workers wearied, there appeared
Out of the dust a mount-like place—a mansion
Of mortar and burnt brick—like Paradise.
They plied their picks ; far down a doorway showed.

---

[1] Reading with P.   [2] *Cf.* Vol. vi. p. 250.

An archmage, seeing, entered by the door,
He and another uninvited guest.
They found a single chamber long and wide,
And many cubits high.   Within it stood
Two buffaloes of gold and, fronting them,
A golden laver strewn with emeralds
And rubies mixed.   They seemed two Signs of Taurus,
Were hollow, and were filled up with pomegranates,
With apples, and with quinces that contained
Fine-watered pearls, each like a water-drop.
The buffaloes had jewel-eyes, and heads
Decayed with age.   Ranked round them there were
      lions
And onagers, some having ruby eyes,
And others crystal.   There were golden pheasants
And peacocks, with their breasts and eyes all gems.
The minister, whose wisdom was a crown
Upon the moon, on seeing that spectacle,
Went to the Sháh and cried excitedly :—
" Arise.   Enough to dower thy treasuries
Is here !   A chamber filled with precious stones
Is manifest, whose key high heaven hath kept ! "
      His lord said : " One of counsel and of might
Would write his name upon his treasures.   See
Whose name is there and when they were amassed."
      On hearing this the high priest went and saw
The impress of the signet of Jamshíd
Upon the buffaloes, and notified
The monarch of the world : " I have beheld,
And ' Sháh Jamshíd ' is on the buffaloes."
. 1509   The Sháh said : " O high priest in all regards
More learned than sages ! wherefore make mine own
The treasures that Jamshíd laid up of yore ?
May nothing e'er be added to my wealth
Unless by justice and the scimitar.
Bestow the whole upon the poor.   God grant

That no mishap befall us. For my troops
No share is requisite, our valour openeth
The earth to us. As is the use of kings
'Tis needful that we count up all this wealth,
Sell all the gems for cash, and then assemble
From desert and from settlement the widows,
The orphans, and the impoverished men of name—
Those lost to aspiration, fame, and ease—
Then take the sum of such, including those
That, troubled by their debts, should have a share,
And give to them the money and the goods
To assoil Jamshid the world-lord's soul, but I
Am youthful still, and sound in wind and limb ;
Why should I seek his treasures ?   Let one tenth
Be for the finder, who sought out the Sháh,
But never let him hope for joy hereafter
That beareth off the cerecloth from Jamshid.
To compass toil in consort with my troops,
And treasure and renown from Rúm and Chin,
That is for me and for my steed, Shabdíz,
And for my trenchant scimitar. No shifts,
Or shirks, for me ! "
                              He went back to the treasure
Won by his sweat and toil, assembled all
The warriors of the realm, and gave his troops
A whole year's pay. He held a feast that spring,
Adorned his hall of jewelled tracery,
And, when the red wine shone in crystal cups,
And he himself was jocund and right glad,
He thus harangued his friends : " Exalted ones,
Who know the token of the throne of kings !
Down from Húshang as far as famed Naudar,
Who was a memory of Farídún,
And on again right up to Kai Kubád,
Who placed the crown of greatness on his head,
See who of all these mighty men is left,

And who remaineth to applaud their justice ?
Now, since the circle of their years is cut,
Their reputation is their monument,
Which saith that this had spirit, that had not,
And one doth blame them, and another praise.
We all shall pass in turn, and not to walk
1510 The world for ill is well.   Why should I need
The treasure of those gone ?   Why should my heart
Expand toward dínárs ?   I will not set it
Upon this Wayside Inn, or make my boast
Of crown, or clutch at treasure.   If the days
Pass in delight why should the wise eat grief ?
Whene'er a liege of mine, a countryman
Or courtier, shall complain of mine oppression
Then may my head and crown and treasure perish."
  There was an ancient man, hight Máhiyár,
Whose years had reached eight score and four.   He
    rose,
On hearing this, and spake thus : " O just lord !
Tales have we heard of Farídún, Jamshíd,
And others more or less renowned, but none
Hath heard of Sháh like thee—the lowly's hope,
The Glory of the great—and were the sea
Large as thy heart 'twould rise in waves of gems,
For from thy soul the radiance of Surúsh
Proceedeth, dwarfing all a wise man's wit.
Thou hast so lavished treasure in the world
That no one great or small hath seen the like.
When men spake of the era of Jamshid,
And of the treasure of the buffaloes,
None wotted where it was—beneath the dust,
Or in the dragon's breath—but having found it
Thou didst not look thereon, for thou didst scorn
This Wayside Hostelry.   Good sooth ! no king
Hath seen, nor will a hundred see, such jewels
As these in any sea, yet these and all

The buffaloes and onagers thou gavest
Without exception to the poor ! May crown
And girdle never lack thee. Health be thine,
Be victor thou and fortune's favourite.
The ink would blacken many a royal roll
To tell this tale and yet not reach the end.
Thou being gone thy name will live in praise
When folk recount the story of thy days."

§ 11

*How Bahrám, returning from Hunting, went to the House
of a Merchant and departed displeased*

One day, another week, he went to hunt,
When indisposed, and took his bow and arrows.
The plain grew sultry with the blazing sun.
He came back from his hunting leisurely,
And reached a merchant's house, to whom he said,
On looking round and seeing none beside :
"Canst give us lodging since thou wilt not find us
A trouble ? "
      Having helped him to dismount   C. 1511
The merchant found a place for him. The Sháh,
Complaining of the cohc, gave the merchant
Some drachms, and said : "Toast some old cheese
  with almonds."
 The merchant did not do as he was asked,
Not having almonds by him, but, at night-fall
And at his leisure, got a hot roast fowl,
And served it to Bahrám upon a tray,
Who said : " I asked thee for old cheese, besought thee
To bring it, and thou hast not brought it me
Although I gave thee drachms and had complained
Of colic."
    Said the merchant : " Foolish fellow !

Thy soul is starving through thy lack of wit.
Since I have brought to thee this hot roast fowl
Mere shame should stay thee asking aught beside."

Bahrám thereat ceased longing for old cheese.
Grieved at his words he ate, referring not
To what had passed.   When it was sleeping-time
He slept and said naught further to the merchant.

Now when the sun rose o'er the heaving deep,
And when the Cloak pitch-hued had disappeared,
The wealthy merchant said to his apprentice :—
" O simpleton ! why didst thou buy a fowl
Not worth a drachm for more and wrong me so ?
Had't been a proper fowl then he and I
Had fallen not out last night, or hadst thou spent
A quarter of a drachm in buying cheese
He would have been to me like milk and water
To-day."

The apprentice answered : " 'Tis all one.
Know that the fowl is at my charge.   Be thou
And he my guests, so quarrel not with me
About the bird."

Now when Bahrám arose
From pleasant sleep he sought his docile steed
To saddle it and go back to his palace,
And from his palace raise his crown to Saturn.
The apprentice, seeing him, said to Bahrám :—
" Give to thy slave thy company to-day."

The Sháh returned, sat down again, and mar-
velled
At fortune.   Then the youth went out and fetched
Two hundred almonds and addressed his master :—
" Bestir thee, sir ! and have these almonds toasted,
Make ready too some cheese and some new bread,
For such the cavalier asked yesterday,
Bring food and spread the board."

He went before

Bahrám and said : " O cavalier ! I bring thee
All hot what yesterday thou didst require,   C. 1512
And there is more to follow in due course."
    Thus saying he set off to the bázár,
A different sort of purchaser.   He bought
More almonds, sugar, fowl, and lamb to make
An ample meal, wine, saffron, musk, rose-water,
And hurried home.   He brought the board all spread
With dainty meats.   A sprightly youth was he
And well disposed.   The eating done, he brought
Forth cups of wine, first serving king Bahrám,
And thus, till blithe and jocund, they proceeded
From eating to the cup.   The Sháh addressed
His entertainer thus : " Bahrám will be
Inquiring for me, but do ye drink on,
Grow drunk, and budge not till ye prove yourselves
Wine-worshippers."
                    Then rubbing down and saddling
Shabdíz he started, blithe with wine, for court,
First saying to the merchant : " Toil not so
In quest of gain, O thou that sellest dear !
Thou wouldst have sold me for a quarter drachm
Yestreen, sewn up the eyes of thine apprentice
Because he bought a fowl above the price,
And have put me within the dragon's maw."
    He spake and sped back to his royal seat.
Now when the sun displayed its crown in heaven
The guardian of the world sat on his throne
Of ivory and bade the chamberlain
Seek out the merchant and conduct him thither
With his apprentice.   One of them was glad,
The other glum.   Bahrám, on seeing the apprentice,
Made much of him and seated him rejoicing
Among the lords.   They brought to him a purse,
And made his awe-gloomed spirit like the moon.
Then to the merchant said Bahrám : " Know this :

Thou shalt be slave for life to thine apprentice,
And, further, pay him twice in every month
Three score drachms from thy savings. With thy
      goods
He shall be entertainer and make laugh
The hearts of noble men."

                          Then to the high priest :—
" The king that disregardeth this world's doings,
How can he know what man is truly great,
Or how discern the evil from the good ? "[1]
  So now, O sage that seekest wisdom's way !
If thou must have a saw hear what I say :—
" Avoid all avarice if man thou be,
Or be indeed below humanity."

§ 12

How Bahrám slew a Dragon and went to a Yokel's House

. 1513   Bahrám abode a season with his lords,
With sparkling wine, with cup, and minstrelsy.
Spring came, the ground seemed Paradise, the air
Sowed tulips on earth's face, all tracts grew full
Of game, and in the brooks the waters seemed
Like wine and milk.   The deer and onager
Paced in the dales or clustered on the sward,
The blackbirds haunted all the river-banks,
And all around them bent pomegranate-blooms.
" 'Tis long," the nobles said to Sháh Bahrám Gúr,
" Since we have hunted onager."

                          He answered :—
" Choose we a thousand horsemen from the host,
And let them bring the cheetahs and the hawks,

---

[1] In C the next section begins here. We follow the arrangement in P.

The falcons and the noble peregrines,
Go to Túrán and pass a month in hunting."
   The royal hunter went. He found the world
All hues and scent. His gallant chieftains swept it
For onager, gazelle, and mountain-sheep—
A labour that extended o'er two days—
What while Bahrám had wine in hand ; the third,
When Sol illumed its crown, when earth grew golden,
And hill and stream became as ivory,
The valiant Sháh went to the chase and saw
A dragon like a lion. From its head
Hair hung down to the ground, and it had breasts
Like those of women. Then Bahrám Gúr strung
His bow and shot forthwith a poplar arrow
Against the dragon's chest. He shot another
Straight at its head, and gore and venom flowed
Adown its front. The king dismounted, drew
His sword, and carved up all the dragon's breast.
It had gulped down a youth and frozen him
In blood and bane. Bahrám bewailed him sorely
What while the venom blinded his own eyes.
He took the corpse out of the dragon's maw,
Ne'er may its head and breast unite again.
He rode off dizzied, suffering, and longing
For sleep and water, reached a settlement,
Arriving at a house-door from the waste,
And saw a woman shouldering a pitcher.
She veiled her face from him. He said to her :—
" Can I lodge here or must I toil on still ? "
   She said : " Brave horseman ! treat this house as
     thine."
On hearing this he rode his courser in.
His hostess called her husband. " Bring a wisp,"
She said, " and rub his steed. At feeding-time
Feed from the sack."
                 She went to her own chamber, C. 1514

Swept out the house and laid down mat and pillow,
With blessings on Bahrám, went to the cistern,
Drew water, and berated to herself
Her spouse the while : " The fool will ne'er bestir
Himself on seeing some one in the house.
This is not women's work, but for my part
I, soldier-like, can only grin and bear it ! "
   She brought and spread the board with vinegar
And salad, bread and curds. Went Sháh Bahrám,
And bathed his face, for he had been o'erwrought
In fighting with that dragon. So he ate
A little, then lay down and groaned, his face
Concealed beneath a kerchief made in Chín.
   The woman, when she woke, said to her spouse :—
" O knave with unwashed face ! thou shouldest slay
A lamb because this cavalier is great,
And of the royal seed, hath kingly bearing,
And moon-like Grace, and he is like to none
Save Sháh Bahrám."
              Her mean spouse said to her :—
" Why such to-do ? Thou hast no salted meat,
No fire-wood, and no bread, and spinnest not
A-nights as others do. When thou hast killed
A lamb, and he—this cavalier—hath eaten
And gone, then go, buy, mingle with the throng ;
The winter, cold, and blast undoubtedly
Will come on thee no less."
              So spake her spouse.
She hearkened not, for she was good and wise,
And in the end her husband slew a lamb
At her entreaty for the cavalier.
When it was slain she made a pot of broth,
And lit a fire with half-burnt sticks, then brought
The tray with eggs thereon and water-cresses,
A roasted leg of lamb and everything
That she had cooked. Bahrám, when he had washed

His hands, his dinner done, felt indisposed
For slumber and still ailed.   Now when the night
Foregathered with the sun the woman fetched
Wine and a harp.   " O woman of few words ! "
The Sháh said, " tell to me some old-world tale
That while thou art reciting I may quaff
To chase away my pain and cares.   I give thee
· Free speech about the Sháh for praise or blame."

That woman of few words said : " Yea, 'tis well,
For he is first and last in everything."

Bahrám responded : " He is so indeed,
But he is just and good to nobody."

That dame of spirit said : " O honest man !
This place hath many folk and many homes,
And always cavaliers are passing through
From public offices and ministers.
If one of them shall call a man a thief
The accused will have much trouble afterward.
The cavalier to compass some few drachms
Will make the poor man's life a misery,
Or one may smirch some honest woman's fame,
And make her fall to folly.   This is loss,
Because the treasury is none the richer.
This is our trouble with our Sháh, the world-lord."

C. 1515

The king grew full of thought at that account—
How those in power were wronging his good name—
And then the pious Sháh thought with himself :—
" No one doth praise the just.   Henceforward I
Will play the tyrant for a while that love
And justice may grow manifest from ill."

Vexed by dark thoughts he passed a sleepless night,
His heart allied to tyranny the while.
Now when Sol rent its musky-scented veil,
And showed its face in heaven, the woman left
The house and bade her spouse : " Bring pot and fire,
And in the water put all kinds of grain

Before the sun shall see it.   Mind it well
While I go milk the cow."

                      She brought the cow
From pasture, got much grass, and threw it down
Before her ; then she tried the udders, crying :—
" In God's name who hath neither mate nor peer ! "
   She found the udder milkless, and the heart
Of that young hostess aged.   She told her husband :—
" Good man ! our monarch's heart hath changed in
     purpose,
The world's king hath become tyrannical !
A secret change came o'er his heart last night."
   He said : " What words are these ?   Why go and
     croak ? "
She thus replied : " My dear one ! what I say
Is sober truth, for when the Sháh, the world-lord,
Hath grown unjust the moon may shine not forth
In heaven, the udders are dry, the musk-bags lose
Their scent, adultery and guile are rampant,
The tender heart becometh flinty, wolves
Devour folk on the waste, the sage doth flee
The fool, and eggs are addled 'neath the hens
What time the Sháh becometh tyrannous.
The pasture of this cow had minished not,
Her watering-place supplied her as before,
Yet is her udder dry, her lowing changed."
   On hearing this the Sháh forthwith repented,
. 1516 And prayed to God : " O Thou who art supreme,
Almighty, and the Arbiter of fortune !
If e'er my heart shall turn away from justice
Then be the throne of kings no longer mine."
   That blessèd dame, who worshipped holy God,
Tried with her hand the udder once again,
She tried it in the Lord's name, saying thus :—
" Cause Thou the milk to flow."

                      The milk flowed forth.

The good wife cried : " O God, our Succourer !
Thou hast recalled to justice the unjust,
For, if not so, this virtue were not his."
   Then said she to the master of the house :—
" The justice of the unjust is restored.
Laugh and rejoice ; this is the Maker's boon
To us."
            Now when the porridge had been cooked,
And man and wife had done that chare, the good dame,
And after her the master of the house,
Who bare the tray, went to their guest. Upon it
There was a bowl of porridge, oh ! how good
Had it been but some broth ! The Sháh ate somewhat,
Then spake thus to that kindly dame : " Take thou
This whip outside and hang it where folk pass.
Choose out a proper bough because the wind
Must harm it not, then note the passers by
With one eye on the whip."
              The good-man went
Forthwith, he hung the whip upon a tree,
And kept his eye thereon a while. There came
Innumerable troops along the road,
And all that saw the whip there hailed Bahrám.
They lighted down before that lengthy whip,
And passed saluting. " 'Tis the Sháh, none else !"
The good-man told his spouse. " Naught but the
    throne
Could fit a face like that ! "
              Then full of awe
Both ran to him and cried : " O Sháh l O great !
O mighty one ! O sage, high priest and world-lord !
A humble woman and her gardener-spouse
Have been thy poor hosts in this house. Withal
They did not do their best. We ne'er suspected
That 'twas the Sháh, that such an one as he
Would come to this place as a guest, would come

To this poor home of ours."

Bahrám replied :—
" Good friend !   I give to thee this march, the land,
And village.   Be thou ever hospitable ;
Be that, and give up garden-work."

He spake,
And laughing left the house, gat on his steed
C. 1517   Wind-footed, and from that poor village reached
His jewelled halls.   The nobles of Írán
Went thither for the chase, three hundred strong,
And each with thirty servants in his train
Of Turkman, Rúman, or of Persian strain.

§ 13

How Bahrám went to the Chase and espoused the
Daughters of the Thane Barzín

The third day after this the Sháh went forth
With escort, the equipment for the chase,
Ten camels all in housings of brocade
With stirrups silver and with dossers gold,
Ten camels with the Sháh's pavilion,
And his brocaded seat.   In front of these
Were seven elephants which bare the throne
Of turquoise hued like Nile ; its feet were all
Of gold and crystal ; 'twas the throne itself
Of Sháh Bahrám Gúr.   Every swordsman there
Had thirty pages who had golden belts
And bridles, while a hundred camels served
To bear the minstrels wearing massive crowns.
The falconers had eight score hawks with them,
And ten score noble peregrines and falcons.
Among them there was one bird black of hue,

More precious in the Sháh's eyes than the rest,
With sable talons and with yellow beak,
Like gold a-gleam on lapis-lazuli.
They called it a tughral. Its eyes were like
Two goblets full of blood. The Khán of Chín
Had sent it with a throne and crown, with amber,
A golden torque inlaid with emeralds,
With two score armlets, and with thrice twelve earrings,
Three hundred camel-loads of rarities
Of Chín, and fifteen score of ruby signets.
Behind the falconers they led eight score
Of cheetahs for that Lustre of the world—
The Sháh—with jewelled torques and chains of gold.
Thus came the king of kings upon the plain,
And raised his crown o'er Jupiter. The sportsmen
Made for the river whither used the Sháh
Auspiciously to fare each seventh year.
As they drew near they found the river full
Of water-fowl. He had the tabor beaten,
And the tughral flew off. The imperious bird
Was all impatience ; in its claws a crane
Was helpless quarry, and a pard had been
Its proper prey. At length it soared from sight,   C. 1518
And bound a crane, then soared again and flew
Like shaft from bow, the falconer pursuing.
The Sháh was vexed that it had flown away,
And followed by the tinkling of its bells.
He came upon a spacious pleasure-ground,
With mansion rising in a coign thereof,
And thither went with certain of his men,
The rest remaining on the hunting-field.
On entering Bahrám Gúr saw a garden
As 'twere a mountain-skirt. Upon the ground
Brocade was spread, and all the place was full
Of slaves and wealth. A pool was in the centre
Whereby an old man sat. Three girls like ivory

Sat by him wearing turquoise crowns.   Their cheeks
Were like the spring, their statures tall, their eye-
   brows
Arched, and their tresses lassos ; each girl held
A crystal goblet, and Bahrám Gúr saw them.
His eyes were dazzled at the spectacle
Just as his heart was gloomed for his tughral.
On seeing him that wealthy thane grew pale
As fenugreek with fear.   A wise old man
Was he, Barzin by name, but ill-affected
Toward the Sháh.   As swift as wind he left
The hauz,[1] approached the Sháh, and kissed the
   ground,
Then said : " O monarch of the sun-like face !
May heaven revolve according to thy will.
I do not dare to say to thee : ' Abide
With thy two hundred horsemen on my march.'
Still, if the Sháh take pleasure in my garden,
The glory of Barzín hath reached the moon."
   " To-day," the world's king answered, " the tughral
Escaped us.   I am vexed about that fowler,
Which hunted birds as leopards hunt their quarry."
   Barzin replied : " I saw a sable bird
Just now with golden bells and pitch-hued body,
Its beak and talons turmeric in hue ;
It came and settled on yon walnut-tree :
By thy good fortune it is come to hand."
   The Sháh said to a servant : " Go and look."
He went like wind and cried : " Glad ever be
The world-lord !   The tughral is on a bough ;
E'en now the falconer is taking it."
   The hawk thus found, the old man said : " O Sháh
Without a mate or equal on the earth !
Oh ! may thine entertainer prove auspicious,
And all the wearers of a crown thy slaves.

   [1] See Vol. i. p. 203 note.

Call for a wine-cup in our present joy, C. 1519
And, when thou art refreshed, ask what thou wilt."
    The king of kings dismounted at the pool,
And old Barzin grew glad.   With that there came
Bahrám's chief minister and therewithal
The captains of the host and treasurer.
Barzín brought forth a golden cup and first
Drank to the monarch of the world, then brought
And offered to the Sháh a cup of crystal,
Who seeing took and drained the proffered draught
Below the inscription-line, whereat Barzin
In high delight had wine-jars set about
The place, and in his cups said to his daughters :—
" My clever chicks ! no chieftain of the host,
But Sháh Bahrám hath visited this garden !
So come, thou songstress ! let us have a song,
And thou, my moon-faced daughter ! bring thy
        harp."
    All three drew near the Sháh, and on their heads
Were jewelled crowns.   One danced, another played
Upon the harp, the third possessed a sweet
And soothing voice.   While they made minstrelsy
The king of kings in high contentment drained
His goblet dry.   He said thus to Barzin :—
" What girls are these who live with thee in joy ? "
    Barzin thus answered him : " O Sháh ! may none
Behold the age without thee.   Know that these
Are mine own daughters and my heart's delight.
One is a caroler, another harpeth,
The third observeth measure in the dance.
I need not aught, O Sháh ! for I have money,
Domain, and pleasure-ground, and my three daughters
Are, as the Sháh perceiveth, like glad spring.
O moon-face ! " said he to the songstress, " fear not,
But sing a song about the Sháh."
                    The Idols

Took heart to sing and play.   The songstress sang :—

> " O moon-faced king ! the moon in heaven
>   Alone is like to thee,
> The royal throne thine only seat.
>   Thou with thy moon-like blee,
>
> And teak-like stature art the pride
>   Of throne and crown.   Oh ! rare
> For those that see thy face at morn,
>   For those that scent thy hair l
>
> Thy loins are tiger-like, thy limbs
>   Are mighty, thy crown's Grace
> Is as the cloud-rack high, and like
>   Pomegranate-bloom thy face.
>
> For rapture of thy love hearts laugh,
>   Like ocean is thine own ;
> Like cloud thy hand.   As thy fit prey
>   I see the lion alone.
>
> Thou splittest with thy shaft a hair,
>   And by thine equity
> Convertest water into milk.
>   When hostile armies see
>
> Thy lasso and thy puissant arm
>   Their hearts and brains are rent
> However mighty their array,
>   Howe'er on battle bent."

1520

Bahrám Gúr, having heard the ditty, drained
The massive crystal cup and thus addressed
Barzín : " O noble sir, experienced much
Is this world's heat and cold ! thou wilt not find
A better son-in-law than me who am
'Mid kings a hero and the king of men.
Bestow thy daughters on me—all the three—

And I will raise thy coronet to Saturn."
"O king!" Barzín replied, "may wine and bearer
Find favour in thy sight. Who will dare say
That he hath such a Venus in his house ?
If now thou wilt accept me as a slave
To serve before the throne of king of kings
Then will I pay my service to thy crown,
Thy throne, thy Grace, thy fortune, and thy state ;
Moreover my three daughters are thy handmaids
To stand before thee as thy slaves. The Sháh
Approved of them as such or ever he
Saw these three Moons afar. As teaks are they
In stature and as ivory in hue,
Fit for the throne and to adorn the crown.
Now will I tell the monarch of the world
What fortune I possess for good and ill :
Of clothes and carpets, stuffs and draperies,
Good sooth have I stored up in mine abode
Two hundred camel-loads or more as well
As necklaces and bracelets, crowns and thrones,
All for my daughters' pleasure."
                                 Hearing this
Bahrám replied : "Leave what thou hast in store,
Where now it is, and seek mirth with the wine-cup."
    The elder answered : "My three moon-like daughters
I give thee by the rites of Gaiúmart
And of Húshang. Dust are they 'neath thy feet,
And all the three live but to do thy will."
    The eldest daughter's name was Máh Áfríd,
The second's Farának, and the cadette's
Was Shambalíd. Approving them at sight
The Sháh preferred them 'mongst his lawful wives,
And bade a noble of his escort bring
Four golden litters,[1] and, when all three Idols
Were set therein, they were encircled there

---

[1] The fourth was for himself and needful. See below.

By forty Rúman slaves—their devotees—
Who called down praises on them as they went.

While they departed to their golden home
The glorious Sháh caroused. A servant hung
His whip above the court-gate, for the escort,
Save by the token of the whip, ne'er knew
Where Sháh and nobles were. When any one
Beheld the handle and its lengthy thong
He used to run thereto and do obeisance.
Bahrám drank on until he was bemused,
Then glorious took his seat within a litter,
And went back to his women's golden house—
The house that was perfumed with ambergris.
On his return he tarried for a week,
And much he feasted, lavished, and held converse.
The eighth day he went hunting with Rúzbih,
And with a thousand cavaliers. He saw
That all the plain was full of onager,
Drew from its case his royal bow, and strung it,
Invoking God who giveth victory.
'Twas springtide and the onager were pairing.
From all the world they met confronting there,
And rent each other's hides, the face of earth
Was reddened with their blood. Bahrám abode
While two bucks fought together furiously,
Then when the valiant buck that gained the day
Was covering a doe he laughed to see
The onagers, took hold upon his bow-string,
Shot, piercing the buck's flank so that the arrow
Went home up to its plumes, and skewered buck
And doe together, thrilling all his escort.
All who beheld that shot acclaimed the Sháh :—
" Oh ! be the evil eye far from thy Grace,
And may thy whole life be a festival.
Such might as thine the age ne'er saw till now ;
At once Sháh, warrior, and king art thou."

§ 14

How Bahrám slew Lions, went to the House of a Jeweller,
and married his Daughter

The Sháh, on urging thence his steed Shabrang,
Came on a forest and beheld before it
Two savage lions, strung and drew his bow.
The arrow, striking on the lion's breast,
Was buried to the plumes.   Forthwith Bahrám
Turned to the lioness and, shooting, pinned
Her breast and loins together, but exclaimed :—
"The shaft was featherless, the point was blunt,   C. 1522
If point there were."
                    The escort praised him, saying :—
O famous king of earth ! none ever saw,
Or will see, on the throne of king of kings
A Sháh like thee, who with unfeathered arrows
O'erthrowest lions, and with plumed uprootest
A mount of flint."
                    The monarch with his meiny
Rode on along the meadow-land and saw
A forest full of sheep, their herds in flight
For fear of harm.   The chief herd, ne'er at ease
For terror of wild beasts, perceived Bahrám,
Who said to him : " What man is driving sheep
To this unlikely spot ? "
                    The head man answered :—
" Great sir ! none cometh to this pasturage
Except myself.   They are a jeweller's :
I drove them from the mountains yesterday.
The owner is a wealthy man not troubled
By fear of loss.[1]   He owneth gems by ass-loads,
Gold, silver, trinketry.   He hath withal
One only daughter, skilful on the harp.
Her tresses cluster on her head in curls.

---

[1] Reading with P.

He will take wine from her hand only.   None
Hath seen an old man like him.   How could he
Have kept his property but by the justice
Of Sháh Bahrám ?   The great king of the world
Is not concerned for gold, and his archmages
Are not unjust ; but say who slew these beasts,
For may the Ruler of the world uphold him ? ''

    Bahrám replied : '' This pair of lions fell
Beneath the arrows of a valiant man,
Who, having slain these gallant beasts, departed
With seven other gallant cavaliers.
Where is the jeweller's mansion ?   Point the way,
And hide it not from us.''

                    The chief hind said :—
'' Proceed and thou wilt reach a brand-new seat.
The jeweller thence fareth to the city,
To Sháh Bahrám's own palace, but, what time
The sun doth don its Sable Silk, returneth
To banquet.   Revelling and sound of lyre
Will reach thine ears if thou wilt bide a while.''

    Bahrám, on hearing this, called for his steed,
And for apparel suited to a king,
Then parted from his minister and escort.
Good sooth ! but he was full of eagerness !
Rúzbih said to the chiefs : '' So now the Sháh
Is going to the village, there to knock
Upon the portal of the jeweller !
C. 1523   And, mark my words ! will ask of him his daughter,
And crown her doubtless with a crown of gold,
Will take her to his ladies' golden house,
And send that other three back to Barzín ! [1]
He never hath enough of chambering ;
His consort flitteth ere the night is over !
He hath above a hundred ladies' bowers !
'Tis ill to have a king of kings like this.

               [1] See previous section.

Just now a eunuch reckoned up nine hundred
And thirty damsels wearing jewelled crowns
Within the palace, all provided for !
The Sháh demandeth tribute from all lands,
And Rúm will be exhausted in a year.
Alack ! for shoulders, breast, and height like his,
And face that brightened all the company !
None will behold his like in strength and stature,
Who pinneth with one shaft two onagers ;
But dalliance with women marreth him,
He soon will be as feeble as a ghost !
His eyes will darken and his looks grow wan,
His body slacken and his cheeks turn blue.
To sniff at women maketh hoary heads,
And hoary heads have naught to hope on earth.
As polo-playing maketh stoop the upright,
So womanizing causeth every ill.
Once in a month is intercourse enough,
While more is waste of blood. A wise youth too
Should husband vigour for his children's sake.
In this excess there is excess of loss,
And slackness is afflictive to a man."
    They went back to the palace, talking still,
And one remarked : " The Sun hath lost his way."
    Bahrám Gúr, with one slave to mind his horse,
Fared through the gloom of night and, when he neared
The jeweller's abode, heard sounds of harping,
Whereto he urged Gulgún, his steed, forthwith
Toward the merchant's house. He knocked and asked
Admittance, all the while invoking Him
Who made the sun. A kindly handmaid said :—
" Who's there ? Why knock thus at this time of
    night ? "
    Bahrám replied : " This morning as the Sháh
Was coming from the hunting-ground my horse
Went lame, and I perforce got left behind.

Here in this thoroughfare the folk will steal
A steed like this and my gold harness too,
So I need help."
                        The handmaid went and told
Her lord : " A man requesteth shelter, saying :
' My steed with its gold harness will be stolen,
And I shall go away undone.' "
                                    He answered :—
" Then ope the door.   Hast never seen a guest
Come here before ? "
                        The maid made haste to open,
And said : " Come in, my son ! "
                                    The Sháh on entering,
And seeing such a place and such attendance,
Said to himself : " O just and only God !
Thou art Thy servant's Guide to what is good.
Ne'er may I be but just in conduct, never
Be covetise and arrogance my creed,
Let every act and deed of mine be just,
And let my subjects' hearts rejoice in me :
Then, if my knowledge and my justice wax,
My memory will shine when I am dead.
May all my subjects, like this jeweller,
Enjoy the sound of harp and revelry."
    On entering the lofty hall he saw
The jeweller's famed daughter from the door.
The thane, on seeing him, arose and came
With bows profound, and said : " Good ev'n to thee.
May all thy foemen's hearts be rooted out."
    The host spread out a mat and laid thereon
A cushion, gazing at his guest with joy.
One brought a sumptuous board with viands hot
And cold thereon.   One came—a faithful liege—
And was instructed to secure the steed.
Elsewhere they lodged and fed Bahrám Gúr's servant.
They set a low seat for the host himself,

. 1524

Who took his place close to his guest the Sháh,
And then began to offer his excuse,
Thus saying to Bahrám : " Brave paladin !
Since thou art entertained within my house
Conform thyself to my rough usages.
When we have eaten we must drink and then
Rest sweetly. 'Tis dark night, the wine is royal ;
When thou hast drunk thy quantum thou shalt sleep,
And, when thou wakest at the break of day,
Must haste back to the service of the Sháh."
    Bahrám replied : " Night dark when one alighteth
On cheery host like thee ! We must not prove
Ingrate to God ; the hearts of thankless men
Are full of fear."
              The handmaid, who was all
Astonied at the aspect of the guest,
Brought water, bowl, and napkin. Hands were washed.
Then came the wine-cup's turn, and with the wine
Came mirth, contentment, and tranquillity.
The handmaid brought a flagon and strong drink,
Red wine, a cup, and flowers of fenugreek.
The thane first reached out for the cup and drank,
Then washed it out with musk and with rose-water,
And gave the cup that cheereth to Bahrám.
" What," said he, " is my boon-companion's name ?
Now will I make a covenant with thee,
And I will take Bahrám, the Sháh, as surety."
    The king laughed heartily thereat and said :—   C. 1525
" Gushasp, the cavalier, am I, and hither
Came I attracted by the sound of harp,
And not to drink or while away the time."
    " This girl of mine," his host replied, " exalteth
My head to heaven and is at once my harper,
And my cup-bearer, and withal she singeth,
And dissipateth care. My Heart's Delight
Is named Árzú—my heart's delight and server."

He said to that tall Cypress : " Bring thy harp,
Come in thy loveliness before Gushasp."
    The harpist, tall as a pomegranate-tree,
Moved stately to the king of kings and said :—
" O chosen cavalier who hast in all
The semblance of a king ! know that this house
Of feasting is thine own, my sire thy host
And treasurer.   May thy dark nights be joyous,
And be thy head exalted o'er the rain-clouds."
    He said to her : " Sit down, take up thy harp,
And let us have a song immediately.
To-night old Máhiyár shall be a youth,
And pledge his soul as hostage for his guest."
    The harpist clasped her harp and first she played
The Magians' chant, and as the silken chords
Rang out an odour as of jasmine filled
The room.   She sang to Máhiyár, her sire,
And thou hadst said : " How plaintive is her harp ! "

              " Thou art as a cypress
                  That lippeth a stream,
              And white locks encircle
                  Thy cheeks' rosy gleam.

              Thy tongue is warm-spoken,
                  Thy heart loveth peace,
              Oh ! ne'er may thy foemen
                  Of ill have surcease.

              Thy soul's food be wisdom.
                  Thy bent is as great
              As Farídún's.   On thee
                  As handmaid I wait.

              Árzú am I titled,
                  I joy in our guest,
              Like monarch whose troops are
                  With victory blest."

This ditty done, toward the guest she turned,
Turned toward him with a song and plaintive chords :—

" Sincere and brave, high-starred and king-like one !
    They that ne'er saw Bahrám, the cavalier,
    The well approved, to every bosom dear,
Should look upon thy face, and all is done.

His only semblance in the host thou art,
    Tall as a cypress with a reed-like waist,
    A cypress with a pheasant's carriage graced,
An elephant in bulk with lion's heart.

Two miles in fight thou flingest forth thy spear,
    Thy cheeks as though pomegranate-blossoms shine
    (Who was it washed, say'st thou, those blooms in
        wine ?)
And as a camel's thighs thine arms appear.

Thou tramplest Mount Bístún. Heaven toiled to
    mould   C. 1526
    A man like thee. None see I to compete
    In strife with thee. As dust beneath thy feet
Oh ! may Árzú's form be while life shall hold."

    The girl's proficiency with song and harp,
Her looks, her stature, and accomplishments,
So wrought the world-lord that thou wouldst have
    said :—
" His heart hath grown a magazine of woes,"
And at the time when Máhiyár grew drunk
Before him he addressed his host, thus saying :—
" Give me thy daughter as my lawful wife
If thou wouldst be commended for just dealing."
    " Wilt thou accept," said Máhiyár to her,
" The presents of this lion-hearted man ?   .
See if he pleaseth thee, and if 'tis well
For thee to go with him."
                          Árzú replied :—

" Good, noble father ! [1] if thou wouldst bestow me
On any then my partner is Gushasp,
The cavalier.   One that doth look upon
A man like this will bid Bahrám ' Avaunt ! ' "
   His daughter's words misliked him and he said
Thus to Bahrám : " O horseman of the fray !
Regard her carefully from head to foot,
Her industry, her knowledge, and discretion ;
See if she be approved of thee at heart ;
Report of her is better than assumption.
She is at once accomplished and no beggar ;
I do not specify exact amounts,
But shouldst thou count the gems of Máhiyár
They would exceed those in the royal coffers.
Be not precipitate, take rest to-night,
And, if needs must, another cup of wine,·
For great men make no compacts in their cups
Especially about their lady-loves.
Wait therefore till the sun shall rise on high,
And till the nobles' heads have roused from
    sleep,
Then will we call far-seeing elders in—
Disinterested men and scholarly.
At night 'tis out of order and ignoreth
The precedents of Farídún, the Sháh.
Ill-omened 'tis to marry in one's cups
Or handsel any business."
                  Said Bahrám :—
" Absurd !   'Tis ill to draw, or go by, omens.·
This harpist pleaseth me to-night, so strive
To deem the matter an auspicious one."
   The sire said to his daughter : " O Árzú !
Dost thou approve him as to looks and manners ? "
   She said : " Yea, I approved of him when I
Far off beheld him with such head and eyes.

          [1] Reading with P.

Complete the work and leave the rest to God :
The sky is not at feud with Máhiyár."
    Her father answered : "Thou art now his wife.
Know this that thou art under coverture."
    He gave her to Bahrám Gúr who espoused her ;   C. 1527
By dawn the matter had been consummate.
The Sháh's attendant hung the royal whip
Upon the door of Máhiyár, Arzú
Went to her chamber while on every side
Folk still were sleeping. Máhiyár departed
To make all ready for the cavalier,
Gushasp, and told a servant : "Shut the doors,
And send off some one to the flock in haste.
They must not serve the board without a lamb,
And one well fattened too. Wait on Gushasp,
And, when he waketh, bring him ice and sherbet,[1]
Take too a bowl of camphor and rose-water
To scent his chamber. As for me, my cups
Have left me just as I was yesterday ;
Old jewellers shirk not their wine."
                      He spake,
And, drawing up his cloak about his head,
Wooed rest and sleep.
            When bright Sol showed its crown,
And earth became like shining ivory,
Troops armed with shields and double-headed darts
Went to seek traces of the royal whip.
The escort gathered round the door as though
The Sháh's own court, and all that recognised
The whip came forward and saluted it.
The porter, seeing that great gathering,
The throng of swordsmen and of javelin-men,
Went, roused his sleeping lord, and sobered him,
Thus saying to him : "Rise, bestir thyself ;
This is no time to sleep or place to sit,

---

[1] *Fakká'.* See Vol. i. p. 43 *note.*

Because the world's king is thy guest within
This sorry house of thine ! "
                              The jeweller's heart
Throbbed wildly at the words. He cried : " What
    say'st thou ?
How tracest thou the footsteps of the king ? "
   Then fully realising what was said
He sprang up from the bed-clothes with a shout,
Enraged against the porter, " These," he cried,
" Are not the words of wisdom and of age."
   " Experienced man ! " the slave said, " who on earth
Made thee the monarch of Írán ?   So vast
A host is at thy gate that, wouldst thou pass,
There is scant room, and every Jack of them,
On coming up, saluteth our old curtain ! [1]
At dawn, before the sun began to shine,
The cavalier's attendant came and hung
A whip all gold and jewels o'er our entry,
Where we pass through it, and round that long whip
There is a world of folk from hill and dale.
So now be up and doing, be not slack,
And let not wine affect thee."
                              Hearing this,
The shrewd old man was troubled : " Why did I
Get drunk last night before the king of kings,
And let my daughter share the wine with us ? "
   Then going to the chamber of Árzú
He said : " My gracious Moon ! it was Bahrám,
The king of kings, that last night visited
The jeweller !   On coming from the chase
He hither turned his rein.   Now up and don
Brocade of Rúm and set upon thy head
Thy last night's crown.   Make him an offering
Of jewels worthy of a king—three rubies
Of royal worth—and, when thou shalt behold

. 1528

---

[1] The felt curtain at the door-way. *Cf.* p. 69.

His sun-like face, enfold thine arms before him,
Keep thine eyes fixed on him and think of him
As thine own soul and body. Answer meekly
When he shall question thee, and let thy words
Be modest and discreet. I shall not come
Unless he calleth me and giveth me
A place among his followers. I sat
At table with him like his peer ! Oh ! would
That I had no bones in me ! Furthermore
I cottoned with the Sháh when in my cups !
Wine maketh old and young to misdemean."
    Just then a slave came hurrying and said :—
" The Sháh, that ardent spirit, is awake."
    Now when the Sháh woke safe and sound, he went
To bathe him in the garden, went to pray
Before the sun, confiding all to God.
Returning thence to the reception-room
He bade a server bring a cup of wine,
Heard that his retinue had come, dismissed it,
And called Arzú on whom his heart was set.[1]
Arzú appeared with wine and offerings—
A handmaid with her necklace and her earrings—
And with a lowly reverence kissed the ground.
The Sháh smiled on her greatly pleased and said :—
" Whence such behaviour—first to make me drunk,
Then run away ? Thy song and harp suffice
For me, a woman's presents are for others.
Come sing to me thy ditties of the chase,
Of spearhead-blows, and royal combatings."
    Anon he said : " Where is the jeweller,
For we got drunk together yesternight ? "
    The daughter, when she heard this, called her father,
Mazed at the Sháh's good-nature. Came her sire   C. 1529
With folded arms before the sun-like king

---

[1] Árzú means " *Desire*," and there is a double use of the word in the original : " Because he had a desire for Desire."

Of kings, and said : " O Sháh ! O chief ! O wise !
O great ! O mighty one ! O warrior !
O archimage ! may this world ever be
At thy dispose and everywhere thy name
Associate with the crown.   The man that quaffeth
The draught of foolishness should hold his tongue.
My fault was due to ignorance.   Methinketh
That thou must deem me mad.   Vouchsafe to pardon
My fault and make my face and faring bright.
I stand—a foolish slave—before thy door ;
The king of kings will deem me less than man."
    Bahrám replied : " The wise man never taketh
The drunkard seriously ; one should not eye
Or savour wine if it make sad the face.
I saw thee not ill-tempered in thy cups.
Now listen to the singing of Árzú,
And proffer as thine own apology
The tulips and the jasmine of her song.
Let her descant what while we quaff, not counting
The ill of days not come."
                    He kissed the ground,
Did Máhiyár, then brought and spread the board,
And, good man that he was, he fetched withal
The nobles that were stationed at the gate ;
Howbeit Árzú went off to her own bower,
Her visage puckered at those stranger-guests,
And stayed till heaven grew sombre, and the stars
Came out around the moon.   The eating done,
Árzú was called and set upon a seat
Of golden work.   The Sháh bade her to take
Her harp and sing to him the song that he
Had asked of her already.   Thus she sang :—

" O monarch undaunted ! the lion in shame
Will slink from the wood at the bruit of thy name.
Sháh, victor, host-breaker art thou.   In thy mien

The tints of the tulip on jasmine are seen.
In stature no ruler on earth is thy peer,
In looks thou transcendest the moon in her sphere.
A host on the war-stead, beholding in fight
Thy helmet, will rive, heart and brain, with affright,
And longer discern not the depth from the height."

When they were blithe with wine and, eating done,
Were quaffing draught on draught, Rúzbih appeared
Before the Sháh.   They lodged him in the village.
Rúzbih had brought a litter and withal
Two score of eunuchs, all moon-face and charming.
Those Rúmans' faces seemed brocade of Rúm,
And freshened all the country round.   Árzú,
A crown of jewels set upon her head,
Toward the bower of Sháh Bahrám Gúr sped.

§ 15
*How Bahrám went to the Chase and passed the Night
in the House of Farshídward*

The king of kings, attended by Rúzbih,   C. 1530
Went from the chief's house with a gladsome heart.
He passed the night and went at dawn to hunt.
Troops fared o'er all the roads and trackless wastes,
And thus abode a month.   They pitched the tents
And camp-enclosure, and swept all the field
Of game.   None slumbered there, it was all wine,
Game, flesh, and harp, and lyre.   They kindled fires
About the plain and burned wood green and dry.
There came a swarm of dealers from the city,
Who tarried at the camp for trafficking :
The crowd made bright the waste.   At quarter price
They bought one onager or ten gazelles,
And whosoever was in want of meat,
For cooking for his guests or for his children,

Might carry home ground-game and water-fowl
By ass-loads.

When a month had passed Bahrám
Grew eager for his wives' society,
And led his people from the hunting-ground.
Folk could not see the way, the cavaliers
Raised such a dust ! but swift as dust they sped
Till day's cheeks turned to lapis-lazuli.
The Sháh observed a town in front of him
With groups of houses, roadways, and bázárs,
And ordered that his escort with the baggage
Should push on, leaving not a soul behind.
He asked : " Where is the chief man of the place ? "
And then made thither straightway.   He beheld
A shattered entry broad and deep.   The owner
Came and saluted him.   The Sháh inquired :—
" Whose ruin is this and wherefore in such plight
Amidst the town ? "

The master said : " 'Tis mine,
And ill luck is my guide.   I have not here
Kine, raiment, victuals, manhood, understanding,
No feet, no wings.   Me thou hast seen, now view
My house—one fitter for a curse than blessing."
    The aspiring Sháh alighted, scanned the house,
And hands and feet both failed him, for the place
Was all sheep's droppings though both great and
        vaulted !

.1531   " Bring me," he said, " thou hospitable man l
Somewhat whereon to sit."

The other answered :—
" Why mock thy host so wantonly, O marchlord !
Had I some draperies my guest would praise me,
But I have none, no clothing, food, or carpets.
Pray lodge thee somewhere else ; here all is poor."
    The Sháh said : " Fetch a cushion then that I
May sit awhile."

" The place is ill," he answered.

" Good sooth l wouldst thou haye bird's milk ? "
Said Bahrám :—
" Bring fresh milk and new bread if thou canst get it."
" Imagine," said the other, " that thou hast
Partaken and gone off with ' Fare thee well.'
I should not be so lifeless had Ì bread,
Though life were better far than bread to me."
Bahrám said : " If thou hast no sheep how come
These droppings here ? "
" 'Tis night," the other answered.
" My head is all a muddle with thy talk.
Select some mansion with a curtained entrance ;
The master of it will commend thy choice.
Why shouldst thou be with an unfortunate,
Who maketh leaves his pillow for the night ?
Thou hast a golden sword and stirrups, thou
Shouldst sojourn not where there is fear of thieves,
For thieves and lions haunt old hulks like this."
The Sháh said : " If a thief should rob me now
Thou wouldst not be responsible, but give me
A lodging for the night, 'tis all I need."
" Then need it not," the owner made reply ;
" None lodgeth in my house."
" O wise old man !
Why art thou," said the Sháh, " so short with me ?
Still thou wilt give me, I presume, cold water,
O noble one ! "
" Didst thou not see," rejoined
The householder, " more than two bow-shots long [1]
The pool ?   There drink and take whate'er thou wilt.
Why seek for aught in this impoverished house ?
Good sooth ! hast never seen a poor man barred
From working by decrepitude ? "
Bahrám
Rejoined : " Thou art not one of the first water,

[1] Or " hence." So Mohl.

Chief though thou be ; so strive not with a soldier.
What is thy name ? ''
He answered : '' Farshídward,
A man without land, raiment, sleep, and food.''
 Bahrám asked : '' Why endeavour not for provand
And comfort ? ''
Said the master of the house :—
'' He that bestoweth all may end my days.

. 1532 If only I can see my desolation
Relieved of thee I will make prayer to Him.
Why cam'st thou to an empty house that never
Saw good condition and a high estate ? ''
 When he had spoken thus he wept so sorely
That Sháh Bahrám fled from his cries.   He laughed
At that old man and took the road again,
While all his escort followed in his train.

§ 16

How a Bramble-grubber revealed the Case of Farshídward, and
 how Bahrám bestowed that Householder's Wealth upon the
 Poor

Bahrám, on quitting that famed township, came
Upon a bramble-brake.   A man, who held
A mattock in his hand, was grubbing there.
The monarch left his retinue, drew near him,
And said : '' O enemy of brambles ! whom
Know'st thou of most account in yonder town ? ''
 He answered : '' Farshídward—a man of greed
That doth not suffer him to sleep or eat.
He hath, may be, a hundred thousand sheep,
More camels, steeds, and asses.   Earth is full
Of his amassed dinárs, but would that he
Had neither skin nor marrow to his body !

A famished paunch and nakedness are his ;
He hath no child, no kin, no friends, no goods.
A captive in the hands of Greed and Need
His person is all misery and wasted
Through eating not, but if he were to sell
For gold his tilth 'twould purchase gems enough
To fill a house ! His shepherds swill down flesh
With milk, but he himself hath millet-bread
Without e'en cheese l He never saw two coats
At once ; he is a tyrant to himself."
　　The Sháh said to the grubber : " Thou dost know
The number of his sheep, but knowest thou
Where those flocks are and likewise where his steeds
And camels are at large ? "
　　　　　　　　　The grubber said :—
" O thou ! it is not far from here to where
His camels and his sheep are, but my heart
Is troubled at the ill that he may do me."
　　Bahrám Gúr gave the grubber some dinárs,
And said : " This day shall gentle thy condition."
　　He bade one of his escort come to him,
A man that knew his way about, by name
Bihrúz, a horseman brave and popular,
And sent with him a hundred cavaliers,
Selected men well suited to the work.
He chose withal a scribe, an honest man
And skilled accountant. " Go," he told the grubber, C. 1533
" Thou didst grub brambles, now reap gold. One
　　hundredth
Of all that wealth is thine. Show to these men
The way."
　　　　　　The grubber's name was Diláfrúz,
A man of stately mien and stalwart form.
Bahrám bestowed on him a noble steed,
And said : " Thou must companion with the wind."
　　He was the Light of hearts but he became

The Lustre of the world [1] and carried out
His task triumphantly. He led the troop
O'er hill and plain past countless flocks of sheep.
Upon the mountains were ten caravans
Of camels, each with its own caravaneer.
The scribe wrote down of draught and of milch cattle
Twelve thousand, and the number of the camels
And steeds as twice ten thousand. All the waste
Was dinted with their hoofs. Beside the stream
There were three hundred thousand camel-loads
Of potted butter and curds fresh and dried. [2]
Height, waste, and level were one mighty cache,
But none had heard thereof. Bihrúz, the son
Of Húr, reported to the king of kings,
Bahrám Gúr, praising first almighty God,
The All-victorious and All-nourisher,
And next the king of kings who had released
Men's hands from toil, and then proceeded thus :—
" O monarch of the world ! thou art the joy
Of all folk great and small because thy justice
Surpasseth bounds. Our treasury hath suffered
Through silence as to this man's wealth. 'Tis well
That all things in the world should have their
    bounds,
Well that the Sháh be boundlessly rejoiced.
A wretch there is named Farshídward, unknown
In feast and fight to great and small alike
Throughout the world, not fearing God or Sháh,
And thankless in respect of what he hath.
While thus he streweth o'er the world his wealth
He is a lack-all, wretched, secretive,
Who is as unjust as the Sháh is just.
Blame not my words and counsel. Let this wealth
Inaugurate a treasury ; 'twill need

---

[1] He was, *i.e.* his name was, Diláfrúz, but he became Gítiáfrúz.
[2] For winter use.

Three years to order it. I have invoked
To mine assistance certain other scribes,
And settled them upon this fertile mount,
But, though the writers' backs are bent, not yet
Is manifest the sum of this man's treasure ;
Moreover he possesseth, so folk say,
Still greater buried hoards of gold and jewels.
Here in the mountain am I with both eyes
Upon the road to know the Sháh's commands.
My salutation to him. May he live   C. 1534
What while his name is all in all to all." [1]
    He sent a cameleer post haste to bear
The letter to the Sháh. Whenas Bahrám Gúr
Had read it he was troubled in his heart,
Grew downcast, wept, and bent his warrior-brows.
He called for Rúman pens and silk of Chín,
And bade a scribe approach. He first gave thanks
To God almighty, the omniscient Guide,
" The Lord of knowledge and of Grace, the Lord
Of diadem and kingship," then wrote thus :—
" I should by rights attach this man. He hath not
Amassed these hoards by thievery and bloodshed,
Hath not incited others to do wrong,
But he hath been ungrateful and not had
The fear of God within him, hath kept ward
O'er all this treasure to the detriment,
By such amassing, both of heart and soul.
Wolf is as good as sheep upon yon plain
Since neither yieldeth profit or return.
A buried gem is nothing but a stone,
Affording no one either food or raiment.
We shall not found a treasury on his toils,
Or fix our heart upon this Wayside Inn.
Evanished from the world are Farídún,
Íraj withal, Túr, and, amidst the mighty,

----

[1] Lit. " is (both) warp and woof."

Sám, Sháh Káús, and Kai Kubád, besides
The other potentates whose names we cherish,
And mine own sire who filled my heart with pain
As being neither just nor generous.
None of these great men is in evidence ;
Herein there is no striving with the Lord.
Collect this treasure and distribute it,
But touch not thou one hair. To every one
That hideth his necessities and looketh
Long vainly for remission from his ills ;
To old men past their work and despicable
In rich men's eyes ; to those that have spent all,
And now in trouble breathe forth chilling sighs ;
To those that have renown but not dínárs ;
To traders reft of friends ; to little ones
Whom thou beholdest orphans, their sires dead,
And they themselves in want of gold and silver ;
To women that have neither spouse nor raiment,
That know no handicraft and no employment,
Give all these treasures and irradiate
The lives of those poor souls. This done, neglect not
The hidden treasures, but bestow the hoards
Of Farshídward upon the mendicants
· 1535   For their relief. Dínárs and gems are dust
To him since he must needs go bury them.
May turning heaven be thy companion,
All justice mayst thou be and self-restraint."
    They set the Sháh's seal on the document,
And thereupon the courier turned and went.

§ 17

How Bahrám went to the Chase and slew Lions

Bahrám bade slaves set up the imperial throne
Within the pleasance, then in spring-tide beauty.

They brought the turquoise throne at his command,
And set it 'neath a blossom-shedding tree,
They brought forth wine and cups, and minstrels went
Toward the pleasance with the chiefs. The king
Said to his counsellors : " This is the time
Of jollity for men. We all must couch ;
Death treadeth under foot the rolls of fame,
The hall and palace. We shall have enough
Of our own company within the charnel,
Men both of mien and stature though we be.
The king and beggar carry when they die
Naught but their good and ill away with them.
What toil soe'er men bear is only loss,
For, when they perish, that will perish too.
That praise of us remaineth is enough,
For crown and girdle are another's share.
Thou needest innocence and uprightness
That thine enjoyments prove not scath to thee.
My years exceed already eight and thirty,
And many a day hath fleeted in delight,
But, after two score years, grief for the day
Of death is instant with us. If one hair
Turn white upon our heads we must forgo
All hope of joy ; when musk becometh camphor
'Tis ruined ; camphor suiteth not the crown.
Two years more will I spend in feast and sport,
Then, when my strength is somewhat broken, go
Before God's presence, don the woollen robe,
And be not thankless for His mercies to me,
For I have passed my days in joy and had
My share of royal crown. Now for the rose,
The apple, the pomegranate, and the quince !
Let not the golden goblet fail of wine ! [1]

[1] The Emperor Bábar (A.D. 1483–1530) in his diary made similar
good resolutions, which he did not keep: " As I intend, when forty
years old, to abstain from wine ; and as I now want somewhat less than
one year of being forty, *I drink wine most copiously.*" EHI, iv. 226.

But when I see the apples amber-checked,
The heavens dappled like a leopard's back,
The fragrant camomile producing seed,
And wine as ruddy as the reveller,
When air is pleasant, neither hot nor cold,
Earth fresh and water blue, what time we don
Our autumn furs, I must to Jaz to hunt,

. 1536   And hold a hunting-bout upon that plain
To make me a memorial in the world.
Meanwhile the onager will grow plump-necked,
And compass lion's heart and tiger's strength.
We must take dogs and cheetahs, hawks and falcons,[1]
For that far faring since it is the spot
For onager and archery, and there
No moment will we rest from chevying.
The plain that I have set mine eyes upon
Is lower Jaz.   There tamarisks are tall
As spear-shafts, there too we shall find the lion,
And have a hunting if we bide our time."
　He waited till the clouds of Shahrivar
Arose, then all the world was filled with troops.
From every clime an army keen for strife
Set face toward the monarch of Írán,
Who chose among them chiefs of note as hunters,
And carried with him to the chase a force
Of thirty thousand mounted Scimitars.
They took with them pavilions, tent-enclosures,
Tents, beasts, and shielings, while the underlings
Went on before Bahrám Gúr to dig wells,
To furnish them withal with wheel and bucket,
And run the water into troughs.   The Sháh
Came later with his meiny to the chase.
He saw the plain well stocked with onager,
The woods alive with lions, and thus said :—

---

[1] Two sorts of falcons are mentioned in the text—the charkh and the sháhin (falco sacer and falco peregrinator ?).

" Wine is our quarry to-night, for on the sand
Are many lion-tracks, and we must have
A lion-hunt to-morrow.   Rest ye then
In health of body and in merry pin,
And let us drink till daybreak, till the sun—
The lustre of the world—is bright again.
Our scimitars shall fell the lions first,
Shall fell those valiant dragons.   When the woods
Are cleared of lions then the onager
Shall yield himself a servant to my shafts."
    He stayed that night and, when the morning dawned,
Approached the forest with his men, whereat
A lion, lusty-grown with battening
On onagers, rushed forth, and brave Bahrám
Said to his friends : "Though I have bow and arrows,
And mastery therewith, I will assail
Yon lion with the scimitar that none
May call me coward."
                                  Donning a shrunk vest
Of wool he mounted on his battle-steed.
Now when that dragon of a lion saw him
It reared, brought down its claws, and sought to strike
The charger on the head.[1]   The warrior heeled
His steed and with his trenchant scimitar,
What while the lioness made off apace,
Struck at the lion's head and clave the beast   C. 1537
Down to its middle, filling lions' hearts
With fear ; yet gallantly another one
Came roaring, one whose mate was suckling cubs.
He smote that lion's neck and parted head
From trunk.   One said to him : " O sun-faced Sháh !
Hast thou not any mercy on thyself ?
The wood is full of lions and their young—

---

[1] Blanford describes a lioness attacking his horse much in this way,
and remarks that Persian sporting pictures generally represent the lion
as leaping, not rearing. EP, ii. 32.

Cubs that are sucklings. Let the lions be,
For in the autumn-time they breed. This forest
Is three leagues deep, and if thou wert to spend
A year in taking lions wouldst not clear it ;
So why impose such labour on thyself ?
The Sháh, when first he sat upon the throne,
Fought lions only as the compact was.[1]
Now thou art Sháh, the world is thine, so why
Fight with them still ? Thou cam'st for onager."

   " Old sage," the Sháh said, " let to-morrow dawn,
And heigh for onager and shaft and me !
But cavaliers and nobles now alive
Can rival me in archery, so when
We give its due to manhood we must take
Account of iron mace and scimitar."

   The archmage said : " Hadst thou ten horsemen
      with thee,
And like thee in the fight, then Rúm and Chin
Would have no crown and throne, and men of wisdom
Would ship their goods off. Be the evil eye
Far from thy Grace, and be it thine to feast
Among the roses."

                     Then with archimages,
And captains of the host, the Sháh departed
Toward his tent-enclosure from the wood
What while the troops acclaimed him, saying thus :—
" Ne'er may the crown and signet-ring lack thee."

   That paladin then entered his pavilion,
His escort quitting him, and washed his hands
Of sweat. He had with him a trusty steward,
Who draped a fresh tent for him. There they set
Musk, camphor, and rose-water, and spread musk
Withal upon the sleeping-place. Each tent
Had golden tables laid with services
Of ware of Chín where lamb and other meats

---

[1] See Vol. vi. p. 405 *seq.*

Were served by the chief server. Sháh Bahrám Gúr,
The eating done, called for a mighty cup
Of crystal, which a fairy-faced cup-bearer
Brought and consigned it to the just king's hands,
Who said : " Ardshír, the great king, he whose fortune
Made old folk young, was founder of our house,
And we are underlings if we be worthy
E'en of that title. Both in fight and feast,
At counsel and at board, give none but him
The title of world's lord. What time Sikandar   C. 1538
Came to Írán from Rúm and wrecked the land,
Since he was both ungenerous and harsh,
And slew kings six and thirty, monarchs' lips
Are full of curses, and earth's surface full
Of vengeance, on him.[1] Farídún they praise,
And he is cursed by stirrers up of strife.
Throughout the world may only good proceed
From me to small and great. Bring me a herald,"
He added, " one of goodly voice and leading,
Let him go round the host and thus proclaim
O'er way and waste alike : ' Whoe'er shall lay
Within the region of Barkúh and Jaz [2]
Unlawful hands on aught, from jewels, gold,
Dinárs, and furs to mean and worthless chaff,
Him will I horse face tail-wards and will have
Two of the soldiery to lead him hence.
His feet shall be made fast beneath his steed,
And to the temple of Ázargashasp
Will I dispatch him there to supplicate
All-holy God and worship in the dust
Before the Fire. I will bestow his goods
On those whom he hath robbed and wronged withal.
If any horse shall injure growing crops,
Or harm fruit-bearing trees, the horse's owner,

---

[1] The Persian pre-Muhammadan view of Sikandar. *Cf.* Vol. vi. p. 15.
[2] Reading with P.

Be he a noble or of no account,
Shall not escape a year's imprisonment.
My work is but to carry from the desert
My portion, then go home again rejoicing.' "
　　The more part of the traffickers of Jaz,
And of Barkúh, went out upon the plain,
And with their various packs produced a scene
About the host like a bázár in Chin.

§ 18

How Bahrám went to hunt the Onager, showed his Skill before
the Princes, and returned to Baghdád and Istakhr

Whenas the sun next day displayed its crown
The world-lord went to hunt the onager ;
The soldiers strung their bows, the Sháh himself
Rode in the rear.　He said : " If one should take
His bow to shoot at any beast the arrow
Should strike the buttocks and come through the
　　breast."
　　A paladin replied : " O king ! consider
Who in this noble host can shoot like that
Among thy friends or foes unless indeed
Thou shoot in person.　May thy head and crown
For ever live.　When thou tak'st mace and arrow,
And scimitar, thy warriors are awe-struck
At thy commanding height and royal Grace,
While other archers' hands lose all their strength."
　　The Sháh said : " 'Tis of God.　If He withdraw it
What strength hath then Bahrám ? "
　　　　　　　　　　　　　　　He urged Shabdíz,
And, nearing a buck onager, let fly
His arrow, when the moment came, and skewered
Together chest and buttock.　As it died

1539

The nobles of the golden belt came up ;
They marvelled at his shot, and all applauded.
They could not see the arrow's point and feathers,
For they were hidden in the onager.
The warlike cavaliers and soldiers bent
With faces to the ground before Bahrám,
What while a paladin exclaimed : " O king !
Ne'er may thine eye behold the ill of fortune.
Thou art a horseman but all we ride asses,
And are but ill at that l "
                              The Sháh replied :—
" Not mine the arrow, for the All-conqueror
Assisteth me.   None in the world is viler
Than one whose prop and helper God is not."
    He urged his charger onward, thou hadst said :—
" Yon courser is an eagle in its flight ! "
A gallant onager appeared.   Forthwith
The Lion reached out for his scimitar,
And with a sword-stroke clave the beast asunder
In equal halves.   Chiefs, nobles, and attendants
Armed with the scimitar, came up to him,
And, when they saw that stroke, a sage exclaimed :—
" What swordmanship and might are here ! Oh l may .
The evil eye ne'er look upon this Sháh.
He hath no semblance save the moon in heaven,[1]
Beneath him are the heads of this world's chiefs,
While heaven is lower than his scimitar,
And arrow-point."   .
                         The troops that followed him
Cleared all the plain of onager.   He bade
Make rings of gold and grave his name thereon.
He ringed the creatures' ears and let them go ;
Six hundred too he branded in a batch,
Then freed them for the honour of his name,
And for his will and pleasure, while a man

---

[1] " il ne laissera peut-être pas la lune dans le ciel." Mohl.

Went round the host proclaiming thus : " Let none
Sell to the merchants any onagers
On this broad plain but give them as a gift."
    They brought him from Barkúh and from the chiefs
Of Jaz abundance of brocade and furs.

· 1540 These he accepted and then bade remit
Those countries' tax and toll though both could pay.
Their poor and those that earned their bread grew rich
By reason of his bounty.   Many too
Had thrones and crowns.   He went home from the
    chase,
And passed a week in mirth among his men.
It was his wont to hold an open court
Upon the riding-ground, and thither used
To fare the troops, the men of eloquence,
The wise, the needy, and the suppliants.
" O ye that seek your rights ! " he used to say,
" Take shelter from your enemies with God,
While ye that have not slept through toil for me,
And yet have had no portion of my wealth,
Come to the king upon the riding-ground,
And haply he will make your fortunes new.
If any one is old, past work, and weak,
Or, being young, is crippled by disease ;
If any of the people be in debt,
And worried by the stress of creditors ;
If any children are left fatherless,
And yet ask not of those possessed of wealth ;
Or if the children's mothers are in want
In secret and conceal their poverty ;
Or if, again, a wealthy man hath died,
And left behind young children in this land,
Whom an executor, devoid of fear
And reverence for God, is plundering,
Keep nothing of this kind concealed from me ;
I want not people that conceal their wants.

I will enrich the poor, I will restore
The souls of misbelievers to the Faith ;
I will defray the debts of those who have
No money and whose hearts are sad, and open
My treasury's door to modest indigence.
If wrong befall from officers of mine
Defrauding children that have lost their sires,
Those doers of injustice will I gibbet
Alive for wronging one of noble race."
   The Sháh, advanced in wisdom and glad-hearted,
Went from the hunting-field toward Baghdád,[1]
And to his presence came the haughty chiefs,
Both alien and those akin to him.
He bade his retinue disperse and sought
His own delightsome palace.   They adorned
The bower of Barzín, the handmaids there
Were clamorous for musk and wine, the Idols
Got ready song and harp, the hall was cleared
Of strangers.   What with harp and wine and pipe,
And sound of song, the vaulted heaven seemed
To greet the air.   All night from every chamber
They brought forth bands of dancers that the Sháh
Might be not sad of heart.   He spent two weeks   - C. 1541
In mirth, and oped his treasury day and night,
Gave largess, and departed for Istakhr,
Placed on his head the glorious, royal crown,
Unlocked the bower of Kharrád, and furnished
The Idols there with treasure and with drachms.
If any in that golden women's house
Had not a crown aloft an ivory throne
The monarch of Írán growled mightily,
Bit at Rúzbih his lip in indignation,
And said : " The tribute from Khazar and Rúm
I give, when paid, to these, but for the nonce
Now requisition ass-loads of dinárs,

---

[1] *Cf.* Vol. vi. p. 254.

And treasure-loads from Ispahán and Rai.
A women's house when in such case as this
Will grow all desolate and not befit
The fortunes of the monarch of Írán."
    They spread brocade upon the floor, and caused
Fresh tribute to be paid in every land.
The world thus passed awhile an easy life—
No war, no toil, no conflict, and no strife.

§ 19

How the Khán of Chín led forth a Host to war with Bahrám,
and how the Íránians asked Quarter of the Khán and
submitted to him

Anon news came to Hind, Rúm, Turkistán,
Chín, and all parts inhabited : " The heart
Of Sháh Bahrám is given up to sport,
He taketh no account of any one,
He hath no outposts, no men are on guard,
And on the marches are no paladins.
For love of sport he suffereth all to drift,
And knoweth nothing of the world's affairs."
    Now when the Khán of Chín heard this he levied
Troops from Khutan and Chín, paid them, and set
His face toward Írán.   No one took thought
About Bahrám while Cæsar for his part
Marched forth in force from Rúm.   When tidings
      reached
Írán from Rúm and Hind, from Chín and all
The settled regions : " Cæsar hath assembled
And led an army forth while troops are seen
Advancing from Khutan and Chín," the chieftains,
The warriors old and young within Írán,
All came before Bahrám Gúr, full of wrath,
Of rage, and bitterness, and bluntly said :—

" Thy glorious fortune hath displayed its back.
The heads of kings should be intent on fighting,
But thy heart is intent on sport and feasting ;
The crown and throne are worthless in thine eyes,
So are Írán, the treasure, and the host."
  The Sháh, the ruler of the world, thus answered   C. 1542
Those archimages, his admonishers :—
" My helper is the Master of the world,
One who is wiser than the wisest sages.
I by the conquering virtue of great kings
Will guard Írán against the claws of Wolves ;
By fortune, host, wealth, scimitar will I
Avert this pain and travail from the realm."
  He toyed on just the same, his nobles' eyes
Were full of blood through him, and all folk said :—
" This Sháh will alienate all good men's hearts."
  Yet Sháh Bahrám's heart was awake and full
Of trouble at the tidings.   Secretly
He organised the host while folk at large
Knew not his privy purpose.   All Írán
Was in dismay at what they saw of him
Their hearts were riven by anxiety ;
They all were in despair about the king,
And held his rule and person in contempt.
  Now when the Khán was drawing nigh Írán
News of him reached the monarch of the brave,
Who called to him the aspiring Gustaham,
And spake much of the Khán and of his host.
This Gustaham was paladin in chief,
And minister, and fight came as a feast
To him.   The Sháh called Mihr Pírúz withal,
Son of Bihzád, he called too Mihr Barzin,
Son of Kharrád, Bahrám, son of Pírúz,
Son of Bahrám, Ruhhám and Kharzarwán,
Which twain were of Sásánian lineage,
One king of Rai, and of Gílán the other,

Who stood up stoutly on the day of battle,
With Rád, son of Barzin, approved in fight,
Who was the ruler of Zábulistán,
Káran too and Burzmihr and Dád the grim,
Son of Barzin, while of the Íránians
He chose him out a hundred thousand men,
Men of discretion, well beseen in war,
Committing to a scion of the race
In power—Narsi, the brother of the Sháh
So pure of Faith—those cavaliers and throne
And crown that he might guard the treasury
And realm. Narsi, that man of noble mien,
Possessed of Grace and Faith and loving looks,
Took up the charge, and thereupon the Sháh
Chose from the host twelve thousand cavaliers
Fit for the day of battle—veterans
With ox-head maces and in coats of mail—
And marched thence to Ázar Ábádagán ;
But, as he took from Párs so small a host,
The mighty and the common folk alike
Thought : " Sháh Bahrám is fleeing from the fight,
And making off toward Ázargashasp."
    What time Bahrám set face toward the Fire
From Cæsar came an envoy swift as wind.
. 1543 Narsi received and lodged him fittingly
Within the palace.
                        Now the host approached
The high priest to get knowledge of Bahrám,
And said : " Why scattereth he his treasures thus
Instead of heaping them like other Sháhs ?
He squandereth gold everywhere because
He knoweth not its worth. Both citizens
And soldiers are dispersed, and all have sought
Some course of betterment."
                        At length, when words
Had waxen old, all folk agreed to send

A man of reputation to the Khán
Of Chin, " Because," said they, " ere evils come
With war and pillage we must try all means
To save Írán : the master of the house
Is lost."
        Narsi replied : " This is not well ;
The world hath not a bed for such a stream.
Shall I ask quarter of the king of Chin ?
I will clothe earth with men and elephants.
There are arms, treasure, and courageous men,
Whose swords would send dust out of fire itself.
Why this despair concerning Sháh Bahrám
Because he started with a little band ?
Why have your thoughts turned evil thus ? If ye
Think ill then ill will come."
           The Íránians heard,
And answered him perversely, saying : " Bahrám,
Departing hence, took not a host with him,
And must we not resign our hearts to grief,
For when the Khán shall come to fight Irán
Our land will lose both scent and hue ? The foe
Will trample on us shamefully, Narsi
And all the host will be o'erthrown. All means
Will we endeavour to maintain our place
And standing here."
        There was an archimage,
A skilful, learnéd, single-hearted man,
Humái by name, and him the Íránians chose
To gird his loins and undertake their cause,
Then wrote the Khán upon their own behalf
A cringing letter which began : " Thy slaves
Are we and bow down to thy will and pleasure.
We send thee of the produce of Írán
Together with our homage and excuses,
With gifts too, toll and tribute, for we have
No power to stand against the king in war."

So from Írán the blest Humái arrived
With certain nobles—men of honest counsels—
And gave the Khán the message of the chiefs,
Whereat his heart rejoiced. Humái withal
Spake of the swift remove of Sháh Bahrám,
And of his hasty flight without a host,
Before the noble Khán whose heart and soul
Expanded like a rose. He told the Turkmans :—
" Now we have saddled the revolving sky !
Who ever took Írán without a fight
As we have by our counsel, wit, and patience ? "
He gave great presents to the messenger,
Drachms and no few dínárs, and wrote this answer :—
" May wisdom company the pure of soul.
I do agree to what hath been proposed
By this ambassador of honest men.
When with my host I reach Marv I will make
The clime like pheasant's plumes,[1] and streams run
      milk [2]
By justice, prudence, and magnificence.
I will await the tribute from Írán—
The Lions' gifts and taxes. I shall come
To Marv, or rather I shall pass it by,
Not wishing to cause damage by my troops."
The messenger returned in haste and told
His converse with the Khán who led his host
To Marv, the world was black with horsemen's dust.
When he had rested he concerned himself
With feasting ; no one thought about Bahrám.
At Marv there was no rest or sleep for sound
Of harp and lyre, the troops were all abroad.
There was no watch, no prospect of a shock,
But all was sport, wine, parties, twang of lyre,
And feeling night and day secure from war.

[1] Because " tadarv," pheasant, rhymes with " Marv."
[2] Reading with P. and T.

The Khán was looking for the Íránians' tribute,
Wroth that it came so late. Bahrám for his part
Slept not but guarded well his host from foes,
Kept his spies busy both by night and day,
And threw in feast and wine no time away.

§ 20

How Bahrám attacked the Host of the Khán and took him

As soon as tidings came to Sháh Bahrám :—
"The Khán and his great host are all at Marv,"
He led his soldiers from Ázargashasp,
Each with two horses but no baggage-train.
With Rúman helmet, morion, and cuirass
He hurried on like wind by day and night,
His soldiers rushing like a mountain-stream,
And reached Ámul by way of Ardabil.
Departing thence he marched on to Gurgán,
Enduring all the chieftains' toil and pain,
And thence came to the city of Nisá ;
One from Bisá preceded him as guide.
O'er mount and waterless and wayless tracts,   C. 1545
At times unwonted, through the night till morn,
He marched and had the watch out night and day.
Thus swifter than a pheasant [1] in its flight
He drew toward Marv. A runner from his scouts
Arrived and told : " The Khán attendeth not
To state-affairs but followeth the chase
At Kashmíhan with wicked Áhriman
As minister."
              Bahrám rejoiced to hear it ;
His travail seemed but wind. There for a day
He rested and, when steed and Sháh and troops

----
[1] See p. 88, *note.*

Were all refreshed, reached Kashmíhan. At dawn,
What time the Lustre of the world arose
Above the hills, all ears were filled with blast
Of trumpet and all eyes with glint of flag-tops,
The din of battle went up from the chase,
And filled the ears of Sháh and troops. The clamour
Split mighty lions' ears. Thou wouldst have said :—
"The clouds are hailing," wouldst have said : "The
    moon
Is raining blood," so sanguine was the dust
Upon that battlefield ! The Khán, aroused
And dazed, was ta'en by Khazarwán. Withal
Three hundred of the noblemen of Chin
Were captured and fast bound on saddle-back.
The Sháh advanced on Marv from Kashmíhan,
Thin as a reed with riding for so long.
The few of Chin that yet remained at Marv
They slew. He followed up the fugitives
For thirty leagues ; behind him was Káran
Of Párs. Returning to the hunting-ground
He gave the booty to the troops. When thus
He raised his head in triumph over Chin
He recognised in all the power of God,
Who to his other good had given the boon
Of might, and is the Lord of sun and moon.

§ 21

*How Bahrám took a Pledge from the Túránians, how he set up
    a Pillar to delimit the Realm, and placed Shahra upon the
    Throne of Túrán*

Bahrám Gúr stayed to rest at Marv and when
Both Sháh and war-steed were refreshed he chose
Bukhárá for the next attack, for he

Had changed from gentleness to bitterness.
He reached Ámwi [1] in one day and one night,
Intent on conquest not on chase and sport.
He reached it in the night's first watch and crossed   C. 154
The river [2] and the desert of Farab.
Whenas the air was golden with the sun,
And doffed its skirt of lapis-lazuli,
The world was like a falcon's wing with dust
What time the world-lord passed by Mái and Margh.
He smote the Turkman host and set on fire
Their fields and fells, the stars concealed themselves
Behind the moon's skirts while the fathers made
Their way across the bodies of their sons.
All of the Turkmans that were leading men,
Both veteran and youthful swordsmen, came
Afoot in evil case before Bahrám,
With full hearts abjectly, and said : " O Sháh !
O mighty one l   O favourite of the stars !
O chief of all the nobles of the world !
Since now the Khán is captive that broke faith
Shed not the blood of those that did no wrong,
For tyranny becometh not the great.
If thou demandest tribute it is well,
But why behead the guiltless ?   All of us,
Both men and women, are thy slaves and are
Thy vanquished in the fight."

                   The Sháh's heart burned
For them.   He sewed up with the hand of wisdom
The eye of his displeasure.   In concern
That man of God restrained his warriors' hands
From shedding blood.   His favour thus secured,
The man of wrath appeased, the leading chiefs
Agreed to pay a heavy tribute yearly.
The Sháh was well content ; he took the tribute,
And further sums in lieu of pillaging.

---

[1] Probably the modern Charjui.   [2] The Oxus.

He turned and reached the city of Farab,
His cheeks were flushed and smiles were on his lips.
He paused, allowed his troops to rest a week,
And called to him the potentates of Chin.
He reared a column of cement and stone,
Which none, save by the Sháh's command, might pass
Out of Írán, Khalaj, and Turkistán.
He made the line between them the Jíhún.
There was among the troops one Shahra hight,
A man of wisdom, rank, success, and fame.
Bahrám made him the ruler of Túrán,
And made his throne the crown upon the moon.
When Shahra sat upon the silver throne
He girt his loins and opened wide his hands,
Set too the golden crown upon his head,
And through the land joy universal spread.

§ 22

How Bahrám wrote to announce his Victory to his
Brother Narsí and returned to Írán

C. 1547   The business of Túrán achieved, and when
The Sháh's heart was released from care, he bade
A scribe attend him, called for pen and ink
And silk of Chin, and wrote Narsí a letter
About the Turkman war and what his troops.
Had done. It thus began : " The nobles praise
Through me—a slave—the Maker of the world—
The Lord of victory and mastery,
The Lord of Saturn, Mars, and Moon, the Lord
Of lofty, circling heaven, the Lord of mean
And miserable dust. The great and lowly
Are underneath His governance, and all
That is to be is subject to His word.

I have indited from the coasts of Chín
A letter to my brother in Írán,
And this same letter, writ on painted silk,
Is meant too for our chiefs and folk at large.
Those that were not engaged against the Khán
Must hear the tale from us who fought with him.
His army was so vast that thou hadst said :—
' The dust thereof hath smeared the sky with pitch ! '
The coasts became as 'twere a sea of blood,
The unjust's fortune drooped, and he was taken
Because [1] the turning sky was weary of him.
Now have I brought him on a camel bound,
With wounded liver and with blood-filled eyes.
The necks of all the proud are bent, their tongues
Are gentle, and their hearts are hot within them.
Those now pay tribute who were enemies,
And they that erred have come back to the way.
I and my host, as my well-wishers would,
Will follow this dispatch."
                                  The wind-foot camels,
Foam-scattering, parted like a thunder-clap,
And when the letter reached Narsi the heart
Of that prince throbbed with joy. The high priest
    came
With all the heroes of the royal race
Before Narsi, the palace rang with joy,
And all gave ear to that report. The nobles
Were pricked at heart for shame before the Sháh
By reason of their fault. Among the chiefs
Six score and ten and more went to Narsi
To proffer their excuses, saying thus :—
" Perverse suggestions and the Div's behest
Have led us to transgress the World-lord's way.
To such a host as that one would presume
That God would ope Heaven's gate. 'Tis marvellous,

---

[1] Reading with P.

. 1548   Surpassing thought and all the providence
Of wise and learnéd men ! In thy reply,
'Mongst matters fair and foul, vouchsafe to give
A place to our excuse. Although the chiefs
Have erred the illustrious Sháh may pardon them."
    Narsi agreed and said : " So will I do
As to release the Sháh's heart from revenge."
    He wrote at once an answer to the letter,
Disclosing matters fair and foul, and said :—
" The Íránians in their pain and misery,
And for the sake of country, children, treasure,
Went for protection to the Khán of Chin,
Despairing of their own illustrious Sháh ;
'Twas not through enmity, offence, or strife ;
No other Sháh had gained their preference.
Now if the conqueror, the king of kings,
Will pardon he will make their dark night day.
Me they selected as the advocate
To urge their cause, and bade me : ' Plead for us.' "
    An archimage, by name Burzmihr, agreed
To go upon that embassage, approached
The monarch of the world, and told him all.
The Sháh was well contented by the words,
The fire of his fierce anger ceased to fume.
Then from Chaghán, Khatlán, Balkh, and Bukhárá
The chieftains went with tribute, and the archmages
From the Gharchís with sacred twigs, and pleaded
Before the worshippers of Fire, and thus
From year to year all those that had the means
Went to the court with taxes and with tribute.
    When the Fire-fane was ready and the place
To hold the feasts of New Year and of Sada
The Sháh approached Ázar Ábádagán,
He and his nobles and his men of name ;
They went to make their prayers before the Fire,
And all the archmages offered reverence.

The Sháh gave largess to the worshippers,
And passing thence proceeded to Istakhr,
Which was the glory of the king of kings.
From ox-hides and from sheep-skins, borne before him
Upon the backs of elephants, were scattered
A thousand quintals and eight score of largess ;
Part was in drachms, the rest in gold dínárs—
Coin that an archimage of Párs would call
In ancient Persian " paidáwasís." [1]   Then
He brought his scented leather bags of coin,
And lavished gold and silver. If he saw
Upon a journey any broken bridge,
Or heard of any hostelry in ruins
From his officials, he would give command
For their repair out of his treasury
Without forced labour.   On the poor withal,
And those that toiled to earn their daily bread,
He lavished drachms, for bounty never irked him,   C. 1549
While, thirdly, on the honest folk, the widows,
And infant orphelins, he showered silver.
Fourthly, on those too old for work or warfare,
And, fifthly, on all those of noble birth
That were despised by wealthy folk, and sixthly
On folk that coming from a lengthy journey
Paraded not their poverty, he lavished
A treasure, and looked round him to do good.
All booty he made over to his troops,
And had no notion of amassing wealth.
He bade a pious archimage to bring him
The crown worn by the Khán of Chin.   They took
The jewels out and used them and the gold
To grace a Fire-fane's walls and decorate
The throne-top of Ázar.   Thence he departed
To Taisafún where dwelt Narsi with those
Archmages that advised him.   All the chiefs,

---

[1] The " paidáwasi " was a silver coin = to five dinárs.

The great men of Irán, and governors,
Came forth to meet the Sháh, and when Narsi
Beheld that royal head and crown, the flags
Resplendent, and that mighty host, he lighted,
With all the great men and august archmages,
And did obeisance to Bahrám who bade him
To mount again, and grasped him by the hand,
Then went up to the golden throne and sat
What while the chiefs stood girded in his presence.
He lavished treasure on the indigent,
They opened wide the prison's narrow doors,
The age was filled with jollity and justice,
The hearts of all were strangers to distress.
He banished toil and grief from every clime,
He made a banquet for the great, and all
That hasted to attend the royal board
Received a present worthy of a lord.

§ 23

How Bahrám wrote a Letter of Directions to his Officials

The third day at a feast made for the nobles
A scribe was brought and set before the Sháh,
Who, when his visage was relaxed with wine,
Wrote, joying in his lovingkindliness,
A letter which began with praise of one
That hath with knowledge laved his soul, made wisdom
The jewel of his heart, won opulence
By his own toil and hardihood, acknowledged
That all good is from God, hath sought for wisdom,
Made friends of sages, knoweth that from justice
Naught will proceed but good, and knocketh not
Upon the portal of malignity :—

C. 1550

" If one complaineth of mine officers,
My noble chieftains or my men of war,
They have no prospect but the cell or gibbet,
And, if slain, vile committal to the dust.
Endeavour to make others' travail small,
Give joy and happiness to mourners' hearts,
Because the world hath stayed, will stay, with none ;
Be just and inoffensive, that sufficeth.
I am exemplary of what I say,
And an incentive to all righteousness,
For what a multitude of troops assailed
Me and this noble company, while I
Departed with a little host, and those
Who were mine enemies are now my friends !
One noble personage—the Khán of Chin,
A world-lord having signet, crown, and throne—
I captured, and the Turkmans' fortunes fell.
All-holy God made me victorious,
My foemen's heads have come to dust.   Be service
My sole employ, mine every thought be right.
I will impose no tax for seven years
On subject or compeer.   I write this letter
In our old tongue to chiefs and to officials
That they may treat my subjects in accord
To righteous precedent and take no thought
Of doing wrong.   Dispatch to me the names
Of those that are in want within your towns,
And in their portion have no day of joy,
And well will I content them.   Furthermore,
If there be any men of noble birth,
Who can recall to memory better days,
Them also with my treasures set past need,
And magnify the wise.   The folk in debt,
And empty-handed, who are everywhere
Looked down upon and scorned, them too relieve
Of debt and write their names upon the roll.

Pray ye to God to keep our heart thus true
To custom and the Faith, joy in this precept,
And well entreat the underlings. Moreover,
Despise not your own slaves, for they, like you,
Are God's. Let one of wealth, and fit therefor,
Entrust to learnéd men his children. Make
Their spirits rich in knowledge and encrown
Their heads with wisdom. Keep your hands afar
From others' wealth, be ye without offence,
And worshippers of God. Be diligent,
Break not our fealty,[1] and eradicate
The stumps, the suckers, and the roots of evil.

C.'1551   Seek not to do your neighbours injury,
Especially the magnates and the rich :
Make God your refuge, keep His ordinance,
And your souls pledges of your love for Him.
Whoever hath grown great from nothingness,
And raised himself to independency, _
Call him not great, such greatness dwindleth soon.
Be just, be worshippers of God, and wash
Perverseness and injustice from your hands.
All ye that have ! withhold not from the poor ;
Incline to holiness and act aright ;
Break not the hearts and backs of suppliants ;
Mishap is nigh to all things done amiss.
God's favour be upon the soul of him
To whom humanity is warp and woof."

    When they had written thus on lustrous silk
The scribe dipped into musk his pen and wrote
The heading thus : " The monarch of the world,
The heart of justice, knowing good and ill,
The lord of pardon, Grace, and puissance,
Bahrám Gúr, the all-bounteous king of kings,
To his marchlords and those beneath his rule—
The wise and understanding, warlike chiefs."

                  [1] Reading with P.

Then runners, cavaliers, and cameleers
Went with the letter everywhere with guides,
And when it came to all the provinces,
To every nobleman and chief, all said :—
" Thanks be to God, the world-lord is devout."
  Thereat the women, men, and children went
In all lands from their houses to the plain,
And all invoked a blessing silently
Upon that upright monarch of the world,
Then set themselves to feast and called for wine,
And harp and minstrelsy. They feasted half
The day, the other half they toiled.

At springtide

It was proclaimed before the court at dawn :—
" Let those of substance eat and give away.
Let them thank us for that which they enjoy,
And let the poor come to the treasury,
And carry thence five drachms of proper weight,
Together with three mans [1] of bright, old wine
Hued like pomegranate-blossom or like gold."
  The world disposed itself to merriment,
The shouts of revellers filled town and hamlet
Until they bought a coronal of roses
For two dínárs and gave without complaint
A drachm for a narcissus-spike. The old
Grew young of heart with joy, the streams ran milk.
The Sháh thanked God on seeing all the world   C. 1552
Thus glad.

One day he thus addressed Narsi :—

" Depart hence with the signet and the crown.
I have bestowed upon thee Khurásán ;
Cause it to flourish ; joy our subjects' hearts ;
Be nothing if not just ; stint not thy hand
Within this Place of Passage.[2] If our father

---

[1] *Cf.* Vol. i. p. 290 *note*.
[2] " n'interrompe jamais le passage à travers cc pays." Mohl.

Sought ill he quaked therefor like naked men
Beneath an autumn-blast."

                He bade prepare
A robe of honour for Narsi, thus voiding
An opulent treasury, and said to him :—
" God shelter thee, and be the sun's throne thine."
   The journey took two se'nnights, then Narsi
Assumed in peace the rule of Khurásán.
   When he had gone one week the Sháh, whose heart
Was freed from care, bade, and the high priest went
Before him, bringing certain of the nobles.
The Sháh addressed him, saying : " Cæsar's business
Is dragging on, and his ambassador
Is waiting long for his dismission.
What sort of man is he, and from the standpoint
Of wisdom where is he, for wisdom straighteneth
The soul ? "

           The high priest answered : " Blest be thou,
Lord of the world, and dowered with Grace divine.
He is advanced in years, discreet, and modest,
A man of goodly speech and gentle voice,
A pupil of the school of Falátún,[1]
A man of wisdom, learned, and nobly born.
He left Rúm, full of energy, but now,
Since he hath been here, he hath grown depressed,
And torpid like a snake in winter-time,[2]
With weak frame and with cheeks of reed-like hue.
His servitors are all like sheep before
A hunting cheetah, but regard not us ;
Such are their manhood and their valiancy
They think none in this land a man at all."
   Bahrám Gúr answered thus the high priest : " God
Bestoweth Grace and diadem and might.
If He hath given me victory, and turned
My fortune's night to day, still Cæsar too

     [1] Plato.   [2] Literally, " in the month of Dai."

Is of imperial race, is great, is sprung
From Salm whose head was crowned by Farídún,
And can recount his lineage sire by sire.
He acteth in a manly, prudent way,
And hath not turned to madness like the Khán.
At audience we will call the envoy in,
To see if what he saith be to the point,
And then I will dismiss him graciously,
For men are useful to me in this world ;
One is for war and bringeth troops, another
For feasting and doth bring a golden crown.
I must maintain the honour of Írán,
The man that treateth with great men is great."
    The high priest praised him lovingly and said :—   C. 1553
" Live happily so long as heaven revolveth.
He shall not speak save to exalt thy fame :
Mayst thou be chief among the men of name."

§ 24

How Bahrám called before him the Envoy of Cæsar, and how
the Envoy questioned and answered the Archmages

The next day when the sun displayed its crown,
And rays proceeded from the vaulted sky,
The monarch of the world sat on his throne,
And called the envoy in before his lords.
That old man sage, experienced, eloquent,
Of understanding and retentive mind,
Approaching with dejected head and arms
Enfolded, kneeled before the monarch's throne.
Bahrám both greeted and made much of him,
Set him upon the turquoise throne and said :—
" Here thou hast sojourned long ; art thou not weary
Of looking on this land ? War with the Khán,

Which closely partnered me, withheld me from thee ;
Now all our case is altered, and thy sojourn
Exceedeth bounds. To that which thou shalt say
We will reply, deriving from thy words
Good rede.''
                    The ancient envoy praised him, saying :—
'' May time and earth ne'er lose thee. Every king
Possessed of wisdom joyeth in the words
Of sages ; sages are more nigh to God ;
Those that think evil have the darker day.
Midst this world's chieftains thou art chief, who art
At once Sháh, chief, and best. Thy tongue's a balance,
Thy words are jewels, and who e'er will see
Gems weighed 'gainst gold ? Thou art possessed of
        knowledge,
Of counsel, sense, and Grace, and all the methods
Of conquering kings ; thou art possessed of wisdom
And holy rede, and master of the wise.
Though Cæsar's envoy I am thy slave's slave.
I carry Cæsar's greeting to the Sháh :—
' May this head, throne, and crown for ever be.'
And furthermore I have it in command
To ask seven questions of thy men of lore.''
    The Sháh replied : '' Proceed ; the highest honours
Await the eloquent.''
                    He bade the high priest
Come to his presence with the famous sages,
But sighs were on his lips the while in view
Of what the man might ask. '' What are,'' he thought,
'' The seven mysterious things whereof this Rúman
Would question us ? ''
                    The high priest with the learned,
Men mighty in all lore, came, and the spokesman
Revealed the secret, telling to the high priest
The words of Cæsar : '' What is ' the within '
In thy nomenclature, what ' the without,'

. 1554

O guide, who hast no other name therefor ?
What is ' the above,' my lord, what ' the beneath ' ?
What is ' the infinite ' and what ' the vile ' ?
What hath most names and ruleth everywhere ? "
   " Haste not," the high priest answered thus the sage,
" And turn not from the path of understanding."
   He then proceeded : " O thou man of wisdom !
Give ear to each reply that I shall make :
There is one answer only to thy words.
As to thy question touching ' the without,'
And ' the within,' it is an easy one :
The heaven is ' the without,' air ' the within ' ;
They are the Glory of the Omnipotent ;
God, touching this world, is ' the infinite,'
For lore to turn thee from Him is ' the vile ' ;
' The above ' is Paradise, Hell ' the beneath,'
And he is wicked that doth fear not God.
Next as to that with many names whose will
Prevaileth everywhere : O ancient ! wisdom
Hath many names, and wisdom compasseth
The will of kings. One man may call it love,
Another faith, but in its absence all
Is pain and tyranny. The eloquent
Term it uprightness and the fortunate
Astuteness ; 'tis at whiles long-suffering,
At whiles trustworthiness, for speech therewith
Is safe. So divers are the names of wisdom
That they exceed accompt. Allow that naught
Surpasseth it ; it is the chief of goods,
And knoweth this world's hoarded mysteries,
Which mortal vision cannot penetrate.
Again, the stars that glitter in the sky
Are what the master can afford to slight
For understanding of the Maker's work.
The eye that gazeth cannot reckon them.
And heaven above is unattainable

As being measureless, so thou mayst scorn
Such reckonings and processes of Fate.
One that can follow not an arrow's course,
Shrewd though he be, will marvel still thereat ;
Then what can be more futile, favoured sir !
Than to compute heaven's stars ?   This much I know,
And if another replication be
'Tis that the Maker's mysteries are vast."

. 1555   When *Cæsar's* spokesman heard he kissed   the
    ground,
And offered praise.   " World-ruling Sháh," he said,
" Ask nothing more of God, for all the world
Is thine to bid, the heads of all the great
Are under thy control, the world hath not
A king like thee in mind, thou praised by all
The high-born nobles ! while thy minister
In knowledge passeth sage and archimage.
All the philosophers are slaves to him,
And at his wisdom hang their heads."

                                        Bahrám,
On hearing, showed his pleasure, his heart brightened.
He bade a robe of honour be made ready
Of things most valued in his treasury,
And gave the archimage withal ten purses
Of drachms with raiment, steed, and much besides,
And then the envoy of illustrious Cæsar
Went from the royal presence to his lodging.
    When Sol displayed its hand upon the sky
The king of kings sat on his golden throne,
And Cæsar's envoy came to court, and with him
The high priest wise and worshipful.   They went
With joy before the king of kings, conversing
On many matters, and the Sháh's high priest
Said to the envoy : " Matchless, peerless sage !
What thing is so injurious that we
Must weep at its occurrence ?   What know'st thou

So useful to the world that men become
Exalted when it chanceth ? "
                                   Said the envoy :—
The wise aye will be great and powerful.
The person of the foolish is more vile
Than clay and undeserving of all good.
Thou spakest of the unwise and of the wise,
And hast received, maybe, the right response."
    The high priest said to him : " Consider well,
Reflect, and put not fish upon the dry."
    The envoy said : " O man approved by all !
One well may quote the sayings of the wise,
But, if thou knowest another answer, speak,
For knowledge giveth increment to fame."
    The high priest answered : " Think, for speech
        resulteth
From thought and brain, and know thou that the death
Of one least harmful is the greatest loss
Of all, but thou mayst joy when bad men die,
Albeit death is common to us all.
This then is profit and the other loss :
Let wisdom judge the answer of us both."
    The Rúman gave assent to what he heard ;
Those words seemed excellent to him ; he smiled,
Did reverence to the Sháh and said to him :—
" How happy is the country of Írán !
For others look not on a king of kings   C. 1556
Like thee, or on a high priest such as thine.
Thou art the world's high crown in understanding,
In priests thou art the greatest of the great.
Wouldst thou from Cæsar tribute ?   Be it so,
Because thy minister is sovereign
In wisdom," and his words rejoiced the king,
Whose heart grew fresh as roses in the spring.

§ 25

How Bahrám dismissed Cæsar's Envoy and charged his own Officials

The envoy left the presence of the Sháh,
The night came on, the Sable Banner rose,
The men of lore were weary of discourse,
The valiant monarch sought his ladies' bower.
    The circling vault of heaven rested not,
But roused the sleepers from their drowsihead,
The fountain of the sun set up its flag,
The world-Sháh's head woke lightly from repose,
The chamberlain unlocked the audience-door,
The king sat down upon the throne of gold.
He bade a robe of honour be made ready,
The envoy summoned. Indian scimitars
With golden scabbards noble steeds betrapped
With gold, dínárs, gems, musk, and spicery,
Beyond that ancient man's imaginings,
The shrewd Sháh gave the envoy, then was busied
With his own folk's affairs. By his command
The high priest, who was counsellor withal,
Approached him with a noble company,
And he apportioned all the land among
Those warlike paladins, gave drachms and steeds
And signet-rings and casques, and, to the greatest,
Thrones, crowns, and provinces. He filled the world
With right, and small and great rejoiced in him.
He banned the unjust with chilling words, unlargessed,
And, after, thus harangued the archimages :—
" Ye sages worshipful and pure of heart !
The world for us hath many memories
Of doings of the Sháhs unjust and just,
Whose hands oft-times were stretched for ill what while
Their persons lurked mid ease and luxury.[1]

          [1] Reading with P.

The world was frighted by these evil men,
The hearts of all the good were rent in twain ;
All hands were occupied with evil-doing,
And none was instant in the cause of God ;
The Div's work everywhere prevailed ; hearts ceased
To fear the Master of the world. The head   C. 1557
Of virtues and the hand of ill, the door
Of understanding and the quest of wisdom,
Are laid upon the Sháh's neck, and in him
Especially are seen both right and wrong.
My sire, who stretched his hand out to injustice,
Was not a holy man, wise or devout.
Hold not his actions strange, for rust attacked
The bright steel of his heart. Consider too
The experience of Jamshíd and Sháh Káús
For having sought the guidance of the Div.
My father in like manner followed them,
And washed not his dark soul in wisdom's stream.
His subjects writhed, and many lost their lives
Through his severity. Now he hath gone,
Hath left behind him but an evil name,
And hath no praise from any, yet let us
Give blessings to his soul, for God forbid
That it should writhe through our vindictiveness ;
And now that I am seated on his throne
His way will doubtless be to Paradise.
I ask the world's Lord to bestow upon me,
Alike in public and in private, strength
To treat my subjects with humanity,
And make pure musk out of the darksome dust,
That when therewith my body shall conjoin
None wronged by me may pluck me by the skirt.
Put ye too on the robe of uprightness,
With hearts washed clean from wrong, for none is born
Unless to die, be he of Persian, Arab,
Or Rúman race ; death's charge is lion-like,

And from its claws none can withdraw the neck ;
It maketh quarry of the rending lion,
The dragon's body 'scapeth not its toils.
Where are the heads and crowns of kings of kings ?
Where are the mighty and the glorious chiefs ?
Where are the cavaliers and haughty ones ?
I see no trace of them within the world.
Where are its fair who joyed those chieftains' souls ?
Know thou that all whose cheeks are 'neath the shroud
Are wedded to the dust.   Let all of us
Have hands both clean and good, and not commit
The world to evil ways.   I swear by God,
The Lord of all, who gave to me the Grace,
With crown and throne, high birth and quality,
That if an officer of mine shall wrong
The mean or mighty by a pinch of dust
I will consume his body in the fire,
Or hang him to a gibbet by the neck.
If in the watches of the night a thief
Shall steal a poor man's quilt I will make good
His loss from mine own treasury with brocade,
And wash the hearts of mourners from their woe ;
While if a sheep be taken from the flock
In dark night or in snow-storm I will give
. 1558   Instead thereof a steed of noble race,
And God forbid that I should ask for thanks.
If in a war against mine enemies
A cavalier is wounded in the fight
I will assign him yearly maintenance,
I will not leave his children in distress.
Praise ye the Judge that knoweth what is good
Throughout eternity.   Let none lay hand
On water or on fire except the priests
That are fire-worshippers.   Slay not draught-oxen,
For they are of avail in husbandry,
Unless past work and worthless to their owner.

Pack-oxen too must not be slain, the land
Else will grow void of grace. Deliberate
In all things with the men of lore and break not
The hearts of children that are fatherless.
Be alien from the promptings of the Div,
In fight ensue not feast. If I require
My subjects to pay taxes I abjure
God, throne, and crown. Since Yazdagird, my father,
Did evil, to redress that wrong have I
Disseminated justice. Let your hearts
All joy to do it and in gratitude
Observe the Cult of Fire. God may forgive him,
And guide him out of Hell to Paradise.
Give pleasure to the young, break not the hearts
Of lieges, keep from drunkenness in age,
For 'tis unseemly in the old to tope ;
Sin ye not therefor, for in age 'tis well
To make your preparations to depart.
If God, the righteous Judge, approveth us
Let not the future trouble you to-day ;
Let there be pleasure in my subjects' hearts,
And let the nobles' heads be free from grief."
  The chiefs, on hearing and considering well
His words, all wept that such an one was theirs,
A Sháh so wise and shrewd, acclaimed his worth,
And hailed him as the great king of the earth.

§ 26

How Bahrám went with his own Letter to Shangul,
King of Hind

A wise wazír rose to his feet and said :—
" O judge of what is just and right ! the world
Hath ceased to fear malignants, toil and stress
Have left our coasts. Howbeit famed Shangul

Among the folk of Hind is still perverse ;
His bands of plunderers infest the earth
From Hindústán up to the coasts of Chín.
He will lay hands for ill upon Írán,
And thou shouldst apprehend this.   Thou art Sháh ;
Shangul but wardeth Hind, so why should he
Take toll of Sind and Chín ?   Consider this,
And note his plans, for ill must not ensue."
    The Sháh, on hearing this, was full of thought,
The world before him seemed a tangled brake,
And thus he answered : " I will deal herewith
In secret, not consulting any one.
I will myself alone observe his troops,
The conduct of his kingship and his throne,
Approaching him an as ambassador,
And not acquaint the Íránians and the lords.
O holy archimage ! write to Shangul
A firm but courteous letter."
                                    Thereupon
His pious minister went with a scribe,
And others that were indispensable,
And canvassed all the case, brought paper, ink,
And pen, and wrote a letter full of counsel,
Instruction, knowledge, and the praise of God.
It thus began : " From God be praise on those
That seek His praise who is the Lord of all
That is and is not.   All things have their peers,
But God is One.   Of all that He bestoweth
Upon His slaves, on sovereign and subject,
Naught is more great than wisdom which illumeth
Both.   He whom wisdom gladdeneth will walk not
The world for ill, and he that chooseth right
Ne'er will repent thereof ; he cannot savour
Ill from the stream of knowledge.   Wisdom looseth
Man from mishap ; may none be wrung therewith.
Wisdom's first token is that one should dread

Ill-doing all one's years and know oneself ;
Then must he search the world with wisdom's eye,
For wisdom is the diadem of kings,
And jewel of the men of name withal.

    Thou know'st not thine own measure but dost plunge
Thy soul in blood. Now, seeing that I am
The monarch of the age, both good and ill
Are laid to me. Do thou so reign that right
May be preserved, for ill is manifest
On all sides. 'Tis not kingly to make raids,
And cotton with the ill-disposed. Thy grandsire
Was vassal to us and thy sire a slave
Before our Sháhs, and none of us allowed
Arrears in tribute out of Hindústán.
Now mark the fortune of the Khán of Chin,   C. 156
Who came thence 'gainst Írán. He gave to spoil
All that he brought, and writhed for his ill deeds.
I see thee also thus disposed, the same
Perversity, same Glory, and same Faith.
Now I have arms and treasures for the war,
My soldiers are devoted and arrayed ;
Thou canst not stand against my gallant men,
And there is not a general in Hind.
Thou art conceited of thy might, preferring
Thine own rill to the river. Now behold !
I have dispatched an envoy to thee, one
Of knowledge, eloquence, and high degree.
Send tribute or make war and fortify
The passes. Be our blessing on his soul
Whose warp and woof are equity and wisdom."

    Whenas air's breath had made the writing dry
The writer of the letter folded it,
And then the scribe addressed it on this wise :—
" From this world's king, the monarch shrewd of wit,
The lord of government, the lord of might,
The world's possessor, generous Bahrám Gúr,

Who on the day of Ard in month Khurdád
Received from Yazdagird the royal crown,
Chief of the marches, guardian of the realm,
To whom Sakláb and Rúm are tributary,
This to Shangul, who ruleth over Hind
From Sind up to the river of Kannúj." [1]
    The monarch sealed the letter with his signet,
And then made ready for the chase, but none
Of all the host knew of his purposes .
Except the nobles of his company.
Thus he drew nigh to Hindústán and crossed
The river of magician-land.[2] On nearing
The palace of Shangul he gazed upon
The hall of audience with its gate and curtain.
It rose aloft in air, and at the gate
There was no lack of arms and equipage,
For there stood cavaliers and elephants
Amid a din of gongs and Indian bells.
He stood there all amazed and lost in thought,
Then on this wise addressed the curtain-keepers,
The servants and officials of the gate :—
" An envoy to this court am I, deputed
By conquering Sháh Bahrám."
                  The chamberlain
Went to the royal presence from the curtain.
They raised it by the king's command and brought
The envoy in with all respect. Bahrám Gúr
Advanced with stately step, and saw a chamber
With crystal roof. On drawing near Shangul

C. 1561 [3] Bahrám beheld him seated on his throne
Of majesty, and crowned. The steps that led
Up to that golden throne were all of crystal.
There sat the king in all his Grace and might,

---

[1] The Ganges is meant.   [2] Hindústán. *Cf.* Vol. i. p. 163.
[3] The first five couplets on this page are read, as in P, in the following
order : 4, 5, 1, 2, 3.

Arrayed in silver broidered with gold thread
Beset with many a gem. Bahrám beheld
The monarch's brother on an ante-throne,
And wearing on his head a jewelled crown.
The minister sat by : the monarch's son
Stood there before the throne. The Sháh drew nigh
Thereto, did reverence, and paused awhile,
Then quickly loosed his tongue. " I have," he said,
" A letter written in our tongue on silk,
Sent to the king of Hind by Sháh Bahrám—
The world's lord who possesseth crown and throne."
    The king, on hearing what Bahrám said, bade
To bring a golden ante-throne. They set him
Upon that seat of gold, and from the gate
Called in his comrades. Seated thus he said :—
" Exalted king ! I will unloose my lips
When thou commandest. May both good and greatness
Be ever thine."
                Shangul replied : " Proceed,
For heaven's blessing is on those who speak."
    Bahrám rejoined : " That Sháh of royal race,
Whose like no mother in the world hath borne,
The exalted prince, the glory of the state,
Whose justice turneth bane to antidote,
To whom all potentates are tributary,
Whose prey is lions in the chase, and who,
On taking up the scimitar in fight,
Converteth deserts into seas of blood,
In generosity like clouds in spring,
In whose sight treasures and dinárs are vile,
Hath sent the king of Hind an embassy,
And letter writ on silk in Pahlavi."

§ 27

How Shangul received the Letter from Bahrám and made Reply

The king, on hearing this, asked for the letter,
And marvelled at that chief.   A noble scribe
Read it, whereat the monarch's face became
Like gall.   He said : " O man of eloquence !
Haste not to speak, and act not haughtily.
Thy Sháh displayeth his imperiousness,
Witness thy journey hither.   Should one ask
For tribute out of Hindústán the wise
Would disavow him.   If thy master speaketh
Of host and treasure, and of giving land
And cities up to woe . . . well, other kings
Are cranes, I am an eagle ; they are dust,
I am a sea.   None fighteth with the stars,
Or seeketh fame by warring with the sky.
Worth is much better than the useless talk
That maketh wise men hold thee in contempt.
Ye have not manhood, knowledge, realm or city ;
Your share of sovereignty is only loss.
My whole land is a hidden treasury
Whereon mine ancestors have laid no hand,
Beside my store of mail for man and steed,
Which, if my treasurer should bring it forth,
Would ask for elephants to bear the keys,
If mighty elephants could carry them ;
And should I count my swords and coats of mail
The stars would seem contemptible in sum
To thee.   The earth will not sustain my host,
My throne, and mighty elephants.   If thou
Shouldst multiply a thousand thousand-fold
'Twould be the sum of those that call me king.
Mine are the jewels of the hills and seas,
I am the present mainstay of the world.

1562

The founts of aloe, musk, and ambergris,
The hoards of undried camphor and the drugs
That cure the suffering, whoe'er shall ail
Throughout the world, are plenteous in my realm,
As well as silver, gold, and jewelry,
While fourscore kings with crowns of gold up-gird
Their loins at my behest. My land is full
Of mountain, stream, and chasm ; not e'en a div
Would find his way across it. From Kannúj
Up to the marches of Írán and thence
Right to Sakláb and Chín the chiefs are all
My men and cannot choose but homage me.
The watchmen of Khutan, of Hind, and Chin
Use in their challenges no name but mine ;
All speak the praises of my crown and grow
More serviceable. In my women's bower
The daughter of Faghfúr of Chin invoketh
God's blessing on me—me of all the world.
By her I have a lion-hearted son,
Whose scimitar despoileth mountains' hearts.
No one since Kai Káús and Kai Kubád
E'er hath concerned himself about this land.
Three hundred thousand warlike troops withal
Acclaim me. Of allies I have twelve hundred,
Who all are wholly in my confidence ;
All are my kith and kin by long descent,
And stand before me here in Hind. Their war-cry
Would make the lions of the jungle gnaw
Their claws. If there were any precedent
For chiefs to slay an envoy out of wrath
Thy head and body would I part, and let
Thy raiment wail for thee."

Bahrám replied :—   C. 1563

" As thou art great, O king ! sow not the seed
Of wrath. My Sháh said : ' Say to him : " If thou
Art wise choose not the pathway of perverseness." '

Produce now from thy court two men of lore,
Of fluent tongue, and happy in discourse,
And if in rede and wisdom they excel
One of these men with me then I have done
With this thy land, for wise men spurn not words ;
Or else choose out among the warriors
That wield in Hindústán the massive mace
A hundred horsemen to fight one of us,
And we, what time thy wit and worth shall stand
Revealed, will ask not tribute from thy land."

§ 28

*How Shangul prepared a Feast for Bahrám, and how
Bahrám displayed his Prowess*

Shangul, on hearing this, said to Bahrám :—
" Thy counsel sorteth not with manliness.
Abide a season and relax thyself,
Why parley to no purpose ? "
                                    They made ready
A splendid hall.   Bahrám reposed till noon,
And when the Crown that lighteneth the world
Had reached its height the feast was all prepared
According to the bidding of the king,
And zealous servants were about the hall.
When they had spread the board before Shangul
He bade a servant : " Summon to the feast
The envoy of the Íránian king, the man
Of fluent utterance and novel aims.
Bring his companions too and seat them where
Ambassadors are placed."
                                    Bahrám came quickly,
Sat at the board and oped his hand to bread,
But shut his lips to speech.   The eating done,

They set themselves to quaff and called for harpists
And wine. The scent of musk rose from the feast,
The hall was spread with golden carpetings.
   Now when the lords were merry in their cups,
And recked not of the future, king Shangul
Bade two strong men attend, men fit to wrestle
Against the Div. These noble athletes came,
And girt their loin-cloths round them. Those two
    youths
Contended lustily and strained and writhed
Together. Now Bahrám took up a cup
Of crystal and the wine confused his brain.
He spake thus to Shangul : " O king bid me   C. 1564
To gird me for a bout, for when I wrestle
Against the strong I am away from harm
And drunkenness."
                Shangul said smiling : " Rise,
And, if thou shalt o'ercome them, shed their blood."
   Bahrám, on hearing this, rose to his feet,
And boldly bending down the upright form
Of him whose waist he clutched (a lion so
Might seize upon wild onager) he flung
His foeman down so that his bones were broken,
And all the colour left his cheeks. Shangul
Was in amazement at the victor's mien,
His stature and his shoulders and his strength,
Invoked God in the Indian tongue and deemed
Bahrám to be a match for forty men.
   When they were all bemused with pleasant wine
They left the hall of jewelled tracery
And, when the vault of heaven donned musk-hued Silk,
Both young and old slept after banqueting.
Shangul went to his sleeping-place, the wine
Had turned his looks and thoughts from king Bahrám.
   Now when the musky-scented Veil was changed
To gold, and in the sky the sun appeared,

The king of Indians mounted on his steed,
And went forth to the Ground with polo-stick
In hand. His servants bore his bow and arrows,
And for a while he rode to please himself,
Then ordered Sháh Bahrám to mount and take
His royal bow in hand. Bahrám replied :—
" I have a number of Íránian horsemen
With me, O king ! and they are fain to ply
The arrow and the polo-stick when bidden
By the most noble king."
                              Shangul replied :—
" The arrows and the bow are doubtlessly
The mainstays of the cavalier. Do thou,
Who hast such limbs and neck and might of hand,
String up thy bow and shoot."
                              Bahrám Gúr strung
His bow and urged his steed with shouts. He took
And shot an arrow that destroyed the mark.
The sportsmen and the warriors 'gan to call
Their blessings down upon him, one and all.

§ 29

How Shangul suspected Bahrám and kept him from Irán

Shangul, misdoubting of Bahrám, thought thus :—
" This stature, Grace, and skill in archery
Resemble not a mere ambassador's
Of Hindústán, of Turkistán, or Persia,
But, be he of the Sháh's race or a noble,
'Twere well I call him brother," smiled and said
C. 1565   Thus to Bahrám : " Famed, high-born prince ! thou
          art
No doubt the Sháh's own brother, being dowered
With vigour, strength, and skill in archery,

Because the Grace of kings, the might of lions,
Are thine.   Art thou then but a gallant chief ? "
   Bahrám said : " King of Hind ! discredit not
Ambassadors.   I am not of the seed
Of Yazdagird or Sháh.   To call him brother
Would be a crime in me.   A stranger I,
Come from Irán, no seeker after knowledge,
No sage.   Dismiss me for the way is long,
And I must not incur the Sháh's displeasure."
   Shangul replied : " Be not importunate,
For I have somewhat still to say to thee.
Thou must not be so eager to depart,
For hasty going prospereth not.   Abide
With us and set thy heart at ease.   If thou
Wilt have not mellowed wine then take it crude." [1]
   He said thereafter to his own adept :—
" I have a secret for thee.   If this man
Be not sib to Bahrám, or in degree
Above his paladins, 'twill prove a marvel
To wise men's hearts.   We must not trust his words.
Address him courteously and say : ' Abide ;
There is no cause for thee to leave Kannúj.'
Sayst thou : ' He will detect deceit herein ? '
If words of mine may terrify his heart
It will be better far for thee to speak,
And talk to him in convenable terms.
Say thus to him : ' 'Tis well for thee to gain
More estimation with the king of Hind.
Now if thou will abide with him, and further
His subtle policy, thou shalt possess
The goodliest march of Hind because the king
Hath thee in high esteem.   'Twill be a land
Of never ending springtide where the streams
Breathe of the rose.   The fortunate ne'er quit
Kannúj where twice a year the fruit-trees bear,

---

[1] Couplet omitted.

Where there are treasures, gems, dinárs, and drachms,
And where drachms can be had hearts are not sad.
The king is gracious and for love of thee
He smileth when he looketh on thy face.'
What time ye meet speak thou whate'er thou knowest
To this effect and then inquire his name,
For that will joy my heart. Should our land please
    him
Our favours would surpass his excellence,
We would appoint him captain of the host
Anon, in favour highest in the land."

'. 1566   The king's experienced minister departed,
Informed Bahrám, and pointed him his way,
Then asked his name because without his name
No answer would suffice. Bahrám changèd colour,
On hearing this, perplexed for his reply.
At length he said : " O man of eloquence !
Make me not wan of visage in two realms.
I will quit not the Sháh for any treasure
However much I may be pinched by want.
The teachings of our Faith are otherwise,
As are our estimations, wonts, and ways,
And every one that turneth from his king
Is lost by such revolt. No man of wisdom
Is eager for addition ; bad and good
Are transient with us. Where is Faridún,
The master of the crown, he that restored
The age ? Where are those chiefs of royal race,
The world-lords Kai Khusrau and Kai Kubád ?
Thou hast withal some knowledge of Bahrám,
The young, ambitious, and imperious,
Who, if I cross his purpose, will avail
To bring the world in ruins on my head,
Leave Hindústán not field or fell but bear
Off to Irán the dust of Wizard-land.[1]

        [1] *Cf.* p. 112 and *note.*

My better plan is to return to court,
And to the purview of the conquering Sháh.
If thou wouldst have my name it is Barzwí ;
My monarch and my parents call me so.
Communicate mine answer to Shangul,
For I have stayed long in an alien realm."
    The minister, on hearing this reply,
Told all that he had heard before the king,
Who frowned and said : " He holdeth him aloof,
But I will take such order that this Light
Of hosts shall end his days."
                                    There was a wolf [1]
Within the monarch's coasts of bulk so vast
That it withstood the wind. The lions fled
The woods before it, and the swift-winged vultures
The sky. Thereat all Hind was full of fear :
Its howlings deafened those most keen of ear.

§ 30

How Bahrám fought with the Wolf at the Bidding of Shangul and slew it

Shangul said to Bahrám : " O man approved !
All enterprises prosper in thy hands.
A wood near by my city troubleth me.
There is a wolf there like a crocodile,
And rendeth lions' hearts and leopards' hides.
Let it be thine to go against this wolf,   C. 156
And pierce its hide all over with thine arrows.
The world may find rest then and by thy Grace,
Victorious one ! Thenceforth in mine esteem,
And that of all this noble company,

---

[1] Perhaps for "gurg," wolf, we ought to read "karg," rhinoceros.
The word is spelt both with g and k in C. and is made to rhyme with
"marg," death, and "tagarg," hail. *Cf.* NIN, p. 55, *note.*

Thy station shall be such that evermore
The folk of Hind and Chin all shall acclaim thee."
  Bahrám, the honest, said : " I need a guide ;
Then by God's strength, when I behold the beast,
Thou shalt perceive its garment [1] soaked in blood."
  Shangul provided him a guide that knew
The creature's lair and haunt, and then Bahrám
Went with his trusty guide toward the wood
Of that blood-shedding wolf. Much spake the guide
About its lair, its height and breadth and bulk,
Showed where it was and went back while Bahrám
Approached apace. Iránians thronged behind him
With loins girt for the fray, but when they saw
Afar so vast a wood, the monster's bulk,
And lair that it had made, all said : " O Sháh !
Adventure not ; thou wilt surpass the bounds .
Of hardihood because, however brave
Thou art in fight, none hath fought rocks and moun-
    tains.
Say to Shangul : ' This may not be. I have
No sanction for this combat from the Sháh.
I fight when I am bidden so that he,
On hearing of it, may advance my rank.' "
  Bahrám replied : " If holy God hath given
My dust to Hindústán how can I die
Elsewhere ? That is beyond me."
                            That brave youth
Strung up his bow, and thou hadst said : " He holdeth
His own life cheap ! "
                  He sped toward the wolf
With head all rage and heart resigned to death.
He grasped his royal bow and, having drawn
Some poplar arrows from his quiver, poured
His shafts like hail till by that token anguish
O'ercame the wolf. On seeing the beast's end nigh,

---

[1] Garment for skin as in Job xli. 13.

Bahrám, exchanging bow for sword, smote off
Its head, exclaiming : " In the name of God,
Who hath not mate or peer and gave to me
Such Grace and might !   By His command the sun
Is bright in heaven."
                    He bade bring wain and oxen
To carry that wolf's carcase from the wood.
They bore it.   When Shangul saw it afar
He had his banquet-hall decked with brocade,
And when the mighty king sat on his throne
He set Bahrám upon the seat of honour
While all the chiefs of Hind, and cavaliers   C. 1568
Of Chin, applauded him.   The lords all came
With offerings and spake thus to Bahrám :—
" None ever did a deed to equal thine ;
Its brilliancy is more than eyes can bear."
     As for Shangul he was both glad and grieved,
Appearing cheerful and depressed, by turns.
     There was a dragon, an amphibious beast,
Which haunted streams and sunned itself ashore ;
It, with its breath, could suck huge elephants
Down,[1] and raise waves upon the dark blue sea.
Shangul spake thus to his companions,
His clever confidants : " By turns this envoy,
This lion-man, doth please and trouble me.
If he remained he would be my support,
The ruler of Kannúj and of my realm,
But if he goeth from me to Írán
Bahrám will devastate Kannúj ; with such
A servitor to such a lord this land
Will lose both hue and odour.   All the night
Have I been musing o'er his case and framing
A fresh device—to send him to that dragon,
Which surely he will 'scape not.   Then shall I

---

[1] " il enveloppait avec sa queue un éléphant de guerre " (Mohl).
Cf. Vol. v. p. 233 and *note.*

Be censured not on his account if he
Will fight with dragons."
                    So he called Bahrám,
Told stories of the mighty men, and said :—
" God, Author of the soul, hath led thee hither
Out of the country of Írán to purge
The ills of Hindústán as is the way
Of men of name.   A matter fraught with pain
And travail is confronting us, of travail
At first but treasure in the end.   If thou
Accomplish this depart on thy return
With my good wishes home."
                    The Sháh replied :—
" I may not leave the way of thy behests,
But will perform thy bidding faithfully
Unless the heaven itself shall turn awry."

§ 31

How Bahrám slew a Dragon

Shangul said to Bahrám : " Within my realm
There is a dragon—an exceeding bale—
Which fareth both by land and stream to hunt
The lashing crocodile.   Thou mayst devise
A scheme to rid thereof the realm of Hind,
Whose tribute thou shalt carry to Írán,
For all the country will assent thereto,
And likewise gifts therefrom of aloe-wood,
Of swords, and goods of all kinds, with the tribute."
    Bahrám replied : " Great king and sovereign,
Whose word is law in Hind ! by God, the Just
And Holy One's, command I will cut off
The footing of the dragon from the earth,
But must be shown its lair whereof I know not."

Shangul accordingly dispatched a guide
To show it to Bahrám who went his way
With thirty horsemen, nobles of Írán
And swordsmen. Hasting to the stream he saw
The dragon mid the gloom, its form, its writhing,
And furiousness, fire flashing from its eyes.
The nobles of Írán with loud exclaims,
And shrewdly troubled at that dragon, said :—
" Hold not this dragon as thou didst the wolf,
O king ! the other day. By one mishap
Give not Írán up to the wind, rejoice not
Thy foemen here."
                        The bold Bahrám replied :—
" I must entrust my life to all-just God.
If I am doomed to perish by this dragon
My time will be not lengthened or decreased
By hardihood."
                        He strung his bow, he chose
Shafts dipped in bane of milk,[1] and 'gan to shower them
Down on the dragon, wheeling all the while,
Like horsemen in the fray, to left and right.
He sewed up with steel points the dragon's mouth,
Whose venom scorched the brambles, then he shot
Four arrows at its head, and blood and poison
Poured down its breast. The dragon's body failed
By reason of those shafts, and all the ground
Ran with its gore and bane. Then lightly drew
Bahrám his sword of watered steel and pierced
The dragon's heart right dourly, hacked its neck
With sword and battle-ax, and flung to earth
Its lifeless form. The dragon overthrown,
He turned in duty to the Lord and said :—
" O Judge who judgest righteously ! 'tis Thou
That slewest this great dragon, for who else

---

[1] *Corruptio optimi pessima.* We shall have an instance later on, in the reign of Núshírwán, of milk being turned to poisonous uses. See p. 320 *seq.*

Hath might enough ?   Thou art Thy servants' refuge
From every ill."
                  He sought the king of Hind,
The noble chieftain of the Sindian host,
And said : "The king is freed from these attacks
By His decree—the Judge and Nourisher's."
  Shangul grieved, hearing this, because Bahrám
Was in the saddle still.   He bade that wains
And oxen should convey the dragon's carcase
To plain from forest, while all Hindústán
Invoked upon Írán the All-Just's blessing :—

. 1570   " For there a cavalier like this was born
To fight with dragons.   One who hath such limbs,
Such stature and such bearing cannot be
But equal to the king in his degree."

§ 32

*How Shangul became troubled about Bahrám and
gave a Daughter to him*

All men rejoiced except Shangul whose heart
Was pained, the matter made his visage wan,
And when night came he summoned his wise men,
Both those of his own kin and aliens,
And thus he said : " This man of Sháh Bahrám's,
Who hath such might, such limbs, and mastery,
Do what I may, is worsted by no toil !
Now if he goeth from us to Írán,
And cometh to the monarch of the brave,
He will depreciate my host and say
That here in Hindústán there is no horseman,
And so my foemen may grow insolent.
I will behead the envoy, will destroy him
By stealth.   What say ye ?   What do ye advise ? "

"Bring not thy heart, O king!" the wise men
    answered,
"To sorrow by such deeds. For thee to slay
The ambassadors of kings would be an act
Unwise and senseless. No one e'er conceived
A thought on this wise. Compass no such plan.
Thou wilt be execrated by the chiefs,
And people should respect their sovereign.
By putting this man's head within the shears
Thou wilt bring longsome trouble on thy land.
Forthwith will come an army from Írán,
And with a potentate like Sháh Bahrám;
None of us in these regions will survive,
And thou wilt have to wash thy hands of kingship.
This man is our deliverer from the dragon,
And slaying should compensate not his toils;
Here hath he killed the dragon and the wolf;
Give him more life, not death."
                   On hearing this
Shangul grew gloomy, for the sages' words
Perturbed him. Passing thus the night, at dawn
He sent a messenger to Sháh Bahrám,
And, when they were together privily
Without a minister or counsellor,
Said : "O thou Joy of hearts! thou hast prevailed.
Attempt no greater feat. I will bestow
My daughter on thee as thy wife, for thus
Shall I be profited in word and deed.
This done, abide with me, for thou wilt have   C. 1571
No colour to depart. I will appoint thee
The captain of the host and give thee kingship
In Hindústán."
         Bahrám was in amaze,
And mused upon his throne, his birth, and glory.
"There is no remedy for one's own acts,"
He thought, "and this thing cannot bring reproach;

Besides by this I may preserve my life,
And look again upon Íránian soil,
For, as the case is, we have tarried long ;
The lion is taken in the fox's net ! ''
    Thus said he to Shangul : '' I will obey
Thy hest and make thy word my rule of life.
However of thy daughters choose me one,
Who, when I see her, may obtain my praise.''
    The king of Hind, on hearing this, rejoiced,
And decked his halls with painted silk of Chin.
Shangul's three daughters came like jocund spring
In all their bravery, their scents, their colours,
And looks, and then he bade Bahrám Gúr : '' Go,
Prepare thy heart to see a novel sight.''
    Bahrám Gúr went immediately, beheld
The hall, and of those moon-faced maids chose one
Like jocund springtide, Sapínúd by name,
All grace and modesty, all wit and charm ;
On him Shangul bestowed her—one that seemed
A straight-stemmed cypress and a smokeless lamp—
Then chose the richest of his treasuries,
Gave to the moon-faced maid the key thereof,
Called for Bahrám's companions, cavaliers
Of noble rank and masterful, and gave them
Dinárs and drachms and every kind of wealth,
With camphor, aloe-wood, and ambergris,
Steeds, golden trappings, girdles, and for those
Of highest rank, gold crowns, while for Bahrám
He had a turquoise crown and glorious throne
Of ivory prepared, and decked his palace
Of jewelled tracery. All men of name
Within Kannúj resorted to that place
Of feasting, waiting on their king with joy.
They spent a se'nnight thus with wine in hand,
All glad and jocund in the banquet-hall,
With Sapínúd beside Bahrám, the king,
Like wine in crystal goblet glittering.

§ 33

How Faghfúr of Chín wrote to Bahrám and how he replied

Intelligence came to Faghfúr of Chin :—
" A man of Grace and courage from Írán
Hath reached Shangul as an ambassador,
And verily is of heroic race.
Great exploits have been wrought in Hind and by   C. 1572
The hand too of this valiant lion-man
Through resolution and the might of fortune.
Naught but the crown and throne befitteth him,
And on him hath Shangul bestowed a daughter,
So that his diadem might reach the moon."
    That mighty world-lord wrote to Sháh Bahrám
A letter superscribed : " From him that is
The monarch of the world, the head of nobles,
And crown of chiefs, to that ambassador
Of Persia who with thirty comrades reached
Kannúj," and then proceeded : " I have had
Accounts of thee, thou famed and glorious man !
About thy wisdom, prudence, and advice,
And how thou standest steadfast everywhere,
So that the wolf and that notorious dragon
Could 'scape not from thy shafts and scimitar.
The lady given to thee is my kin,
Her dust is worth the whole of Hindústán,
And thou hast raised thy head on high by thus
Affining with this mighty potentate,
While in Írán 'twill magnify the Sháh,
Whose crown well may bediadem the moon,
Because his envoy took fit comrades, reached
Kannúj, and clasped a Moon upon his breast.
Now bear the toil, come hither, and abide
Within this land so long as thou mayst wish.
I will illume mine eyes with seeing thee,
    VOL. VII.

And make thy rede the breastplate of my soul.
Thou shalt go hence at will.   I will not bid thee :—
' Abide awhile.'   So with a robe of honour,
And wealth, depart with joy, thou and thy chiefs,
Well furnished.   'Tis no shame for thee to come
To me ; I have no quarrel with the Sháh.
On no wise be remiss in coming hither,
And, when thou wouldst depart, then tarry not."
    This letter reached Bahrám Gúr and perturbed him.
He called a scribe, wrote his reply, and planted
A tree within the orchard of revenge.
The letter thus began : " I have received
Thy words.   Thou canst have seen no land but Chin,
For thou hast superscribed thy letter thus :—
' From him that is the monarch of the world,
The most exalted of the glorious chiefs.'
It is not so ; new-fangled majesty
Like thine I do not recognise.   Bahrám Gúr
Alone is king of kings ; we know none other.
No man remembereth any king like him
In courage, knowledge, Grace, and lineage.
Him I acknowledge, as victorious world-lord,
And know him greater than all other kings.
Again, for what thou saidst about my deeds,
And of my toil endured in Hindústán,
C. 1573 That too was all the star of Sháh Bahrám,
Who hath Grace, throne, and fame.   Accomplishment
Is the Íránians' own, they hold fierce lions
Of no account.   They all are single-hearted,
They worship God, and in their blest estate
They fear no ill.   Again, if king Shangul
Bestowed his daughter on me I achieved
That honour by my courage.   He is great,
By his own coúrage driveth wolf from sheep,
And, thinking good to make affinity
With me, bestowed on me his worthy child.

Again, for what thou saidst : ' Arise and come,
And I will guide thee unto every good,'
The Sháh sent me to Hind, and shall I go
To Chin for painted silk ?   If I propose
A course like that he will approve it not.
Thou sayest further : ' I will send thee home
Enriched with treasures.'   God hath set me past
The need of clutching after others' goods.
I praise Bahrám for all his bounty to me,
And offer up thanksgiving to my God
Three watches of the day and of the night.
And fourthly, all the praise that thou hast lavished
Upon me in excess of my deserts,
This I accept from thee, O king of Chin !
And will report it to the Sháh.   May God
Give thee so many blessings that the sky
May not distinguish 'twixt their warp and woof."
    Bahrám dispatched this letter to the king
Of Chin when he had sealed it with his ring.

§ 34

*How Bahrám fled from Hindústán to Írán with the
Daughter of Shangul*

When with the daughter of Shangul Bahrám
Consorted she found out that he was Sháh ;
By night and day she wept for love of him,
And kept her eyes upon his face.   Her father
Heard of her love and ceased to doubt Bahrám.
    One day the pair sat happily, discussing
Things great and small, and Sháh Bahrám spake thus :—
" I know that thou dost wish me well, so I
Will tell to thee a secret ; keep it close.
I would quit Hindústán.   Dost thou consent

Thereto ?   I will take thee withal, but none
Among this folk must know.   Within Írán
My state surpasseth this and, furthermore,

• 1574   The Almighty is mine aid.   If thou wilt go
Thy wise decision will promote thy weal,
In every place thy title shall be ' queen,'
And thine own sire shall kneel before thy throne."
   She said : " Exalted one ! seek what is good,
And turn not from the way of understanding.
The best of womankind is she through whom
A smile is always on her husband's face.
If my pure purposes are not conformed
To thy command I joy not in thy life."
   Bahrám replied : "Then frame a scheme but tell it
To none."
                She said : " O worthy of the throne !
I will, with fortune's aid.   Not much removed
There is a place where festivals are held,
For in the forest there my father feasteth.
It is a place that men deem fortunate,
And thither gather idol-worshippers.
Hence to the forest is a score of leagues,
And one must weep before the idols there.
That is a place for hunting onager,
A place too for the worshippers of God.
Both king and host will set forth to the feast ;
He will not leave a soldier in the city.
Go then if thou art minded to depart :
Let feasts grow old but be thou young for ever.
Wait for five days, then when the world's Light shineth,
And he shall quit the city, get thee ready
To go thyself."
              His wife's words pleased Bahrám,
Who slept not till the dawn for thought.
                        Now when
The sun displayed its hand upon the sky,

And dark night packed, he mounted on his steed,
And rode forth with his weapons to the chase.
He told his wife : " Make ready and tell none ;
Let us prepare and set out on our way."
    Bahrám departed, neared the stream,[1] and saw
The baggage of some merchants on the road.
They recognised him, and he bit his lip,
For they were of Írán—bold travellers
O'er sea and land.   He bade them offer him
No reverence ; not even had he told
His comrades what he purposed.   To the merchants
He said : " Shut fast your lips ; on that depend
Our profit and our loss, for if in Hind
This secret be divulged the Íránian soil
Will be as seas of blood.   Enlarged is he
Whose lips are shut, the tongue must be confined,
And both hands open.   By a mighty oath
Will I bind fast your tongues till I regain
My throne.   Say thus then : ' May we turn away
From God, the Holy and Supreme, and follow
The Div if ever we desert the counsel   C. 1575
Of Sháh Bahrám and contemplate ill-doing.' "
    When this oath had been taken and confirmed,
So that the Sháh's heart was relieved from care,
He said : " Guard well my secret, tendering it
Like life itself, if ye desire to turn
My bondage [2] to a crown ; but if the throne
Be void of me armed hosts will come from all sides,
And leave no merchants here, no Sháh, no thane,
No host, no throne, no crown."
                    When they perceived
The import of his words they came with cheeks
All wet with weeping.   " May the nobles' lives
Thy ransom be," they said, " and youth and kingship
Thy habit.   If the treasure of thy secret

---

   [1] The Indus, according to Mohl.   [2] Reading with P.

Should be revealed our country would resemble
A sea of gore !   Who dareth contemplate
Such things and turn his wisdom to an ax,
His counsel to a hatchet ? "

                   Hearing this,
The Sháh 'gan praise those honourable men
Of Grace and Faith, and fared home ill at ease,
Committing to God's charge his soul and body.
He tarried till the banquet-hall was decked,
And till the nobles had departed thither,
But when Shangul himself prepared to go
Bahrám's wife said to him : "Barzwí is sick,
Would be excused, and saith : 'Be not concerned
For me, O king !   The banquet-hall to one
That aileth is distasteful, and the king
Must know thus much.' "

               "Let none," Shangul replied,
"That aileth think of banqueting."

                     At dawn
He left Kannúj and hurried to the place
Of feasting.   When 'twas night said Sháh Bahrám :—
"'Tis time to go, good wife ! "

                   He seated her
Upon her palfrey and invoked God's name
O'er her in ancient Persian, donned his mail,
And mounted too, his lasso in the straps,
And mace in hand.   He hurried to the river,
And found the merchants sleeping.   Rousing them
He gat a skiff in readiness wherein
He seated Sapínúd.   With day begun
They came to land, and brightly shone the sun.

§ 35

How Shangul followed Bahrám, learned who he was,
and was reconciled to him

A horseman from Kannúj sped with the tidings   C. 1576
Of Sháh Bahrám's departure, and Shangul,
Who heard it from that loyal servant, quitted
The chase as swift as fire. He hurried on
Until he reached the river where he saw
Both Sapínúd and brave Bahrám. He grieved,
Crossed o'er in dudgeon, and upbraided thus
His child : " O wicked wanton ! thou hast passed,
Bold as a lioness, across the river
To go Írán-ward with this lusty knave,
To desert waste from cultured paradise,
Without my knowledge. Now thou shalt behold,
Since thou hast left my pillow secretly,
The impact of my double-headed dart."
    Bahrám replied : " O thou of evil mark !
Why didst thou urge thy steed as madmen do ?
Thou hast had testimony that in war
I am as with the cup and boon-companions.
A hundred thousand men of Hindústán
Before me would not equal, as thou knowest,
One horseman like me and my thirty comrades,
Famed, clad in mail, and wielding Persian swords.
I will fulfil the Indians' eyes with blood,
And will not spare a soul."
               Shangul was ware
That he had spoken sooth because his prowess
And valiancy could not be overlooked,
But answered him : " I have foregone my children,
My kindred, and allies, have held thee dearer
Than mine own eyes, and as the diadem
Upon my head, and given thee her whom thou
Thyself didst choose. The right is on my side,

The wrong on thine.   Instead of good faith thou
Hast chosen outrage.   Ever hast thou heard
Of good faith paid thereby ?   Shall I tell thee :—
' One of my kin and wise in mine esteem
Hath gone off cavalierly, gone conceiving
Himself a king ? '   What hath a Persian's heart
In common with good faith ?   He sayeth ' yea '
And meaneth ' nay ' !   Thou'rt such a lion's whelp,
In good sooth, as would bathe in their hearts' blood
Its nurses and, when fangèd and sharp of claw,
Would purpose combat with its fosterer ! "
    Bahrám made answer : " When thou knowest me
How shalt thou call me ill in thought and deed ?
I shall be unreproached for having gone,
Thou wilt not term my heart and conduct evil.

The king of kings am I both of Írán
And of Túrán, the leader of the folk,
The mainstay of the brave, and will requite
Hereafter thy deservings and behead
Thy foes, hold thee as father in Írán,
And vex thee not with tribute for thy realm.
Thy child shall be the Lustre of the West,
And Crown of dames."
                  Astounded at his words
Shangul took off his Indian turban, spurred
His steed, and from the front of that great host
Approached the Sháh to make excuse, embraced
The king of kings with joy, and sought to amend
What had been said.   He was rejoiced to see
Bahrám, prepared the board, and brought the cup.
Bahrám revealed the secret to Shangul,
Discoursed of the concernments of Írán,
And said : " Such circumstances and such thoughts
Were those that guided me in this affair."
    They both of them arose, the drinking done,
And each asked pardon of the other one.

§ 36

How Shangul went back to Hind and Bahrám to Írán

These two kings—one a worshipper of God,
The other an idolater—joined hands,
And pledged themselves : " Henceforth we will not
    sever
Out hearts from right, will raze each root of guile,
Keep faith for aye, and listen to the words
From sages' lips."
              Shangul too bade farewell
To Sapínúd, he made his breast the warp
And hers the woof. The two kings quickly turned
Their backs on one another and flung down
The rancour of their hearts upon the dust.
One land-ward went, the other river-ward,
Apace and glad.
           When tidings reached Írán :—
" The Sháh himself with those escorting him
Hath come back from Kannúj," the people all,
As they were minded, decked the roads and cities,
And everywhere strewed money, musk, and saffron.
When Yazdagird received the news he gathered
The scattered troops. He and Narsi, the high priest,
And all the sages, went to meet the Sháh.
When Yazdagird beheld his sire Bahrám
He lighted down and bent him to the dust.
Narsi, the monarch's brother, and withal
The high priest had cheeks dust-stained but glad hearts.
On such wise Sháh Bahrám came to his palace,
Committing soul and body both to God.
He rested when the world grew dark and while   C. 1578
The moon was like a silvern shield, but when
Day rent night's raiment, and the world's Light
    showed,

The king of kings sat on his golden throne,
Gave audience but refrained his lips from speech.
Came all the nobles with the men of lore,
And princes of the empire, then the world-lord
Rose on his throne and spake words just and holy,
First spake of the Creator, then discharged
His debt [1] to wisdom, and thus said : " Revere
The Almighty in whose ken the manifest
And hidden are, Him praise, and unto Him
Address thy supplications midst night's gloom,
For he hath given power and victory,
And is the Lord of shining sun and moon.
All ye that would gain Paradise abstain
From evil and foul deeds.   Where there is justice
With bounteousness and righteousness the heart
Will turn from guile and loss.   Let none henceforth
Fear me though he possesseth hills of gold,
And mines of silver.   From your hearts expel
All fear and seek addition of all good.
The peasant and the thane are one to us
When we are judge.   When we gave crown and
        throne
To any know that 'twas from God and fortune.
I will strive not to fill my treasury,
I would drive not my people from their homes.
One treasure only—justice—will I hoard
That after death my spirit may rejoice.
Thus too, God willing, will my heart grow bright,
And fortune smile.   Hereby I shall increase
Our blessings and direct you to fair fortune.
He who hath borne oppression from my troops,
Officials, kin, and cavaliers of war, .
And doth acquaint me not, but keepeth hidden
That knavery, is guilty of the crime ;
Will one so futile e'er endeavour greatness ?

[1] Reading with P.

I call to God for justice on the man
That hath concealed the moon behind a cloud ;
But if your will is other, for men's motives
Are diverse, tell me boldly ; haply I
May bring to pass your long-conceived desires.
Attend to me, do what I bid, and find
Your souls' peace in my counsels.''
                              Thus he spake,
Resumed his seat upon the throne, rejoicing,
And set the crown of greatness on his head.
The nobles praised him, saying : '' May the crown
And signet ne'er lack thee.   Realm, crown, and throne C. 157c
All glory in a Sháh that is both wise,
And of victorious fortune, but with thee
Thy hardihood, thy knowledge, and thy Grace
Are greater than the throne of king of kings.
A Sháh like thee the world remembereth not
For manliness, for treasure, and for justice.
To bless thee is incumbent on us all,
Both young and old, and we will glorify thee
To God and in the presence of our folk.
No Sháh hath sat upon this throne of gold
Like thee in justice, victory, and might.
Thou raisest from the dust the dead by justice,
By goodly speech, and by munificence.
May God almighty be thine aid, and may
The head of fortune's star be in thy lap.''
   The mighty men and sages prosperous
Went from the monarch's throne with songs of joy.
Then mounting with his troops he drew anear
The precincts of Ázargashasp.   He lavished
His gold and jewels on the mendicants,
On those especially that hid their want.
The high priest of the Fire-fane of Zarduhsht
Came muttering prayers with sacred twigs in hand.
The Sháh brought Sapínúd to him, and he

Instructed her in custom, Faith, and rite,
In limpid water and the good religion
Bathed her and banned from her dust, rust, and soil.[1]
The Shán unlocked the prisons and began
Bestowing gifts of drachms on every man.

§ 37

How Shangul with seven Kings visited Bahrám

Now from his child—the consort of the Shán—
Shangul heard of the doings of her spouse,
And was desirous to behold Írán—
The dwelling of the noble monarch's daughter.
He sent an Indian·eloquent and noble
As envoy to request the Shán to grant
Another treaty to be stored away
For record, and the world's lord had one drawn
Like shining Sol in jocund Paradise.
The envoy took withal a letter written
In ancient Persian by the Shán's own hand,
And went his way.[2] Now when he reached Shangul,
And when the monarch of Kannúj had seen
Bahrám Gúr's letter, he prepared to journey
From Hindústán, but hid it from his kindred
In Chin. Seven monarchs followed in his train,
Escorting Rái[3] Shangul upon his way—
The monarch of Kábul, the king of Hind,
The king of Sind with troops, the famous king
Who ruled Sandal, the monarch of Jandal,
A potent prince, the monarch of Kashmir,
A man of mastery, and last of all
The great and glorious monarch of Múltán,

·1580

---

[1] " la débarrassa de la poussière et de la rouille *de l'idolâtrie* " (Mohl).
[2] Reading with P.   [3] Rái = Rája.

All coveters of honour, all with crowns,
All wearing torques and earrings, all with escorts
And camp-equipment, all of them renowned,
Of high estate and rank, all exquisite
With silver, gold, and gems ; their parasols
Were all of peacocks' plumes, their elephants
Had housings of brocade, their escorts glittered
O'er miles with offerings for the Sháh and gifts,
Such that dinárs seemed worthless in his eyes.
Thus king Shangul and those seven kings withal
Proceeded stage by stage, and, when they neared
Írán with all their precious equipage,
The Sháh, informed of their approach, arrayed
A host to go to meet them while the chiefs
Of every city went to welcome them.
The king of kings in wisdom old, and wary
Though young in years, advanced to Nahrawán.
The two illustrious and exalted kings
Drew near to one another, both of them
Alighted from their steeds and, as they met,
Both offering greetings and apologies,
Embraced. Both retinues alighted too :
The world was full of babble. Much talk passed
On matters great and small when thus the kings
Of these two kingdoms met. They both remounted,
As did their worshipful and famous troops.
Bahrám Gúr set him up within his halls
A golden throne draped as the custom was,
Set wine upon the board and furnished minstrels.
The whole place rang with song. He spread a board,
An arrow-flight in length, with roasted lambs [1]
And fowls. The eating done, he held a revel
In royal wise—all colour, scent, and beauty.
The handmaids and the slave-boys stood around,
Throne, hall, and palace were like Paradise,

---

[1] *Cf.* Vol. vi. p. 238 and *note*.

The wine-cups were all crystal, there were chargers
All golden, musk, and scents. The revellers
Wore jewelled crowns and shoes depict with gems.
Shangul was in amazement at the palace,
And as he drank he pondered : " Is Írán
A paradise or garden where one's friends
Exhale the scent of musk ? "

                    Thus to the Sháh
Said he in private : " Let me see my daughter."
. 1581   Bahrám bade eunuchs of the company
Conduct him to that Moon. The noble king
Went with them and beheld another palace
Like spring. When he beheld her on her throne
Of ivory, crowned with an amber crown,
He came and kissed her on the head, and laid   .
His cheek to hers and wept exceedingly
For love of her as did the Fair o'er him.
He stroked her hand and speaking of that hall,
That palace, and reception-room, he said :—
" Behold a paradise ! Thou hast escaped
A wretched palace and a foul abode."
    The gifts that he had brought with him—the
        purses,
The crowns, and slaves withal, the gems and raiment,
Whose value none knew how to estimate,
He gave to her. He gave great largess too,
And that blithe home was like a garth in spring.
Departing thence he went back to the Sháh,
Disposed for drinking by his happiness.
Now when the lords were merry with the wine
Shangul departed to his couch to sleep,
And, when the Veil of musky hue appeared
With stars to spot it like a leopard's back,
The revellers betook them to sweet slumber,
While all the attendants stood with folded arms.
    Thus was it till that golden Cup appeared,

Which thou wouldst call the sun, flung off the cloak
Of lapis-lazuli, and strewed the waste
With topazes ; then valiant Sháh Bahrám
Went forth to hunt and took the Indian kings,
Went to the chase with cheetahs, hawks, and falcons [1]
Imperious. For a while they did not irk
Their hearts, not one of them felt pain and grief
As for a month they hunted on the waste
Gazelle and onager. Then they returned
With instancy to wine and festival.
Thus king Shangul, when hunting and when feasting,
Ne'er was long absent from the world-lord's side,
Or at the riding-ground, at merrymake,
At banquet and at polo, turned his face
For one day from the Sháh. A long while passed,
The Indian king prepared to journey home.
He sought his daughter with a loving heart,
And stayed with her a while. He bade a slave-boy
Bring pen and paper to him, then he sought
For phrases scented with black, pounded musk,
And wrote in Indian a righteous rescript,
As it were ancient Persian. First he praised
Him who had washed the world of its distress,
Had spread abroad integrity and right,   C. 1582
And flung black lies and loss upon the Div :—
" I serve upon the way of use and Faith,
Not that of anger or for vengeance sake.
I have bestowed my daughter Sapínúd
As wife on Sháh Bahrám, that noble prince.
May he live ever as the king of kings,
And be the great ones of the world his slaves.
As soon as I shall quit this Wayside Inn
Let king Bahrám become Rái of Kannúj.[2]
Transgress not the commandment of that king,
And carry my dead body to the fire.

[1] *Cf.* p. 76, *note.*   [2] *Cf.* p. 140, *note.*

Give up my treasury to Sháh Bahrám,
And therewithal crown, kingdom, throne, and casque."
  This deed of gift in Indian characters
On silk he gave to Sapínúd as hers.

§ 38

*How Shangul returned to Hindústán, and how Bahrám
remitted the Property-tax to the Landowners*

Shangul abode for two months in Írán,
And then dispatched a noble to the Sháh
To ask permission to depart, both he
And his illustrious counsellors, for home.
The king of kings consented that Shangul
Should start on his return to Hindústán,
And bade an archimage to choose among
The treasures of Írán—dinárs, gems, silver,
Gold, thrones and crowns, swords, girdles and brocade,
And stuffs uncut—unbounded, countless gifts
To give Shangul while for his suite he furnished,
To each in his degree, steeds and brocade
Of Chin, dismissed them happy and content,
And went three stages with Shàngul.   Besides
The gifts he gave them provand to the coasts
Of Hindústán.
                    When Sháh Bahrám returned
He sat in peace upon the throne, but mused
Of death and of ill fortune till his heart
Ached and his face grew wan.   He bade a scribe—
A noble archmage who was his vizír—
To come to him and bade him to inspect
The treasury and reckon up the gold,
The gems, and raiment, for astrologers
Had told him, and the words had troubled him :—

" Thy life will last three score of years, the fourth score
Will make thee weep at death," and he had said :—
" The first score years will I devote to pleasure,   C. 158`
Will set joy as a shoot within my soul,
And in the next will justify the world
By equity and liberality
In public and in private. I will leave
No corner waste and will provide for all.
In the third score I will entreat the Lord ;
Perchance He will direct me on my way."
    The astrologer said sixty years and three,
But of the three the reckoning was not clear,
And so the Sháh desired sufficient treasure
To meet the presage of the astrologer,
Else would he have not self-reproach and travail ?
    The treasurer went to the treasury,
On hearing this, and laboured at the account.
He toiled exceedingly till he had told
The total to the monarch's minister,
Who thereupon went to the famous Sháh,
And said : " For three and twenty years to come
In sooth thou wilt need naught. I have allowed
For provand, largess, and thy famed troops' pay,
For envoys that arrive from other kings,
And from thine own famed provinces, and thou
Possessest for these years a treasury filled
With silver, gold, and goods."
                 On hearing this
Bahrám took thought, he was too wise to sorrow
Beforehand, and replied : " My sway is ending.
This world, if thou reflectest, hath three days.
Since yesterday is over, and to-morrow
Not come, to-day I stoop not under care.
As I have means of largess and a throne
Of ivory I will have no more tax."
    He bade that no tax should be asked thenceforth.

From small and great. He set up in each city
A man to rouse the drowsy and check strife
Wherefrom proceedeth naught save evil deeds.
He gave those wise archmages what was needful
By way of provand, clothes, and draperies
Out of his treasury, and said to them :—
" Ye must hide nothing good and bad from me.
Be ye the arbitrators of disputes,
Make no demands that make yourselves vexatious,
Report both good and ill, and cut my fears
Concerning evils short."
                    This thing obtained
Throughout the world, and nothing good and bad
Remained concealed. . Those sages ordered all,
But still from every province letters came,
Which said : " Through bounty,[1] idleness,[2] and wealth
The brains of men are ceasing to be wise.

C. 1584   There is such strife and bloodshed in the world
That young men set no value on the great ;
The young men's hearts are filled with many things,
But not with thoughts of Sháh and archimage.
Their faces they have turned from gain to guile,
They have grown troublesome and combative.
The peasants, landowners, and unemployed,
All give themselves to battle and contention."
    When letters of this kind arrived the Sháh
Was heart-pierced at the bloodshed. In each province
He chose officials, wise and understanding
As was befitting, and provided them
Out of his treasury with food and raiment,
The means for largess, and its allocation,
And for six months established offices,
Requiring of his subjects drachms in payment,
And stamping " tax " on silver thus received.
The officers wore crowns and had great state.

_____
[1] Or, with Mohl, " les dons *du roi*."   [2] Reading with P.

For six months he received, for six gave back
To wretched mendicant and man of birth.
He strove in this way to keep men of war
From bloodshed and inaugurating ill.
Again his agents wrote : " Munificence
Hath robbed the world of its security,
For they that have the money pay no tax,
But only meditate more bickerings.
Instead of being crass they have grown cruel,
They are all troublesome and quarrelsome."
   Now when Bahrám Gúr had perused this letter
His heart was troubled at such deeds. He bade :—
" Treat in accord to God's decree all those
That shed blood or employ deceit, that all
May find the means of livelihood."

                     He chose
A marchlord full of justice and of knowledge
For every province as was fit. He gave them
A court-allowance for a year, invoking
The Giver of all good. Much time passed by,
And then the monarch had a letter sent
To those truth-speaking men and correspondents,
Whom he had scattered through the world, to ask :—
" What is there in the world unprofitable,
And bringeth injury upon this realm ? "
   They wrote in answer : " Through the monarch's
     gifts
No man observeth rule and precedent.
There is no thought or care for tilth or toil
Wherefrom man's worth deriveth. We behold
Draught-oxen straying and the herbage lush
In tilth and springing crop."

                 The Sháh rejoined :—
" Till midday, when the world-illuming sun
Is at its height, the tiller of the soil
Must rest not from his work. The other half

Is for repose and sleep. If men are fools
We can but weep for them. If any lacketh
. 1585   Fruits, seed, and oxen be not stern and harsh
Toward him but kind and aid him from my treasures
That none may be distressed by indigence.
So likewise if the weather causeth loss,
And nobody is sovereign o'er the weather,
Or locusts anywhere conceal the earth,
And eat the herbage to the naked soil,
Give compensation from the treasury.
Proclaim this edict in the provinces.
If there are sterile routes or if the land
Be but a waste and all uncultivate,
And whether it be owned by rich or poor,
From such as I describe demand not aught,
And if a man, one of my servitors,
Or mine own foster-sire, shall take one mite
Him will I bury on the spot alive :
God give him neither home nor dwelling-place."
　　They sealed the letter with the royal ring,
And sent the camel-posts a-hurrying.

§ 39

How Bahrám summoned Gipsies from Hindústán

Thereafter he sent letters to each archmage,
Gave clothing to the mendicants, and asked :—
" In all the realm what folk are free from toil,
And who are mendicants and destitute ?
Tell me how things are in the world, and lead
My heart upon the pathway toward the light."
　　An answer came from all the archimages,
From all the nobles, and the men of lore :—
" The face of earth appeareth prosperous,
Continuous blessings are in every part,

Save that the poor complain against the ills
Of fortune and the Sháh. ' The rich,' they say,
' Wear wreaths of roses in their drinking-bouts,
And quaff to minstrelsy, but as for us
They do not reckon us as men at all.
The empty-handed drinketh with no rose
Or harp.' The king of kings should look to it."
    The Sháh laughed heartily at this report,
And sent a camel-post to king Shangul
To say thus : " O thou monarch good at need l
Select ten thousand of the Gipsy-tribe,
Both male and female, skilful on the harp,
And send them to me. I may gain mine end
Through that notorious folk."
                              Now when the letter
Came to Shangul he raised his head in pride
O'er Saturn's orbit and made choice of Gipsies,   C. 1586
As bidden by the Sháh who, when they came,
Accorded them an audience and gave each
An ox and ass, for he proposed to make
The Gipsies husbandmen, while his officials
Gave them a thousand asses' loads of wheat,
That they might have the ox and ass for work,
Employ the wheat as seed for raising crops,
And should besides make music for the poor,
And render them the service free of cost.
The Gipsies went and ate the wheat and oxen,
Then at a year's end came with pallid cheeks.
The Sháh said : " Was it not your task to plough,
To sow, and reap ? Your asses yet remain,
So load them up, prepare your harps, and stretch
The silken chords."
                    And so the Gipsies now,
According to Bahrám's just ordinance, ·
Live by their wits ; they have for company
The dog and wolf, and tramp unceasingly.

§ 40

How the Time of Bahrám came to an End

Thus passed he three score years and three, and had
No equal in that age. With New Year came
The scribe—the wise archmage, his minister—
And said to him : " The treasury of the king
Of mighty men is void, and I have come
For thy command. Those that enjoyed this wealth
Expect us not to levy any tax."
    The monarch answered : " Take no further pains,
For I have passed beyond the need thereof.
Resign the world to its Creator—Him
Who manifested forth His works. The heavens
Will pass away, but God abideth ever
To guide both thee and me to what is good."
    He slept that night, and early in the morn
A countless crowd resorted to his court.
They brought together all that were required,
And young prince Yazdagird approached the Sháh,
Who gave him in the presence of the lords
The crown and bracelets, torque and ivory throne.
Intending to devote himself to God
He cast away the crown, he left his seat,
And hasted to resign the world's affairs.
At night-fall he was eager for repose,
And, when the sun displayed its head above
The deep, fear filled his archimage's heart,
Who thought : " The Sháh ariseth not from sleep
Unless he hath withdrawn him from the lords."
C. 1587   Then Yazdagird drew near his sire and spied
What froze the breath upon his lips—Bahrám
With faded cheeks lay dead on gold brocade !
    The day of gloom is as it was of yore,
Sear not thy heart with greed and lust of more.

At death the cores of stones and iron quail,
' And here thy strivings are of no avail.
Thou shouldst be inoffensive and humane ;
Why seek addition with its biting bane ?
Woe for that great Sháh and his equity !
Oh ! never derogate his memory.
Of fifty monarchs of seed royal sown,
Who girt their loins upon the Íránian throne,
Bahrám Gúr had no like in eminence,
In justice, puissance, and excellence.
Thou wouldst have called king Rustam but vizír
To him though Rustam sent his arrows sheer
Through mounts of iron, yet was there no delay
When Sháh Bahrám Gúr's term had passed away.
What profit had he from his valour's day ?

    For forty days the Sháh bewailed his sire,
The host wore raiment black and blue, and when
The charnel closed o'er that famed warrior Sháh
" He bore off bounty," thou hadst said, " with him."

    Sun, moon, and Venus, Saturn, crown, and throne,
A Sháh, like this one, ne'er will look upon.
Woe for that royal mien, that height, and Grace !
Woe for that lofty star, that hand, and mace !
He decked the throne and crown, from Rúm and Chin
Took toll and tax, yet passed as he had been
Some starving mendicant !   When all was done
What profited his halls aloft the sun ?
He and the pauper fare the selfsame path,
And each of grief and pain a scantling hath.
The dear delights of earth, the sovereign sway,
What boot they ?   Soon thy rule will pass away.
Blest is the pious mendicant and wise,
Whose ears oft feel the world's rough pleasantries,
For, when he passeth, he will leave behind
A good name and a good conclusion find.
His portion is in heaven, and in God's sight

He will have honour, not be in my plight,
In miserable case, calamitous,
With all that I possess sent Hell-ward thus
Beyond recall ! No hope in heaven I see,
My hand is void, both worlds have ruined me !
   Now, if I can collect my thoughts again,
The rule of Yazdagird shall be my strain.

XXXVI

YAZDAGIRD SON OF BAHRÁM GÚR

HE REIGNED EIGHTEEN YEARS

NOTE

The length of the reign of this Sháh (Isdigerd II, A.D. 438–457), as given by Firdausí, appears to be about correct. From the point of view of popular tradition he seems wholly to have been overshadowed by his famous father, and his reign consequently is all but a blank in the Sháhnáma. Historically it was full of incident, and Firdausí's statement—

> "He sent out countless hosts on every side,
> And kept the world secure from enemies,"

though it may be only a conventional statement, is correct enough. He began his reign with a war with Rúm. This was soon over, but was followed by long wars with the Huns and the Haitálians. Within the empire there were persecutions of the Jews and Christians, and about A.D. 450 serious trouble in Armenia. Yazdagird, as we have seen,[1] continued his father's minister, Mihr Narsí, in power. According to Mas'údi he fortified the passes in the Caucasus.[2] He was known to his subjects by two titles— "The Clement"[3] and "The soldier's friend."[4]

Of the two sons of Yazdagird it is not certain historically which was the elder, but as Pirúz was successful in the struggle for the throne that followed on the death of his father, he in any case would have been made out to be the elder in order to regularise the succession, and the elder he is according to all the Oriental authorities. In dating his coins he ignored the short reign of his brother Hurmuz.[5]

---

[1] See p. 4.   [2] MM, ii. 193. *Cf.* Vol. i. pp. 16 and *note.*
[3] ZT, ii. p. 127.   [4] RM, I, ii. 363.   [5] NT, p. 426.

§ 1

How Yazdagird sat upon the Throne and exhorted the
Captains of the Host

· 1588   When Yazdagird became the world's great king
He gathered unto him the scattered troops.
There was a conclave of the wise and noble,
The great men and the princely archimages.
The atheling sat on the golden throne,
He shut the door of toil, the hand of evil,
And thus began : " He that committeth not
A wrong is not in danger of the avenger,
But when a heart is darkening with envy
The Div will be called in to medicine it,
For envy causeth greed and grief and want,
And is a cruel and revengeful div.
Impute not to a foeman's heart and hand
That which displeaseth thee. Humanity
Is wisdom's brother. Wisdom is the crown
Upon the head of knowledge. What time thou
Conferrest benefits on any one
Din it not into him and break his heart.
If thou dost good and art longsuffering
Thou art not worthless in a wise man's eyes.
If now victorious fortune shall assist me
In furthering my wishes in the world
I will prepare a roll of righteousness
Without an entry of deceit or wrong."
    He ruled the world in justice for a while ;
The age rejoiced in him and he rejoiced.
He sent forth countless hosts on every side,
And kept the world secure from enemies.
When eighteen years had passed above his head,
He grieved because his fortune was bedimmed,
Convoked to him the magnates and the sages,

Caused them to kneel before the golden throne,
And thus addressed them : "This untoward sky,
Not knowing fosterling and fosterer,
And heeding not the crowns of potentates,
Pursueth every quarry in its path ;
So now my time is drawing to its close,
And all my strength is broken. I bestow
The crown, the signet-ring, the host, and all
The treasures of Írán upon Hurmuz ;
Pay due observance, execute my bidding,
And make my will the music of your souls.
Although Pirúz hath Grace divine and stature,
And is the elder brother of Hurmuz ;
Yet see I in Hurmuz deliberation,
With wisdom, modesty, and aptitude."

He spake and lived a se'nnight afterwards ;   C. 1589
Then passed ; the throne wept over him awhile.

Be thy years twenty-five, be they five score,
Soon will this fleeting show be thine no more,
Regard then as a transitory thing
Whatever falleth to thy reckoning.

XXXVII

HURMUZ

HE REIGNED ONE YEAR

NOTE

The earliest coins of Pirúz date from his third year as he reckoned it, counting from his father's death, so the reign of Hurmuz (Hormisdas, A.D. 457–459) lasted about two years.[1] Hurmuz probably had the advantage of being on the spot at the time of Yazdagird's death, but Pirúz may have had the better right to the throne,[2] and seems to have owed much to the services of a leader named Ruhhám—a scion of the great Mihrán clan which was of Arsacid descent.[3] The name is a familiar one to students of the Sháhnáma as that of one of those secondary heroes many of whom—real personages in the Parthian epoch—have been reflected back to the mythical periods of the poem.[4] Ruhhám, as we have seen, was one of the Twelve (eleven) Champions.[5] Whether Pirúz also received formal help from the Haitálians is doubtful, but plenty of nomad tribes would be willing to take service with him for a consideration, and if they happened to be within the Haitálian sphere of influence would be regarded as Haitálians themselves by tradition. For the consideration required in the text Tabari substitutes Tálikán.[6] This is much more probable. Tirmid is mentioned because it would represent the traditional notion of the Oxus being the boundary between Írán and Túrán. On the other hand settlements in the desert, such as Tálikán, were valuable both for trade and in war.[7] Firdausí's statement that Pirúz pardoned Hurmuz is supported by Dínawarí and Mír Khánd, but two out of the three accounts in Tabari say that Hurmuz was put to death. The third says that he was imprisoned. In all probability he was executed.[8]

---

[1] NT, p. 426.   [2] See p. 153.   [3] NT, pp. 114, 139 and *notes*.
[4] See Vol. iii. p. 9.   [5] See Vol. iv. p. 102.   [6] NT, p. 116 *seq.* and *notes*.
[7] *Id.*   [8] *Id.* 117 *seq.* and *notes*, RM, I, ii. 364.

§ 1

How Hurmuz, Son of Yazdagird, ascended the Throne

Hurmuz succeeded to his father's throne,
And set upon his head the crown of gold,
While, thou hadst said, Pírúz was all one rage
With tears of envy mounting to his eyes.
He went incontinent with troops and treasures,
And many chiefs, to the Haitálian king,
Who was a princeling of Chaghán, a man
Of high ambition and possessed of troops,
Of treasure, and of power, hight Faghánísh.
To him Pirúz said : " O good friend of mine !
Two sons were we—the glories of the throne.
Our father gave the younger of us twain
The royal crown and, having acted thus
Unjustly, died. If thou wilt give me troops
I have myself wealth, weapons, majesty,
And might of hand."
                              The monarch of Chaghán
Replied : " 'Tis well, thy sire was king himself.
I will point out the way to get thy rights,
And furnish thee with troops upon these terms :
That I shall have Tirmid and Wísagird,
To which effect I hold a covenant
From Yazdagird."
                              Pirúz said : " Yea, 'tis well,
And thou deservest greater sovereignty."
    The monarch gave him thirty thousand swordsmen—
A noble army of Haitálians—
Wherewith Pirúz, the Sháh, arrayed a host
That darkened sky and moon with flying dust.
He fought with king Hurmuz who could not long
Endure the stress of war but presently
Was taken, and his father's crown and throne

Grew worthless to him.   When Pirúz beheld
His brother's face he yearned for love and union,
Bade him remount and sped to grasp his hand,
Dispatched him to the palace and declared
His own conditions.   Said Hurmuz to him :—
" Thank God that those who worship Him are wise.
My brother taketh from me crown and throne ;
Be victory both in name [1] and deed his own."

[1] Pirúz means victorious.

XXXVIII

PÍRÚZ

HE REIGNED ELEVEN YEARS

ARGUMENT

Pírúz becomes undisputed Sháh. His inaugural speech. The land is troubled by a severe drought which Pírúz takes measures to mitigate. The breaking of the drought. Pírúz builds cities and, in violation of the treaty of Sháh Bahrám Gúr, makes war upon the Haitálians, is defeated, and killed.

NOTE

The reign of Pírúz (Perozes, A.D. 459–484) lasted much longer than eleven years, and seems to have made a deep impression on the popular mind by reason of its accumulation of mishaps. The expedition against the Haitálians was preceded by a few months by a total eclipse of the sun [1]—a portent of disaster that well may have helped to bring about its own fulfilment. Mír Khánd tells us that this Sháh's sobriquet was " The Valiant." [2]

A relic of Pírúz—a cup engraved with a representation of that Sháh engaged in hunting—is said to be still in existence.[3]

§ 1. Drought is common enough in Írán, and the record shows that this particular one must have been of exceptional severity. According to Tabarí the relief measures adopted by Pírúz to cope with the emergency were so efficient that only one man perished through want.[4] Tabarí of course is merely giving the statements of his authorities without comment.

§§ 2–4. According to the account in Tabarí, Pírúz built three cities—Rám-Pírúz (the Pírúz-Rám of *Firdausi*) in the territory of

---

[1] On Saturday, January 14th, A.D. 484. NT, p. 425.
[2] RM, I, i. 368. [3] RSM, p. 329. [4] NT, pp. 119, 122.

Rai, another called Rúshan Pirúz, and a third named Shahrám-Pírúz (Firdausí's Bádán Pirúz) in Ázarbáiján.[1]

The tradition given in the Sháhnáma of the war between Pirúz and the Haitálians is dominated by the memory of the beloved and popular Bahrám Gúr. We have seen how that Sháh, after his triumphant campaign against that people, set up a pillar that was to mark the boundary between them and the Íránians.[2] The presumption in the poem is that the arrangement then made continued in force till Pírúz refused to be bound by it any longer. His refusal brought death upon himself and disaster on his host. Clearly this was a judgment upon him for violating the treaty made by his grandfather. Naturally if Pirúz had been successful a different popular estimate would have been formed upon his conduct, but as matters turned out he was manifestly a wrong-doer for having left his grandsire's way and he merely got his deserts. Consequently on this occasion right was on the side of the enemy, and for a time the tradition becomes almost pro-Haitálian. Between the memory of a great popular Sháh and the occurrence of a great national disaster practically nothing remained, and the two are linked together as cause and effect. Historically, as we know from other sources, the case was very different. Bahrám Gúr's son and successor, Yazdagird, had plenty of trouble with the Haitálians,[3] and so had, it would seem, Pírúz himself before the final disaster overtook him. Once, if not twice, he had been forced to conclude an unfavourable peace with them, had found himself in their power, and his son, Kubád, had on one occasion to remain two years in captivity until a heavy ransom had been paid. If the story of the help given by the Haitálians to Pirúz against his brother, Hurmuz, at the price of the cession of Tálikán be unhistorical it was probably at one of these conclusions of peace that the place was ceded.[4] Popular tradition may have preferred to represent Tálikán as being yielded to secure the throne for the rightful heir rather than as the consideration for a disgraceful treaty later on. Pirúz violated his own compact, not Bahrám's, and perished in consequence. There are three accounts of the disaster in Tabari. They are in accord in essentials, and two of them attribute the proximate cause of the overthrow of Pirúz to the trench dug by the Haitálian king who in these accounts is called Achshunwar or Akhshunwar approximately, but in the absence of diacritical and vowel points the precise form is uncertain. According to one account it was the evil practices of the

---

[1] NT, p. 123.   [2] p. 92.   [3] p. 153.
[4] pp. 156, 157, NT, p. 119, *note.*

Haitálian king that impelled Pírúz to declare war, and four sons and four brothers perished with him.[1] The second, which comes from Ibn Mukaffa,[2] states that there were two campaigns. In the first of them Pírúz was led astray by an Haitálian chief, who had had himself purposely mutilated in order to deceive the Sháh, and forced to sue for peace. Subsequently wounded honour induced him to tear up the treaty and renew the struggle in spite of the advice of his counsellors; he perished, and his baggage, women, money, and papers fell into the hands of the enemy.[3] In the third account mention is made of Bahrám Gúr's pillar, and Pírúz is said to have had it thrown down and dragged in front of him by fifty elephants and three hundred men that he might not be charged with passing it. This account also states that a daughter of Pírúz was among the captives taken by the Haitálians. Their king put her into his haram, and she had a daughter who afterwards married her uncle Kubád.[4] There can be no doubt but that a terrible disaster befell the Íránian arms in this campaign and, as we shall see presently,[5] the memory of it was reflected back upon the mythical past and the story retold in connexion with the overthrow of a Pishdádian Sháh.

§ 1

How Pírúz sat upon the Throne and made an Oration

Pírúz, at ease about Hurmuz and free C. 1590
From care, came, sat upon the royal throne,
As well became a Sháh that worshipped God,
And at the outset thus harangued the chiefs :—
" Ye worshipful and noble lords ! I ask .
The Judge that needeth naught to grant to me
Long life, a due regard for great and small
As their conditions are, abundant wisdom,
And happy days. Longsuffering is the crown
Upon humanity ; the hasty man
Is ever in abasement. Wisdom's pillars

---

[1] NT, p. 120.
[2] For whom see Vol. vi. p. 17; NT, p. 121, *note.* [3] *Id.* p. 123 *seq.*
[4] *Id.* p. 128 *seq.* and *notes.* [5] p. 171.

Are equity and mercy, its adornment
Is bounty's gate, the tongue of eloquence
Its glory, while its plumes are hardihood
And fortitude. How shall mere high estate,
If wisdom fail, enjoy the throne of greatness ?
E'en sages are but mortal and possess not
More Grace than had Jamshíd who died, what time
His crown had reached the moon, and gave another
His royal seat. None can abide on earth
For aye. Take refuge then with God from ill,
And all is said."

               Wise and untouched by evil
He ruled one year with justice and good counsel.
Next year the face of heaven was dry, the water
Shrank in the streams till it became like musk.
The third and fourth year it was even so,
And all men were in misery through the drought ;
The mouth of heaven became as dry as dust,
And river-water was a precious drug ;
There was no room to stand, such multitudes
Of men and beasts lay dead. The king of kings
Beheld that portent, took off tax and toll,
And in each city where he kept his stores
Bestowed them freely on both small and great.
A proclamation issued from the court :—
" Distribute, O ye men of name and might !
Such grain as ye possess and heap instead
Your treasuries with coins struck by Pirúz.
Whoe'er possesseth hoarded stores of grain,
Or sheep or oxen roaming at their will,
Let him dispose thereof at his own price,
For lives are perishing for lack of food."

C. 1591   He sent another letter in all haste
To every officer and potentate :—
" Ope wide your barns to all folk everywhere
That are in need. Should young or old and feeble

Die lacking bread—a victim to the famine—
I will pour out his blood that hath the barn,
For he hath scorned God's work. His waist will I
Cleave with the trenchant scimitar and wreck
His life."
                He ordered folk to quit their homes,
And coming plainwards lift their hands in plaint.
A cry of bitter weeping and distress,
Of pain and consternation rose to heaven ;
On hill and waste, in desert and in cave,
They called on God for mercy. On this wise
For seven years both small and great beheld
No verdure anywhere. With Farwardín,
The eighth year, rose a glorious cloud which rained
Pearls on the parched up soil. The scent of musk
Rose from the gardens while the hail that fell
Lay in the mud like pears within a bowl ;
The rainbow was resplendent in the sky,
The age escaped the ill of evil men,
And everywhere the bow was strung again.

§ 2

*How Pírúz built the Cities of Pírúz-Rám and Bádán-Pírúz,
and how he went to war with Túrán*

Now when Pirúz had 'scaped that day of stress
He sat in peace upon the throne of kingship,[1]
He built himself a city which he bade
Call Pírúz-Rám, the world hath good thereof,
For 'tis the pleasance of the glorious Sháhs.
He built withal Bádán-Pírúz, far-famed,
A place of peace and joy, now Ardabil,
Where Cæsar hath of right his boundary.

---

[1] The previous section ends here in C.

Whenas Pirúz had prospered all these parts,
And made thereby the hearts of wise men glad,
He gave a largess to his noble troops,
And gat him ready to attack the Turkmans.
In that campaign Hurmuz was in the van
With troops new-levied ; after Sháh Pirúz
Kubád led [1] on the army like a blast ;
Pirúz' pure son was he, wise, and a bough
That brought forth fruit.   Balásh, the younger son,[2]
A man of Grace and justice, sat rejoicing

C. 1592   Upon the throne while one of Párs, a man
Of high renown called by the king Sarkhán,[3]
Was bidden by Pirúz : " Abide thou here
As upright minister before Balásh." [4]

   Pirúz set forward with his troops, his treasure,
And gear of war, to fight with Khúshnawáz.
Now brave Bahrám had marked the boundary
By setting up a column on the plain
With this inscription by the king of kings :—
" Let not a Turkman or Íránian
Transgress this boundary on any wise,
Or pass across the river."

               When Pirúz,
The lion-queller, reached that spot he saw
The mark set by the monarch of Írán,
And thus addressed his chiefs : " By this same token
Will I erect with scimitar and treasure
A tower against the Turkmans so that none
May suffer from the Haitálians.   When 'tis raised
On the Tarak, and when their chiefs shall bring
The former treaty, I will say : ' Bahrám Gúr
Did thus by manhood, wisdom, might, and Grace,
But I will leave no trace of Khúshnawáz,
Haitálian or Turkman, high or low.' "

---

[1] Reading with P.   [2] *Cf.* p. 170.
[3] Súfarai, for whom see pp. 170, 173 *seq.*, 185.   [4] Couplet omitted.

When Khúshnawáz, son of the Khán, had heard :—
" The Sháh and all his host have crossed Jíhún
Against the treaty that Bahrám Gúr made :
Fresh war and strife have come upon the land,"
A veteran scribe was called by his command.

§ 3

The Letter of Khúshnawáz to Pírúz

He wrote a letter to the king of earth,
With [1] praises of him from the righteous Judge,
Then said : " Since thou departest from the pact
Made by just kings I will not call thee royal.
Thine ancestors had acted never so,
Those rulers of the world elect and pure.
By breaking thus the compact of the Persians,
And flinging to the dust the mark of greatness,[2]
Thou forcest me to break the treaty also,
And draw the scimitar in self-defence."
He wrote at large and sent too many gifts.
A noble cavalier and eloquent
Went with the letter which when Sháh Pirúz
Had read he raged against that famous prince,
And bade the envoy : " Rise and get thee gone,
Return to that base man and say to him :—
' Bahrám concluded terms of peace whereby   C. 1593
The country was your own to the Tarak,
But now thou hast the whole to the Jíhún,
Hill, dale, and desert, all alike are thine.
Behold l I lead a vast, a noble host,
And warriors bent on fight, and I will leave not
For long on earth the shade of Khúshnawáz.' "

---

[1] Reading with P.
[2] " la marque *de la frontière* établie par les grands " (Mohl).

The envoy came like flying dust and told
What he had heard. When Khúshnawáz had hearkened
Thereto, and read what had been writ to him,
He called his scattered followers to horse,
Led forth the army to the battlefield,
And set upon a lance's point the treaty
Accorded to his grandsire by Bahrám
To this effect : " Our frontier is Jihún."
He chose a man of mark among the troops—
One who was shrewd of heart and eloquent—
And said : " Approach Pirúz with courteous words,
Hear his reply, and say : ' I will confront thee
Upon the march with thine own grandsire's treaty—
That man of lofty fortune, thine own guide—
Set on a spearhead like a shining sun
Before the host that all possessed of wisdom
May look upon the patent of the just.
I shall be praised while thou wilt be condemned,
And called "The impious Sháh." God and his wor-
　　shippers,
And subjects everywhere, will not approve
That any one should seek to do injustice,
And break the treaties of the kings of kings.
None like to Sháh Bahrám for equity
And manhood e'er set crown upon his head.
God is my witness, and it is not well
To have to make appeal to Him, that thou
Art with injustice seeking war with me
In falling thus upon me with thy host.
Herein thou wilt be not victorious,
And likewise get no fruitage from good fortune.
Henceforward I shall send no messengers :
God will avail to aid me in this fight.' "
　　The envoy came dust-swift with this dispatch,[1]
And to Pirúz repeated all these words.

---

[1] We have not been told that Khúshnawáz wrote one.

When that haught Sháh had read what Khúshnawáz
Had written in the letter he was wroth,
And said thus to the envoy : " One of years
And world-experience would speak not like that ;
But if from Chách thou comest o'er the river
My spearheads are prepared to welcome thee."
   The messenger returned to Khúshnawáz,
Spake with him privily at large, and said :—
" I see not in Pírúz a reverence
For God ; he hath not wisdom for his guide ;
He careth only for revenge and strife,
And walketh not according to God's will."
   When Khúshnawáz had heard these words he sought c. 1594
To God for shelter, making supplication,
And saying : " O Thou Judge that judgest right,
And art the Master both of wind and dust !
Thou knowest that iniquitous Pírúz
Is not in prowess better than Bahrám.
He speaketh words unjust and fain would win
Addition by the scimitar. Break Thou
His foot-hold from the earth. Oh ! may he have
No strength, no wit, no heart ! "
                       Around his host [1]
He dug a trench which he made shift to hide ;
'Twas lasso-deep and twenty cubits wide.

§ 4

How Pírúz fought with Khúshnawáz and was slain

This done, he called on God and marched his powers
From Samarkand. On that side Sháh Pírúz,
The frantic, led his troops on like a blast ;
On this side Khúshnawáz with fearful heart

[1] *i.e.* where he intended to make his stand.

'Prayed privily before the holy Judge.
The drums and trumpets sounded in both hosts,
The air was ebon with the armies' dust,
And from them both such showers of arrows rained
That blood ran down like water in a stream.
Then, like a dust-cloud, Sháh Pirúz advanced
With mace and Rúman helm, and as he drew
Anear to Khúshnawáz,[1] the Turkmans' chief
Retreated, turned his rein, and showed his back.
The foeman followed fiercely. Sháh Pirúz
Spurred forward with few followers and fell
With others—chiefs and Lions of the day
Of battle—in the fosse, such as Hurmuz
His brother, glorious Kubád and others—
Great men and princes of the royal race—
Till seven had fallen headlong, men of name
With golden casques. Then Khúshnawáz returned
Rejoicing to the fosse and lifted thence
The living while the throne bewailed their fortune.
Now Sháh Pirúz, that chief of chiefs endowed
With Grace and state, had broken head and back,
While of the princes, save Kubád, none lived :
Thus host and empire went adown the wind.
Then Khúshnawáz advanced with heart content,
And head exalted with his warrior-host,
And gave to spoil the baggage and the foe,
For right and left were indistinguishable.
They made some prisoners and what numbers more
Were stretched by arrows on the sombre soil !

· 1595 'Tis not for world-lords to be covetous,
    For hearts that covet are the dark dust's mate ;
The never-resting sky ordaineth thus
    Alike for subjects and for king's estate,
And wringeth its own fosterling, be he
    A fool or wisdom's pillar. None can stay

---

[1] The sentence thus far has been translated from P.

Upon this earth of ours eternally.

Make right thy provand : naught is left to say.
When Khúshnawáz had crossed the fosse his troops
Lacked not for wealth. They bound Kubád with
    fetters
Of iron, heedless of his throne and race.

When tidings reached the people of Írán
About the fosse and how Pirúz had fought,
A wail of anguish went up from the land
For all those princes—men of high degree—
And when the tidings had been certified
Balásh descended from his golden seat,
Plucked out his royal locks and strewed sad dust
Upon the throne. Within Írán the host,
The cities and the women, men, and children,
All wailed, all rent the hair and tore the face
For grief, talked of the Sháh and yearned for him ;
All sat in dole and woe while great and small
Took thought what course to choose and whether they
Should quit Írán and see where fell the fray ?

XXXIX

BALÁSH

HE REIGNED *FIVE* YEARS AND TWO MONTHS

ARGUMENT

Baláush becomes Sháh. Súfarai leads forth a host against the
Haitálians to avenge the death of Pirúz and defeats them. Terms
of peace are arranged, Kubád and the other captives are released,
and Súfarai returns with them in triumph to Írán. After some
years Súfarai dethrones Baláush and makes Kubád Sháh.

NOTE

Baláush (Balas, A.D. 484–488) seems to have been the brother, not
the son, of Pirúz and the uncle of Kubád.[1] The name is identical
with the more familiar Vologeses. Baláush being on the spot and
regent at the time of the death of Pirúz naturally became Sháh.
Tabari says that he had to fight for the throne with his brother
(really his nephew), Kubád, who fled to the Haitálians. The real
struggle however appears to have been with Kubád's brother, Zirih,
who was defeated and slain.[2]

§§ 2 and 3. Pirúz having expiated by his own death his violation
of the treaty made by his grandfather, Sháh Bahrám Gúr, with the
Haitálians, popular tradition is at liberty to resume a patriotic
attitude and set forth how Pirúz was avenged and Íranián honour
vindicated. Unfortunately the account does not appear in the
oldest authorities and seems to be unhistorical. Írán at that time
was much oppressed by, if not actually tributory to, the Haitálians.[3]
Súfarai's triumphant campaign seems to have been invented as a
salve to the national honour and, incidently, as a glorification of

---

[1] NT, p. 133 *note*.   [2] *Id.*
[3] *Id.* 119 *note*. That the scene of Súfarai's victory should be laid
at Kashmíhan, where Bahrám Gúr had triumphed, is in itself sus-
picious. See pp. 89, 90.

the great family of Káran to which he belonged. The story of
his success appears, as Nöldeke has pointed out, to have been
reflected back into mythical times and told in connexion with
Naudar, the Pishdádian Sháh. Certainly the parallel is very
complete. In both cases the Íránian host is overthrown by a
Northern foe; in both the Sháh perishes; in both the scene is laid
in the same neighbourhood; in both the defeat is avenged by a
Káran, and in both cases the prisoners are rescued.[1] In Tabarí's
account Súfarai appears as Súkhrá.[2] As a leading Íránian of the
time he may have been instrumental in bringing about a peace
with the Haitálians after the death of Pirúz, and this perhaps may
be regarded as the historical measure of his achievement.[3]

Balásh appears to have been somewhat after the type of
Yazdagird, son of Shápúr, in character,[4] mild and tolerant,
approved by the Christians and hated by the Magi who, it is
said, were scandalised at his attempt to introduce the Roman
fashion of public baths, which of course involved a profanation of
the sacred element. As his treasury was exhausted he was unable
to look to the army for support, and after a reign of four years was
dethroned and blinded. According to other accounts he died
a natural death.[5] Mír Khánd says that he was known as
"the beloved."[6]

§ I

How Balásh ascended the Throne and harangued the Íránians

Whenas Balásh had mourned one month, with dust
Upon his head and lacerated cheeks,
The people and the high priest came to him
With valiant warriors and famous sages.
They spake with him at large by way of counsel
In profitable words, then seated him
Upon the throne of kingship, showering gold
And jewels over him abundantly.
When seated on the throne he said : " O chiefs !
Acquire the secrets of the sages' hearts,

---

[1] See Vol. i. p. 345 _seq._, and NIN, p. 9.   [2] NT, p. 120 _note_.
[3] _Id._, and RSM, p. 332.   [4] See Vol. vi. p. 371.
[5] NT, pp. 133 _seq._ and _notes_; RSM, p. 336 and _note_.
[6] RM, Pt. I, Vol. ii. p. 371.

And ye shall have advancement at my hands
When my dark counsels brighten.   Frustrate not
The purpose of well-doers in the world.
As for the wicked and malicious man,
He shall not partner me, but first will I
Enrich him with advice and, if that faileth,
. 1596 Crown him with blood.   When any subject plaineth
To us 'gainst some one of this loyal host
The heart of the unjust one will I break,
And rase him utterly, both root and branch.
See that ye take no freedoms with your Sháh,
And in especial one that is devout,
For he by turns is bane and antidote ;
So choose the antidote and leave the bane.
Of all things seek to please the Sháh and never
Approach his throne unless with joyful looks.
When he is wroth excuse thyself and bless him,
Just or unjust.   Whene'er thou sayest : ' I
Am wise, and I am mighty in all knowledge,'
Know that thou never wast more ignorant,
So be not thine own enemy.   If now
Ye shall obey the counsel that I give
By hearkening to my profitable words,
Ye shall receive the treasures of wise Sháhs :
I never yet saw knowledge injure any."
    The chieftains marvelled at his understanding,
And called down praises on him, while the troops
Spake thus to one another : " From this Sháh
Will fall a lustre on the throne and crown.
God grant that he escape the evil eye,
And ill befall the persons of his foes."
    They went forth from his palace well content,
Committing to God's care his soul and body.
Their hearts were full of love, their tongues of praise :—
"May such a Sháh have endless length of days."

§ 2

*How Súfarai had Tidings of the Slaying of Pírúz, how he wrote
a Letter to Khúshnawáz, and how Khúshnawáz replied*

What time Pírúz was going to the war
He sought a paladin—a man of counsel
And weight—to watch o'er crown and throne, and be
A friend to young Balásh. Now Súfarai—
A man of great estate and good withal—
Was fitted for that task, experienced,
A native of Shiráz, a general,
A man exalted both in heart and head,
And likewise marchlord in Zábulistán,
Kábulistán, Ghaznín, and Bust. When tidings
About Pírúz, uncounselled and unguided,
Came his eye-lashes drenched his cheeks with tears,
He rent his raiment of a paladin,
The warriors doffed their helmets and sat mourning
Through sorrow for the Sháh, while Súfarai
Exclaimed : " How shall Balásh, youth that he is,
Seek vengeance for Pirúz ? " for well he knew
That that would naught avail and that the throne   C. 1597
Of kingship was in evil case. He gathered
His scattered soldiers, beat the kettledrums,
And dust rose from the plain. There came to him
A hundred thousand warlike, vengeful swordsmen.
He paid, equipped the host, and joyed the hearts
Of all that sought for vengeance. Then he called
A sweet-tongued envoy watchful, wise, and shrewd,
And, seared and sorry, wan and weeping, wrote
A letter of wise counsels, instancing
Jamshid and Kai Khusrau and Kai Kubád,
Dispatched it to Balásh, and said : " O Sháh !
Be not aggrieved at death ; it is a grief
That all must taste ; choose patience and choose fame.

What came from wind returneth with the breath :
Some call it justice and some tyranny.
Now with the approbation of the king
Will I make ready for revenge and strife
Because the sun and moon cry out in heaven
For vengeance for the blood of Sháh Píruz."
  With that the envoy went upon his way,
And Súfarai, all wreakful, for his part
Arrayed his army like a pheasant's plumes,[1]
And from Zábulistán advanced toward Marv.
He chose him out a wary messenger,
Who by his words could mollify the heart,
And spake on this wise to a scribe : " Arise,
Because thy pen hath stirring work to do,
Indite to Khúshnawáz and say : ' O fool,
And knavish doer of the work of divs !
Thou art in God's sight guilty, and thy shirt
Shall wail for thee.   Whoe'er did deed like thine,
Thou faithless one ?   Thou shalt behold anon
The sword of tribulation.   Thou hast slain
A man without offence—the king of kings,
The grandson of the world-lord Sháh Bahrám—
And hast set up a new feud in the world,
A feud to be forgotten nevermore.
Why, when the din of tymbals rose, didst thou
Not come and fawn upon him like a dog ?
Thy grandsire was a poor man of thy tribe,
Thy sire was like a slave before Bahrám.
Lo ! I have come to Marv to seek revenge,
And I will waste the Haitálians utterly.
The captives and whatever booty came
Within thy grasp upon that battlefield,
I will exact all with the sword of vengeance,
And bear to Marv Túrán's dust, suffer not
The world to be thy son's, burn all thy kith

----

[1] *Cf.* p. 88, *note.*

And kin, cut off thy head by God's command,
And make thy kingdom like a sea of blood.
But this is not revenge ; why talk I long ?　　　　C. 1598
When Khúshnawáz, in that he slew Pírúz,
Shall rot in darksome dust his soul shall plead
His cause from Hell.' "
　　　　　　　　The envoy with the letter
Of Súfarai went like a mighty lion,
Came in an angry mood to Khúshnawáz,
Appeared before his throne, did reverence,
And gave the letter, while the captains present
Withdrew.　The monarch gave it to a scribe,
And said : " Read out to me in confidence
Both good and ill."
　　　　　　　　The scribe thus answered him :—
" This letter is all arrow, mace, and sword,"
And sorely grieved was valiant Khúshnawáz
At that long letter writ by Súfarai,
Then set himself without delay to answer
The good and ill there written and began :—
" I live in fear of God and fortune's changes.
A worshipper of His would not have broken
The compact of the Sháhs.　I sent Pírúz
A letter of advice besides the treaty
Of that great king,[1] but he despised my words,
And spurned the old king's pact.　When he assailed me,
And put me to a shift, and when the hosts
Met face to face, the stars raged at Pírúz,
And by no will of ours thy Sháh was slain.
Or e'er he broke the pact of righteous Sháhs
His youth had not another day of joy ;
He found [2] no favour in the Maker's eyes ;
Thou wouldst have said : ' Earth took him by the
　　heel.' [3]

---

[1] Bahrám Gúr.　See p. 166.　　　　[2] Reading with P.
[3] " *Foot* " in the original.

The man that breaketh his forefather's treaty,
And flingeth underfoot the head of right,
Is like Pirúz upon the battlefield,
Pashed in a dusty ditch. So shalt thou be
If thou shalt come ; my wealth and warriors fail not."
   Departing with the letter and apace
The envoy in a week reached Súfarai,
Who read and loosed his tongue in malisons.
Then from the plain the people heard the blare
Of trumpets and the clash of brazen cymbals,
And Súfarai led forth to Kashmíhan
A host so great that Sol was lost in heaven.
'Twas thus they crossed the stream—an armament
That made itself at home where'er it went.

§ 3

How Súfarai fought with Khúshnawáz, and how Kubád
was released from his Bondage

C. 1599   When tidings came to Khúshnawáz he marched
Out to the desert and prepared for war.
He reached Baigand and chose a battlefield
That hid the wilderness from circling heaven
With troops.
              On his side vengeful Súfarai
Came onward like a blast. When it was night
That leader of the army occupied
All the approaches with fresh elephants.
The outposts went their rounds in both the hosts,
The world resounded with the warriors' shouts,
The challenge of the sentries and the clang
Of bells rose from both armies, front and rear,
Till Sol rose o'er the peaks and made the dales
And deserts like white crystal. Both arrays
Prepared for strife ; each raised the flag of greatness.

Then dragons' livers sundered at the shouting
Of valiant warriors while feathered shafts
Made air all vultures' plumes, and earth became
A bath of chieftains' blood.   Where'er one gazed
Lay heaps of warriors slain.   Then Súfarai
Charged from the centre with his troops amain,
While Khúshnawáz on his side with his sword
Of vengeance spurred down from his vantage-ground ;
But when he saw that fortune proved unkind
He turned his rein and showed his back, pursued
By Súfarai as 'twere a raging blast,
Who followed with a head-transfixing spear.
He captured many nobles ; many more
Were slain by arrow and by scimitar.
He sped till he reached Kuhandizh and saw
No lack of slain and wounded on the way.
Then from the ramparts Khúshnawáz beheld
His troops spread o'er the desert's hills and dales ;
The way was strewn with dead and things of price
So that the plain was decked out like a garden.
    The soldiers carried off to Súfarai
The harness, lances, coronets of state,
The battle-gear, the girdles, steeds, and slaves,
And made a heap as high as Mount Alburz.
He paid no heed to all that Turkman spoil,
But gave the whole in largess to his troops,
And thus harangued the host : " To-day's affair
Hath prospered for us to our hearts' content
Through fortune's favour, but what time the sun
Shall lift its hand in heaven we must not bide
Inactive on the plain but march like lions   C. 1600
Upon yon hold to avenge the king of kings."
    His troops agreed and each man spake his mind.
Thus fared it with them till in arching heaven
The sun's resplendent diadem appeared,
Whereat the tymbals sounded in the camp,

And Súfarai bestrode his steed.   An envoy
Reached that proud chief from Khúshnawáz to say :—
" From battle, strife, and bloodshed naught resulteth
But travail and contention.   Shall we then,
Who are two men of wisdom, young, and brave,
Send both our souls to Hell ?   If thou wilt seek
Again the way of wisdom thou shalt learn
That all that happened was the work of God.
It was not through the blast that Sháh Pírúz
Was slain but rather that the stars foreclosed
For him his years and months.   He was to blame
For breach of pact, for choosing colocynth,
And spurning honey.   Now what was to be
Hath come upon our heads.   Blest is the man
That walketh not the round of violence.
The captives and whatever spoil there was,
The gold, the silver, and the uncut gems,
The steeds, the weapons, and the crowns and thrones,
Left by Pirúz when fortune quitted him,
Both his own treasures and his troops' as well,
Will I send to the general of the Sháh
That thou mayst go victorious to Írán,
Mayst go back to the monarch of the brave.
I will not trespass on Írán ; do you,
For your part, keep the treaty of Bahrám.
The king of kings apportioned earth aright :
Túrán and Chin are ours, Írán is thine."
    When Súfarai had heard the embassage
He called the soldiers to his tent-enclosure,
And in their presence bade the messenger :—
" Repeat before the host the foeman's words."
    He came and gave them, keeping nothing back.
Then Súfarai addressed his army thus :—
" What in your view should be our policy
Herein ? "
        The troops replied : " 'Tis thine to bid,

And thine to stipulate the terms of peace.
None knoweth better in Írán than thou :
Thou art our king, our leader, and our lord."
    Thus to his noble chiefs spake Súfarai :—
" The only policy for us to-day
Is this—to seek no more to fight with them.
I will lead back the army to Írán
With speed, because Kubád,[1] son of Pírúz,
One of the royal race, is in their hands
With the high priest Ardshír and army-leaders,
Both young and old. If we fight Khúshnawáz
The matter will be long and profitless,
And they will slaughter their Íránian captives,   C. 1601
Kubád, the world's heir, and Ardshír. Howbeit,
Unless Kubád had been in jeopardy,
Ne'er had my heart and brain recalled to mind
The high priest ; but if evil from the Turkmans
Befall Kubád Írán will be all outcry,
And this shame current with our warriors
Until the Resurrection. We will give
A courteous answer to the messenger,
And take fair counsels in the cause of peace.
We then perchance may see Kubád again,
(God grant that no one else be king of kings !)
Ardshír the high priest and the other captives,
Both young and old."
         His soldiers blessed him, saying :—
" That is the treaty, precedent, and Faith
For us."
        The paladin then called the envoy,
And thus addressed him with a dulcet tongue :—
" It was the act of God—enough ! This world
Designeth evil and appriseth none.
The great men of Írán that have been taken
Are these—Kubád and the high priest Ardshír.[2]

---

    [1] Kaikubád in the original.   [2] Reading with P.

These with the rest that have their feet in fetters
Dispatch to me in honourable fashion.
Moreover all the booty in your hands—
Dinárs and crowns and wealth of every kind—
Dispatch in full to me, and let it come
In presence of the chieftains of this host.
We will not stretch our hands to spoil and slay
Because we have no need and worship God.
Within ten days we will recross Jihún,
And take no warlike step thenceforth.   Give ear
To that which I have said and tell it all,
On thy return, to Khúshnawáz."

                   The envoy
Returned forthwith to Khúshnawáz in triumph,
And gave the message.   Khúshnawáz rejoiced,
And instantly released Kubád from bonds
With the high priest Ardshír and all the other
Íránian prisoners, collected all
The booty found upon the day of battle,
Besides the throne and crown of Sháh Pírúz,
And what was scattered 'mongst his troops, and sent
All by a trusty man to Súfarai.
   Now when the soldiers looked upon Kubád
They joyed to see him, the high priest Ardshír,
And all the other captives young and old.
The mighty men came from their tents and all
Stretched out their hands to heaven in gratitude
That they beheld the king of kings' own son
Unhurt with all the rest that most they prized.
Forthwith the chief broke up the camp, took horse,
And glad and triumphing repassed Jihún
With that renowned high priest and with Kubád.[1]
   When tidings reached the country of Írán
About that fortunate and glorious chief,
About his war and strife with Khúshnawáz,

C. 1602

            [1] See p. 179, *note*.

And all his wonder-working policy :—
" He hath returned glad and victorious
From war, Kubád hath been released from fetters,
And Súfarai hath brought withal Ardshír,
The high priest, and the Íránian prisoners ;
Just now he crossed o'er the Jihún, his host
Is on the plains and mountains of Írán,"
Such shouts ascended that thou wouldst have said :—
" They deafened those that heard." The prudent
    magnates
Arose and gat themselves in readiness
To go forth with their welcome while Balásh
Prepared a golden throne to seat Kubád,
And that chief paladin. When Súfarai
Arrived within the realm the great men all
Met, while the Sháh prepared the welcoming,
Set forward with such forces as he had,
And when he saw Kubád released from bonds,
Glad and victorious, embraced him quickly
With joy and cursed the people of Haitál
And Chin. They passed within the royal palace
With hearts still sore and eager for revenge.
Balásh commanded and they spread the board,
And called for wine and harp and minstrelsy ;
But there was little gladness at that feast
Through sorrow for magnanimous Pírúz.
The singers lauded Súfarai and sang
Upon the harp the war against Túrán.
He was the Cynosure of all the chieftains,
Who entertained high hopes and joyed in him.
The country rallied to him, those at least
That longed to take revenge on Khúshnawáz.
The hearts of all the paladins rejoiced
In Súfarai ; they freed their souls from care.
    Thus was it till four years had passed away,
And he had not his equal in the world.

Naught happened but according to his will,
And what he would he did.   Now when his word
Prevailed throughout the world he had Balásh
Removed, albeit gently, from the throne,
And said to him : "Thou rulest not the realm ;
Thou knowest not the good men from the bad ;
Thou turnest all the empire to a jest
Through thy perversity and carelessness.
Kubád is wiser far than thou and hath
Much more authority within the realm."
    Balásh withdrew to his own house, for he
Dared not make answer : " Get thee gone," but said:—
" This throne will vex not when I sit thereon ;
'Tis free from travail, pain, and malison."

XL

KUBÁD SON OF PÍRÚZ

HE REIGNED FORTY-THREE YEARS

ARGUMENT

Kubád ascends the throne and harangues the chiefs. Súfarai continues for a time at the head of affairs and then is disgraced and executed. The Íránians revolt in consequence, hand Kubád over to Súfarai's son, Rizmihr, and make Kubád's brother, Jámásp, Sháh. Rizmihr acts with extreme loyalty, protects Kubád, and escapes with him to the Haitálians. On the way thither Kubád marries a thane's daughter who becomes the mother of Kisrá. Provided with an army by the king of the Haitálians Kubád regains the throne. He wars against Rúm, builds cities, and becomes a convert to the teaching of Mazdak who, however, is worsted in a public disputation by Kisrá and put to death with his followers. Kubád appoints Kisrá, to whom the folk give the name of Núshírwán, his successor and dies.

NOTE

According to Mír Khánd, Kubád (Kobad, A.D. 488–531) was known as "the well-intentioned."[1] Historically the events of his

[1] RM, Pt. I., Vol. ii. p. 371. The nickname may be illustrated by the following story from the Persian Tabari. Kubád was engaged once in hunting at vintage-time and reached a village where he saw a very beautiful vine. Near by was a woman, engaged in baking bread, who had with her a child some three years old. Suddenly the child entered the garden where the vine was, picked a bunch of grapes, and was about to eat them. The woman slapped the child, took away the bunch, and refastened it to the vine. Kubád, astounded at her parsimony, approached the vine and asked the woman whose it was. She answered that it belonged to her. He then inquired whose the child was, and she told him that it was hers. Then he said : " Why have

reign, as set forth in the Sháhnáma, may be revised as follows. Súfarai remained at the head of affairs until the revolt occurred that drove the Sháh to take refuge with the Haitálians. This revolt was brought about by the conversion of Kubád to the doctrines of the heresiarch Mazdak, who had a large and increasing following. Kubád seems to have been sincere in his adoption of Mazdakism, but at the same time used its subversive principles as a means of reducing the power of, and of humbling, the great nobles. The official hierarchy, however, took alarm, Kubád was dethroned and shut up in the "Castle of Oblivion" in Susiana, and Jámásp, his brother, reigned in his stead. Kubád, however, by the help of his sister, wife, or both, or of Súfarai himself, managed to make good his escape to the Haitálians with whom he had stayed for some two years as a hostage during the lifetime of his father.[1] During his second sojourn among them he married his own niece—the offspring, by the Haitálian king, of the captive daughter of Pirúz.[2] Helped by his royal father-in-law Kubád managed to recover his throne and placed Súfarai again at the head of affairs, but at length, finding him too powerful, called in the aid of his rival—Shápúr of Rai, the captain of the host—and had him put to death. Kubád never seems to have abandoned his personal regard for Mazdakism, in spite of the fact that it had cost him the temporary loss of his crown, until nearly the end of his long reign. Probably after his restoration he was content to hold it as a pious opinion only, no longer as a weapon to be used against the nobility or in a manner provocative of the Magi. The Mazdakites, however, not unnaturally became concerned about the future—what would happen on Kubád's death? Accordingly they

---

you taken the bunch of grapes away from it, beaten it, and refused to your own child a paltry bunch." She replied : "We are not free to dispose of our own, for the Sháh has a share, and before some one comes on his behalf to deduct his portion we dare not put hand to it." Kubád said : "Do you only or do all folk act thus?" She answered : "Not I alone, but all in the realm of Kubád." The Sháh was full of pity for his subjects, narrated the story to his ministers, and bade them find a less oppressive way of raising revenue. They recommended that the whole realm should be surveyed and taxed in proportion to its fertility, remoteness, and distance from water. Then the revenue would be in money which could be demanded at any time. The Sháh gave orders accordingly, and the work was begun, but finding that it could not be completed in his own lifetime he charged his son and destined successor, Núshírwán, to see that it was carried through, which he did (p. 224 *seq.*). —ZT, ii. 152 *seq.*

[1] See p. 160.   [2] *Id.* p. 161.

attempted to secure the succession for one of Kubád's sons whom
they knew that they could trust. Kubád, however, had made up
his mind already in favour of another heir, and a great massacre
of Mazdakites ensued. This seems to have taken place at the end
of A.D. 528 or the beginning of A.D. 529. Kisrá in consequence of
the share that he took in exterminating the Communists received
the name of Núshírwán.[1]

This account, from which all irrevelant history has been omitted,
differs widely, as will be seen, from that given in the Sháhnáma:
Mazdak and his evangel have been replaced in their proper his-
torical context, the story of the birth of Kisrá has been omitted,
and so has all reference to Rizmihr, Súfarai's son.

§§ 2 and 3. Tabarí tells us that when, at the instance of Kubád,
Shápúr of Rai overthrew Súkhrá (Súfarai), a saying, which became
a proverb, grew current and ran thus : "Súkhrá's wind is gone ;
now a wind has risen for Mihrán." Mihrán was the name of one of
the great Arsacid families that played an important rôle, and held
high office, in Sásánian times, and its employment in the above
proverb has led Nöldeke to suspect that "Súkhrá" also must be
the title of a family, not the name of an individual, as otherwise
the two halves of the proverb would not have balanced properly.
He is inclined therefore to the opinion that Súkhrá and Zarmihr—
the Rizmihr of Firdausí—were not two individuals standing in
the relation of father and son to each other, but one and the same
person—Zarmihr of the family of Súkhrá of the house of Káran.[2]
This house, like that of Mihrán, was probably of Arsacid descent,
but in Íránian tradition, as we learn from the Sháhnáma, claimed
a much older origin and looked upon Káwa, the smith, who raised
the standard of revolt against the tyranny of Zahhák, as the founder
of its fortunes.[3] However this may be, the rivalry between two
great families, and the employment by the Sháh of one of them to
deliver himself from the overgrown authority of the other would
be natural enough. It is to be noted that Shápúr of Rai is described
in the poem as being descended from Mihrak—the mortal enemy of
Ardshír Pápakán and evidently for some reason or other a very
important personage in Íránian legend. He is said to have been of
Jahram in Párs, while Rai, with which his descendant Shápúr is
associated, was the centre of Arsacid power in popular tradition.[4]
Not very long ago we had a Mihrán as treasurer to Yazdagird son

[1] MM, ii. 196. *Cf.* p. 211 and *note.*
[2] NT, pp. 120 *note*, 140 and *note.*   [3] See Vol. i. p. 154 *seq.*
Vol. vi. pp. 201, 237, 241, 256, 266 *seq.*

of Shápúr,[1] quite lately we found another—Ruhhám—helping Pírúz in his struggle against his brother Hurmuz,[2] presently we shall come upon a third as the opponent of Belisarius,[3] a fourth as a general in Núshírwán's host,[4] while a fifth—Mihrán Sitád—goes on a mission to the Khán.[5]

In Kubád's plans for escape to the Haitálians he associates himself with six others. Seven is a favourite number in Persian story. We have the Seven Climes, the Seven Courses or Stages of Rustam and Asfandiyár, the Fight of the Seven Warriors, the Seven Feasts of Núshírwán, and other instances.[6]

§ 4. According to Tabarí, Kubád fled twice to the Haitálians, once on the occasion of his unhistorical contention with Balásh[7] and again, historically, here. On both occasions he is said to have contracted a marriage on his journey and to have been accompanied by Zarmihr (Rizmihr). This is stated by Tabarí with regard to the first flight and by Dínawarí and Firdausí as to the second.[8]

§ 5. In the above accounts the birth of Kisrá is chronicled in connection with both flights. This duplication does not make the story any the more probable, and, as a matter of fact, Kisrá appears to have been the son of the sister of one of Kubád's generals who served in the Roman war, A.D. 502–506.[9] In view of the subsequent importance of Kisrá it was incumbent that Kubád should ask and receive satisfactory assurances as to the descent of the mother of his son. The name Kisrá is the Arabic form of the Persian Khusrau which, with the exception of twelve years, was the name of the Sháhs from A.D. 531 to A.D. 627, if we leave out of account the usurper Bahrám Chubina.

Jámásp who, according to Mír Khánd, was known as "the proud,"[10] appears to have reigned for two years, A.D. 496–498, and it is to be feared that his brother's treatment of him after his deposition was not so amiable as Firdausí would have us believe. The same remark would apply to Jámásp's adherents, whom also the poet tells us were pardoned. One account at all events states that Kubád "killed the Great" when he regained the throne.[11]

According to Tabari, Zarmihr (Rizmihr) was put to death by Kubád some time after his restoration.[12] The story of the Sháh's ingratitude to the father is duplicated in the case of the son, which

---

[1] *Id.* p. 387.	[2] p. 156.
[3] p. 187.	
[4] p. 251. *Cf.* NT. p. 139 *note.*	[5] p. 350.
[6] See Vol. vi. p. 207.	[7] p. 170.
[8] NT, pp. 135, 145 and *note.*	[9] *Id.* and *cf.* p. 187.
[10] RM, Pt. I, vol. ii. p. 371.	[11] NT., p. 461 and *note.*
[12] *Id.* p. 142.	

in itself is suspicious, as is the almost superhuman loyalty displayed by the latter in § 3. It may be laid to the account of the legitimist view that obtains in this part of the poem.[1] If Súfarai be the Persian commander-in-chief called Seoses in Procopius he was not put to death till about A.D. 519.[2]

Until war broke out in A.D. 502 there had been, with one slight exception in the reign of Yazdagird son of Bahrám Gúr,[3] a period of peace for eighty years between the Persian and Eastern Roman Empires. To both the defence of the passes in the Caucasus against the incursions of northern Barbarians was equally important, and the understanding was that both should contribute equally to that end. This arrangement formed one of the terms of the peace concluded by Yazdagird with the younger Theodosius after the brief war, above mentioned, in A.D. 442. The Romans, however, were very remiss in carrying out their part of the undertaking, and their money contribution was in arrear. Both parties seem to have been inclined to look upon the money as tribute to be exacted or refused according to circumstances, and this added to the difficulty of an agreement which probably is responsible for the notion often found in Íránian legend that Rúm was tributary to Írán. Kubád, after his restoration, found himself in want of money to pay his Haitálian allies and applied to the Emperor Anastasius for the arrears due for the defence of the passes. Anastasius refused, his motive being, it is said, the hope of embroiling Kubád with his northern mercenaries, and the Sháh declared war. At first he was very successful, taking Theodosiopolis in Roman Armenia and Amida in northern Mesopotamia, but the generals whom he left to carry on the war, when he himself was called off to resist an Haitálian invasion, were less successful, and Kubád commissioned his brother-in-law, the uncle of Kisrá, to negotiate a peace.[4] The Persians received a lump sum and gave up the captured cities. Towards the end of Kubád's reign war again broke out, A.D. 526, and lasted till his death. It was in this war that Belisarius rose to fame and fought twice with one of the Mihráns named Fírúz.[5] Procopius, who had become secretary to Belisarius in A.D. 527, gives a correspondence purporting to have passed between the two generals.[6]

Hulwán was situated north-west of Kirmánsháh at Sar-i-pul-i-Zohab.[7] Kubád merely renamed it as he also renamed a town

---

[1] See Vol. vi. p. 251.   [2] NT, p. 145 note.
[3] See p. 153.   [4] NT, p. 145 note; RSM, p. 360 and note.
[5] Cf. p. 186.   [6] RSM, p. 368 seq. and note.
[7] Id. 564 note; NT, p. 138 and note.

called Aragán on the borders of Ahwáz and Párs not far from the
present Bihbihán.   He changed Aragán to Rámkubád.[1]

§§ 6 and 7. In the Vendidád there is a reference to "the ungodly.
fasting Ashemaogha" (heretic), to which the Pahlavi commentary on
the Zandavasta adds : "like Mazdak, son of Bámdát."[2]   In the
late Pahlavi Text known as the Bahman Yasht the names are given
of six priests whom Núshírwán summoned to his aid in his disputa-
tion with Mazdak.[3]   Two of them are recognisable in Firdausí's
Hurmuzd and Mihr-Ázar.   Mazdak's place of birth is quite uncer-
tain, and his historical importance began and ended with the reign
of Kubád.   The poet omits to mention two of Mazdak's principles
—the prohibition of bloodshed and of flesh-eating—but in other
respects his account of that heresiarch's doctrines seems to be sub-
stantially correct—Zoroastrianism with private property and the
family abolished.   To this anarchical Faith doubtlessly he did his
best to win over Kubád's recognised heir, failing in which he schemed
to alter the succession and perished in the attempt.   This seems
to be the obvious explanation of the catastrophe.   Máni and his
followers in their time fared no better.[4]   Núshírwán was far too
able and practical to be led away by Mazdak, and on coming to the
throne tried his best to repair the mischief that had been done.[5]

§ I

*How Kubád sat upon the Throne and made an Oration
to the Íránians*

1603   When glorious Kubád sat on the throne,
And donned the crown of majesty, he went
To Taisafún, departing from Istakhr—
The glory of the great.   Now when he sat
Upon Pírúz's [6] seat he said : "Conceal
Naught from me.   By bright day and darksome night

----

[1] *Id.* 13 and *note,* 146.   [2] DZA, i. 48 and *note.*

[3] WPT, i. 194.   [4] See Vol. vi. p. 359; NT, 465.

[5] NT, p. 163.   For Mazdak and the Mazdakites generally see *id.*
p. 455 *seq.*

[6] Or "victorious" or, with a slight change of reading (P), "tur-
quoise," but the translation given is most in accord to the legitimist
tendency in this part of the Sháhnáma. *Cf.* Vol. vi. p. 251.

The way to me is open unto you.
The man is great who ordereth his tongue
To right discourse and seeketh not deceit,
While since he will be merciful in wrath
The best of men will welcome him as guide.
He setteth up the throne of acceptation
Within the world, receiving from the great
Just commendation. If thou keep'st thy heart
Far from revenge both great and small will praise
    thee,
But when the great king is a double-dealer
His double-dealing is a call to strife.
First hear a matter through for thus apprised
Thou wilt reply aright. When any sage
Is covetous his knowledge will not fruit ;
When he is headstrong it will be to him
Like water in a salt marsh. Furthermore
'Tis well to get a soldier's heart and bear
Reproach submissively.[1] The rich, hard man
Is lower even than a mendicant ;
But when a foolish mendicant hath sway
His rule is simple madness. He that knoweth
His own defects will not be eloquent
On those of others. Patience is the pillar
Of wisdom : to be wroth is but to make
Oneself despised. Submission to God's justice
Will make thee rich, sincere, and honourable,
For thou art freed from care. The body of him
That hath no greed is better than a treasure,
While that man whose viaticum is knowledge
Will die in person but in name live ever ;
So put ye all your hands to good alone,
And walk not on this whirling world for ill."

---

[1] Mohl, with a very slight change of reading, translates : "Celui qui recherche l'affection de l'armée prend un ton modeste, même en blâmant." *Cf.* p. 44.

The nobles all called blessings down on him,
And showered emeralds upon his crown.
He was a youth of sixteen years, and bore
As yet but little part in government,

C. 1604   While Súfarai took order for the world.
Kubád ruled in the palace'; all affairs
Were managed wholly by the paladin.
He suffered no one to approach the Sháh,
Who had no archmage and gave no command
Or counsel. Súfarai ruled all the land.

§ 2

How Súfarai went to Shíráz, how the Íránians slandered
him to Kubád, and how Kubád slew him

Thus in the cup the wine was tulip-like
Until Kubád was twenty-one [1] years old ;
Then Súfarai came in before the king
For licence to go home and thereupon
He gat him ready with his retinue,
Struck up the drums, and started for Shiráz,
Returning to his country, full of joy,
As one that had obtained his whole desire.
All Párs was as it were a slave before him,
And, save the throne of empire, all was his.
His thoughts were these : " I have set up the Sháh,
And done him homage as my sovereign,
So now if any man shall slander me
He will rebuke that man and banish him."
    He levied tribute on the provinces,
On all the men of name and all the chiefs.
When tidings of his just and unjust deeds
Came from Shiráz to glorious Kubád,

                    [1] Reading with P.

The people said : " The Sháh hath but the crown,
And not the troops and treasure in Írán,
Hath no authority, is not consulted ;
The world is all the slave of Súfarai."
    All those that shared the secrets of Kubád
Repeated to him what the people said,
And added : " Why, exalted king ! art thou
Contented merely to be king in name ?
His treasury is better filled than thine :
Thou shouldst release the world from his oppression.
All Párs hath grown as 'twere a slave to him,
The great men have become his thralls."
                      These words
Seduced Kubád's [1] heart, which became forgetful
Of all the services of Súfarai ;
He said : " If I shall send an army forth
He will revolt and seek to be avenged,
I shall but use my wealth to make a foe,
While he will cause much trouble and much toil.
The people all are talking of his deeds,
Unwitting of his secret purposes.
I know not any warrior of Írán
To march against him with a host to battle."
    A wise man answered thus : " Think not that he
E'er will be recognised as king. Thou hast
Both lieges and a leader of the host   C. 160
That can lay hand upon the circling sky ;
So when Shápúr of Rai is on the march
The heart of wicked Súfarai will rive."
    The Sháh took courage when he heard these words,
Forgot the merit and presumed the guilt ;
Then bade a veteran mount as swift as wind,
And, on the plea of faring forth to hawk,
Go to Shápúr of Rai, cause him to mount
Forthwith upon his steed, and summon him

---

[1] See p. 179, *note.*

From Rai to court.　The messenger, who took
A spare steed, went swift as an autumn-blast
To Rai as he was bidden by the king.
The chamberlain there saw and questioned him,
Took the king's letter, went before Shápúr,
Gave it, and introduced that noble horseman.
Shápúr, who was descended from Mihrak,
Smiled when he read the letter of Kubád,[1]
For Súfarai had not a foe like him
In public and in private.　Thus apprised
Shápúr convoked his lieges and led forth
His army in all haste to Taisafún.
When he had brought his army to the Sháh
They gave him audience instantly.　The world-lord,
On seeing him, received him graciously,
Caused him to sit upon the turquoise throne,
And said : " I have no portion in this crown,
Am noted 'mongst the foolish in the world.
All power is with Súfarai ; I see
But sovereignty in name.　Late in the day
My body shrinketh from the weights that press
With justice or injustice on my neck.
E'en were my brother master of Irán
'Twere better than this unjust Súfarai."
　　Shápúr replied : " O king ! be not aggrieved
At heart on this account.　Thou shouldest write
A letter in harsh terms to him, for thou
Hast Grace and fame, high lineage and support.
Say : ' Of the crown of king of kings my share
Is travail and an empty treasure-house.
Thou takest tribute, and I bear the blame.
I will not have thee call me Sháh henceforth.
Lo ! I have sent to thee a paladin
In that thy conduct causeth me to wail.'
When he shall get a letter thus conceived,

---

[1] *Id.*

And I am there with troops prepared for fight,
I will not leave him time to wink an eye,
Or speak a word to him unless in wrath."
    They called to them a scribe and seated him
Before Shápúr, who said again the words
As spoken in the presence of the Sháh :
The writer wrote them, grieving secretly.
Shápín, whenas the Sháh had sealed the letter,
Led forth his host, then added famous chiefs,   C. 1606
Disbanded from the armies of the king,
And with those nobles eager for the fray
Set face toward the city of Shíráz.
When Súfarai had tidings of the matter
He marched at once, and with a mighty host—
Picked cavaliers in mail—went out to meet
Shápúr. They met, and those two haughty chiefs
Alighted from their steeds. Now when Shápúr
Sat down with Súfarai they talked at large
Of projects good and ill. Shápúr then gave
The letter of the king, and matters reached
A cruel, shameful pass ; the paladin,
When he had read the letter, changed his favour,
Was stunned and dark of soul. Then said Shápúr,
The letter being read : " I must be plain :
The   world-lord   ordered   that   thou   shouldst   be
    bound,
Complaining much of thee before the nobles,
And thou wilt gather, having read his letter,
That he is resolute."
                 The paladin
Replied : " The monarch of the world is ware
What toil and hardship I have borne for him,
That marching from Zábulistán with troops
I set him free from bondage by my valour,
And suffered no calamity to come
Upon him. I had influence with the Sháh,

And with the chieftains of the Íránian host,
But since bonds are to be my recompense,
And my resistance will be troublesome
To thee, I ask no respite.   Bind my feet :
The fetters of Kubád will profit me.
Doth he not shame before God and the host,
For I shed freely my warm blood for him ?
What time the Sháh was in captivity
I swore by God a mighty oath, and said :—
' My hand shall look but on my falchion's hilt,
And I will cloud the sun in fight, till I
Shall give my head or bring down from the throne
The head of Khúshnawáz between the shears.'
And now he biddeth me be bound !   Is't right ?
Receive I but derogatory words ?
Still turn not aught from his commands, for know
That bonds but ornament a hero's feet."
   Shápúr, on hearing this, made fast the fetters,
Then bade the trumpet sound and gat to horse.
From Párs he carried Súfarai before
Kubád, who thought not of past services,
But bade men bear him to the prison-house,
Near where the madmen were, and gave command
To carry from Shíráz to Taisafún
What wealth soever he possessed—his folk,
His treasures, and the produce of his fields—
By those appointed to the treasurer.
C. 1607   Now when a week had passed Kubád consulted
The archmages how to deal with Súfarai,
And thus a counsellor addressed the Sháh :—
" The whole of Taisafún is on his side—
Troops, courtiers, thanes, and populace alike.
If he abideth in Írán unscathed
Thou mayest wash thy hands of sovereignty.
The foeman of the Sháh is best when killed,
His hater's fortune best when overturned."

Now when the Sháh had heard the archmage's
    counsel
He took a new course and despised the old,
Gave his command that Súfarai be slain,
The hearts of all his kindred wrung with pain.

§ 3

How the Íránians put Kubád in Bonds and committed him to
Rizmihr, the Son of Súfarai, and how Jámásp, the Brother
of Kubád, was set upon the Throne

Now when these tidings reached the Íránians :—
" He of the elephantine form is dead,"
A cry of anguish went up from Írán,
Men, women, children, all alike bewailed ;
The tongue of every one was steeped in curses,
And secret thoughts found public utterance.
Írán was all convulsed, the dust went up,
While all folk made them ready for the fight,
And thus they said : " Since Súfarai is gone
Let not Kubád's throne be within Írán."
    The soldiers and the citizens agreed,
They would not bear the mention of Kubád,
But marched upon the palace of the Sháh,
Vexed at his ill advisers, for redress.
These men—all malice and intent on evil—
They took, dragged from the palace, and then sought
With diligence for traces of Jámásp,
His younger brother and a noble youth,
One whom Kubád had cherished tenderly.
They chose him, seated him upon the throne,
And called down blessings on him as their Sháh ;
But made Kubád's feet fast in iron fetters,
Unheedful of his Grace and noble birth.

Now Súfarai had one son well beloved,
A wise man, holy and illustrious,
A youth without offence, Rizmihr by name,
Whose fame had made his father well content.
To him the people gave Kubád in bonds,
As unto some malicious enemy,
And thought : " Through grief the loving son will take
Revenge upon the king for Súfarai."
    The good Rizmihr, the worshipper of God,
Laid not his hand for ill upon the world-lord,[1]

C. 1608 But did obeisance to Kubád and spake
No words to him about his evil deeds,
Whereat the world-lord marvelled much, began
To bless Rizmihr, and thus excused himself :—
" My foes have troubled much my star and moon,
But, if I find deliverance from bond,
I will reward thee for all ills endured,
For I will banish anguish from thy heart,
And cause the eyes that look on thee to shine."
    Rizmihr made answer to him thus : " O king !
Let not thy soul be grieved on this account,
For when a father acted not aright
His son should bear the sorrow of his death.
As touching mine own self, I am thy slave ;
I stand before thee as a servitor,
And at thy bidding I will swear that never
Will I break off my fealty to thee."
    So spake Rizmihr and as the monarch heard
His heart began to throb for very joy,
His soul regained its confidence and grew
Right joyful at the words of that wise man.
He made Rizmihr his confidant and said :—
" I will not hide my thoughts from thee.   Five men
Are sharers in my secrets.   None besides
Hath listened to my voice.   Now we will summon

---

[1] *Cf.* p. 187.

These five and ope to them our secret plan
If it appears that we have need of them,
While if from fetters thou shalt set me free
Know this—my policy shall profit thee."

§ 4

*How Kubád escaped from Ward with Rizmihr, how he wedded
the Daughter of a Thane, and how he took Refuge with the
Haitálians*

The good Rizmihr, on hearing this, anon
Released Kubád from fetters.   From the city
They fared forth to the plain by night, unseen
By foes, and made toward the Haitálians,
Wrung with anxiety and hurrying.
On this wise sped the seven like flying dust
Until with dizzy heads they reached Ahwáz,
And entered on their steeds that wealthy town—
A town wherein a famous chieftain dwelt.
Dismounting at the dwelling of the thane
They tarried there and breathed themselves awhile.
He had a daughter moonlike, crowned with musk,
And, when Kubád beheld her face, all wisdom
Fled from his youthful brain.   He went forthwith,
And told Rizmihr : "I have a privy word
For thee.   Haste to the thane.   Tell him from me :— C. 1609
'This moon-faced damsel—could she be my wife ? '"
   Rizmihr went instantly, informed the thane,
And said : "If thy fair daughter is unmated
I will provide her with a noble spouse,
And thou shalt be the master of Ahwáz."
   The illustrious thane made answer to Rizmihr :—
"My pretty daughter hath no husband yet,
And, if she please thee, she is thine to give :
Give her to him that longeth after her."

The wise Rizmihr came to Kubád and said :—
" May this Moon bring good fortune to the Sháh.
Thou sawest her unawares and didst approve,
Thou didst approve of her just as she was."
    Kubád then called to him that fairy-faced ;
The gallant warrior set her on his knee,
And having with him one, and but one, ring—
A signet-ring whose worth was known to none—
He gave it to her, saying : " Keep this signet ;
The day will come when I shall ask for it."
    He stayed a se'nnight for that fair Moon's sake,
And parted on the eighth day with the dawn,
Went to the king of the Haitálians,
Told what had chanced, the Íránians' deeds, and how
They all had girded up their loins for ill.
The king replied : " The wrongs of Khúshnawáz
Have surely brought thee to this strait to-day.
On these conditions will I give thee troops,
Who are crown-wearers, every one of them,
That if thou shalt recover crown and treasure,
Chaghán, its wealth and state, its march and rule,
Shall be all mine, and thou shalt keep my terms
And stipulations."
                Said Kubád while smiling
At him who thus dictated terms : " I never
Will give that land a thought and, when thou wishest,
Will send thee troops in numbers numberless.
What is Chaghán that I should look that way ? " .'
    When they had made their pact the Haitálian king
Unlocked his treasury and gave Kubád
Dinárs and arms, and two score thousand swordsmen,
All famed as warriors and cavaliers.
Thus to Ahwáz from the Haitálians went
Kubád ; the whole world rang with that event.

§ 5

How Kubád returned from Haitál to Írán, how he had Tidings of the Birth of his Son, Núshírwán, and reascended the Throne

Kubád approached the thane's abode and saw
In every street a scattered populace,
Who all apprised him of the joyful news :—
" Thy spouse brought forth a son to thee last night   C. 161c
But little less resplendent than the moon,
And may he bring good fortune to the Sháh."
    Kubád, on hearing, went within the house
In great content.   They named the boy Kisrá.
Now afterwards Kubád asked of the thane :—
" From whom art thou descended, noble sir ? "
    He said : " From·valiant Farídún who took
The kingship from the kindred of Zahhák :
Thus said my father and my mother too :—
' We give our reverence to Farídún.' "
    Kubád was pleasured yet more at the words,
And instantly resumed the royal crown.
He had a litter brought and, when his spouse
Was seated there, departed on his march ;
He led the army on to Taisafún
In high displeasure with the Íránians.
    Now in Írán the while the ancient chiefs
Sat with the sages and the notables.
They said : " Between these two—both Sháhs and
    proud—
The matter will prove wearisome for us.
Hosts are upon their way from Rúm and Chín,
And they will cause much bloodshed in the land."
    Then one of that assembly said : " Ye chiefs,
Exalted and heroic warriors l
'Tis needful that we go out to Kubád,

Who, it may be, will not recall the past,
And bring to him Jámásp, the ten years' child,
To turn the hailstones of his wrath to pearls ;
So haply we may swerve aside and 'scape
From pillaging, from bloodshed, and from war."
    All went to meet Kubád and said to him :—
" O Sháh of royal race ! if thou hast hurt
Men's hearts, and they have washed their hearts and
    eyes
In petulance, now act as pleaseth thee
Because the world-lord ruleth o'er the world."
    They all drew near to him in haste, afoot,
Dust-covered, and with gloomy souls. The Sháh
Forgave the evil doings of his lords,
Accepting their excuse in lieu of bloodshed ;
He pardoned too Jámásp : the nobles blessed him.
He came and sat upon the royal throne :
Jámásp became his liege. Kubád bestowed
The conduct of the realm upon Rizmihr,
And gave him great advancement. By his means
The kingship was well ordered, and the world
Fulfilled with justice and prosperity.
    Thus matters fared until Kisrá grew tall—
A stripling bold and lusty. Then Kubád
Entrusted to wise governors his son,
That fresh and fruitful Bough. Kubád directed
All matters in Írán and in Túrán,
And raised his crown of greatness to the sky.
Thereafter he led forth his host to Rúm,
Which proved as 'twere a lump of wax to him :
C. 1611 He made a thorn-brake of those fields and fells.
Two cities asked for quarter at his hands,
One Hindiyá, the other Fárikín.
He taught the Zandavasta there, established
The Faith, and instituted Fanes of Fire,
His power, the feasts of New Year's Day and Sada.

He fixed his royal seat at Madá'in,
And wrought much good and ill. He built a city
Betwixt Ahwáz and Párs, and founded too
A hospital. He called the city's name
Arash ; the Arabs call it now Hulwán.
They opened everywhere canals that flowed
A-brim, and peace and rest on earth abode.

§ 6

*The Story of Kubád and Mazdak, and how Kubád
adopted the Faith of Mazdak*

Then there arose a man by name Mazdak,
Learned, eloquent, judicious, and commanding,
Of noble birth, a trafficker in knowledge,
And brave Kubád gave ear to him. This man
Became the king of kings' chief minister,
The treasurer and the guardian of the treasure.
Then famine visited the world through drought,
A famine that afflicted great and small ;
No sign of snow appeared upon the sky,
And none saw snow or rain-fall in Írán.
At length the nobles of the world begged bread
And water at the portal of Kubád.
Mazdak returned them this reply : " The Sháh
Will manifest to you a way of hope,"
Then came himself in haste before the king,
And said to him : " O upright Sháh ! I fain
Would question thee upon a point if thou
Wilt condescend to answer."
                        Eloquent
Kubád replied : " Say on and make my lustre
Fresh in the world."
                        " A man," Mazdak rejoined,
" Is bitten by a snake ; his life is passing ;

Another man hath got the antidote
Whereof the bitten can obtain no share.
What then should be the guerdon of the man
That hath it ?   Money will not purchase it."
    The Sháh replied : " He is a murderer,
And should be slain to avenge the other's blood
Before my gate whenever the pursuer
Shall take him."
                    Hearing this Mazdak went forth
To those petitioners and told them thus :—
" I have discussed the matter with the Sháh.
Wait till the dawn, and I will show you how
To right yourselves."

. 1612   They went away, returning
At dawn with stricken hearts in deep affliction.
Mazdak, when he beheld those chiefs from far,
Ran from the portal to the Sháh and said :—
" O thou victorious Sháh and eloquent,
Unsleeping, and the glory of the throne !
Thou gavest me an answer, when I spake,
And by that answer oped my bolted door,
So now with thy permission I will speak
A word to guide thee."
                    " Speak," the Sháh replied,
" Lock not thy lips because thy words will help me."
    Mazdak said : " Noble king ! suppose a man,
Whom thou hast bound, but they withhold from him
All food until he dieth, thus perforce
Surrendering sweet life.   Now how should one
Be punished who had bread yet left that captive
In destitution ?   Will the great king say :—
' This man was wise and holy ? ' "
                    Said the Sháh :—
" Rend such to pieces, for through his neglect
He is a murderer."
                    On hearing this

Mazdak, when he had kissed the ground, went forth.
And from the portal thus harangued the crowd :—
" Go to the magazines where grain is stored,
And help yourselves while if the owners ask
Its value give them gold."

His own possessions
Within that city he gave up to pillage
In order that all folk might have their share.
Then all the hungry rabble fared in haste
To plunder every magazine of corn,
Owned by the citizens or by Kubád,
Who had none left to bless themselves withal.
The officers, when they perceived this, went
Before the watchful world-lord and thus said :—
" The mob have sacked the Sháh's own granaries,
But all the fault recoileth on Mazdak."
    Kubád bade call that man of eloquence,
And talked with him about the pillaging.
Mazdak replied : " Mayst thou be fortunate,
And may thy words be wisdom's daily food.
I only told the wretched market-folk
The words which I had heard the monarch speak.
I asked the Sháh about the snake and poison,
And of the man who had the antidote.
The Sháh returned this answer to his servant
Concerning him that had and him that sought it :—
' If any die of snake-bite in the city,
Unhelped by one who hath the remedy,
For such they shall require that niggard's blood.'
The Sháh's authority must not be slighted.
Bread is the antidote for hungry men—
An antidote not wanted by the full.
If thou art one that judgest right, O Sháh !
Shall not the corn in store be put to use ?
To hunger have a multitude succumbed,   C. 1613
Whose deaths are due to idle granaries."

Kubád was much affected by the words :
These righteous words aroused his brain to action.
Then, questioning Mazdak and hearing him,
The Sháh perceived him learned in heart and brain
In all things that the prophets, the archmages—
Those righteous dealers—and the great had spoken.
The teaching of Mazdak perverted him,
And exercised unbounded influence.
The multitude came thronging to Mazdak—
The many that had wandered from the way :
He said to them : " The man of empty hand
Is equal to the man possessed of wealth.
No one should have a superfluity,
The wealthy is the warp, the poor the woof ;
To right the world all men must have sufficient ;
The rich man's plenty is abominable ;
The women, goods, and houses are for all ;
The empty-handed and the rich are one.
I will take order that the holy Faith
Be manifest, the lofty from the low.
Whoever is of other Faith than this,
The malison of God is on that div."
He treated mendicants, both old and young,
As though they were the equals of himself,
He took from this man and bestowed on that ;
The archmages were astonied at his doings.
Kubád himself gave ear and was converted,
And of all things was joyful in his words.
He set Mazdak at his right hand although
An archimage unknown to all the host,
And unto him the mendicants resorted
With those that earned a living by their toil ;
His Faith began to flourish in the world,
And no one dared to seek revenge on him,
The rich renounced the things that made them glad,
And gave to mendicants what wealth they had.

§ 7

*How Núshírwán rejected the Faith of Mazdak and slew
him and his Followers*

It happened that Mazdak at dawn one day
Went from his house and came before the Sháh,
And thus he said : " Of those that hold our Faith,
As well as of our lieges pure of heart,
A crowd of chiefs are at the door ; shall I
Admit them or shall they depart ? "
                                        Kubád,
On hearing, bade the chamberlain admit them,
Whereat Mazdak said to the noble Sháh :—
" This house is narrow and the crowd is great,
In sooth the audience-hall will hold them not ;   C. 1614
Let the Sháh go and see them on the plain."
    Kubád commanded that his throne be brought,
Brought from the royal palace to the waste,
And there a hundred thousand Mazdakís
Proceeded joyfully before the Sháh,
And thus Mazdak addressed the king of earth :—
" O thou above all knowledge and acclaim !
Know that Kisrá accepteth not our Faith,
But is it fit that he should turn therefrom ?
We must obtain from him an undertaking
In writing to give up his evil course.
There are five things that turn men from the right,
And e'en the sage can add no sixth.   Now these
Are anger, vengeance, jealousy, and need ;
The fifth is greed, which is predominant,
And if thou conquer these five divs the way
Of God will be made manifest to thee.
From these five things it cometh that our women
And wealth work havoc with the good religion,
But will not meddle more if thou wilt keep it

Intact. The twain cause jealousy, greed, need,
While anger and revenge conspire with them,
And thus the Div perverteth wise men's heads :
The twain should be a common property."
    This spoken, by the hand he grasped Kisrá,
What while the Sháh looked on in wonderment.
The noble prince in wrath withdrew his hand,
And turned his eyes in anger from Mazdak,
To whom Kubád said smiling : " Why art thou
Concerned for the religion of Kisrá ? "
    Mazdak rejoined : " The way of righteousness
Is not in him. He is not of our Faith."
    The Sháh then questioned of Kisrá and said :—
" What way is there except the good religion ? "
    Kisrá replied : " If I shall have the time
Allowed me I will prove this theory false.
When both the fraud and falsehood shall appear
My truth will show out more conspicuously."
    Mazdak rejoined : " Thou askest of the Sháh—
The lustre of the world—how many days ? "
    He said : " I ask a period of five months.
The Sháh shall have his answer in the sixth
On all points."
              They agreed and so departed.
The exalted Sháh returned to his own palace.
Kisrá dispatched a man to every quarter
To look for sages and auxiliaries.
An envoy went to Khurra-i-Ardshír
To cause the old Hurmuzd to come to court,
While from Istakhr came Mihr-Ázar of Párs
With thirty friends. These seekers after knowledge
Held session and discussed the case at large,
And then these men of lore and ancient sages
Presented their conclusions to Kisrá,
C. 1615 While he, when he had heard, went to Kubád,
Discoursed with him about Mazdak, and said :—

" The time now hath arrived when I would make
Investigation of the good religion.
If then Mazdak be right, and if the Faith
Delivered by Zarduhsht shall prove in fault,
I will accept the true Faith of Mazdak,
And make my soul's choice his,[1] for when the way
Of Farídún, of Esdras, and of Christ,
And all the Zandavasta, shall prove wrong,
And when the doctrine of Mazdak shall stand,
The world must take him for its only guide.
If, on the other hand, his words are false,
And he ensueth not God's holy way,
Then turn thee from the pathway of his Faith,
Put far from thee this sorry Creed of his,
And give him with his followers to me ;
God grant that none of them keep brain and skin."
  He took as witnesses Rizmihr, Kharrád,
Bihzád, Bandwí, and Fará'in, and thence
Departed to his palace and observed
The righteous covenant that he had made.
At dawn, what time the sun displayed its crown,
And earth was like a sea of ivory,
The world-king's son, that man of eloquence,
Set forth with chieftains and with archimages.
They went together to the royal palace.
Their speech was fluent and their quest the Way.
That youth—the Joy of hearts—came to Kubád,
And oped the case, whereon an archimage
Addressed Mazdak before the throng and said :—
" O seeker after wisdom ! thou hast framed
A new religion in the world and made
Community of women and of goods.
How will a father recognise his son,
The son in like wise recognise his father ?
When every man is equal in the world,

---

[1] " j'arracherai de mon âme cette ortie " (Mohl).

And great and little are no more discerned,
Who then will serve, and how can any rule ? [1]
Who then will labour for us, thee and me,
And how shall good men be discerned from bad ?
When one shall die to whom will appertain
His house and goods when toiling slave and Sháh
Are equal ?   This will desolate the world ;
Such evil must not come upon Írán.
When all are masters who will be the servant ?
When all have treasure who be treasurer ?
None of the leaders of the Faith spake thus,
And thou art mad although thou hidest it.
Thou leadest all mankind to Hell, and thou
Accountest not all evil-doing wrong."

Kubád, when he had heard the archmage's words,
Was wroth and then gave sentence on the case.
The illustrious Kisrá supported him,
The impious one grew full of fear at heart,
C. 1616   While all the people there assembled cried :—
" Let not Mazdak remain before the Sháh ;
He hath made havoc of the Faith of God ;
Let him not tarry at this famous court."

The Sháh became abhorrent from that Faith,
The heads of all its chiefs grew full of care.
He gave up to Kisrá Mazdak forthwith
With all that held that doctrine and that way—
As many as three thousand men of name.
The king at that time thus addressed his son :—
" Do with those chiefs as seemeth good to thee,
And henceforth mention not Mazdak."

Kisrá
Had at his court a pleasure-ground whose wall
Was higher than a crow could fly.   Around
The circuit of that wall he dug a trench
Wherein he set those men at intervals.

[1] For an exemplification of this see p. 26 seq.

They planted them like trees and firmly fixed
Their feet aloft, their heads below.   Kisrá
Addressed Mazdak on this wise : " Visit thou
The entrance of my noble garth.   The seed
That thou hast scattered all this while hath brought
Fruit forth to thee, O thou insensate one !
Thou shalt see trees such as none e'er beheld,
Or heard described by shrewd men heretofore."
    Mazdak went, oped the portal of the garden,
And thought maybe to see fruit-bearing trees,
But seeing what he did he gave a cry,
And then all consciousness abandoned him.
Kisrá gave orders for a lofty gibbet
To be set up and at the top to fasten
A twisted lasso.   Thereupon he hung
That impious wretch head-downwards and alive,
And after slew him with a shower of arrows.
If thou art prudent follow not Mazdak !
The chiefs felt reassured about their wealth,
Their women, children, and their pleasances.
Kubád remained ashamed for many days,
And cursed Mazdak, gave mendicants much largess,
And offered gifts before the Fane of Fire.
He gladdened at Kisrá exceedingly
Because that Bough of his bare fruit of gems.
From that time forth the father sought alway
The son's advice and heard what he would say.

§ 8

*How Kubád nominated Kisrá as Successor, and how the
Great gave him the Name of Núshírwán* [1]

Now when Kubád had reigned for forty years
The grief of death's day came upon his heart.

[1] Reading with P.

He had a writing fairly drawn on silk
In that befitting and engaging script,[1]
He and first he offered praise to that just Judge,
" Who gave us Faith, accomplishment, and wisdom,
Whose word is certain, whatsoe'er He saith,
Alike in secret things and manifest.
None hath beheld His height of sovereignty,
And His elect ne'er are contemptible.
All ye that see the writing of Kubád !
Give heed but to the counsel of the wise.
I have bestowed the honourable throne
Upon Kisrá. Fair fortune will be his
When I am dead. May God accept my son,
And may his foes' hearts be fulfilled with smoke.
By this our signet-ring we do require
Of archimages, chiefs, and other subjects
That ye in no wise shall transgress his bidding,
But joy in him and fill your treasuries."
   He set his golden signet on that writing,
And placed it with the archmage Rám Barzin.
Kubád had come to four-score years and yet,
Old as he was, he did not wish for death.
Is any in the world content to die
Since no man knoweth what will come thereby ?
He died and left the world as his bequest ;
His travail, ease, and pleasures passed away.
Who profiteth by what he hath amast
Since empty-handed go he must at last ?
They draped the body with brocade and called
For rose and musk, for camphor and for wine.
They made for him a royal charnel-house,
A golden throne and crown of majesty.
They set the Sháh upon the throne of gold,
Barred up the way thereto for evermore,
And thenceforth looked not on him.   Thus he passed

[1] Pahlaví.

O'er this world, as thou mightst have said, like wind !
How canst thou trust then in this ancient sky
Since it will end thee irremediably ?
 The mourning being o'er, the high priest spread
The royal document upon the throne,
The magnates and archmages of Írán,
And all the famous sages, met in conclave,
The document was read before them all,
And with rejoicing they enthroned the heir.[1]
 Now when Kisrá ascended his new throne
The people hailed him as their new-made Sháh,
Called praises down on him as sovereign,
And time and earth submitted to his sway.
His throne revived the world, and at the stream   C. 1618
The sheep drank water with the wolf.[2] Folk said :—
" May this Sháh live for ever. May his Grace
Surpass Jamshíd's."
       His goodness and his justice,
His institutions, Faith, and far-famed knowledge
Were such that people called him Núshírwán,[3]
For love and signet were both young with him.
 The story of Kubád is at an end,
And henceforth to Kisrá my thoughts I bend.

 [1] In the text the reign of Núshírwán begins here, and there is no division before § 3.
 [2] Reading with P.   [3] *i.e.* " Of immortal soul." *Cf.* p. 185.

XLI

NÚSHÍRWÁN

HE REIGNED FORTY-EIGHT YEARS

ARGUMENT

The poet tells of the accession of Núshírwán, his internal administration, his repression of marauding tribes, his first war with Rúm, the revolt and death of his son Núshzád, of the rise to power and wisdom of Búzurjmihr, the fall of Mahbúd, the Sháh's marriage with the daughter of the Khán, Búzurjmihr's discourse on good words and deeds, the introduction into Persia of the game of chess and the Fables of Bidpai, the legend of the invention of the former and that of the game of nard, the fall and the restoration to favour of Búzurjmihr, the wisdom of Núshírwán, his last war with Rúm, his appointment of his successor, and death.

NOTE

Kisrá, surnamed Núshírwán (Chosroes I, A.D. 531–578), ruled contemporaneously with three Eastern Roman Emperors—Justinian (A.D. 527–565), Justin II (A.D. 565–574), and Tiberius II (A.D. 574–582). Justin resigned the rule to Tiberius, the captain of the guards, in A.D. 574, but did not die till A.D. 578, the year of Núshírwán's death. Núshírwán was perhaps the greatest of the twenty-nine Sásánian Sháhs, at least it is not easy to assign that title to any other unless we reserve it for the founder of the dynasty, Ardshír Pápakán, who has to his credit the overthrow of a long-standing foreign domination, the re-establishment of a national dynasty, and all the toil of political reconstruction that his successful revolt against the last Arsacid involved.

It will be seen that the poet had plenty of material for this portion of his undertaking. The subject-matter falls naturally into certain well-defined divisions; accordingly we have broken up the reign, as in the case of that of Gushtásp,[1] into Parts, but there is no such arrangement in the original.

Kisrá will be referred to throughout by his popular title of Núshírwán.

The principal historical events recorded by *F*irdausí in his account of the reign may be placed in approximate chronological order as follows :—

> The fall of Mahbúd.
> The reorganisation of the kingdom, finances, and army.
> The chastisement of barbarous frontier-tribes.
> The fortification of *D*arband.
> The first war with Rúm (A.D. 540–562).
> The revolt of Núshzád (A.D. 551).
> Núshírwán's marriage with the daughter of the Khán.
> The introduction into Persia of the *F*ables of Bidpai (about A.D. 570).
> The birth of Muhammad (about A.D. 571).
> The second war with Rúm (A.D. 572).

The first eight of these are included in the present volume.

---

[1] Vol. v. p. 9.

PART I

NÚSHÍRWÁN'S ADMINISTRATION OF THE REALM, HIS WARS WITH FRONTIER-TRIBES AND WITH RÚM, AND THE REVOLT OF NÚSHZÁD

ARGUMENT

Núshírwán ascends the throne and makes an oration to the people. He divides the realm into four provinces, and takes order for all matter civil and military. He builds a wall in the Caucasus and represses the Aláns and the men of Balúch and Gílán. He espouses the cause of Munzir, the Arab, against Cæsar, invades Rúm, takes cities, and compels Cæsar to sue for peace and to pay tribute. On a false report of the Sháh's death his son, Núshzád, a Christian, attempts to seize the crown. Núshírwán writes to his general, Rám Barzín, instructing him how to proceed, and Núshzád is defeated and slain.

NOTE

§ 2. Núshírwán's accession to the throne was not universally popular and gave rise to a formidable conspiracy in favour of one of his nephews.[1]

§ 3. Núshírwán's division of his empire into four satrapies differs in details in the different authorities, but seems to have been suggested by the names of the four winds. According to Dínawarí the East included Khurásán, Sístán, and Kirmán ; the North Ispahán, Kum, Media Magna, and Ázarbáiján ; the South Párs and Ahwáz ; the West 'Irák to the Roman frontier.[2] Firdausi includes the Khazars in the South division—a mistake. They lived beyond the Caucasus.[3] He includes too Rúm in the West division on the assumption, for which there was certainly some justification at this time, that Rúm was tributary to Írán. A peace or truce concluded between Justinian and Núshírwán involved almost as a matter of course a money-payment from the former to the latter. It did not follow that Justinian always got the worst of the bargain. For instance, in the definite treaty of peace between the two

---

[1] See p. 316.   [2] NT, p. 155, *note*.   [3] See Vol. iv. p. 316.

empires in A.D. 562, Núshírwán's renunciation of Lazica (Mingrelia and Imeritia), and consequently of his dream of a fleet and of assailing Rúm by sea, was well worth the thirty thousand pieces of gold to be paid annually by Justinian though it did lay the Emperor open to the imputation of being tributary to the Sháh. Traditional instances of such payments crop up in the Sháhnáma as far back as the days of Dáráb and Failakús.[1]

The popular version of the origin of Kubád's resolve to alter the system of taxation has been given already.[2] It was left to Núshírwán to carry it out. According to Tabari the taxes imposed were as follows :—On every garíb of corn-land, *i.e.* sown with wheat or barley, a ground-tax of one drachm was imposed, on every garíb of vineyard eight, and of lucerne seven ; on four Persian date-palms, six common date-palms, provided that they grew in plantations or in numbers, and on six olives, one drachm. Single, scattered trees were not taxed. On all men between the ages of twenty and fifty a poll-tax varying, according to the fortune of a man, was imposed. The people were arranged in classes and paid twelve, eight, six, or four drachms according to their means. The taxes were paid yearly in three instalments at intervals of four months. Schedules of the taxes were drawn up, one of which was kept at the royal chancery, one sent to each collector, and one to each district-judge. The judges were priests and were charged particularly with the duty of seeing that the collectors did not exceed the tariff, and also, in cases where the crops had been damaged, with the duty of remitting taxation to a proportionate amount. The nobility, soldiers, priests, scribes, and others in the royal service, were exempt from the poll-tax.[3] They were supposed to render their due to the State in other ways.

§ 6. Farídún had his capital in Mázandarán. See Vol. i. pp. 177, 230. For the vegetation of that region, which is very luxuriant, see Vol. ii. pp. 27, 31.

For the fortifications at Darband, see p. 187 and Vol. i. p. 16. Mas'údí's two accounts of Núshírwán's wall, as given in the French translation, are as follows:—"Appelé dans le pays d'El-Bab et dans le Caucase par les incursions des rois du voisinage, il bâtit sur le mer (Caspienne), à l'aide d'outres de cuir gonflées, une muraille de rochers, qu'il consolida avec le fer et le plomb. Ces outres s'enfonçaient dans l'eau, à mesure que le construction s'elevait ; lorsqu'elles s'arrêtèrent sur le fond et que la muraille

---

[1] See vol. vi. p. 24.   [2] p. 183, *note.*

[3] NT, p. 244. A garíb is said to have been equal to 3600 square ells and a drachm to 88 centimes. *Id.* pp. 242, 245, *notes.*

dépassa le niveau de l'eau, des plongeurs, armés de poignards et de coutelas, crevèrent les outres ; la muraille, entrant profondémont dans le sol sous-marin, atteignit alors la hauteur du rivage. Elle existe encore aujourd'hui, en 332,[1] et toute la partie de cette muraille dont les assises plongent dans la mer est nomée *el-kaïd* (la chaine), parce qu'elle arrête les bâtiments ennemis qui tenteraient d'aborder sur cette côte. On continua le même travail le long du rivage, entre le Caucase et le mer ; on pratiqua des portes donnant sur le territoire infidèle, et l'on prolongea la muraille sur le mont Caucase, ainsi que nous l'avons dit ci-dessus, en décrivant cette montagne et la ville d'El-Bab."[2]

The other account referred to is this :—"Le Kabkh est une grande chaîne de montagnes qui renferme, dans sa vaste étendue, un nombre considérable de royaumes et de tribus : en effet, on n'y compte pas moins de soixante et douze peuplades, qui ont chacune leur chef et parlent une langue qui leur est propre. Ces montagnes sont sillonnées de gorges et de vallées ; c'est à la tête de l'un de ces défilés que se trouve. la ville de Bab-el-Abwab, bâtie par Kosroës Enouchirwân, sur un point intermédiaire entre le pays montueux et la mer des Khazars. Le même souverain construisit cette célèbre muraille qui, d'une part, s'avance dans la mer, jusqu'à une distance d'environ un mille des côtes, et, d'autre part, s'élève sur les sommets abruptes des montagnes et descend dans leur gorges profondes, sur une longueur de quarante parasanges, jusqu'à ce qu'elle aboutisse à une place forte nommée Tabarestân. De trois milles en trois milles à peu près, suivant l'importance de la route sur laquelle elle s'ouvrait, il plaça une porte de fer, près de laquelle il installa, dans l'intérieur de l'enceinte, une peuplade chargée de veiller à sa garde et à celle de la muraille. Ce rempart devait opposer une barrière infranchisable aux attaques des tribus voisines du Kabkh, telles que les Khazars, les Alains, les Turcs, les Serirs et les autres peuplades infidèles."[3]

One of the terms of peace made between Núshírwán and Justinian, after the death of Kubád, was that Persia should be paid the sum of eleven thousand pounds of gold towards the maintenance of the defences in the Caucasus and should undertake the actual defence herself.[4]

For Sikandar's wall, built, according to the legend, with a similar purpose, see Vol. vi. p. 163.

§ 7. Núshírwán's dealings with the Aláns and the folk of Gilán

---

[1] A.D. 943.　　　　　　　[2] MM, ii. 196.
[3] *Id.*, p. 1.　　　　　　　[4] RSM, p. 382.

are historical, but Firdausí substitutes the Balúchís, who made themselves very troublesome in his time, for another tribe, mentioned in his authorities but unknown to him, which dwelt north of the Caucasus.[1] It is very unlikely that any of the Sásánian Sháhs ever got as far East as Hindústán.

·§§ 8–10. The accession of Núshírwán found Persia and the Eastern Roman Empire at war, but a year or two later he concluded what was known as the "the endless peace" with Justinian. The title was somewhat unfortunate, as in A.D. 540 war again broke out owing, according to Firdausi and Tabarí, to the treatment of Munzir, prince of Hira (A.D. 505–554), by the Romans. He was Núshírwán's protégé and had a dispute with Hárith bin Jabala, the Ghassánian and Justinian's protégé, about a pasturage for sheep south of Palmyra. Hárith, as Tabarí states, attacked Munzir, made a great slaughter of his people, and carried off much booty. Munzir appealed to Núshírwán, who could get no accommodation from Justinian, and war ensued between the two empires.[2] Historically of course there were other reasons, one of the chief being that Justinian, secured on his Persian frontier by the "endless peace," had availed himself of the opportunity and the services of Belisarius to extend and almost double his possessions by conquests in the West. "Both his friends and his enemies said, with hate or admiration, 'The whole earth cannot contain him; he is already scrutinising the æther and the retreats beyond the ocean, if he may win some new world.'"[3] Justinian's success threatened to upset the balance of power. Probably, too, there were always "pin-pricks" going on between the two empires.

§ 11. The Fire-temple visited by Núshírwán before beginning his campaign was probably not one at Tabríz but the more famous one at what is now Takht-i-Sulaimán, about one hundred miles to the South. It was to this latter that the Sásánian Sháhs were wont to resort at important epochs in their lives.[4]

It will be noticed that a Mihrán commands the centre of Núshírwán's host—another instance of the prominent part played by this family of Arsacid descent in Sásánian times. *Cf.* p. 185.

§ 12. Crossing the Euphrates Núshírwán marched along its western bank till he reached Sura, the Greek τὰ Σοῦρα and the Shúráb of Firdausí, which was taken without difficulty, sacked, and burnt. The Sháh then advanced to Hierapolis, the Áráyish-i-Rúm of the Sháhnáma, which was allowed to ransom itself for two

[1] NT, p. 157, *note.*   [2] *Id.* p. 238; BLRE, i. 418.
[3] *Id.*   [4] *Cf.* pp. 5, 86, 94.

thousand pounds of silver.[1]   Hierapolis sounds somewhat like Aráyish, which means "ornament," so it would seem that the poet converted the name of that city into Aráyish-i-Rúm or "Ornament of Rúm."

§ 13. On leaving this city Núshírwán, according to Firdausi, encountered and defeated a Rúman army led by Farfúriyús. Historically, the Persians in their advance on Antioch, in the course of which they held Chalybon-Beroea (Aleppo) to ransom, appear to have been unopposed. The occupation of Kálíniyús (Callinicus) did not take place till the third campaign (A.D. 543) when the city made no resistance, and the inhabitants were led away captive. It was situated on the eastern bank of the Euphrates. In A.D. 531, however, Belisarius, after foiling an attempt of a combined force of Persians and Arabs to raid Antioch, was worsted in a battle at Callinicus ; so the two campaigns may have become confused in tradition. Germanus, Justinian's nephew, had been at Antioch before the Persians reached and stormed it in A.D. 540, but had withdrawn as he considered the existing fortifications could not be held with success. The taking of Antákiya (Antioch) was Núshírwán's crowning achievement in this his first campaign against Rúm, and he returned home by another route, compelling Various cities to ransom themselves on his way. Farfúriyús is probably Firdausí's rendering of a Byzantine title. Belisarius took no part in the campaign of A.D. 540 ; he only returned from Italy in that year.

§ 14. That Núshírwán built a new Antioch on the Tigris, not far from Ctesiphon, as a residence for his Roman captives is no doubt historical, though we need not commit ourselves to Tabarí's statement that the new town was so exactly a reproduction of the original that the captives, on arriving, went to their own houses as naturally as if they never had left home.[2] The cordwainer from Callinicus would be a later arrival.[3] The new Antioch was also known as Rúmiya or "The Rúman" and by other names.

§ 15. Negotiations for peace had been going on even during the first year of the war, though they came to nothing, but five years later a suspension of hostilities was agreed upon for five years. Justinian had to give Núshírwán two thousand pounds of gold.[4] Firdausi does not carry the story of the war further. Peace was made, after the resumption of the war which was followed by another five years' truce, definitively in A.D. 562.

---

[1] RSM, p. 387. [2] NT, p. 165.
[3] See above. [4] RSM, pp. 391 *seq.*, 404.

§§ 16–19. The revolt of Núshzád, "Immortal-born," is historical, and the circumstances attending it may be stated fairly correctly perhaps as follows. He seems to have been Núshírwán's eldest son, and to have been brought up as a Christian by his mother, who was in that Sháh's seraglio and of course a Christian herself. On account of his religion, or for some other reason, he was interned by his father at Gund-i-Shápúr,[1] which contained a strong Christian element and was the seat of the Nestorian Metropolitan—the next in rank to the Patriarch.[2] When the news, false as it turned out, of his father's death reached him he had every reason to bestir himself. In the circumstances there was a likelihood of his being passed over in the matter of the succession. His father's known disapproval, the rivalry of his brothers, and his own religion, were obstacles which had to be faced promptly if at all, while as the eldest-born it was only natural that he should aspire to the vacant throne. At the time when his rising occurred (A.D. 551) there was a five years' truce in force between Persia and the Eastern Roman Empire, so it is not likely that he got much help from that quarter. Probably Justinian never heard of the affair till it was all over. The Christian inhabitants of Gund-i-Shápúr naturally would support Núshzád, and it is interesting to find that the leader of his troops is Shammás—a word meaning a Christian priest or deacon. The general Persian opinion of Christians is shown by the word "tarsá," which means a Christian because its primary meaning is "cowardly," but it does not appear that Firdausí shared that view; on the contrary, when obviously putting his own words into the mouths of his characters, he treats the Church militant, especially the episcopacy, with much respect.[3] It is very unlikely therefore that the derogatory words concerning Christianity in the utterances of Núshírwán and Pirúz were the poet's own. Neither are they characteristically Muhammadan. Firdausí found them in his authorities translated from the Pahlavi. Historically, Núshzád does not appear to have fallen in the fight: he fell into his father's hands, was blinded probably, imprisoned, and disappeared from history. The concluding scene of the story may be regarded therefore as the poet's own contribution to it. There is nothing polemical there, but all is characterised by dignity and good feeling.[4]

---

[1] See Vol. vi. p. 295. [2] NT, p. 41.

[3] *e.g.* Vol. i. p. 378. *Cf.*, too, the parable of the kerchiefs where Christianity is meant by the "Faith of Yúnán," which is described as being "good." Vol. vi. p. 95.

[4] For Núshzád generally see NT, p. 467.

§ I

The Prelude

" O lofty Cypress, thou that ravishest
The heart ! oh ! wherefore art thou thus opprest ?
With pleasure, Grace, and luxury anear
Why is thine ardent heart fulfilled with fear ? "
Said to the questioner the Cypress-tree :—
" I was in joy ere age o'ermastered me.
I yield me to the puissance of three-score,
Forbear then and contend therewith no more,
For it hath dragon's breath and lion's claw,
And whomsoe'er it flingeth it will gnaw.
It hath the might of wolf, and thunder-breath,
In one hand care and in the other death.
It maketh stoop the Cypress that subdued
All hearts, it maketh jasmine amber-hued ;
It giveth saffron's tint to cercis-bloom,
And, after saffron's tint, a toilful doom.
The runner's foot is bound though fetterless,
The precious body turned to wretchedness ;
The lustrous pearls begin to fail with me,
And stoopeth too the noble cypress-tree ;
My melancholy eyes bewail and run
Through their debility and travail done ;
My blithe, glad heart is full of pain, and thus
These days of mine have grown ungenerous.
Or ever man is weaned his death is nigh,
And people call him old !   The sovereignty
Of Núshírwán was forty years and eight ;
To look for youth at sixty is too late
For thee, so seek an end to thine affairs,
And wound thy heart no more by gainful cares." [1]

---

[1] There is no break here in the original.

§ 2

How Núshírwán ascended the Throne and made an Oration
to the Íránians

When Núshírwán [1] assumed the ivory throne,
And donned the crown—the lustre of the heart—
The great men of the world were gathered there
What time the Sháh sat with his counsellors.
That chief of famous men then loosed his tongue,
Invoked the righteous Giver of all good,
And said : '' Be our hearts filled with praise and love
Toward the almighty Ruler of the sky,
From whom are good and ill, fame and desire,
By whom I am made sorrowful and glad,
Of whom are Grace and strength. By His command
The sun is bright in heaven. We will not quit
His counsels and His covenant, or reckon
Our breaths but at His bidding. He that doth
That which is just upon the throne of power
Will have fruition of good fortune here ;
But he that harboureth an ill intent   C. 1619
Will bring disaster on himself at last.
Whate'er ye ask of us we will reply,
And in our answer will advise you well.
None wotteth of the secrets of the heart ;
That is a way too strait for me to find ;
But still if justice be the Sháh's employ
It surely will rejoice the hearts of all.
Delay not till the morrow this day's work ;
How know'st thou what to-morrow will bring forth ?
The rosary in bloom to-day will have
But worthless flowers for thee to cull to-morrow.
In days when thou art hale be not unmindful
Of malady, of suffering, and of loss ;

[1] Kisrá in the original, but henceforth we write Núshírwán.

Think of the day of death which closeth life,
And how with death we are as leaves with wind.
When thou art slack to act thou makest all
Thy policy unsound.   When envy swayeth
The heart of man no leech can cure that ache.
When passion mastereth wisdom is't not proof
Of madness ?   Furthermore none honoureth
The quarrelsome and talkative.   The path
That leadeth thee to guile is gloomier,
To right is straiter.   Skilful as thou art,
If thou art lazy and perfunctory
Thy work will turn out ill.   Whene'er the tongue
Is wedded to deceit it hath no lustre .
From heavenly fortune.   Feckless folk resort
To lying, and we can but weep for such.
Whenas the Sháh is first to rise from slumber
He will be safe from foes and hale of body.
Be wise and have withal enough to eat,
But more than this is anguish, toil, and greed.
Whenas a Sháh is just and liberal
The world is full of goodness and of peace,
But if he thwarteth justice in its course
He eateth colocynth and drinketh blood.
All ye in this assembly ! hear what I
Proclaim to you, learn it, observe it well,
And all your years fare side by side with fortune :
Full many a crownéd monarch have we scanned,
And our choice is the path of right and wisdom ;
Yet must ye listen to my minister,
For good and ill appear not save through him.[1]
Whoever cometh to this court of mine
With just cause whether in or out of season,
No minister of mine will I approve
That keepeth such a matter hid from me.
As for the officers about my court,

---

[1] Reading with P.

And valiant cavaliers among my troops,
As we stint not the stipend due to them
So must they tender mine own name and fame.
Let all be done humanely and uprightly
Without defect of justice. Every one,
That, being an Íránian, girdeth him
To do his service in this court of ours,
Shall have both treasure and kind words from us
If he shall prove a shrewd and modest servant ;
But if his underlings shall be oppressed,
And he shall be unwise and fear not God,
He shall be punished for his wickedness,
And we should grieve not o'er the fall of one
So despicable. Keep within your hearts
The laws of holy God and fear not us,
For He is King of kings, Lord of the world,
Victorious, and One whose word is law,
The Illuminer of crown and sun and moon,
Who showeth us the way of righteousness.
Lord of the world is He, the Judge of judges,
And higher than the thoughts of every man.
He hath created heaven, space, and time,
And hath adorned our souls and hearts with love.
He is the Guard of crown and lofty throne,
And when thou seekest help will succour thee.
'Tis He hath fired your hearts with love of us,
His will hath blinded, heart and eye, our foes.
Well-being is all subject to His hest,
All goodness underneath His providence.
All from the stubble to the seventh heaven—
Air, fire, and water, and our gloomy earth— ·
Bear witness to His being and afford
Thereof a clear assurance to thy soul.
Whate'er we praise is under His command,
And all our worship dedicate to Him."

C. 162

When Núshírwán had spoken all the world
Was lost in wonder at him.   To their feet
All rose with praise anew the Sháh to greet.

§ 3

How Núshírwán divided his Realm into four Parts and wrote
a Decree to his Officers on the Administration of Justice

The king of kings called unto him the wise,
And settled the affairs of all the world.
The world itself he parted into four,
Assigning that which was inhabited.
He first of all for Khurásán took thought,
And filled thereby the nobles' hearts with joy.
The second part was Kum and Ispahán—
The seat of magnates and the place of chiefs—
Wherewith Ázar Ábádagán, whereon
The Íránians lavished offerings, was comprised.
That Sháh of wary heart [1] included too
Armenia up to Ardabíl and Gíl.

. 1621   The third from east to west was formed of Párs,
Ahwáz, and of the marches of Khazar.
'Irák together with the land of Rúm
Came fourth—a splendid realm and populous—
And in these marches to the indigent,
Who had to toil to satisfy their needs,
The Sháh made largess of his hoarded treasures,
And all folk blessed him.
                        Now of former Sháhs—
Sháhs greater or inferior to himself—
All had required a portion of the crops,
And no man thitherto had 'scaped the tax.
The royal portion was a third or fourth

---

[1] Reading with P.

Until Kubád came and required a tenth.
He meant to have reduced it further still,
And strove to make the lowly like the lord,
But fortune gave him not the time.[1]   Whilst thou
Art in the stream ne'er trust the crocodile.
The crown of worship came to Núshírwán,
And he remitted all the tenth forthwith.
The sages, chiefs, great men, and archimages,
The shrewd of heart, assembled—all the rulers.
They had the land partitioned and surveyed,
And laid thereon a land-tax of one drachm
So that the owners might not be distressed.
All that lacked seed or beast, when they should be
Preparing for the crops, were subsidised
Out of the treasure of the king of kings
So that they might not let the ground lie fallow.
Land, if untilled, was left out of account ;
The previous usages were done away.
On each six fruiting vines a drachm was levied,
Date-palm plantations paid an equal tax,
While each ten stems of olives and of walnuts,
And other trees that bear their fruit in autumn,
Brought one drachm to the treasury, and this
Was made the only burden of the year.
To fruits that ripened in the month Khúrdád
No heed was paid in taxing.   From the men
Of means who neither owned nor tilled the soil
The tax-collector every year received
A payment varying from ten drachms to four ;
But no one was oppressed because the money
Was paid in three instalments annually,
And thus a third part of the tax was paid
Each four months to the exchequer of the Sháh.
The royal scribes and officers employed
Within the taxing-office passed all count.

[1] *Cf.* p. 183, *note.*

The Sháh had these above-named tolls and imposts
Recorded by the archmages in three ledgers,
Whereof he gave one to the treasurer,
And made that minister account for it ;
The second was for sending through the realm.
To all officials and the men in power ;
C. 1622   The third was handed to the archimages
To keep account of all the revenue.
All that concerned tax, toll, and husbandry
Was done by order of the Sháh himself,
And he had agents scattered everywhere
To keep him cognisant of good and ill.
He filled with justice all the face of earth,
And cultivated all the barren lands ;
Both great and small slept safely on the waste,
And sheep and wolf came to one trough.   He bade
To draw up in the olden tongue a letter—
One that will pleasure thee to hear from me.
It thus began : " From Núshírwán, the chief—
The king of kings, the worshipper of God,
A Bough fruit-bearing from the Tree Kubád—
Who hath assumed the crown of majesty,
And in especial prospered all the land,
For God, the just Judge, gave him Grace divine,
To all the officers of revenue—
Thralls of the shadow of our Grace and throne—
Our well weighed greetings unto you whose birth
Hath been exceeded by your own deserts.
Here at the outset of our task we first
Give praises to the Maker of the world.
Know that the man is wise and shrewd of heart,
Whose praise is of the righteous Judge of earth,
Well knowing that He hath no need of us,
And that all secrets are revealed to Him,
Who when He willeth to exalt a man
First maketh him superior to all want.

He bade me judge, but He is Judge Himself,
And higher than all height eternally.
In God's sight king and subject are as one,
And saving service none hath aught to do ;
From the abyss of earth to heaven above,
And from the sun to dark and sorry dust,
The ant's foot beareth witness that He is,
That we are bondslaves and that He is king.
All His commands to us are righteousness ;
It is the Div that causeth lies and loss.
Now if my portion of the spacious world
Had been a garden only, park, and palace,
My heart had chosen naught but love and justice,
And kept a smiling face for everything ;
But now the expanse of all the world throughout
From east to west hath God, the Holy One,
Bestowed upon me as my sovereignty—   ·
All from the bright sun to the darksome dust—
And I must practise naught save love and justice
Although I furrow mine own face thereby.
If careless be the shepherd and the waste
Thus vast the sheep will 'scape not from the wolf.
As for my subjects, whether country-folk
Or those devoted to the Cult of Fire,
Be they in drouthy dust or ship at sea
By day or night alike, or be they merchants,
Engaged in voyaging over wet and dry   C. 1623
With monies and with lustrous pearls and musk,
The sun must shine not from the arch of heaven
Upon them save in justice and in love.
Now this hath been the custom of our race
That son should have his father's crown and this
The world hath recognised as just and right
With one consent in public and in private.
We have imposed a land-tax and a tree-tax
For sustentation of the throne and crown.

Now when they bring this letter to you may
Urmuzd prove fortunate to you. Whoever
Herein transgresseth by a single drachm,
Or doth injustice for a single breath,
I swear by God, who hath bestowed upon me
The diadem of Grace, that I will saw
That man in twain ; such is God's chastisement
On those whose evil seed hath come to fruit.
Observe this letter and this ordinance,
And turn not from the glorious Way and Faith.
Demand with justice and with courtesy
The instalment of the tax due each four months ;
But where the locusts have been ravaging,
Or sunbeams beaten on the parched-up earth,
Or where the blast or lightning of high heaven
Hath brought disaster on the cultured fields,
Or if rain falleth not at the New Year,
So that the jocund crops are vexed with drought,
Demand no tax upon those fields and crops,
Because the spring-clouds have not watered them,
And pay the seed sown and the labourers' hire
Back to the farmers from the treasury.
The lands whose owner is deceased and hath
No kith and kin must lie not waste, for they
Are underneath the shadow of the Sháh ;
Else will the foe make scorn of my resources
With such a pretext ready to his hand.
Give what is needed from the treasury,
For God hath set me out of reach of need.
If lands within my power lie desolate,
Unsheltered by the shadow of my wing,
Whoe'er he be that is responsible,
And doth neglect the task, hard though it be,
Him, whether lord or underling, will I
Hang from the gibbet on the spot. The great—
The Sháhs of yore—had other usages,

With their officials rested right and wrong,
The world lay open to the cavaliers,
Who wantonly mocked wisdom and ne'er rested
From adding to their wealth.   My wealth is justice ;
The people of the land compose my host ;
I will not cast a glance upon dinárs.
To win by equity the world's regard,
And to respect the worth of men of birth,
Are dearer to me than the wealth of foes   C. 1624
That seek to win my kingdom and my throne.
The general that selleth men for gold
Shall get no entry to my court whereat
They are esteemed that follow justice, love,
Law and the Way.   When my shrewd officers
Assemble at the office of the archmage,
And falsehood showeth in the words of any,
He shall receive no grace from us henceforth.
I do not love the man that is unjust ;
The leopard and the oppressor are as one.
All they that have ensued the way of God,
And bathed their dark souls in the stream of wisdom,
Shall have a lofty station at our court,
High estimation with the archimages,
And from their God for that which they have sown
The recompense of jocund Paradise.
We are ourselves exempt from need of wealth
Whereby the soul is minished and accursed.
He that doth eat the flesh of mendicants
Will find, no doubt, some nurture in their skins.
A pard is better than a king like that,
Who hath no modesty, no rule, no Faith.
The way of right is open to us.   Why
Knock we in folly on the door of loss ?
To do ill closely, justice openly,
So that the fame thereof may come to us,
Will have not God's approval, or be held

In high consideration at our court ;
But he hath God's approval and our own
Whose love and justice are as warp and woof."
    If thou art just, O monarch ! thou wilt give
The world a record of thee that will live,
For every one will praise eternally
The Sháh that brought the world prosperity.

§ 4

How Núshírwán required Bábak to muster the Host

Of all the Sháhs that erst had throne and crown,
And had been great in treasure and in troops,
There was not one more just than Núshírwán,
And may his soul be young for evermore.
None was more worshipful for manhood, throne,
For diadem and knowledge. He possessed
An archimage, Bábak by name, a man
Of wisdom, shrewd of heart, and fortunate,
Made him the muster-master of the host,
And bade him to prepare himself an office
Of ample size before the palace-gate,
And higher than its top, and furnish it
C. 1625   With carpets that were worthy of a king
To seat the clerks engaged upon the work.
A proclamation issued from his office,
And all the folk gave ear : " Famed warriors !
Mount and attend the portal of the Sháh,
All ye that would have guerdon at his hands !
With iron helmets set upon your heads,
Arrayed in mail and bearing ox-head maces."
    The troops came to the office of Bábak,
The air was darkened by the horsemen's dust.
Now when Bábak reviewed the host he missed [1]

-----
[1] Reading with P.

The standard and the chief of all the noble.
He left the office, mounted on his steed,
And bade the soldiers go back to their quarters.
The turning sky continued on its course,
And when the radiant sun displayed its face
It was proclaimed before the palace-gate :—
" Ye mace-men of the army of Írán !
Go all in full array with arms and bows
And lassos to the office of Bábak."
    They went with lances, helms, and coats of mail ;
The army's dust ascended to the clouds.
Bábak looked round upon the host but, since
The Sháh appeared not in his Grace and state,
Thus spake : " Return glad and victorious
In love and duty, each man to his quarters."
    Again the third day rose the proclamation :—
" Ye men of name, of Grace divine and wisdom !
Let there not be one horseman of this host
Without his helmet and cuirass of war,
And let him come and pass before this gate,
And see his name upon the muster-roll.
Let those that are distinguished by a crown,
By Grace, by majesty, and lofty fortunes,
Know that this muster is without respect
Of persons, reticence, and modesty."
    The king of kings gave ear thereto and heeded
The proclamation from Bábak's diván,
Then smiling called for coat of mail and helm,
And held erect the flag of majesty.
The Sháh, with iron helmet on his head,
Proceeded to the office of Bábak.
The chain-mail hung down from his Rúman helm,
And was secured by many a fastening.
Within his hand he had an ox-head mace,
Within his belt four shafts of poplar-wood,
A bow on arm and lasso on the saddle.

While round his loins he had a golden girdle.
He urged his charger, gripping with his thighs,
And laid the massive mace upon his shoulder ;
Then, lightly wheeling both to left and right,
Displayed both steed and rider to Bábak,   '
Who when he had inspected them approved,
And, having come up to the king of kings,
. 1626 Said thus to him : " O Sháh ! mayst thou be blessed !
May wisdom be the provand of thy soul !
Thou hast adorned the kingdom's face with justice,
Such that with us 'tis thy memorial.
What I have said was boldness from a slave,
But never must thou turn from what is just ;
So now, I prithee, wheel thee to the right
With all the skill whereof thou art the master."
    Then Núshírwán again urged on his steed
To right and left as 'twere Ázargashasp.
Bábak looked on amazed and oft invoked
The Maker of the world. A horseman's pay
Ran from a thousand to two thousand drachms ;
Four thousand were the most that any had.
Bábak paid to the Sháh just one drachm more.
Then from the office-door 'twas cried : " Exhibit
The charger of the first of warriors—
The horseman of the world, the famous Sháh,"
While Núshírwán laughed heartily, for fortune
Was young with him and he a youthful king.
Now when Bábak had left the royal office
He came before the noble Sháh and said :—
" Great Sháh ! if I, thy slave, made bold to-day
The purpose of my heart was right and just :
Let not the Sháh take notice of my harshness ;
It is not harshness to discharge one's duty,
And blest is he who meant not to be harsh."
    " O man of wisdom ! " said the Sháh to him,
" Keep thyself ever in the path of right,

Whereof thou break'st the heart by self-regard.
Know that thou art the dearer in mine eyes ;
But mine anxiety is for myself—
How, when the army is engaged in fight,
I shall comport myself upon the field."
  Bábak made answer to the noble Sháh :—
" No crown and signet will behold thy like,
While painter hath observed not limned in hall
A hand and rein like thine, O king ! Oh ! may
High heaven accord to thee thy full desire,
Oh ! may thy heart be glad, thyself unscathed ! "
  Thus to the archimage said Núshírwán :—
" Our justice shall make old folk young again.
The king must leave as his memorial
Within the world but righteousness alone.
What need have we for such a treasury,
Such toil and greed, and to confine our soul
Within this Wayside Inn ? The need, since here
Is no abiding, is to eat and drink.
I have been troubled with the world's affairs,
Although I kept these matters to myself,
Because my royal crown hath enemies,
And Áhriman doth compass me about.
Methought : ' I will bring troops from every side,
And summon warriors from every province,
But for the levy I have need of treasure,   C. 1627
Which I have but to labour to amass ;
Still if this bringeth evil on the poor
I must refrain my heart from this desire.'
So I revolved this matter in my heart,
And, having come upon a wise resolve,
I wrote a letter to the paladins,
The mighty men, and prudent archimages,
To all the nobles and the potentates
In all the provinces, and thus it ran :—
' All ye possessed of wisdom and of sense !

Bring up your sons for military service,
Dispatch them to the field equipped for war,
And look to me for honour and reward.
They must be able to distinguish hand
And rein from stirrup on the hills and dales,
And learn to battle with the enemy
With mace and scimitar, with bow and arrow,
Because a youth unskilled availeth naught
Although he be descended from Árish.' [1]
The muster-master went forth from the court,
With money for the chiefs, to every province,
And now in sooth I have adorned the face
Of earth with men prepared to take the field.
I have more knowledge, policy, and method
Than former Sháhs, and greater armaments."

The archmage, when he heard the Sháh speak thus,
Called praises down upon the crown and throne.

The payment was delayed for forty days,
And then the athelings, equipped for war,
Went to the office and received their pay
While joyance was the order of the day.

§ 5

*How Núshírwán harangued the Íránians, and how the
Kings acknowledged his Supremacy*

Now when the sun displayed its shining face,
When circling heaven unlocked the garden-gate,
And when the Mound of Fenugreek appeared
While dark night's tresses vanished, Núshírwán,
All smiles, glad-hearted, and of youthful fortune,
Sat on his throne, while all that sought redress
Flocked to his court. The king harangued thein
      thus :—

[1] For whom see Vol. v. p. 12.

" Acknowledge that ye have not any helper
Save holy God, the Lord of all, our Guide,
Who leadeth us in both worlds by the hand.
Fear not the throne and crown, the court is open
To all, and ye soe'er that come thereto
By day and night keep not your lips from speech.
If we are quaffing wine in company,
Or busied with advisers, or at polo,
Or on the hunting-field, the way is open
For you to us. Let access be withheld
From none because I am asleep, awake,
At work or play. Let none of you withdraw
From us to sleep with wants unsatisfied.
My heart will be rejoiced and bright whenever
I break the travail of the oppressed. Please God,
No officer of mine, no man at arms,
No servitor, shall sleep with heart aggrieved,
For from his grievance harm will come on me.
However trifling or obscure the matter
The Maker will require it at my hands.
For tolls and imposts, other than the archmages
Are now concerned with in mine offices,
No gold or silver shall be asked of you,
So sleep all unafraid of me henceforth."
  Then sunward from the face of earth applause
Rose from the hall : " May Núshírwán have Grace,
And all his years the crown of king of kings !
Ne'er may the throne, the state, and famous crown
Of sovereignty be void of him ! "
                                    They went
Their ways, glad and rejoicing, and earth's face
Grew like the garden of Iram.[1] Thou hadst not
Seen any one despondent in the world,
While from the clouds came seasonable rain,
The world resembled jocund Paradise,

C. 1628

[1] See Vol. i. p. 100.

The clouds sowed tulips in the pleasances,
The dales, the plains, and orchards shone like lamps,
The uplands were like garths, garths like the sun.
   Thereafter tidings came to Rúm and Hind :—
" Írán is like fine painted silk of Rúm ;
The Sháh hath decked with armaments and justice
The earth till it is like the shining moon.
No one in all the world doth know the sum
Of all his forces save the Sháh himself.
They all are blithe of heart and dight for war,
Have fame and glory and illume the world."
   The kings of all the realms were sore amazed
At heart ; their souls were dark through Núshírwán.
Ambassadors arrived from Hind and Chin,
And all kings called down praises on the Sháh ;
They saw that they could counter not his might,
And hasted to pay tribute with good will,
Bare them as underlords to Núshírwán,
And gathered slaves and purses for his service.
With golden maces and with golden crowns
The envoys went upon their way.   They reached
The court-gate of the monarch of the world,
And brought the toll and tribute of their lords.
The court appeared adorned like Paradise
Through all those purses, slaves, and audience-seekers.
Thus for a while the heavens turned above,
Consorting with the Íránian king in love.

§ 6

How Núshírwán went round his Empire and built a Wall
in the Pass between Irán and Túrán

. 1629   Then Núshírwán, the wise, made this resolve—
That he would sojourn for a while abroad

To make the circuit of the jocund world,
And bring whate'er was hidden to the light.
He beat the kettledrums, marched forth the host,
And sun and moon were both astound at him.
What with the troops and jewels, gold and silver,
The golden girdles and the golden shields,
Thou wouldst have said : " No gold is left within
The mines, no gems or lustrous pearls remain ! "
  He led his host toward Khurásán at leisure,
All heedful of Sásánian precedent.
Whenever he passed settlements he pitched
His camp and camp-enclosure on the waste,
And when the blare of clarions rose there went
A herald first afoot who thus proclaimed :—
" Ye subjects of the monarch of the world !
Is any privily aggrieved at us ?
Sleep not despairing of the Sháh, allow not
Your souls to fail with care."
                                      He led the host
Thus to Gurgán and bare with him the crown
And throne of chiefs. Know, justice is no loss :
Sháhs should have prowess, rede, and noble birth.
  Now when the nightingales were full of song
They went thence toward Sari and toward Ámul,
Where hill and plain were clothed with forest-trees,
Which filled the Íránian monarch's heart with thought.
He left the plain and mounting to the heights,
Still seated on his Arab bay looked out
O'er mountain and o'er forest, and observed
Rose, hyacinth and game, and water there,
And thus he said : " O Thou almighty Judge,
The World-lord, Conqueror, and Fosterer !
Thou art the Maker of the sun and moon,
The Guide and the Revealer of the way.
Thou mad'st the world of such delightsomeness
That we distinguish not 'twixt earth and Heaven.

Whoe'er shall worship any save Thyself
Will send his soul to Hell.   It was for this
That pious Farídún forwent Írán,
And made his dwelling here, so passing fair
Is this place and delightsome to the heart,
Where water is rose-water and the soil
Is spicery."

            One said : " O righteous judge !
If this were not a highway for the Turkmans
Our hearts would be not empty of delight,
Such are the wealth and glory of this place ;
But as it is we cannot raise our necks
For constant murders, sack, and harryings.

'. 1630   There are not many left or even few
Of fowl or men or cattle on this spot.
This is the only route between the realms,
And causeth loss to the Íránian folk.
There came much toil and strife in former times,
But then the Turkmans' route was through Khárazm.
Now for the merchant or the thane to raise
His head would be in vain.   However, now
That thou hast led an army to these parts,
Avert this ill from us and bar the way.
Thy treasures will be more, not less, thereby :
Now is the time to render us a service."

  The Sháh, whenas he heard the suppliant,
Showered tear-drops from his eyes and thereupon
Addressed his minister and said to him :—
" A very grievous toil confronteth us.
Henceforth 'tis not for us to fare and feast,
Or even tender our own crown, for God
Will sanction not the wrong in us that we
Shall be in happiness while thanes are grieving.
Such mountains as these are, such spacious plains,
All fit for gardens, grounds, and palaces,
And filled with cattle, game, and running water,

So that the soul is freshened by the sight—
We must not let the Turkmans lay them waste,
And desolate the country of Írán.
My kingly office, prudence, policy,
Humanity itself, will brook it not.
Men will invoke not blessings on our heads
What time Írán is lying desolate."
  He bade his minister : " From Hind and Rúm
Select men famous in those cultured lands
From all the provinces, foreseeing men,
Such masters in their craft as thou canst find,
And build me from the sea a lofty wall,
On broad foundations and ten lassos high,
Of stone and mortar, starting from the deep,
And rising to the fountain of the sun.
In this way surely we shall form a bar,
And loss from foes will come not on Írán.
Use no forced labour, ope our treasury,
And pay to every one what he demandeth.
The labourer, the thane, and man of birth
Must not be incommoded by the blast."
  He made an old archmage the overseer,
And shut out all the desert by the wall,
Wherein they set a mighty iron door,
And all the flock grew fearless of the wolf.
Of frontier-guards he stationed many a post,
And, having made all safe, led on the host.

§ 7

*How Núshírwán chastised[1] the Aláns and the Men of
Balúch and Gílán*

Thence from the sea he went toward the Aláns,　　C. 1631
And finding there a ravaged, barren march

---

[1] Literally, " rubbed the ears of."

He thus addressed his chiefs : " It is a shame
For regions in Írán to lie thus waste,
And we must suffer not our foes to say so."
   He chose an envoy from among the troops,
One, as was fitting, wise and eloquent,
To whom he said : " Depart hence with the dawn,
And say thus to the marchlords of yon folk :—
' From mine intelligencers have I heard
All that hath passed in public and in private,
And that ye say : " Why fear we Núshírwán ?
As for Írán it is a pinch of dust."
Now have we come anigh you and set up
Our camp, our camp-enclosures, and our court.
Your wastes are spacious and your mountains high,
Your troops are armed with arrow, mace, and lasso.
Your gorges are the place for ambuscades,
Land, mountain, field and fell, are all your own.
We—general and soldiers—challenge you,
We who are strangers in a foreign land.' "
   The envoy went his way and spake the words
Dictated by the monarch of Írán.
The host of the Aláns assembled—all
The great, the sages, and the counsellors—
A host that found employ in pillaging,
And recked but little for the Íránians.
Írán was wont to stand in awe of them ;
Folk had no raiment, gold, or silver left,
And men and women with their babes and beasts
Were wont to quit their homes and seek the plains.
The envoy told the Aláns, withholding naught,
The message of the monarch of the world,
Whereat the faces of the chiefs grew black ;
The words of Núshírwán amazed their hearts.
The great men and the chieftains of that march
Went forth with contributions and much tribute,
With slaves and raiment, and with gold and silver,

And many a noble steed, while of the folk
All that were men of years and eloquence,
And wisdom-seekers, came to Núshírwán,
Bewailing their past doings.   When they reached
The tent-enclosure of the Sháh with presents,
And gifts, they cried and wallowed in the dust,
Their eyes fulfilled with tears, their hearts with blood.
For shame and self-excusing is no need   C. 1632
When wisdom and the valiant are agreed.
The prudent Sháh was gracious unto them,
And pardoned all that they had done amiss ;
Then ordered that upon the wasted lands—
The lurking-place of lion and of leopard—
They should erect a city with all speed,
With room for sowing and for harvesting,
The whole surrounded by a lofty wall
That ill might not befall from enemies.
The Aláns made answer to the noble king,
And said : " With earrings on as slaves of thine,
And, as the Sháh hath bidden, we will raise
The ramparts of a noble seat."
                                            The Sháh
Marched thence to Hindústán and sojourned there.
At his commandment all folk came to him,
Came seeking to ingratiate themselves,
And for two miles beside the Indus-bank
Were horses, elephants, brocade, and coin.
The great men all with honesty of heart
And loyalty appeared before the Sháh,
Who questioned them and well entreated them,
And placed them in accordance to their rank.
With jocund heart the Sháh departed thence :
Troops, steeds, and elephants fulfilled the world.
He went his way, and tidings came to him :—
" The world is wasted by the Balúchís,
Till from exceeding slaughter, pillaging,

And harrying, the earth is overwhelmed,
But greater ruin cometh from Gilán,
And curses banish blessings."
                              Then the heart
Of Núshírwán, the Sháh, was sorrowful,
And grief commingled with his joy. He said
To the Íránians : "The Aláns and Hind
Were, in their terror of our scimitars,
Like silk. Now our own realm is turned against us :
Shall we hunt lions and forgo the sheep ? "
    One said to him : "The garden hath no rose
Without a thorn, O king ! So too these marches
Are ever troublesome and treasure-wasting.
As for Balúch the glorious Ardshír
Tried it with all his veteran officers,
But all his stratagems and artifices,
His feints, his labours, arms, and fighting failed,
And though the enterprise succeeded ill
He cloaked the failure even to himself."
    This story of the thane enraged the Sháh,
Who went upon his way toward Balúch.
Now when he drew anear those lofty mountains
He went around them with his retinue,
And all his host encircled them about,
And barred the passage e'en to wind and ant.
The troops, like ants and locusts, occupied
The mountain-outskirts to the sandy desert.

. 1633 A herald went his rounds about the host,
Proclaiming from the mountains, caves, and plains :—
"Whene'er the Balúchís are seeking food,
If they be warriors and carry arms,
However many or however few,
Let not a single one of them escape."
    The troops, ware of the anger of the Sháh,
Stopped every outlet with their horse and foot ;
Few of the Balúchís or none survived,

No women, children, warriors, were left.
All of them perished by the scimitar,
And all their evil doings had an end,
The world had quiet from their ravaging :
No Balúchí, seen or unseen, remained,
While on their mountains, so it came to pass,
The herds thenceforward strayed without a guard ;
Alike on waste and lofty mountain-top
The sheep required no shepherd.   All the folk
Around thought nothing of past sufferings,
And looked on vale and mountain as their home.
Thence toward Gílán marched Núshírwán, for there,
And in Dílam, was trouble manifest.
The army stretched from sea to mountain-top,
The air was full of flags, the earth of troops.
The army was extended round Gílán,
And light departed from the sun and moon.
Thus spake the Sháh : " Among the small and great
No trace of Wolf and Lion must be left."
   So mighty was the slaughter in the land
That all the region's face was bathed in blood.
At all the slaying, pillaging, and burning
The men and women sent up wails of woe.
On every side the slain were piled in heaps,
The grasses smirched with brains.   The warriors—
The just, the prudent and the men of weight—
Remaining in Gílán bound their own hands,
And with their women-folk behind, their children
Before them, came lamenting to the king
With bosoms rent and dust upon their heads.
They all assembled at the monarch's court
With bounden hands and wounded bodies, saying :—
" We have turned back upon our evil courses ;
Oh ! that the Sháh would cease from his displeasure !
If he is vexed at heart against Gílán
We will behead ourselves with our own hands.

It may be that the Sháh then will relent
When he shall see the heaps of severed heads."
    When such a cry rose from the court, and when
The Sháh had listened to their supplication,
He pardoned them ; the past was blotted out,
But he required two hundred hostages
Both from Gílán and from Dilam that none
Thereafter might pursue the path of ill.
He left a paladin with them to stay,
And, having ordered all things, marched away.

§ 8

How Munzir, the Arab, came to Núshírwán for Succour
against the Injustice of Cæsar

C. 1634   Next from Gílán he marched toward Madá'in,
Not knowing his troops' number or extent.[1]
Now as he journeyed on appeared afar
A boundless host of wielders of the spear.
A cavalier—one of that great array—
Approached as quick as dust on their behalf,
And, having lighted from his charger, said :—
" Behold Munzir the Arab."
                              When Munzir
Drew near the Sháh all chiefs made way for him.
The Sháh saluted him with signs of joy,
And brightened at his looks.   That veteran
Set loose his tongue, discoursed of Rúm and Cæsar,
And said : " If thou art monarch of Írán,
The guardian and the backbone of the brave,
Why do the Rúmans lord it so and prance
Upon the desert of the cavaliers ?
While if the Sháh be Cæsar's overlord

_____
[1] They were so many.

That haughty potentate should lose his head.
Now if the noble Sháh will give permission
No more will he behold us asking aid,
And in the fight the horsemen of the desert
Shall triumph o'er the cavaliers of Rúm."
    The Sháh was wroth that Cæsar should exalt
His crown, as said Munzir, and, having chosen
Among the troops a man of eloquence,
And learned in Cæsar's tongue, said thus : "Go thou
To Rúm, take not thine ease in peopled parts,
And say to Cæsar : 'If thou lackest wisdom
Thy brains will sorrow for thy policy.
The warrior-lion chasing onager
Will batten on them even in a salt-marsh.
For thee to have thy just dues from Munzir
Sufficeth seeing that Vega is his throne.
Discern then 'twixt thy left hand and thy right,
And, when thou knowest, claim what march is thine.
Since I am the distributor of lands
And realms, am highest in the world and chief,
My conduct shall be worthy of myself :
I will let not the wind blow on Munzir.
Since thou hast stretched thy hand upon the Arabs
In fight take privy heed for thine own self.
Moreover all that sovereignty is mine,
And mine is all between the Bull [1] and Pisces.
If I shall send an army into Rúm
Thy sword of steel will prove a sword of wax.' " [2]
    The ambassador came forth from Núshírwán
As 'twere a torrent, came and gave the message   C. 1635
To Cæsar, but that worthless one recoiled
From what was just, replied evasively,
Imagining a fall from power remote,
And answered thus : "As for that fool Munzir,
Take what he stateth at its proper worth.

---

[1] See Vol. i. p. 71.   [2] Because "múm, ' wax, rhymes with "Rúm."

If he complaineth out of wantonness,
Exaggerating thus the evil done,
Or if a single man complain within
The desert of the wielders of the spear,
I will convert the heights of earth to breadths,
And that unwatered desert to a sea."
 The envoy heard, came swift as dust, and told
The words of Cæsar. Núshírwán enraged
Said to his minister : "The brains of Cæsar
Are wedded not to wisdom. I will show him
Who hath authority, the power to conquer
The world, to levy war, and make a pact.
His overweening and his haughtiness,
His labour, pillaging, and harrying,
He shall repent more dearly than the drunkard,[1]
That thrusteth both hands in the fire at night."
 He then bade blow the trumpets, and a host
Was gathered unto him from every side ;
The din of tymbals went up from the court-gate,
Earth was pitch-hued and air was ebony.
He chose of cavaliers from that famed host
A hundred thousand armed with scimitars,
Entrusted that great army to Munzir,
And bade him : "From the desert of the spearmen
Lead unto Rúm an army of the brave
To set the frontier and the land afire,
For youthful monarch though I be and though
I am but newly famouséd in fight,
Yet fear not Rúm or Rúman, thou ! for I
Regard the Rúman as a pinch of dust.
Now will I send me an ambassador—
A man of eloquence—to him. Henceforth,
If thou experience naught calamitous,
That Cæsar should keep Rúm would pleasure us.[2]

---

[1] Reading with P.   [2] Ending section with P.

§ 9

The Letter of Sháh Núshírwán to Cæsar of Rúm

The Sháh then called a scribe that was at court,
And bade to write a letter unto Cæsar :—[1]
" From Núshírwán, the Sháh of glorious birth,
The world-lord and successor of Kubád,[2]
To Cæsar, the exalted lord of Rúm—
Guard of the marches of that prosperous land."
   The letter opened with the praise of God
From whom alone all greatness must be sought—
" The Master of the circling sun and moon,
The Source of victory and mastery,
Who is above the will of turning heaven   C. 1636
As touching justice, love, and strife. Though thou
Art Cæsar and the lord of Rúm dispute not
Aught with the Arabs, for if thou shalt take
The sheep out of the clutches of the wolf
Thou wilt, as thou art ware, have grievous toil ;
While if thou sendest troops against Munzir
I will not leave thee host or crown or throne.
If any underling grow masterful
He shall be punished by our scimitar.
Step not a single cubit past thy bounds
If thou desirest that our pact shall stand.
If thou shalt pass thy bounds we will pass ours,
And trample under foot thy head and throne.
The greeting of the lord of diadem
And might to those that seek not to cause trouble
By their injustice."
                  Unto this they set
The Sháh's seal and then chose a cavalier,
Such as was needful, from the court, a man
Persuasive, valiant, shrewd, and veteran.

---

[1] In C. the previous section ends here.   [2] *Cf.* p. 170, *note.*

§ 10

How the Letter of Núshírwán reached Cæsar and how he replied

The envoy with the letter of the king
Came to famed Cæsar, gave it, greeted him,
And told him all the mind of Núshírwán.
When Cæsar heard and had perused the letter
He writhed and was astound. His brow grew wrinkled,
His visage wan at what the exalted Sháh
Had said. He called a scribe, wrote his reply,
And made his meaning clear for good and ill.
The letter first grew musky with the ink
What time he offered praise to God almighty—
"The Artist of the heavens over us,
The Source of warfare, peace, and amity.
He giveth in the world one man a crown
With slaves before him better than himself.
Though turning heaven itself be under thee,
And Jupiter beneath thy scimitar,
Search out thy records, for no son of Rúm
E'er hath paid tribute to thy royal race.
King as thou art I am no less than thou ;
I too possess a head, a crown, and realm.
Why must I take so much abuse in fear
Of foot of elephant or din of drum ?
I now ask you for tribute and for toll,
And who is there with power to fight with Rúm ?
The doings of Sikandar in Írán
Thou knowest, and we claim that noble Sháh.
. 1637   Sikandar's sword is still in evidence,
Why pickest thou a quarrel with us thus ?
The javelin-wielding horsemen of the waste
Have pillaged our possessions in their raids :
No longer will we bear their wrongs but raise

The dust in all their borders. Núshírwán
Was neither Maker of the sun, nor hath
He seized the key of the revolving sky,
That there must be no other king of kings,
And his will only current in the world."
　　He gave the envoy no reply in speech,
Not recking of the wrath of Núshírwán,
But, when he set the seal upon the letter,
He spake these words : "Christ and the Cross are
　　with me."
　　The envoy spent no breath on him, perceiving
With grief the answer, and with grief departed ;
Swift as a dust-cloud to the Sháh he sped,
And told him all that Cæsar purposéd.

§ 11

How Núshírwán went to war with Cæsar

The king, when he had read the letter, raged
Against the turn of fortune. Then he called
The archmages and the chieftains, one and all,
And spake to them at large about that letter.
He sat for three days with his counsellors
And paladins—the shatterers of hosts—
And on the fourth day was resolved to lead
His troops to fight with Cæsar. At the gate
Arose the blare of trumpets with the din
Of brazen cymbals and of drums. He paused not,
But went to battle in a righteous cause,
Assembled troops, made up the baggage-train,
And called on God, the Giver of all good.
A dust rose such that thou hadst said : "The sky
Hath smirched its visage in a sea of pitch !"
He clad the surface of the earth with horse-shoes,

While silken flags incarnadined the air.
There was no room on earth e'en for a gnat,
No room for wind left in the firmament.
The hubbub of the horsemen and the dust
Of elephants made earth seem like the Nile.
The world-lord marched with Káwa's flag, with crown,
And golden boots. The army's din was heard
Two miles away. Before the host were drums
And elephants, and on this wise the Sháh,
With chiefs behind him and with chiefs before him,
Sped onward to Ázar Ábádagán.
Now when his eyes beheld Ázargashasp
Afar he lighted down and went afoot,
Requested of his pious minister
The sacred twigs and bathed his cheeks with tears.
. 1638 He made his entry of the Fane of Fire
With wailing. They set up a throne inlaid
With gold, and spread thereon the Zandavasta,
Wherefrom an archimagus read aloud,
According to the ritual, while priests
And chieftains wallowed in the dust before it,
And rent their skirts. The great men showered jewels
Upon the book and muttered laud thereon.
The Sháh approaching offered praise and prayer
Before the Maker of the world, and asked
For victory, for mastery, and guidance
Upon the path of justice. He bestowed
Gifts on the attendants and on mendicants
Wherever seen. He pitched his tent before
The Fire-fane, and his troops arrayed their ranks
Upon each side. He called a prudent scribe,
Discoursed at large, dictating fitting words,
Bade him address by letter graciously
The marchlords of the country of Írán,
And say : " Fear God, be vigilant, and guard
The world against the enemy. Ye lords

And paladins ! be just to those beneath you,
And keep such forces as will foil the foe.
None while my standard shall be out of sight
Must think to slumber in security."
  As from the Fane of Fire he marched towards Rúm
The bruit of him was spread throughout the land,
And all the faithful lieges flocked to him
Until the warriors [1] hid the fields and fells,
And many an aspirant came with gifts
And offerings to the king. Where'er he lighted
There reached him salutations and addresses
From all sides, while where'er he led his host
He still had feast and chase before his eyes,
And 'twas the custom for a thousand chiefs
To come each night to banquet with the king.
When he was near the frontier he made ready
For war and in the first place paid his troops.
His general was Shírwí, son of Bahrám—
A man of rede and self-possessed in battle.
He gave the army's left wing to Farhád,
To whom he proffered many prudent counsels.
Ustád, son of Barzín, was on the right,
Garshasp, the atheling, was o'er the baggage.
Mihrán [2] was at the centre, for his heart
Was steadfast in the fray. The outpost duty
The Sháh gave to Hurmuzd, son of Kharrád,
Enjoining wisdom to his soul and heart,
While everywhere intelligencers went
That nothing might be hidden. Then the Sháh
Called and advised his veterans much and well.
He said to them : " Ye numbers numberless   C. 1639
Of men of high estate and warriors !
If any one of you shall quit my way,
Or draw a breath without my privity,
Shall cause affliction to the mendicants,

---

[1] Reading with P.   [2] *Cf.* p. 185.

Or to the mighty men possessed of treasure,
Shall injure any tree that beareth fruit,
Or do an act unseemly, trample down
The cornfields, or leave station to advance
Before the troops, I swear by God, the Lord
Of Mars, of Saturn, and of Sol, who gave me
The diadem and might, forthwith to cleave him
Asunder with my sword though like a star
He hide him in the clouds.   I am the scout
Before the host, aspirant, central stay,
Guard of the elephants, of troops, and baggage,
Am now upon the left, now on the right.
I fare o'er land and sea, I seek no rest
And sleep in war."
                    A herald named Shirzád
Laid up at heart the words of Núshírwán,
And made in haste the circuit of the host,
Went round about tent and pavilion,
And cried : " Ye troops in numbers numberless !
The bidding of the watchful Sháh is this :
Whoever, save in justice, love, and wisdom,
Shall look upon this gloomy earth of ours,
Men shall pour out his blood thereon as one
That hath departed from the will of God."
    A proclamation did not satisfy
The Sháh who night and day employed himself
In going on his rounds about the host,
Observing everything both good and bad,
Receiving tidings of the world's affairs,
And slighting nothing whether good or ill.
When any soldier died upon the march
The Sháh prepared a charnel at the place,
And all the man's belongings—silver, gold,
His bow, his helm, his lasso and his belt,
Or good or bad, were buried with the dead,
Who in the grave had still his goods with him.

The world was lost in wonder at the height
Of majesty attained by Núshírwán.
In every place where he engaged in battle
He showed his counsel, caution, and good sense,
And used to call a trusty messenger,
Who went to foes preparing for resistance,
And if they entered on the path of right
The wise Sháh treated them with clemency ;
But, if they fought, that valiant Crocodile
Was very wroth, went forth to fight with them,
And gave their fields and crops to spoil.   He wooed
The world with justice and the scimitar.
The conduct of the Sháh was like the sun's,
Which shineth in its course on wet and dry,
Denying unto none its radiance,   C. 1640
When banishing the clouds from circling heaven,
But giving all its justice and its bounty,
Its hue and scent, its lustrous pearls and waters,
Obscuring unto none its light and height,
But joying hearts and simply shining on.
The king of kings by justice, policy,
And Grace took all the world beneath his wings ;
Both war and bounty were mere play to him,
And thus it was that he attained his greatness.
Confronted by the elephant and lion
He ne'er deferred the combat for a day,
And when a foe was instant to appear
In helm and mail before the host for fight,
Him would they slaughter or in scorn would fling
Bound in the dungeons of the conquering king.

§ 12

How Núshírwán took divers Strongholds in his March to Rúm

He marched upon this wise until he reached
A busy city which was named Shúráb,
Wherein Gushtásp dwelt when he went to Rúm.[1]
The Sháh beheld it rising in the air,
Fulfilled with men and goods, with harp and song,
With stone-foundations springing from the deep,
And battlements up-builded to the clouds.
The troops beleaguered it but saw no means
Of access to the gate.   The Sháh set up
The catapults on all four sides, and then
The ramparts of the Christian crumbled down.
From every quarter came the breath of doom ;
Men saw no place of refuge or escape,
And when the shining sun set in the sky
The castle-walls were level with the plain.
The shouts of cavaliers, the dust of troops,
And fume of fire ascended to the moon.
The strong-hold was all trunkless heads and feet,
Elsewhere were headless trunks.   The cries for quarter,
And women's shrieks, rose o'er the drummers' din.
The magnates eminent for wealth or valour
They bound and laid upon the elephants,
While wails of woe and cries for quarter rose.
The Sháh spared none in battle-tide, he spared not
His treasures and dínárs in banquet-time.
He marched thence till another hold appeared,
Wherein were Cæsar's treasures, and it had
A mighty man for castellan.   'Twas called
Áráyish-i-Rúm till that Núshírwán
'. 1641   Ill-ended it.   The watchful Sháh surveyed

[1] See Vol. iv. p. 325.

That hold, unentered yet by hostile troops,
And bade shoot showers of arrows till the air
Was thick with them as 'tis with hail in spring.
The chieftains bravely stormed the walls and flung
Fire on the city and the citadel,
Wherein no living thing remained alive
Or, in the country round, a thorn or briar.
The Sháh gave Cæsar's treasures up to spoil,
And all the crowns and purses to his troops.
He brought the Day of Doom upon that city,
And all folk fled.   Men, women, children, wailed
Till old and young assembling came before
The noble Sháh and cried aloud for succour :—
" The ministers, the treasurers, and treasure,
Are thine, and thine the gain and toil in Rúm ;
We only beg of thee to spare our lives,
We bondslaves of the Glory of thy crown."
    The Sháh bade cease the slaughtering, and he
Provided for these people bounteously.

§ 13

The Battle of Núshírwán with Farfúriyús, the Leader of Cæsar's
Host, the Victory of Núshírwán, and his Capture of Káli-
niyús and Antákiya

Departing thence the Sháh led on his troops,
And left Áráyish-i-Rúm in his rear.
One came and told him : " Cæsar hath dispatched
A host and lo ! it draweth nigh."
                                    On hearing
Of that great power's approach—all spears and mail—
The Sháh proclaimed the tidings to the troops
That all the host might be prepared.   They marched
As 'twere an iron mountain ; battle-cries

Ascended and the blast of clarions.
A courier with tidings from the scouts
Appeared before the monarch of the world,
And told him : " Cæsar hath dispatched an army
Formed of his famous men and warriors.
Their leader is a mighty paladin,
Whose name in Rúman is Farfúriyús—
A haughty cavalier with trump and drum—
And all his troops long for the fight like wolves."
　　While thus he spake before the watchful Sháh
The dust-clouds of the advancing host appeared.
He smiled and answered thus the messenger :—
" The thing is not unknown to us, for we
Already have prepared the host for battle :
Such thoughts ne'er have been absent from our minds.'
　　Then with his lips afoam he gave command
That all the army should draw up in line.

C. 1642　So host with host confronted, and the air
Was hindered in its passage by the dust.
It was a glorious gathering of troops,
Proud chiefs and wielders of the scimitar,
All with loins tightly girded for the fray—
The great, the sages, and the seed of kings.
The swords of all were reeking with fresh blood,
And trenchant of the clouds.　The enemy
Had no more respite than the quarry hath
From leopard springing.　Rúman slain lay heaped
On all sides while the wounded turned from fight.
Farfúriyús himself thus stricken fled
The field with banner rent and drums o'erthrown.
The horsemen of Írán like pards, when they
Clutch on the waste the mountain-sheep, pursued
The Rúmans, sweeping them from dale and desert.
The Sháh marched on again equipped for war,
The soldiers all with mace and sword in hand.
He led his army on along a plain

Until another lofty hold appeared—
A citadel with soldiers, trump, and drum,
And hight Kálíniyús. The eagle saw not
Its battlements, a full moat girdled it,
And all around it stretched a fair domain
Of halls and gardens, grounds and palaces.
'Twas strongly garrisoned by Rúman troops—
All famous men and eager for the fight.
The Sháh encamped his powers two leagues away,
Earth blackened with the dust-clouds of the host,
And war-cries went up from Kálíniyús—
A clamour that bedwarfed the tymbals' din.
The Sháh marked well that city whereunto
His troops for ever thronged increasingly ;
They battled at the gates and showered down
Their shafts and hand-grenades, and when bright Sol
'Gan pale, and half revolving heaven was dark,
No portion of the castle-walls remained :
That city was all level with the ground.
Then from the Sháh's gate proclamation issued :—
" Ye famous men of the Íránian host !
Come from the city, every man, and pass
The night upon the plain.   If any cry
Shall rise from women and from agéd folk,[1]
Or any sound of pillage, rioting,
And combating, shall reach mine ears at night,
So that but one complain of evil usage,
As soon as such appealeth ye shall see
The skin of the offender stuffed with hay."[2]
    When Sol was stretching out its hand from Cancer,
Had put away fatigue and banished sleep,
The tymbals sounded at the monarch's gate,
Those that were highest in esteem set forth,
And from that hold and seat the men and women   C. 1643
Assembled at the gate of Núshírwán :

" No cavalier of all our warriors
Is left," they said, " or magnate in this city ;
They all, though guiltless, have been slain or wounded,
And it is time for pardon from the Shâh,
Because God's justice never will approve
That women, babes, and elders should be captive.
The citadel and city's walls are such
That henceforth thou wilt see but thorn-brakes here.
Since Cæsar was the offender how are we—
The people of Kálíniyús—to blame ? "
     The Shâh gave pardon to those Rúmans : both
The guilty and the innocent escaped.
He left with them an ample store of wealth,
And marched his army with all speed away ;
But all the folk that he saw fit for arms
They bound on elephants and carried off.
Then news to Antákiya came : " The Shâh
Is on his way with elephants and troops."
     Now at that city was a boundless host
Of Rúman warriors and mighty men.
The Shâh accorded to them three days' grace
That he might war not on them wrongfully,
But on the fourth his host came mountain-like—
The warriors of Írán in close array—
While for the sake of women, children, land,
And wealth the cavaliers of Rúm advanced.
They fought three mighty battles in three days,
But on the fourth day when the sun arose
The marches of that prosperous land lay open,
The Íránians saw no Rúman cavaliers,
The soldiers took possession of the place,
And filled it till there was no room to stand.
The great men that had thrones and coronets,
And those that were the treasurers of Cæsar,
Gave up the treasure to the Shâh—the world-lord—
The treasure unto him that bare the toil.

The Íránians set in bonds on elephants
All that were warriors among that folk.
The Sháh dispatched to Madá'in the captives,
And all the wealth of Cæsar, then went round
The city and beheld a country-side
More brilliant than the orbéd moon. The gardens,
The parks, and streams, restored old age to freshness
And youth. The king addressed his nobles thus :—
" Can this be Antákiya or young spring ?
Whoe'er hath seen not jocund Paradise
Whereof the soil is musk, the bricks are gold,
Whose waters are rose-water and trees jewels,
Whose country is the sky, whose heaven the sun,
Should look on this fresh land, and may it be—
This land of Rúm—in full prosperity."

§ 14

How Núshírwán built the City of Zíb-i-Khusrau in the Likeness
of Antákiya and settled the Rúman Captives therein

Then Núshírwán gave orders to construct   C. 1644
A city having palaces and streams,
Like Antákiya, radiant as a lamp—
All rosaries and mansions, parks and gardens.
The great men, bright of heart and happy, called it
Zíb-i-Khusrau.[1] 'Twas like the jocund spring—
A paradise all colour, scent, and beauty.
The captives taken in the towns of Rúm,
Whose hands and feet were galled with heavy bonds,
Were set at large by Núshírwán's command,
And sent to dwell in joy in that new city.
He said : " We have erected this new seat—
All gardens, rosaries, and palaces—

---

[1] The Ornament of Khusrau.

That each might have a dwelling to his mind
And worthy of his name."
                              He gave to each
Goods, and the earth was decked like Paradise.
At sight of all the mansions, streets, and marts
Thou wouldst have said : " Each space is occupied."
A clamorous cordwainer came and said —:
" O unjust Sháh ! there was a mulberry
Within my dwelling at Kálíniyús
Before my courtyard ; from Zib-i-Khusrau
I have not any such advantages,
For there is no such tree before my door."
     So Núshírwán bade men to plant green trees
Before the door of that misfortuned one.
     The Sháh then chose a Christian unto whom
He gave authority, wealth, troops, and said :—
" Zib-i-Khusrau is thine and thine the charge
Of all the stranger-folk and their new home.
Be like a tree that beareth fruit and be
The city's sire at whiles, at whiles its son.
Be bountiful and beautify the place,
Not covetous, and keep the mean in all."
     The Sháh marched forth from Antákiya, leaving
A Christian and experienced man in charge.
     Farfúriyús thereafter brought to Cæsar
Intelligence about Kálíniyús,
And said to him : " The experienced Núshírwán
Came in his state with troops and elephants.
So mighty is his host that seas and mountains
Are all confounded by the horses' dust."
     Then Cæsar writhed for that which he had spoken,
And called to him his prudent chiefs.   His heart
Was full of fear because of Núshírwán ;
All day and through three watches of the night
He canvassed what to do.   Thus spake a priest :—

" Thou'rt ill-advised because thou hast not power

To fight with Núshírwán.   The foe will raise
The dust from this fair realm and bring to naught
The achievements of the Cæsars.   In debate
The feeble-tongued endangereth the state."

§ 15

How Cæsar wrote to Núshírwán and sent Tribute

Now Cæsar heard this and his heart was troubled,
His counsels were o'ercast by Núshírwán.
He chose of the philosophers of Rúm
From regions scathless of the enemy,
A man of eloquence and understanding,
While of the priests three score unsmirched in soul
And wisdom volunteered.   He sent the Sháh
An embassage.   Those magnates took their way.
Their leader was that man of wits, Mihrás—
A warrior old in wisdom, young in years.
There went before them treasures of all kinds
Past reckoning, while Cæsar, who repented
His language in the past, dispatched no stint
Of adulation, counsels, and fair words,
With heavy tribute and with hostages
Both of his own and of his nobles' kin.
Mihrás, when he had come to Núshírwán,
Pronounced his praises in the Rúman tongue,
And thou hadst said : "So shrewd and just is he,
He will produce stars from his sleeves ! "   'Twas thus
He spake to Núshírwán : "Set not, O king !
Such value on the world.   Thou art in Rúm
Now and Írán is void ; it hath not worth
Or Glory.   So, when Cæsar is away
From Rúm, this country valueth not one gnat.
The worth deriveth wholly from the man ;
When he is lost the value is lost too.

If this commotion be but for wealth's sake—
That ruiner of wisdom and contentment—
Lo ! I have brought thee all the wealth of Rúm,
For more than land and treasure is a soul
Serene."
        The king's heart, when he heard this, grew
As jocund as a garden in the spring,
And he accepted what the envoy brought—
The purses of gold coin, and hostages—
Gave commendations to the ambassadors,
Enlarging on the value of the gifts,
And said : " O clear in wisdom ! any one
Whom wisdom feedeth is a mighty man.
If all the soil of Rúm were turned to gold
Thou wouldst outvalue still that noble land."
    They set as tribute on those fields and fells
A hundred ox-hides brimming with dinárs

'. 1646
To be dispatched by Cæsar to the king
Each year with other gifts and offerings.
His troops were not to ocupy Yaman,
Or to require aught of the people there.
Therewith was heard the blare of trump and clash
Of brazen cymbals, and the prudent world-lord
Led back his host.   He went his way to Shám,
And tarried there awhile.   He brought with him
So many implements of war and troops,
So many captives, purses, crowns, and thrones,
That earth's back bent beneath the elephants,
And purses full of drachms.   When he resolved
To quit that land he set in charge thereof
Shírwí, son of Bahrám, and said : " Demand
The tribute due from Cæsar and accord not
Remission for a month or day."
                          Shírwí,
Who kissed the ground, blessed and addressed the
    Shah :—

" Mayst thou be happy and victorious,
And may the royal Tree ne'er pale its leaves."
    When at the monarch's portal had begun
The drum-roll flag and troops fared toward Arman.

§ 16

*The Birth of Núshzád, the Son of Núshírwán, by a
Woman who was a Christian*

Like to the sun was Núshírwán, the king—
    The world's hope and its fear.   Just as above
Sol speedeth on its pathway carrying
    A sword in this hand and in that hand love,
Is all relentless in its hour of rage,
    But in its day of ruth all clemency,
So was this Sháh of royal lineage,
    Who had adorned the world with equity.
Know this—in my regard the monarch's state
    And subject's, if they holy be and pure,
Requireth of necessity a mate,
    Dress, provand, and a privacy secure ;
While if the wife be pious and discreet
    A heaped-up treasure will she prove, and all
The more if locks musk-scented to her feet
    Descend, and she be more than common tall,
Wise, learned, well counselled, chaste, and can express
Herself in fair discourse with gentleness.
The noble Sháh possessed a wife like this,
In height a cypress and in looks a moon,
This Moon-face was a Christian, and her beauty
Engrossed the tongues of all.   She bare a babe
Sun-faced, out-shining Venus in the sky.
The noble mother called the child Núshzád,
And no fierce blast assailed that lovely boy.

. 1647   He grew up as he were a straight-stemmed cypress—
A youth of parts, the glory of the realm.
He knew of Hell, the path to Paradise,
Of Christ, of Esdras, and Zarduhsht, but he,
Believing not the Zandavasta, bathed
His visage in the fount of Christ, preferring
His mother's to his father's Faith : the age
Was lost in wonderment at him.   The king
Was grievously concerned about his son,
Because that Rose bare only fruit of thorns.
They shut the portal of Núshzád's fair palace,
And there imprisoned him.   His prison-house
Was at Gund-i-Shápúr [1] far from his home
And father.   Many criminals and captives
Were with him in that city and in ward.
Now when the Sháh was on his way from Rúm
The turmoil and the journey tried him sorely ;
So weak was he that he could hold no court.
One bare the tidings to Núshzád and told him :—
" The Glory of the empire is bedimmed ;
The watchful world-lord Núshírwán is dead,
Bequeathing to another earth and time."
    His father's death rejoiced Núshzád.   Oh ! may
No pleasure and enjoyment e'er be his !
    He that doth joy when just kings pass away
Must have a gloomy temper.   As to this
    A famous ancient said : " If thou art glad
At my decease see that thou never die."
    From death thou know'st no succour can be had,
The past is one here with futurity ;
    But never death will wreck the soul of one
Whose toil hath favour in the sight of God.
    Call we a reprobate and fool that son
Who in his father's footsteps hath not trod.
    Wet be the seed of colocynth or dry

    [1] Kand-i-Shápúr in the text.   For this city see p. 219.

It will not savour musk, then where the need
    That it should change from what should spring
      thereby
By nature if the gardener sow its seed ?
    When any plant is predisposed to earth,
It parteth with the sunshine and pure air,
    Therefrom no foliage or fruit hath birth,
It liveth for the earth and dieth there.

§ 17

The Sickness of Núshírwán and the Sedition of Núshzád

I have made mention of Núshzád. Take heed
    That thou quit not the path of equity.
If heaven possessed a father then indeed
    He would resemble Núshírwán, so why
Should his own son quit the paternal way,
    And seek the royal dignity and throne ?
Accord thine ear to all that I shall say,   C. 1648
    And I will keep back nothing, O my son !
I have well ordered that I did receive
    From rustic bard, and by that token too
Am fain some memory of myself to leave,
    So be the honour unto whom 'tis due.
This is my wish that after I am dead
    My fame as poet evermore shall last.
On this wise spake a Persian bard whose head
    A hundred years and twenty had o'erpast :—
" He that is hostile to the world's great king
    Not of man's stock but Áhriman's must be."
Now of Núshzád they tell that very thing
    As handed down by ancient legendry.
Whenas the son of Núshírwán had heard :—
" The throne of that right royal Tree is void,"

He oped his palace-door, and from all quarters
Troops gathered unto him—all that had 'scaped
From wisdom's bonds and had been put in ward
By Núshírwán.   Núshzád unchained the mad,
And all the city was in consternation ;
But he assembled of the citizens
All that were Christians, whether priests or prelates,
Assembled many haughty cavaliers
And swordsmen, while his mother gave him wealth—
The treasures lavished on her by the Sháh.
There gathered to him thirty thousand men,
All famous and prepared to fight.   He took
The cities round ; his fame was noised abroad.
He wrote a letter to his kinsman [1] Cæsar,
Made known his dark designs, and said : " Arise
O king ! for thou art lord, friend, of one Faith
With me, and Cæsar.   As 'twere Rúm, Írán,
Its worship and its settlements, are thine,
My father hath been sick and now is dead,
His wakeful fortune hath been overthrown."
    The tidings reached the towns of Madá'in
Of what the son of Núshírwán had done,
Whereat the warden of that march dispatched
To Núshírwán a cavalier to whom
He told what he had heard and what was secret.
The messenger went like a rapid stream,
And came to Núshírwán to whom he gave
The letter, telling all that he had heard,
And of the overt actions of Núshzád.
The Sháh, when he had listened and had read
The letter, grieved thereat and was confounded,
Held session with the noble archimages,
Debating much with them in privacy,
And, when the consultation reached its end
In resolution, bade a scribe attend.

[1] In the Faith. *Cf.* p. 269. .

§ 18

The Letter of Núshírwán to Rám Barzín, the Warden of the March of Madá'in, respecting the Taking of Núshzád

The Sháh, both seared and sore, with frowning face   C. 1649
And sighing lips, then had this letter written
Wherein he first of all gave praise to Him,
Who fashionéd the heavens, time, and earth,
The Artificer of Sun and Moon and Saturn,
The Illuminer of Grace, of crown, and throne :—
" From worthless stubble up to elephant
And lion, from the dust on emmet's foot
Up to the Nile, though men shall roam from earth
To turning heaven they roam beneath God's sway.
No limit can be seen to His behest,
And none will rob Him of the sovereignty.
Of that unpleasing letter have I heard,
Sent by that most injurious son of mine,
And of the criminals who brake from ward,
And are assembled now about Núshzád.
'Twere better one should quit the world than see
A day like this, for all are born to die ;
First Núshírwán and then Núshzád must go.
From gnat and ant e'en to rhinoceros,
And elephant, none can escape the claws
And beak of death. If earth revealed its secrets,
Displaying everything from first to last,
Its bosom would be found fulfilled with kings,
Its breast with blood of cavaliers, its skirts
With men of lore, the creases of its robe
With fair-cheeked dames. Then wherefore set a crown
Or helmet on thy head when death's plumed shaft
Will pierce them both ? No one rejoiceth much
At death of son, albeit all must die ;
But as for those consorting with Núshzád,

Who reckon on the death of Núshírwán,
The death of them would be a cause for joy
If but Núshzád should 'scape the evil day.
Moreover none but misbegotten knaves
Would count upon the death of righteous Sháhs.
Now though Núshzád hath turned his head from us,
In that the Div thus hath conspired with him,
His purpose is not firm in this regard ;
He was inflamed when he obtained his wish.
He could not have the post as well as we,
And thus was ruined by a false report,
For had the crown been void of Núshírwán
Núshzád had been the glory of the realm.
Still such an act is worthy of his Faith,
And suited to an evil soul like his.
C. 1650   I am not moved or fearful in this matter,
In that our son's religion is impure :
Moreover for the wealth that he hath wrecked,
That matter weigheth nothing on my heart ;
While as for all that have combined with him,
And banished from their hearts their awe of us—
The ill-doers, the malignant, and base-born,
Unworthy to be subjects to myself—
We look upon them also with contempt :
Let not their doings make thy heart afraid.
My fear is of the Master of the world,
Who is in wisdom wiser than the wise.
We must not grow unthankful in our souls
To God who is omniscient in good.
Me hath He given triumph and success,
Grace and the diadem of king of kings,
And had my praise been worthy of His gifts
It would have bettered my prosperity.
My son hath found a home and rest elsewhere ;
No single drop of him came from my loins.
With his awakening my foe arrived,

And, I do fear me, toil.   Still if the World-lord
Hath no occasion to be wroth with me
I reck not of such things.   In my regard
All they that are confederate with my son
Are vile and despicable.   'Tis his letter
That, if it bringeth Cæsar, will befoul
My stream.   The twain must be akin, methinketh,
Since they are one in Faith and policy.
The man that quitteth his forefathers' Faith
Is one whose wits are much to seek.   That son
Is best who is of one Faith, not at war,
With his own sire.   Albeit though that insensate
Turn from the right no lip must ope to curse him.
To curse him is in essence to curse us,
Because he is of our own flesh and blood.
Array the host, take order for the war,
But act with moderation and hold back,
While if the matter cometh to a pass,
And if he offer battle, be not fierce.
To capture him is better than to slay :
Perchance he will turn back from evil doing,
And then the stream that reared that noble Cypress
Must come not on it in a bath of dust ;
But if he hold his honoured person cheaply,
If that tall Cypress shall demean itself,
And if he spurn the pillow of delight,
Withhold not thou the mace and scimitar.
A man of rank indulging base desires
Can not be freed from that propensity,
And such a high-born man is base indeed
When he doth fight the monarch of the world.
Fear not to slay him if he would pour out
His own head's blood upon the dust.   He hasteth
To give his faith to Cæsar and put off   C. 1651
Allegiance to our crown, whereby his greatness
Hath grown vile, wretched, and calamitous,

And he hath chosen ruin from high heaven.
In this regard said Mihr-i-Núsh—a sage
Who worshipped God and wore the woollen vest :—
' The man that joyeth in a father's death,
May his be neither happiness nor breath.'
Seek not for light from darkness, else wilt thou
But mingle fire and water in the stream.
Man's only rest is when his toil is done :
It is fate's law and we must acquiesce.
Be not in friendship with the turning sky,
For whiles thou art the kernel, whiles the shell.
Why seek from its pomegranate hue and scent,
For it will rob thee of them both at sight ?
Whene'er the turning sky exalteth thee,
Then is thy time for travail, fear, and loss.
As for the soldiers that are with Núshzád,
And err so greatly from the path of duty,
Know that they are but wind and sport to us,
The mockery of the wise, no mystery.
As for the Christians that are in his host,
And have revolted for religion's sake,
The regimen of Christ is such that they
Are frighted if one lifteth up one's voice,[1]
Desert his precepts and his path, and end
By turning into foemen of the Cross.
As for the other folk—the common herd,
Ill-taught, ill-minded, and adventurous—
They will not fright the heart of any man :
Their counsel and a breath of air are one.
Now if Núshzád be taken in the fight,
Discourse not with him touching these affairs ;
His person must not suffer injury,
His raiment must not show the rents of blows,
Because his women-folk will slay themselves.
His palace will afford the best of prisons

---

[1] The Persian word for a Christian also means a coward. *Cf.* p. 219.

Both for himself and those that follow him.
Bar not to him the portal of my treasures,
Albeit one so dear hath grown so vile,
And as for raiment, victuals, tapestries,
And carpets there must be no stint at all,
For he is fitted but for things like these.
As for those marchlords of the Íránians—
Those that have girded up their loins with him—
When thou hast conquered do not hesitate,
But cleave them through the middle with the sword,
For all that are the great king's enemies
Thou rightly flingest to the crocodiles.
Besides these, all that are opposed to me
At heart—the seed of wicked Áhriman—
Who have forgotten all our benefits,
Thou now wilt test in dealing with Núshzád.
All acted as our watchmen heretofore,

V. 1652

And were in terror of our punishments.
For those on-lookers who have vilified,
And wagged their tongues against, Núshzád, know thou
That they have in especial cursed ourselves,
Preparing trouble in mine evil day.
Do not thou too as they ; thus foemen speak.
Unworthy as he is he is mine own,
Such is the truthful witness of my heart.
The tongue of each man that hath spoken ill,
Or acted with injustice toward him, brand
In presence of the folk.   May such an one
Have neither tongue nor mouth.   As for the man
That warreth to o'erthrow the Sháh, employing
Guile, enmity, hostility, and faith
In Áhriman, such, as the famed Sháh's foe,
Must not be suffered in the realm."
                              They set
The Sháh's own seal upon the letter.   Then
The messenger departed with all speed,

And, when to Rám Barzin he made his way,
Told all that he had heard the great king say.

§ 19

*How Rám Barzín fought with Núshzád, and how Núshzád
was slain*

That done, he gave to Rám Barzin the letter
With its behests for dealing with Núshzád,
To levy troops, make war, and banish ruth.
When the old man had read it, and had heard
The messenger at large, the din of tymbals
Arose at cock-crow at the palace-portal,
A mighty host marched forth from Madá'in,
And Rám Barzin went swiftly to the war.
News reached Núshzád who called and paid his host,
While all the Christians and grandees of Rúm
That dwelt along the march of that fair land
Assembled with Shammás as general :   •
Those warriors' hands all had been bathed in blood.
A shout rose from the portal of Núshzád,
And then the army, like a wind-tossed sea,
Moved from the city out upon the plain,
Their heads all war, their hearts revenge and venom.
When Rám Barzin beheld that army's dust
He blew the trumpets and arrayed the host.
The dust of cavaliers, the charge of chieftains,
The brandishing of mighty maces, rent
The hearts of flints ; none saw the bright sun's face.
. 1653 Then in the centre of the host Núshzád
Set on his head a Rúman helm. His host
Was full of Christian clericals from Rúm ;
The soil was hidden by their horses' hoofs.
Thou wouldst have said : " Earth seetheth, and the air
Is shrieking over it."
                          A warrior,

Beclad in mail and hight Pírúz the old,
Came boldly forth and cried : " O famed Núshzád !
Who wantonly hath turned thy head from right ?
Contend not with the army of the king
Because thou wilt repent thee of this strife.
Thou hast abjured the Faith of Gaiúmart,
The pathway of Húshang and Tahmúras.
The arch-deceiver Christ was put to death
Because he had renounced the Faith of God ;
So choose not him, of all that founded Faiths,
Who so mistook the aspect of his work,
For if the Grace of God had shone in him
How could the Jews have gained the upper hand ?
Heard hast thou what thy sire, that noble man,
The world-lord, did to Cæsar and to Rúm,
Yet now thou wouldst contend with him and raise
Thy head to heaven ! For all thy moon-like mien,
Thy Grace and stature, neck, limbs, hands, and
    mace,
I see no wisdom with thee anywhere,
Such recklessness possesseth thy dark soul !
Woe for this head of thine, crown, name, and birth,
Which now thou wouldst abandon to the blast !
For son to seek his living father's throne,
How should this be ? 'Tis neither use nor right.
To seek the crown, if he be dead, is well ;
To seek to fight him now is criminal.
Save thou be snorting elephant or lion
Thou canst not match Sháh Núshírwán, and though
I have not seen, O prince ! a bridle-hand
Like thine limned in the palace of the Sháhs,
Such foot and stirrups, such a breast and neck,
Such ardour in the fight and such a mace,
Though painter never looked on such a picture,
Or any age on such a prince, yet burn not
The soul of Núshírwán by childishness,

Or stultify the world-illuming crown,
For hostile howsoe'er a son may be
His father will lament when he is slain.
Dismount, ask quarter of the Sháh, and fling
This mace and Rúman helmet to the ground ;
Then if far hence some chilling blast should make
The dark dust settle on thy countenance,
The Sháh's heart would consume for thee, the sun
Weep o'er thy face.   Sow not throughout the world
The seed of enmity, for hastiness
Becometh not a prince.   If thou dost swerve
From mine advice and trust to violence,
And to thy might, the counsel of Pirúz

.1654   Oft will recur to thee, and then the words
Of thine ill counsellors will seem but wind."
   Núshzád made answer : " O wind-pated dotard !
Ask not my troops—exalted warriors—
Or me—the Sháh's son—to cry out for quarter.
The Faith of Núshírwán is naught to me ;
My heart inclineth to my mother—her
Whose constant practice is the Faith of Christ.
I will not quit her Grace and Faith.   Although
Its   Founder—Christ—was   slain,   the   World-lord's
   Grace
Hath not forsaken Him.   That Holy One
Hath passed from this earth back to holy God,
Such was His aspiration when on earth.
I may be slain but shall not fear to die,
For to that bane there is no antidote."
   He answered thus the old Pirúz and veiled
Air's face with shafts.   The warriors of the host
Advanced, the battle-cry and clarion's blare
Went up, Núshzád, the chief, spurred on like fire,
Came as it were Ázargashasp, and brake
The left wing of the army of the Sháh,
Where none remained to fight with him.   He slew

Full many a Lion of the host, whereat,
Grown wrathful, Rám Barzín bade shower arrows,
And fill the air as 'twere with hail in spring.
The din of battle went up on both sides
From all the valiant soldiers there engaged.
Núshzád was wounded in the mellay. Oft
He called to mind the counsel of Pirúz,
And reached in pain the centre of the host,
Pierced by a shaft and pale with agony.
Thus said he to the warriors of Rúm :—
" To fight one's sire is wretched, vile, accursed ! "
    Bewailing and lamenting thus he summoned
A bishop and confessed his heart's desires.
He said : " The evil fortune caused by me
Hath fal!en rigorously upon myself.
Now, since my head will pass beneath the dust,
Dispatch a horseman to my mother. Say
To her : ' Núshzád hath left this world. For him
The days of right and wrong are at an end.
I prithee be not grieved at heart for me ;
Such is the fashion of this Wayside Inn !
Since I have been allotted this dark day
How could my heart be glad and brighten earth ?
All living creatures are but born to die ;
Grieve not for me, for thou art mortal too.
'Tis not my slaying that confoundeth me,
But worse—my sire's displeasure. Let me have
No mausoleum, throne, or stately rites,
But bury me with Christian burial.
I need no camphor, musk, or spicery,
For arrow-stricken I depart the world.' "
    He spake and shut his lips. Thus passed Núshzád, C. 1655
That noble Lion-heart. Now when his troops
Heard of his death they fled the battlefield.
The Íránian leader, hearing that the prince
Was slain, went weeping to his couch in haste.

The troops ceased slaying on the field of fight,
And neither joyed nor spoiled. They saw the prince
Slain and o'erthrown with ignominy, his head
Upon a Rúman bishop's breast : the field
Was filled with wailing for him.   Rám Barzín
Was troubled to the heart and asked the prelate :—
" What know'st thou of the prince's dying wishes ? "
    " Except his mother," thus the bishop answered,
" None must behold his head exposed.   He, seeing
That he was wounded by a shaft, forbade
All obsequies and musk and spicery,
Or coronet, brocade of Rúm, and throne,
Perceiving his to be the slave's dark lot.
His mother now will shroud him and provide
A tomb and winding-sheet with Christian rites,
While his condition now is that of Christ's,
Although he did not die upon the Cross."
    Of all the Christians that were in the land
There was not one but had his visage torn.
A cry rose from the country.   Men and women
Assembled.   From the plain they raised the corpse
Of that young, gallant prince—the Heart and Eyes
Of Núshírwán, the Sháh—upon a bier,
Transporting it three leagues by hand, then set it
Upon two mules which bare it to his mother.
Now when she was aware of what had chanced
Her head and crown descended to the dust.
She came forth to the street unveiled.   A crowd
Assembled round her in the market-place.
They set a camp-enclosure round about,
And all the folk cast dust upon their heads.
They laid him in the earth.   He passed.   He came
From wind and suddenly to wind returned.
Gund-i-Shápúr [1] was all in tears, consumed
With sorrow for the anguish of the Sháh.'
Why writhe so madly in the bonds of greed ?

[1] See p. 219.

Thou know'st that here thou canst not long remain.
Seek to escape, give not the world such heed,
  Smell not its rose so fondly, 'tis but bane.
From Faith and righteousness turn not thy head,
  Or else the wrath of God will chasten thee ;
" A father's wrath," a pious Arab said,
  " Will bring upon thy life calamity."
When sire shall be displeased with son in aught
  Know that in seed and fruit that son is bad.
Oh ! never make thy father's soul distraught
  Whatever trouble thou from him hast had.
When thou'rt secure refrain thy heart from woe,   C. 1656
  Nor on thy heart the fire of trouble fling,
Let not thy passions master wisdom so,
  But act with seemliness in everything.[1]
Now be the world's king happy all his days,
  And may he bear these words of mine in mind.
Mahmúd, the world-lord, who ensueth praise,
  A niche therefor in every heart will find.
Love ever shineth from his Grace divine,
  His crown's top is the pillar of the sky.
Now ask, if cup thou hast, for amber wine,
  And hold not quaffing acting sinfully.
Seek joy and mirth but never be bemused,
Nor think that talk—wise talk—should be abused.

[1] *Four couplets omitted.*

PART II

THE STORY OF BÚZURJMIHR AND OF THE SEVEN BANQUETS OF NÚSHÍRWÁN

ARGUMENT

The Sháh, being disquieted by a dream, sends emissaries through the empire to find an interpreter. One is discovered at Marv in the person of Búzurjmihr, then a youth, who having been brought before the Sháh interprets the dream and is advanced to great honour. The Sháh subsequently gives a series of entertainments at which discussions on wisdom and morals are substituted for the usual diversions of Oriental banquets, and Búzurjmihr again greatly distinguishes himself.

NOTE

Persia, like other nations, has its Wisdom-literature. This comprises apologues, apothegms, proverbs, parables, the interpretation of dreams and dark sentences, astrological forecasts, the solution of problems, the supplying the correct answer to questions relating to religion, morals, conduct, and expediency, and longer discourses thereon, reflections on fate and fortune, on the uncertainty of all terrestrial affairs, on the vanity of striving after wealth and fame, and the importance of leaving behind one a good name after death. All these forms of wisdom find expression in the Sháhnáma, and the poet himself has been not backward in contributing his quota. At the first available opportunity in his work he utters his " Praise of Wisdom "—the first created of God and His best gift to man.[1] A collection of all the passages dealing with such themes and subjects as are mentioned above, and including Firdausí's own reflections on such matters, as have occurred in the poem up to this point, would amount to something considerable, but scattered through a mass of narrative they are apt to be overlooked. In this reign, however, we are confronted by formal collections of primitive Persian Wisdom associated for the most part with the name of Búzurjmihr but to some extent with other great officials and with

---

[1] Vol. i. p. 101. *Cf.* too p. 103, *supra.*

Núshírwán himself. Firdausi availed himself of the opportunity of the conjunction of the just Sháh with the wise counsellor to bring together all that he could find in his authorities and elsewhere on some of the subjects mentioned at the beginning of this note. That a large Pahlavi literature once existed on such matters, and arranged sometimes in the form of question and answer, we know from what is extant. Thus the sage in the "Diná-í Maínóg-í Khirad" ("Opinions of the Spirit of Wisdom") consults the Spirit of Wisdom on sixty-two points and receives answers, e.g. "The sage asked the spirit of wisdom thus: 'Which man is the mightier?' . . . The spirit of wisdom answered thus: 'That man is the mightier who is able to struggle with his own fiends; and, in particular, *he* who keeps these five fiends far from *his* person, which are such as greediness, wrath, lust, disgrace, and discontent.'"[1] The concluding question is: "Which is that good work which is greater and better than all good works, and no trouble whatever is necessary for its performance?" The answer is: "To be grateful in the world, *and* to wish happiness for every one. This is greater and better than every good work, and no commotion whatever is necessary for its performance."[2] These questions and answers are quite of a piece with the sages' gnomes in the poem. There are also extant in Pahlaví the "Pandnámak-í Vadshórg-Mitró-í Búkhtakán" or "Bakhtagán," *i.e.* the "Book of Counsels of Búzurjmihr the son of Bakhtagán," the "Characteristics of a Happy Man," and other texts dealing with similar subjects.[3] There can be no doubt but that Firdausí derived the sententious, gnomic, parenetic, or whatever one chooses to call them, portions of the Sháhnáma, like the narrative, indirectly from the Pahlavi. Four series of such passages occur in the present reign. The first and longest is in the present Part. The second is Búzurjmihr's *Discourse on good deeds and works* in Part III. The third is Núshírwán's answers to the questions addressed to him by the archmages. The fourth is the *vivâ voce* examination that Hurmuzd, Núshírwán's son, has to pass at the hands of Búzurjmihr, by order of the Sháh, before being nominated as his father's successor. One cannot help feeling a sneaking sympathy, reprehensible though it be, with him when we find him signalising his advent to the throne by making a clean sweep of his father's ministers from whose "wise saws and modern instances" doubtlessly he had suffered much in the days of his youth. Nero acted similarly in the case of Burrus and the younger Seneca. Of these four series the third is concerned only partly with Wisdom-literature, some

---

[1] WPT, iii. 81. [2] *Id.* 113. [3] GIP, ii. 113 *seq.*

of the questions dealing with Núshírwán's own conduct on specified occasions. This and the fourth series will appear in Volume VIII.

Búzurjmihr, the son of Bakhtagán, of Marv, the man chiefly associated with the Wisdom-literature of the Sháhnáma, is but a semi-historical figure hardly mentioned by any historian before Firdausí's time with the exception of Mas'údi who died when the poet was a youth. Mas'údi gives twelve maxims of Búzurjmihr's and little else,[1] so that practically we are dependent on what Firdausi tells us, and this, with regard to the incidents recorded, generally has something of the præternatural about it. Búzurjmihr's career begins with a dream, and while sleeping on his journey to the court a snake, which seems an Arab rather than a Persian touch, comes and breathes over him. Moreover, his fall from power is preceded by an omen and his restoration to favour accomplished by another. We never hear of him as being associated with any of Núshírwán's great achievements in administration or in war. He is employed, it is true, upon two missions, once to expound a game—chess—and to propound another of his own invention—nard—and once to negotiate in time of war a loan for his master, which falls through owing to the fact that Núshírwán has a higher conception of the dignity of the office of the scribe than Búzurjmihr himself. His repute seems largely due to Firdausi, who used him as a peg whereon to hang all the old clothes of the Wisdom-literature that the poet was too conscientious to discard but could not dispose of elsewhere. There is, however, a thanksgiving couplet to testify that he was not sorry when the worst of his task was over.[2] If the number seven were not such a favourite in Persian story one might suggest that the Seven Banquets of Núshírwán originated in a perverted reminiscence of the seven Greek philosophers who were entertained for a while at his court when Justinian closed the schools of Athens,[3] and that Búzurjmihr himself is not much more than a native composite reproduction of those hapless and disillusioned sages.

Mohl has some apposite remarks on the Wisdom-literature:

" Ce qui a le plus contribué à la gloire du règne de Nouschirwan, c'est la réputation de son vizir, Buzurdjmihr, qui est en Orient le représentant de toute la sagesse humaine, comme Nouschirwan lui-même est la représentation de la justice. On les a entourés tous les deux d'une auréole de fables, et l'on a mis sous leurs noms tous les contes qui se rattachent par leur nature à la renommée particulière de chacun. On a donc attribué à Buzurdjmihr tous

---

[1] MM, ii. 206 *seq.*, vii. 164.   [2] See p. 379.   [3] GDF, v. 93.

les traits de sagesse et toutes les moralités qu'on a pu trouver, et *Firdousi* les rapporte au long les uns et les autres. Quant aux moralités, le poëte avait évidemment découvert quelques collections où on les avait réunies, et il nous en donne à trois reprises différentes, ou des traductions complètes, ou d'amples extraits. Je crois que les originaux ont dû être composés en pehlewi, et que ces sentences ont éprouvé quelque dommage, soit de la part des copistes, soit de celle des traducteurs, car les questions et les réponses ne paraissent pas toujours s'accorder suffisamment. De plus, les copistes du *Livre des Rois* on évidemment été arrêtés par le texte et ont fait pour le redresser beaucoup d'effort malheureux. . . . Il est très-probable encore que les sentences que nous trouvons dans les moralistes arabes et persans sont des restes de cette antique sagesse des Perses. Les observations et les règles qu'elles contiennent nous paraissent en général bien simples et parfois bien puériles ; mais cela même parle pour leur origine reculée. Elles ont été une fois neuves et frappantes et ont été transmises aux nouvelles générations, entourées du respect qu'inspire en toute chose la réputation d'antiquité. Ce n'est certainement pas dans une monarchie comme celle de la Perse sous Nouschirwan, que commençait à tomber de vétusté, qu'on avait besoin d'inventer des moralités élémentaires." [1]

On the same subject Nöldeke says : " In the discourses on wisdom and riddles which take up so much space in the story of the first Chosrau (Kisrâ) are probably to be found many duplicates of whole passages ; to settle these questions much material besides the Sháhnáma is available, but truly to investigate these wearying fragments would require an unusual amount of patience ! " [2]

§ 1

How Núshírwán had a Dream and how Búzurjmihr interpreted it

Now in the tale of Búzurjmihr will we
    Reveal a cheerier visage. Do not deem
    That there is naught but folly in a dream ;
Know that a dream may smack of prophecy,
And in especial when such visitings

[1] P, Vol. vi. Préface.   [2] NPS, II, p. 29.

Impress the clear mind of a king of kings.
The stars with sky and moon hold conference,
  Their words are whispered and dispersed through
    space,
And clear souls dreaming see the future thence
  As fire is mirrored in the water's face.
One night Sháh Núshírwán, the wise and shrewd,
That lucid spirit, lay asleep and dreamed :
A royal tree grew up before the throne,
And joyed his heart.   He called for harp and wine
And minstrelsy, but on his throne of peace
And joy there sat with him a sharp-toothed boar,
Sat ready-dight for revelry and claimed
To quaff the wine from Núshírwán's own cup.
Sol rose in Taurus and the skylark's note
Was heard on all sides yet the monarch sat
Upon his throne in dudgeon at that dream.
They called the interpreter of dreams and held
A session of the magnates at the court.
The Sháh narrated to those archimages,
The counsellors, his dream.   The interpreter
. 1657 Made no reply, he knew of no such case,
And one that pleadeth ignorance is excused.
The Sháh, thus left unanswered by the sages,
Was instant what to do in his concern,
And sent to every side an archimage,
One enterprising, shrewd of heart, and wise.
He made each take a purse and entertained
High hopes from their return.   In every purse
There were ten thousand drachms that every envoy
Might seek out some interpreter of dreams,
Some man of understanding, some adept,
To solve the world-king's dream and to reveal
The mystery, and then bestow on such
A full purse and the royal compliments.[1]

> [1] Reading with P.

So to all parts a veteran archmage went—
A prudent cavalier and man of lore.
One of these chiefs—Ázád Sarv [1]—came to Marv,
Went through the town and saw an archimage,
Who taught the Zandavasta to some youths
With harshness, anger, and raised voice. The tallest,
An earnest student of the Zandavasta,
One whom they used to title Búzurjmihr,
Was poring lovingly upon the roll.
Ázád Sarv turned his rein, drew near, and sought
An explanation of the great king's dream.
The scribe replied : " 'Tis not my business ;
The Zandavasta is my help to knowledge.
I teach these children but I do not dare
To breathe of aught beyond," but Búzurjmihr
Said blushing to his master, having heard
The envoy's words : " This quarry is for me ;
It is my business to interpret dreams."
   His teacher bawled : " Hast thou thy roll by heart
That thou shouldst thus exalt thy neck in pride,
And set up as a dream-interpreter ? "
   The envoy said to him : " O learnéd man !
He may possess this skill ; abash him not.
This youth's lot may be high through fortune's teaching,
Not thine."
          The master wroth with Búzurjmihr
Cried : " Tell then what thou knowest," but he
   answered :—
" I will speak not till set before the Sháh."
   The envoy gave him money and a steed
With all things needful. They set off from Marv,
As pheasants pace 'neath roses, and discoursed
About the Sháh, his power, Grace, crown, and state   C. 1658
Till at the hour for provand and repose
They reached a spot with water, lighted down

      [1] *Cf.* Vol. v. p. 260.

Beneath a tree and, having eaten, rested.
While Búzurjmihr slept in the shade, his mantle
Drawn o'er his face, his noble way-mate saw,
Being still awake, a snake which drew away
The mantle from the sleeper, vehemently
Breathed over him from head to foot, then clomb
The tree. When that black snake had scaled the stem
The youth awoke, and when the serpent saw
The youth's discomfiture it disappeared
Amid the dusky boughs. The envoy stood
Astound, invoking oft the name of God,
And thought : "This wise youth will attain to great-
    ness ! "
    They left that wood, pushed on, and reached the
    Sháh.
The envoy hurried first before the throne
Of Núshírwán, and said : " Oh ! may thy fortune
Be ever young, O Sháh ! From court I went
To Marv and roamed about as pheasant doth
Within a rosary. Amid the sages
I found a wise youth and have brought him hither
In haste."
               He told withal what Búzurjmihr
Had said and of the portent of the snake.
The world-lord called and told the dream to him.
He heard, grew full of matter, and replied :—
"There is a youth disguised in women's garb
Within thy bower. Now put all strangers forth,
That none may know our purpose, and command
Thy ladies all to pass before thy presence
With measured tread, and then I will demand
Of that bold reprobate how came he thus
Within the Lion's lair, for God will show
The secret fact to be as thou hast dreamed."
    The Sháh put forth all strangers, closed the palace
Of king of kings, and bade the eunuchs bring,

As swift as smoke, the Idols dwelling there.
They came, those Idols of his bower, in all
Their perfumes, tints, and beauty.   All these fair ones, C. 1659
Exhaling jasmine, dainty, modest, passed
With leisured tread before him, but no man
Appeared among them, and like angry lion
Raged Núshírwán.   Then said the interpreter :—
" This should not be ; there is a youth among them.
Bid them to pass a second time all bare,
And probe their practice to the uttermost."
   The Sháh spake thus : " Cause them to pass again,
And put away the veil of modesty."
   They passed the second time and, when all thought
The dream an empty one, a youth appeared
Of cypress-stature and of kingly looks,
But quaking like a willow and despairing
Of his dear life.   Now in the great king's bower
Were seventy girls, all noble Cypresses,
And one of them, with cheeks of ivory,
Was daughter to the governor of Chách.
The youth with jasmine-face and musk-perfumed
Had been her love at home.   He followed her
Where'er she went and served her like a slave.
The Sháh inquired of her : " Who is this man
So cherished by my slave, so favoured, young,
And daring, in the bower of Núshírwán ? "
   " He is not," said the girl, " as old as I.
He is but young.   One mother bare us both.
Our sire was different, our mother one.
There is naught wrong between us.   He assumed
This kind of habit, for through modesty
He did not dare to look upon the Sháh.
Oh ! make it not a pretext that my brother
From shamefastness before thee veiled his face."
   The Sháh said to the youth : " Thou worthless dog !
Both race and family are smirched by thee."

He frowned. He was amazed at that young pair,
Then bade in wrath the executioner :—
" Let the dust hide them."

                      So he haled them back
Behind the curtains of Sháh Núshírwán,
And hung them there—a warning to the rest.
The Sháh gave that interpreter of dreams
Purse, steeds, and robes, and, wondering at his know-
    ledge,
Observed his sayings. They inscribed his name
Among the counsellors, the archimages.
Thus prospered Búzurjmihr, and circling heaven
Showed him its face, while ever day by day
His fortune greatened, and the Sháh's heart joyed
In him exceedingly.

V. 1660
                     That heart was full
Of right ; the Sháh was cultured, heart and brain.
He had residing at his court archmages,
And sages understanding in all knowledge.
Three score and ten—all men of eloquence—
Were lodged and entertained continually.
He used, when not engaged with justice, largess,
Festivity or war, to question them,
And deck his heart with knowledge. Búzurjmihr,
Though still a youth, was eloquent and shrewd
And fair to look upon, surpassing all
The famed archmages, readers of the stars,
And sages, in his knowledge, and became
Exalted over those philosophers.
None was so learnéd in astrology.
In leechcraft he excelled [1] and spake with ease
Of conduct, government, and policies.

                  [1] Reading with P.

§ 2

The first Banquet of Núshírwán to the Sages, and the Counsels of Búzurjmihr

The board was spread one day. The Sháh com-
    manded :—
" Bid the archmages come, the learned, the curious,
The eloquent, the prudent, and observing."
    The archmages vigilant of heart, the chiefs
That were accomplished in all knowledge, came,
And, having feasted, called for wine and drank
Until their spirits rose, not bringing wisdom
To disrepute but to refresh their souls.
The prudent Sháh said to those men of lore :—
" Display the hidden knowledge that ye have ;
Let every one possessed of understanding
Within his heart hold forth and pleasure me.'"
    The wise men bold and mighty in discourse
Set loose their tongues in presence of the king,
Both young and old, as he required of them.
When Búzurjmihr had listened to their words,
And noted that the Sháh held knowledge dear,
He rose, did reverence, and said : " Just judge !
Be earth the bondslave of thine ivory throne,
Heaven lustrous with the Glory of thy crown.
If now the Sháh shall bid his slave unlock
His tongue then I will speak although unworthy,
And, in respect of knowledge, least of all.
No wise man can be blamed for having loosed   C. 1661
His tongue in presence of Sháh Núshírwán."
    The monarch looked upon the sage and said :—
" What reason can there be for hiding knowledge ? "
    The youth forthwith displayed his mastery,
And spread light round him while his eloquence
And counsels fixed the archimages' hearts.

He first displayed his gifts in praise of God,
And then proceeded : " One whose mind is clear
Will utter much in little ; hasty folk
Are talkative and tedious.   When fools' talk
Endureth long the speaker is despised.
Seek worth and not addition, for the world
Is fleeting, and we are but sojourners.
Were our days to endure for evermore
The world would have too many candidates.
While here below humanity is best,
And knowledge in that view will not gainsay thee.
Our inward light we owe to righteousness,
And we must weep o'er darkness and chicane.
The heart of every one is slave to passion,
Which differeth with each, and in the world
Each hath his humour ; it is well that thou
Conform therewith.   All foremost in affairs
Still will be scheming and endeavouring more,
But sages, scholars, and the inly blest
Dwell here below and set their hearts above.
Vex not thyself about the unattained ;
'Tis toil of body and distress of soul.
He that is strong will act straightforwardly,
But lies and double-dealing come of weakness.
If thou lack knowledge silence is the jewel,
While if thou art in love with thine own knowledge
Debate will take that wisdom out of thee.
Rich is the man that hath not greed, and blest
Is he that hath not covetise for mate.
Humanity is brother unto wisdom,
Which is as 'twere the crown upon the soul.
To have a sage for mortal enemy
Is better for thee than a fool for friend.
The man content is rich ; he putteth greed
And care in bonds.   Thou wilt give ear to sages
If thou art humble in thy wish to learn.

When one is masterful in counselling
Men falter not in action. Let the man
That hath forgot his knowledge hold his tongue.
When thou hast wealth in hand with gold and silver,
And steeds caparisoned, in daily cost
Be neither close nor lavish. Choose the mean,
And let thine only guide be rectitude.
The wise man keepeth foes afar, and they
Become his servants. Know thou, he that doth
His best will win in war. Speak not vain words,
For from that fire ensueth naught but smoke.
Spend not thy thoughts upon what ne'er can be,
Because with water thou canst pierce not iron.
A king if he be learned is humble too
Though knowledge make him great and powerful.
He that acknowledgeth God's handiwork
Hath passed the ills of fortune ; he will serve
God more and more, cast out the Div's suggestions,.
Refrain himself from what should not be done,
Afflict not those that should be unafflicted,
And in the last resort incline to God,
Who is our Nourisher and Fosterer."
  Now at that goodly speech of Búzurjmihr
The doctors all grew fresh of countenance,
Rose in the presence of the king of kings,
And proffered praise anew. The company
Were all astound at Búzurjmihr, that one
So young should rise so high. The world-lord mar-
    velled
At him, then summoned the chief registrars,
And bade them set his name first on the roll :
His fortune shone forth like the sun in heaven.
Again the archmages entered on discourse,
While all the sages were in wonderment ;
The youth set loose his tongue, for he was pure
Of heart and of an ardent soul, and thus

C. 1662

He said : " We must not even in our thoughts
Turn from the king, the righteous judge, for he
Is as the shepherd and we are the sheep ;
Again, we are the earth, he is high heaven.
We must not quit our fealty to him,
Must not renounce his way and ordinance,
But joy when he is glad, if we are fain
To proffer to him all the age's due,
Diffuse his excellences in the world,
But keep his confidence inviolate.
Presume not thou upon his dignity,
For e'en the lion's heart is frayed by fire.
We should call e'en a mountain that despised
His bidding foolish-hearted and light-witted.
All evil and all good come from the Sháh,
From him come bond and dungeon, crown and throne.
The world hath from his love its worth and Grace,
While at his wrath our livers seethe within us.

C. 1663   The crowned head is the Grace of God, the sage
Hath joy and mirth therefrom.   Of Áhriman
Is he that joyeth not ; his heart and brain
Are cultured not with knowledge."
                                     They gave ear
To what the young man said, and those outworn
Revived in soul.   With tongues and mouths all praise
That mighty convocation went its ways.

§ 3

*The second Banquet of Núshírwán to Búzurjmihr and
the Archimages*

A se'nnight passed.   That king of ardent heart
Convoked the wise and shelved the world's affairs
Because he wished to hear the words of sages—

Those that were worthy to be called to court,
And were approved by knowledge to the Sháh.
They came, the wise in utterance, both young
And elders of experience. With the doctors
Of ardent soul fared youthful Búzurjmihr,
The exalted one. These doctors sage and shrewd
Sat near the lofty throne and turned their looks
On Búzurjmihr because at him the face
Of Núshírwán grew bright. One of the wisest
Then questioned him concerning fate and fortune :—
" What is their character and who ordained them ? "
   He answered : " One aspireth, being young.
He toileth night and day, and yet his path
Is dark and narrow and his conduit low,
While some mere dolt will sleep on fortune's throne,
And rose-trees scatter roses over him.
Such is the character of fate and fortune,
No toil avoideth their apportionment ;
The World-lord, the All-wise, our Fosterer,
Hath fashioned thus the star of destiny."
   Another said : " What man attaineth greatness ?
To whom is high estate the most becoming ? "
   He said : " The man that hath the better know-
      ledge
Of what is good and putteth it in practice."
   Another said : " What is there best in us ?
Who from the world is worthiest of good ? [1]
   He answered : " Gentleness, munificence,
With magnanimity and courteousness.
The humble man who boweth down his neck ;
His hand will give, expecting no return ;
He toileth and by toil would win the world,
And keepeth step with fellow way-farers."
   " What is the special virtue of the sage,"
Another said, " in moments of dispute ? "

[1] Reading with P.

C. 1664   He answered : " To discern when he is wrong,
And modify his methods and his views."
　　Another one inquired : " How should one act
To make existence more endurable ? "
　　He thus made answer : " Whensoe'er the heart
Is fraught with wisdom there is gladness too.
Then will the man both give and take aright,
And shut the door of fraud and knavery,
Will pardon faults whene'er he hath the power,
And not be hasty or irascible."
　　Another asked of him : " Among the folk
Who is best able to command himself ? "
　　He said : " The man that is not led by passion
Away from nobleness and native worth,
And likewise he that can command his weakness,
Aware that evils follow on excess."
　　Another said : " Is there aught anywhere
More excellent than bounty and good nature ?
Who bringeth speedily his crop to fruit,
And furnisheth two springtides in a year ? "
　　" One," thus he made reply, " that all unasked
Doth deck his soul with generosity,
But one that hath the praise of the receiver
Regard him not as giving but as trading."
　　One said : " What are the adornments of a man,
And which is noblest ? "
　　　　　　　　　Búzurjmihr replied —:
" He that is bounteous toward a worthy object ;
He towereth like a cypress in a garden,
And never withereth, but one unworthy,
Though he be set in musk, will savour not ;
No flower will grow upon that arid thorn.
To question of the dumb or of the deaf,
Though thou art justified, is profitless."
　　" Within this Wayside Inn," another said,
" The sage is not exempt from pain and trouble.

How shall we act that we may win fair fame,
And so begin that nobly we may end ? "
He answered : " Keep from sin ; treat all the world
As though it were thyself ; what thou mislikest
Inflict not on another—friend or foe."
Another said : " Which sayest thou of the twain
Is better—labour moderate or great ? "
He answered thus : " From wisdom's standpoint
    thought
Alone is worthy. If thou needest fruit
Toil in proportion to the work in hand."
" If we must weep o'er those that are to blame,"
Another asked, " who can deserve our praise ? "
He answered thus : " Whoever hath the most
Of hope and fear and awe of holy God."
Another said : " O thou illustrious
In wisdom and whose head out-toppeth heaven !
What is the goodliest destiny for me
From this exalted and unstable sky ? "
That man of eloquence made answer : " His   C. 1665
Who is secure and is exempt from need ;
Him fortune treateth with benevolence
So long as he is just in all his ways."
" What is the knowledge," asked another one,
" Whereby I may be happy in the world ? "
He answered thus : " That of the patient man,
Who holdeth in contempt the impudent,
And his whose brain is not perturbed by wrath,
And who, though wroth, will wink at others' faults."
Another asked : " What man is he, O sage !
That winneth the approval of the wise ? "
Said Búzurjmihr : " The man whom wisdom
    feedeth,
Who mourneth not the lost but giveth up
His darling to the dust without regret,
Pain, or dismay, rejecteth empty hopes

Like willow's fruit, is always glad and gay,
And careless of the processes of time."
    Another said : " What are the faults of kings
Whereby the hearts of righteous men are saddened ?,"
    He answered : " Wise men say that there are four :
The first is terror of the foe in fight ;
The second being niggardly in giving ;
The third rejecting wise advice in war ;
The fourth is hastiness of temperament,
And sleeping not upon their purposes."
    Another one inquired : " What man is faultless,
And what is there to blame in noble men ? "
    " We call one upright," thus said Búzurjmihr,
" When wisdom beareth witness to his words,
While those that seek by cunning and injustice
To shine are blamed for falsehood and deceit.
Between them is the man of violence,
Abusive, with his head fulfilled with strife,
And who, though meek and humble with the king,
Yet madly persecuteth holy men."
    Another said : " What kind of character
Will profit him that seeketh not mishap ? "
    " The speaker of the truth is true in all
His deeds," he answered, " governeth his tongue,
Is modest, and soft-voiced amidst of clamour.
Best is the sage who holdeth it unmeet
To banish wisdom for the sake of passion."
    Another sage inquired : " Who is the man
That can without mishap transact affairs,
Tend his own life, and profit kith and kin ? "
    He thus made answer : " He that from the first
Hath known and sought the door of holy God—
The Source of thy thanksgivings and thy Refuge,
The Lord of day and night, of sun and moon.
Moreover heartily he must obey
The Sháh's behests in public and in private,

Tend his own person dearly and shut fast
Thereon the door of travail and of greed,
Must care for his own kindred, feed the poor,
And give his children teachers, for the world
Must not be trusted to the ignorant,
And when a son is docile to command
'Tis for the father to make much of him."
    " What is the place an upright son should hold,"
Another asked him, " in his sire's esteem ? "
    He thus made answer : " In his father's eyes
A glorious son is dear as life itself :
The father's name abideth after death
Because the son will say : ' My father taught me.' "
    Another asked : " What dost thou see in riches
To grace the heart ? "
                        He made reply : " The man
Of wealth is honoured though the wealth is vile ;
But there is much that is bound up therewith,
Take heed that thou misprize not these my words,
For, first, whate'er thou hast a mind unto
Will by its nature show if thine be good ;
And, next, for thee to have and not employ
Is to treat stones and royal gems as one."
    " Among the kings with fame and lofty crown,"
Another said, " whom callest thou the best ? "
    " That king," he made reply, " with whom the good
Dwell safely while the bad quake at his voice :
The earth reposeth underneath his throne."
    Another said : " What maketh a man rich,
And who in this world is distressed and poor ? "
    He thus replied : " The man that is content
With what the Master of high heaven bestoweth,
While for the man whom fortune favoureth not
There is not any evil worse than greed."
    The famous men were full of wonderment
At him and lauded him with one consent.

§ 4

*The third Banquet of Núshírwán to Búzurjmihr and
the Archimages*

A se'nnight passed.   The eighth day with the dawn
The all-conquering Sháh sat on his throne and sum-
    moned
Before him all the men of understanding,
The wise and eloquent, who all discoursed
At large, but truly none much pleased the Sháh,
Who after said to Búzurjmihr :   " Unveil
Thy shamefast face."
                    That fluent sage set loose
His tongue, displayed his varied lore, and first
He blessed the Sháh, and said :   " Be this crowned head
Victorious," adding : " None becometh great
Unless he shun the pathway of mishap.
If thou wouldst rise to greatness by thy knowledge
Thou needest wisdom in thy choice of words.
1667   In quest of fame one must be brave, the age
Rejecteth faint-hearts.   If thou seek'st the throne
Accomplishments are needed since the bough
That putteth forth its green must bear thee fruit.
When folk make question of accomplishments
'Tis vain to cite mere aptitude,[1] for that,
With these to seek, is not approved and worthless.
In dealing with this point a wise man said :—
' If roses savour not forbear to speak
Of colour ;   none in fire a stream will seek.'
A king is all the richer for his bounty,
And hath no credit for his secret treasures.
If thou hast claimed attainments justify
What thou hast fairly spoken by thy deeds.
The sage is happy being fed by heaven

           [1] Or " high lineage."

With wisdom, and the man of simple heart
Because 'tis free from all deceitfulness.
In this world wisdom is a trusty tree,
And the great king's heart is its first of fruits.
Thou wilt be easy if thou art content,
But practise greed and thou wilt quake therefor.
Do not thy kindness in the sight of men,
For thou wilt have small kindness in return.
Good fortune favoureth the open-hearted,
And he is blest who beareth patiently.
Still if a man would rise he must be furnished
With certain things to aid him in the struggle.
First, rede and erudition ; secondly,
A ripe experience ; thirdly, friends to help
In time of action and to estimate
The chances every way for good and ill,
And to be profitable afterward
In every-day life and emergencies.
He needeth, fourthly, rectitude and wisdom
To purge his heart of falsehood and of fraud,
And, fifthly, if thou art possessed of strength
Toil with thy body ; greatness will result.[1]
The strong unless they labour ne'er will reach
The height of their desires, but over-toil,
Know, endeth in despair.   I will set forth
The five characteristics of the sage,
Which to observe involve him not in trouble,
With seven too of the fool, and 'tis no marvel
If he be irked thereby : and, to begin,
No sage is vexed at loss or prematurely
Is glad, for disappointment will perturb him.
He counteth not upon the unattained
So as to break his heart if he should miss it.
He neither hopeth that which ne'er can be,
Nor saith : ' The willow-bough will bring forth fruit.'

[1] Couplet omitted.

When at his ease from travail and from ill
He recketh of the future, wherefore when
Time bringeth hardship on him he will prove
Beforehand and not slack in enterprise.

. 1668   The fool's way, as I said, is sevenfold :
His wrath is kindled with the innocent,
His treasure opened to the unworthy man
Without return of meed or recompense,
While, thirdly, he is an ingrate to God,
And is not wise and cognizant of good,
But, fourthly, talketh loudly of himself
To every one and, fifthly, is involved
In pain and loss through his own feckless words ;
He trusteth, sixthly, to untrusty folk,
Expecting thorns to bear him painted silk,
And, lastly, uttereth lies in argument,
Endeavouring to shine by impudence.
Know this, O thou exalted sovereign !
That no man getteth aught but harm from ill.
When any one is mute in company
That silence is melodious to the heart.
By hearing some one wise and eloquent
Thou wilt get provand for thy body, counsel
And prudence for thy heart.   Forget not thou
Such words because they crown the throne of knowledge.
If thou wouldst bring that knowledge into bearing
Release thy jewel from its case by speech,
And if thou wouldst extend thy fame draw forth
Thy tongue as 'twere a falchion from its sheath ;
But if thou holdest session with the unwise [1]
The under then will have the upper hand.
By knowledge are the soul and heart illumed ;
See thou go not about to compass lies.
When one of eloquence is holding forth
Abide his words, be not impatient ;

[1] Reading with P.

Thou mayst get wisdom from his utterances,
And afterwards repeat what thou hast heard.
Use not thy wisdom as a means of gain
Though not to do so may result in hardship.
With heart and tongue in an accord of right
The door of loss is barred on every side.
Oh ! may the heart of Núshírwán, the Sháh,
Be open to instruction evermore."
   An archimage of subtle intellect
Then asked : " What are the good and seemly things
That give a man a lustre in the world,
And quittance from the troubles of the time ? "
   He answered thus : " Whoe'er attaineth wisdom
Will gain thereby the fruitage of both worlds."
   " But if he hath not wisdom," said the archmage,
" Since wisdom is God's radiant robe of honour ? "
   Said Búzurjmihr : " Then knowledge is the best,
The learned is mighty midst the men of might."
   " But if," the archmage said, " he hath not sought
That stream and never bathed his soul therein ? "
   Thus Búzurjmihr replied : " The warrior
Must count his body as a worthless thing,
And if he striveth in the day of battle,
And layeth foemen's heads upon the dust,
He will be cherished in the great king's heart,
For ever happy and in good command."
   " But if one is not valiant," said the archimage,   C. 1669
Nor seeketh after knowledge, law, and Faith ? "
   Then Búzurjmihr replied : " 'Twere well that death
Should set the helm of darkness on his head."
   Another asked : " How shall we act that all
Of us may eat the fruitage of the tree
Set by the sage within the garth of spring,
And walk moreover underneath its shade ? "
   Said Búzurjmihr : " The man that barreth up
His tongue from evil vexeth not his soul,

And rendeth not in talk another's skin.
He will be likewise friends with all the folk,
All troubles will be smoothed away for him,
And enemy and friend will be as one."
    Another asked him, saying : " Are the men
That shun the way of failure great or good ? "
    Thus Búzurjmihr replied : " An evil deed
Is like a tree that beareth evil fruit.
Thus if a man speak gently with his tongue
But little harshness will befall his ear,
For know it is the tongue that troubleth men ;
So if thou wouldst be easy weigh thy words.
The man of few words and a loyal subject
Hath only one fit post—before the throne.
Moreover he escapeth ills not come,
As bird or beast escapeth from the net,
While furthermore he triumpheth o'er evil,
Is self-controlled and wise exceedingly.
He leaveth well alone and troubleth not
The inoffensive, letteth no good 'scape him,
And counteth not upon the days to come.
He shunneth foe with more than quarry's speed,
And cleaveth unto friend like shaft and feather.
For any pleasure that will end in grief
The man of wisdom hath but little yearning.
Put ease and indolence afar from thee,
Take pains and make a feast of toil ; without it
Thou wilt win not addition in the world ;
There is no treasure for the indolent.[1]
May this world live in Núshírwán, be he
Its world-lord ever and his fortune young."
    They held discourse at large upon this theme :
The hearts of those grown drowsy were awakened.
The archimages, magnates, and shrewd sages
Blessed Búzurjmihr and gave the Sháh great praise,
Then went rejoicing on their several ways.

      [1] The two following couplets are transposed.

§ 5

The fourth Banquet of Núshírwán to Búzurjmihr and the Archimages

Two se'nnights passed away and then the Sháh
Relinquished public business for a day,
And bade the archimages and great men
Assemble at the palace with the sages.
He asked about the body and its birth,   C. 1670
About wrath, peace, the intellect, and justice,
About the sovereignty, the crown, and power,·
And how good fortune doth begin and end.
He questioned those archimages and inquired
Concerning that which pleased him.   When the others
Had spoken as their knowledge was, but failed
To gratify the Sháh, he next addressed
Himself to Búzurjmihr and said : " Bring forth
The splendid jewel from its hiding-place."
    Then Búzurjmihr gave praises, saying thus :—
" O Sháh most loving and serene of heart !
Know that in all the world no king like thee
For justice, understanding, crown, and throne,
For Grace and mien, for counsel and for fortune,
Hath set the diadem upon his head.
The king that exerciseth self-control
Will be at rest from vengeance and from war
Because to shun unwarrantable deeds
Is better than to get a sorry heart.
How goodly is the saying of the sage :—
' Self-discipline is goodly in a king.'
In seasons of dispute he feareth God,
Inclineth not to vengeance and to prowess,
And maketh wisdom ruler of his passions
When he is choleric.   A monarch's thoughts
Should not displease the Master of the world

Through whom he doth discern 'twixt good and
    evil,
And seeketh Paradise as virtue's meed.
A tongue truth-speaking and a reverent heart
Will be his glory in the world for aye,
While every one that is his counsellor
Will be a man of weight among the people,
Be eloquent, serene of heart, and just,
And give to small and great alike their due
According to the measure of their states.
The man that is the servant of the Shán
Should not be damnified on that account,
And while a monarch holdeth sages dear
His crown will be exalted ; but if he
Shall take the counsel of the ignorant
He will bring down his crown's head underfoot,
For knowledge frighteneth the fool away,
Who in his ignorance is combative.
The world-lord, whose informants are all wise,
Aware of what is going on at court,
And able thus to foil the malcontent,
Will be still glorious.   None must sleep aggrieved
Lest ill befall the Sháh from that mishap,
Who should ban him deserving chastisement,
The misbegotten and the ill-disposed,
Lest such should trouble those that are offenceless.
All captives in the prisons of the Sháh,
The guilty and the innocent alike,
Should be enlarged by the decree of God,
Who thus directed in the Zandavasta.
. 1671   If one be an ill-doer black and base
The face of earth should be relieved of him,
For while his evil day continueth
He will bring ruin on the homes of men.
The world-lord must rejoice in faith and right
So long as he is in the world as Sháh.

'Tis his to cleanse it from the wicked Div
In public and in private by the sword.
The king that ruleth his troops well will be
Untroubled by the griefs of suppliants.
When thou art wary of thy foes in counsel
Thine evil-wishers will lose heart.   Man all
The breaches of the realm ere war betide.
Whenas the Sháh is blamed for anything
Reproach too falleth on the crown and throne,
Through grief the wish is to be quit of him,
And to make wisdom testify thereto.
Let grow the love thou bearest to thy son,
Who is as 'twere the reflex of thy face
In water.   Teach him wisdom and good sense,
And seek but to illuminate his soul.
Unlock for him the portal of thy treasures ;
He must have no cause to bewail himself,
And when he putteth forth his hand to wrong
There is no need to break the prince's heart.
Recall him to the way with gentleness,
And keep a hold upon him from the first.
If in his heart thou find hostility
It is an ill weed ; pluck it from his plot,
For if it bideth 'twill grow strong and fill
The garden of the sovereignty with tares ;
But when the atheling hath Grace and sense
He must not hear the words of evil speakers ;
Still when the hand can reach the miscreants
Haste not to bloodshed save at God's command.
Destruction cometh on the royal crown
Through rascal-ministers and wicked wives.
Give fools a hearing, but when they propose
An unjust action do not thou consent.
'Tis needful to fulfil all righteousness,
And clear thine own heart of perversity.
The sole adornment for the mighty Sháh

Is right, for 'tis the Div that causeth wrong.
Now when the Sháh shall hearken to these.words
He in his heart will witness unto wisdom,
The crown will call down blessings on the king,
The throne of empire be confirmed to him,
Both will rejoice in him, his foes despair
Of fortune ; while this restless sky revolveth
His good name will be his memorial.
Now may the accomplished soul of Núshírwán
Be young while day endureth.''
                                    At his words
The assembly was amazed, compared with them
The counsels of the wise seemed lustreless.
When Núshírwán had listened to this speech
His greatness greatened great although it was.
C. 1672   The counsels given filled his eyes with tears :
He filled the speaker's mouth with lustrous pearls.
Then from the palace with their lips all praise
The company departed on their ways.

§ 6

The fifth Banquet of Núshírwán to Búzurjmihr and the Archimages

Thus seven days passed away.   Upon the eighth,
Whenas the world-illuming sun blazed forth,
Put off its robe of lapis-lazuli,
And decked the world with golden-hued brocade,
The king of kings sat with the archimages,
The veterans, and officers of state—
Ardshír, the high priest and the chief of nobles,
Shápúr and Yazdagird, the scribe, the men
Of science and the readers of the stars,
The wise, the enlightened, and the eloquent.
The youthful Búzurjmihr, the orator,

Came to the presence of Sháh Núshírwán,
And did obeisance to his sovereign,
Who joyed at him and thus addressed the sages :—
" Who wotteth aught whereby the Faith of God
May be confirmed, the royal throne kept scathless ? "
    Thereat the high priest loosed his tongue amid
The chiefs and said : " The justice of the Sháh
Will cause his Grace, his crown, and throne to shine,
And when it openeth his treasury-door
His high renown will last when he is dead.
Moreover he should purge his tongue of lies,
And seek not lustre in the world by guile.
Next he will be both just and merciful,
And make his throne the glory of the age.
Then too the head of the illustrious Sháh
Should be not wrathful with an erring liege,
And, fifthly, he will speak so that his fame
In this world never will grow obsolete ;
He will speak truth in all things small and great,
And never derogate in any thing.
He will esteem withal as his own fortune
The servant of his throne. If wise in words
His speech will be convincing, and his heart
Ne'er satiate of learning and consuming
His brains with thought. All men are set at large
By wisdom and have little cause to wail
At fortune. Wisdom nourisheth the souls
Of sages, wisdom pointeth out the way
To those that seek. Tear not thy heart, O Sháh !
From wisdom's path, for wisdom fostereth
Fame and a noble end. Base and a fool
Is he that ever said : ' I am the man,
Because there is no peer to me in knowledge.' "
    Then Yazdagird, the scribe, spake thus and said :— C. 1673
" O wise and wisdom-loving Sháh ! in Sháhs
It is a thing unseemly to shed blood,

Or suffer trifles to disturb the heart.
Moreover when the king is light of wit
He putteth hand to matters thoughtlessly,
While, further, he is hasty with the wise,
And all the more so through his ignorance.
When lust for vengeance hath possessed his heart
The Div is the associate of his soul ;
So too a judge's words, if he be hasty,
Lead not to fair results.   The warrior,
Moreover, that is fearful of his life
In battle-time, not of disgrace, and he
Whose heart, though he be rich, is mean and narrow,
Were better hidden underneath the ground.
Authority becometh not a beggar,
Since he himself becometh not high rank.
A guileful elder is a hateful thing,
And after death his soul will be in fire.
When any youth is slack in business
The heart of fortune will grow sick of him,
Disease will make him prematurely old,
And may his vigour and his spirit cease."
    When Búzurjmihr had heard these goodly words,
And had adorned his brain with wisdom's lore,
He said : " O Sháh whose face is like the sun's !
May shining heaven be at thy dispose.
Know this : that men of wisdom will sustain
Their souls with knowledge since the hearts of stones
And mountains sorrow o'er the ignorant,
For none respecteth him.   He knoweth not
End from beginning, fame from infamy.
The common folk, still more the wisdom-seekers,
Despise the doings of such men as these—
The lying judge unhonoured by the sage ;
The general who guardeth well his treasure,
And is abandoned by his toil-worn troops ;
The sage that feareth not to do amiss

If he can have enjoyment therewithal :
The leech that aileth ; how can he cure others ?
The mendicant that braggeth of his wealth
While that whereof he talketh is but naught ;
A Sháh who letteth not his people rest,
Or sleep at night, disquieting their hearts,
And yet when favouring breezes blow on thee
Assumeth all the merit for himself ;
A choleric sage who eyeth others' goods,
And lastly he that counselleth a fool,
Or giveth the indolent authority.
They that lack wisdom and acquire it not
Will have occasion to repent their words.
The heart of any man, my gracious lord !
That hath not wisdom wrestleth with desire
In such wise as a flame devoureth brimstone,   C. 1674
Or maketh provand of a bed of reeds.
Long live the heart of Núshírwán, may he
Have this world's chiefs his servitors to be."

§ 7
The sixth Banquet of Núshírwán to Búzurjmihr and the Archimages

The Sháh allowed another week to pass,
Then issued orders to prepare the court,
Came and assumed his seat upon the throne
Of gold, with armlets, crown, and golden girdle.
On one hand was the archmage that was vizir,
And on the other Yazdagird the scribe,
While round him were the other archimages,
The chiefs, and Búzurjmihr the eloquent,
To whom the Sháh : " Why keep the jewels hidden—
Those words which are a profit to the soul,
And make the unprized man of high estate ?

The speaker's treasure is not minished,
While 'tis a pleasure to the listener."
　　Thus spake the archimage to Búzurjmihr :—
" O thou more famous than the turning sky !
Know'st thou the thing whose more will harm, whose
　　less
Will strengthen thee ? "
　　　　　　　　He thus made answer, saying :—
" By eating less thou wilt be easier
In body and withal feed up thy soul,
But by too much well-doing wilt advance
Thy rival."
　　　　　　Then said Yazdagird, the scribe :—
" O man of eloquence and heedful mind !
What are the heart's three [1] secret blemishes
Which men retain although they need them not ? "
　　He answered : " In the first place thou must purge
Thy heart of all censoriousness, for none
In this world publicly or privily
Is free from fault.　A chieftain, jealous of thee,
Will weep [2] on growing thine inferior,
While, thirdly, he that is a slanderer—
The man of double face—endeavoureth
To raise dust e'en from water." [3]
　　　　　　　　　Then the archmage
Inquired : " O thou that art supreme in knowledge !
None in this world is franchised from desire,
Which may be hidden or exposed to all.
Supposing ways to gratify it open,
So that 'tis manifestly in one's power,
In my case which way will advantage me,
And which result in travail, pain, and loss ? "
　　He answered thus and said : " The ways are twain,
And thou canst journey either at thy choice.
1675　One is the way of rashness, full of ill,

---

[1] Reading with P.　　[2] With envy.　　[3] Three couplets omitted.

The other that of wisdom and well-doing,[1]
And therein wisdom is the guide for thee—
A fact that is beyond all questioning.
God's robe of honour is upon the sage ;
Observe what man is worthy of that gift.
No one will purchase one of giant strength
Devoid of wisdom.   In defect thereof
It is not well to live, for God is witness
That wisdom is the very life of life.
The man that hath acquired a base of knowledge
Is fitted for the warfare and the struggle.
First, let thy knowledge make thee turn to God,
Who is and who will be for evermore.
By faith in Him thou hast thy heart's desire,
And hast attained the goal whereto thou spedest.
Another point of knowledge is that thou
Shouldst use discretion in the choice of food.
Strive after purity in food and raiment,
And thus uphold the ordinance of God.
When thou hast need to earn thy daily bread
Run not to misers for their help and treasure,
But let thy choice be of some business
Whose reputation will not sink repute.
Make to thyself a friend of some great man,
Who can assist thee when thou art in straits.
Be silent when thou art in company
If thou wouldst win the praise of every one,
But if thou speak'st speak that which hast learned,
And branded on thy liver.   Weigh thy words,
Not the dinárs within thy treasury,
For to a wise man treasures are but vile.
When thou art speaking let thy tongue be shrewd,
Make it thy shaft and let thy bow be wisdom.
Be not imprudent when a fight is toward,
But guard thy body from the enemy,

[1] Couplet omitted.

And when he hath arrayed the host against thee
Be prudent and preserve thy self-control.
When thou beholdest thine antagonist
Thy face must pale not.   Thou wilt be victorious
If thou art prompt, but slackness will undo thee.
Be wary as thou urgest on thy steed,
And watch the weapons of thine opposite.
If he is eager do not turn away,
And choose thee prudent fellow-combatants ;
But strive not and have sense to quit the fight
On finding that thou art no match for him.
Thus tender too thy body when thou eatest ;
Food should not harm thee ; eating much will do it,
While taking little will increase thy strength.
Make not thyself a carfax at thy meals,
But always leave off with an appetite.
Use wine but use it for refreshment only,
For drunkards hear no praise from any one.
C. 1676 If thou adore God thou wilt be commended,
The world will be a head and thou the eye.
Let all thy converse be of the Creator
With adoration for the base thereof.
Profoundly watch the occasion when to act,
And when to take repose by night and day.
Select the mean in every enterprise,
In making peace as well as waging war.
All wind and water blent with dust art thou ;
Forget not thou the way of holy God.
Think more about thy worship than thy meals ;
Be still a novice though the law is old ;
Incline to good ; acknowledge benefits ;
Attribute all to Him who made the world ;
Prefer not lust to wisdom and advice,
Or wisdom will regard thee not thenceforth ;
Go not about to compass wickedness,
But being wise adorn thyself with virtues.

He that is good in public and in private
Is most to be commended in the world.
Teach to thy son the business of the scribe
That he may be as life to thee and thine,
And as thou wouldest have thy toils bear fruit
Grudge not instructors to him, for this art
Will bring a youth before the throne and make
The undeserving fortune's favourite.
Of all professions 'tis the most esteemed,
Exalting even those of lowly birth.
A ready scribe who is a man of rede
Is bound to sit e'en in the royal presence,
And, if he be a man of diligence,
Will have uncounted treasure from the Sháh,
While if endowed with fluency and style
He will be studious to improve himself,
Use his endeavours to be more concise,
And put his matter more attractively.
The scribe hath need to be a man of wisdom,
Of much endurance and good memory,
A man of tact, accustomed to court-ways,
A holy man whose tongue is mute for evil,
A man of knowledge, patience, truthfulness,
A man right trusty, pious, and well-favoured.
If thus endowed he cometh to the Sháh
He cannot choose but sit before the throne."
　　Whenas the king had listened to these words
His heart grew fresh as roses in the spring,
And he addressed the high priest thus : " Go to,
Give Búzurjmihr advancement.　Claim for him
A robe of honour fitted for his state,
And money : he hath made our hearts elate."

§ 8

The seventh Banquet of Núshírwán to Búzurjmihr and the Archimages

A se'nnight passed, the Sun lit up his crown,
And came and sat upon the ivory throne,
Together with the high priest, the grandees,
The world-aspiring and shrewd-hearted sages,
With Sáda and with Yazdagird, the scribe,
And as their leader the astute Bahman.
Then spake the Sháh to Búzurjmihr and said :—
" Adorn our hearts and show to us the way.
Speak truth about me as thou knowest it,
And seek not this world's honours by deceit.
How should men give obedience to my hest,
Observe my counsels, and act loyally ?
Speak at thine ease and speak without reserve :
Dress not plain words with colour and with scent."
    Thus Búzurjmihr, the shrewd, said to the Sháh :—
" O more exalted than the azure vault !
The service of the monarch of the earth
Is, saith the sage, the path-way of the Faith.
The orders of the Sháh brook no delay,
Because the Shah's heart never must be straitened,
And every one that is his enemy
Is in his soul the liege of Áhriman.
The heart that loveth not the monarch's person
Should forfeit brain and skin. Know that the Sháh
Is the world's peace, and when thou dost aright
He will advance thee. Both for good and ill
The power is his, he taketh not revenge,
And injureth none. Wish not his son to fill
His room but hold his dear face as thy life.
Want never findeth entrance to the soil
Of states whose monarch is their well-beloved.

. 1677

His Grace will fend thee from all ill, for why
His fortunes nurse all virtue.   When a king
Hath God's Grace on his face the world's heart laugheth
For joy.   As thou partakest of his favours
Strive ever to give ear to his commands.
If thou shalt grow disloyal, e'en in thought,
That moment fortune will abandon thee.
If he associate with thee be not proud,
And if he banish thee revile him not.
Mark that a subject toiling for his king
Will in the toil find treasure and renown.
He that shall praise the monarch is of God,
And he that is of God will praise the monarch.
The liege must neither weary of his work,
Nor yet be slack in fight, must keep concealed
The counsel of the Sháh and tell it not
To sun and moon.   One that is slack to do
The Sháh's commands doth outrage to himself.
Accurséd are the blossoms of the tree
That scattereth naught but leaves o'er crown and
    throne.
Calumniate not his lieges to the Sháh,
Or thou wilt minish thine esteem with him :
Great liars get small lustre in kings' eyes.
Let no one utter in the royal presence
Words that are not conformable with wisdom ;
But, if the Sháh shall ask thee, speak, not losing
Thy credit with him by loquacity,
Because there is more knowledge in the world   C. 1678
Than ears can hear in public and in private.
He whom the monarch of the world misprizeth,
That soul will be in pain for evermore,
While he will be in high esteem on whom
The Sháh's lips smile.   If he shall show thee favour
Hug not thyself, old servant though thou be,
For, though thy service may have lasted long,

Know that thou art not indispensable,
And if he favoureth another man
'Tis doubtless one as loyal as thyself.
If he shall be displeased with thee in aught
Make thine excuses ere thou drawest breath,
And if thou wottest naught of thine offence
Lay bare thy heart in presence of the Sháh,
While if thou hast a grievance in thy heart
Break it but show not unto him thy face,
Lest by God's Grace he should discern thy secret,
Discern thy heart perverse and clouded mind.
Thereafter thou wilt get no good of him,
Not hearken to his accents warm with love.
Account the Sháh's court as a sea where lieges
Are sailors, and accomplishments are vessels
With words for anchors and with wits for sails.
A wise man, who is voyaging o'er that sea,
Will make his sails robust because they are
A source of strength and shelter to himself.
The accomplished man, whose wisdom is to seek,
Should tread not on the portal of the Sháh.
Although the Sháh should be a mount of fire
Still would his servants find existence good,
For if such fire burn at the time of wrath
It will but shine the more when gratified.
The Sháh at whiles is milk and honey, whiles
A biting bane.   His acts are like the sea ;
The moon is bright in heaven at his behest.
One getteth from the sea a pinch of sand,
Another hath the pearl within the shell.
Be all the world alive in Núshírwán,
And circling heaven aye subject to his will,
For he doth head the monarchs of the world,
And ornament the empire with all good."
    To Búzurjmihr's oration Núshírwán
Gave heed, heart-joyed to look on him.   The king

Was wont to give his largess on this wise :
If he said " Good ! " the largess was four purses,
But whensoe'er he said : " Good ! very good ! "
The gift amounted in that case to forty,
And when the treasurer reckoned with the Sháh
Each purse was taken at ten thousand drachms.[1]
The king of kings had said : " Good ! very good ! "
A speech equivalent to all that coin.
The treasurer brought with visage sunny-clear
The purses full of drachms to Búzurjmihr.

[1] *Cf.* p. 215, *note.*

PART III

THE STORY OF MAHBÚD AND OTHER MATTERS

ARGUMENT

The poet tells how Mahbúd, sometime chief minister of Núshírwán and a virtuous and blameless man, was done to death by the machinations of Zúrán, the chamberlain, and of a Jewish sorcerer, how too late Núshírwán discovered the plot, put the chamberlain and the Jew to death, and made all the amends in his power. The poet then tells how the presents sent by the Khán of Chín to Núshírwán were plundered on the way by the Haitálians, of the wars that followed and how Núshírwán married the daughter of the Khán. Firdausi then discourses of the justice of Núshírwán, of the happiness and prosperity of the world under his administration, and of the tribute paid to him by Cæsar and other potentates. The Part ends with a discourse of Búzurjmihr's on good words and good deeds

NOTE

§§ 1 and 2. Sháh Kubád had left several sons, of whom Núshírwán was not the eldest, but he was the heir to the throne by his father's appointment, who appears also to have made some arrangement for his recognition as such with the Emperor Justin, or at all events to have suggested it. On Kubád's death his eldest son, Káús, claimed the throne, but the prime minister Mahbúd (Mebodes) was in a position to indicate what Kubád's wishes on the subject had been, and Núshírwán became Sháh. Another brother of his, however, Jam by name, was very popular but disqualified for the throne by a personal defect. In these circumstances a conspiracy was formed to overthrow Núshírwán and make Jam's son, Kubád, Sháh with Jam himself as regent, Kubád being still a child. The conspiracy, which had much influential support, was discovered, and a clean sweep—the usual course in such cases—made of the conspirators and all their male relations with the exception of Kubád, who ultimately escaped to Constantinople and was well received by the Emperor Justinian. There is no account of the conspiracy in the Sháhnáma, but it has been mentioned here because the poisoning incident and the drastic vengeance that followed may have been transferred from it to the story of the fall of Mahbúd as given in the poem. The Western account of the fall of Mahbúd is entirely different.[1]

§ 1. Milk, which "turns" so easily, especially in a hot climate, would be regarded as more sensitive to evil influences than other foods. *Cf.* Burton's *Supplemental Nights*, vol iv. p. 243 and *note*.

§ 2. In view of Núshírwán's tardy repentance and his reparation to the kindred of Mahbúd it is interesting to find a Mebodes in high command in the Persian army in A.D. 578.[2]

§ 3. The account of the building of Súrsán is a doublet of that of Zib-i-Khusrau.[3]

§§ 4–11. At this point the Turks come historically upon the scene under the leadership of their Khán, whom Tabari calls Sinjibú. In A.D. 569 or 570 they threatened to invade Írán, and Núshírwán sent his son Hurmuzd against them. As Hurmuzd was the son of the daughter of the Khán it is evident that the alliance between Sinjibú and Núshírwán must have been entered into at a considerably earlier period. The object of the alliance was to crush the Haitálians, and this was done. Núshírwán occupied their territory up to the Oxus—the old traditional boundary of Írán—while the Khán annexed all to the north of that river, but, according to Persian accounts, withdrew on the approach of Hurmuzd. Firdausi does not mention Núshírwán's wars with the Haitálians, and represents them as being the aggressors. No doubt they would do their best to prevent friendly relations between their two formidable neighbours. Later on the Khán, as Tabarí tells us, hearing from the vanquished Haitálians that Írán had been tributary to them, wished to assert his claim to a similar payment and marched southwards, as mentioned above, with that object. He found, however, the frontier of Írán too well guarded and soon withdrew.[4]

§ 11. For the so-called tribute paid by Rúm to Írán see p. 187, and for the temple of Ázargashasp, p. 5.

§ 13. See p. 278. The formula of Good Thoughts, Good Words, and Good Deeds plays an important part in Zoroastrianism. One of the most beautiful passages in the Zandavasta, Yasht XXII,[5]

---

[1] See NT, p. 147, *note ;* GDF, v. 183 ; RSM, p. 377 *seq.*
[2] *Id.* p. 436.   [3] See p. 259.   [4] NT, p. 159 and *notes.*
[5] DZA, ii. 314 *seq.*

deals with the subject and may be paraphrased briefly and metrically thus —:

> Once Zoroaster asked, so Text and Comment saith,
> " How fares the good man's soul when he has tasted death ? "
> And this was *H*eaven's reply : " The soul still sits anigh
> Its tenement of clay for thrice a day and night,
> And chants the sacred hymns in uttermost delight.
> It sings: 'Oh ! happy he, the man whoe'er he be,
> To whom the Great God grants all that he longed to see ! '
> And after that third night, at breaking of the dawn,
> Mid lovely plants and scents that good man's soul is borne,
> And from the South will come a perfume-laden air,
> The sweetest breath e'er breathed ; and then white-armed and
>   fair,
> Bright, beautiful, and young, a Maid will meet him there ;
> Whereat the good man's soul will question : 'Who art thou,
> For never have I looked on loveliness till now ? '
> And she will make reply : ' Thy Conscience, youth ! am I.
> Good Thoughts, Good Words, Good *D*eeds, have made me thus
>   to be,
> And they were all thine own, and I grew thus through
>   thee.' "

§ I

The Story of Mahbúd, the Wazír of Núshírwán, and how Mahbúd and his Sons were slain by the Sorcery of Zúrán and a Jew

679　This matter ended, I proceed to tell
　　　The story of Mahbúd, the minister.
Cease not from learning for a moment's spell,
　　　And let not knowledge cause thy heart to err.
When thou shalt say : " My lust for wisdom I
　　　Have satisfied and learned all needful lore,"
Fate playeth off some pretty trickery,
　　　And putteth thee to discipline once more.
Now hearken to a rustic minstrel's lay,

Ta'en from the legends of a time long sped ; [1]
I questioned him of ages past away,
  And this is what of Núshírwán he said :—
He had an upright minister, a man
Of vigilance, who was his treasurer,
Whose heart was full of wisdom and whose rede
Was right, whose sole ambition was fair fame.
This man so well disposed was named Mahbúd :
His soul and heart were full of good discourse.
He had two sons like jocund spring who served
Continually before the king, for he,
What time he was about to mutter prayer,
Or use the archimages' sacred twigs, [2]
Ate only what Mahbúd himself provided,
And trusted those two sons. He used to have
His kitchen in Mahbúd's house and demeaned
Himself as guest, and that good, famed man's sons
Themselves brought in the great king's meal. The
    nobles
Were wont to weep for envy of Mahbúd
At court. There was a magnate, one Zúrán,
Whose aspirations all were centred there.
He was an old man and Sháh's chamberlain,
Conspicuous at feasts and audiences ;
His visage ran with tears the whole year through
In envy of Mahbúd and his two sons.
'Twas his endeavour to incense the Sháh
Against the doings of that holy man,
Yet failed to find an opening for slander
To set the monarch's mind against Mahbúd ;
But how should he—that man of wisdom—know
That he possessed an enemy at court
Since never had he cause to pale one whit
For all the words and practice of that knave ?

C. 168c

---

[1] Seven couplets omitted.
[2] See Vol. i. p. 80 *s.v. Báj* and *Barsam.*

A Jew, it happened, borrowed of Zúrán
One day some money to employ in trade.
He came and went, his influence grew, and he
Beeame that gloomy soul's associate.
Thus, as familiar with the chamberlain,
He came to be at home about the court,
And there one day conversed in confidence
Of spells, of court, the monarch of the world,
Of magic, necromancy, and black arts,
Of crookéd practices and villainy.
Zúrán, attending to the Jew's discourse,
And hearing of the secrets of his craft,
Told his own secret to the Jew, and said :—
" Discourse not of it save with me alone.[1]
Thou must perform a deed of sorcery,
And give the age its riddance of Mahbúd,
Because he hath attained to such high state
That he will dominate the age itself.
He careth not for any.   Thou wouldst say,
To put it shortly : ' He is Núshírwán.'
Now he—the world-lord—will not take of food
Save only at the hands of this man's sons,
Who hath become so great through royal favour
That heaven kisseth evermore his skirt."
    The Jew replied : " This cause need not increase
Thy grief.   What time the Sháh and world-lord taketh
The sacred twigs mark well what meats are served,
And see if there be any milk therein.
Meet thou the serving-man and sniff the meats ;
'Twill serve if I but see the milk from far.
Then thou shalt see Mahbúd and his two sons
No more alive.   Though he be brass or stone
That eateth he will perish instantly."
    Zúrán attended to these words.   His heart
Was freshened as he gazed upon the Jew ;

1 Reading with P.

Whene'er he went to court the Jew went likewise ;
They had their secrets, joys, and feasts in common.
A season passed with matters in this stay :
The court was haunted by that evil teacher,
That court whereto each dawn Mahbúd's two sons
Were wont to turn their steps so joyfully.
Behind the curtains of their noble father
There was a pious dame and well advised,
Who, when Sháh Núshírwán desired some food,
Was wont to spread a golden tray for him,
And lay thereon three platters set with jewels ;   C. 1681
The whole was covered with a golden napkin,
And used to come before the exalted Sháh,
Served by the two sons of the good Mahbúd.
The food consisted of rose-water, milk,
And honey.   Núshírwán would eat and sleep.
One day it happened that the two young men
Were going with the tray to Núshírwán ;
It was conveyed upon a servant's head
To whom 'twas usual to entrust the food.
Zúrán, the chamberlain, beheld the tray
When coming to the palace of the Sháh,
And with a smile addressed the two youths thus :—
" Ye trusty lieges of Sháh Núshírwán !
Reveal for once the colour of these meats—
The Sháh's repast—because they savour well :
Withdraw the silken cover just this once."
    The young men readily displayed the food.
Zúrán, who kept his distance, gazed thereon,
And in like manner did the Jew, who came,
When he had marked the colour of the meats,
And said thus to the chamberlain : " The tree
That thou hast planted cometh into fruit."
    The two young men, both wise and vigilant,
Then carried in the tray to Núshírwán,
While after them Zúrán came quick as dust,

And thus addressed the Sháh, that noble man :—
" O Sháh, the just, the favoured by the stars !
Touch not these meats till they be tasted first.[1]
The cook hath mingled poison with the milk,
And may thine enemies partake thereof."
    Sháh Núrshírwán, on hearing, turned his gaze
On those two youths whose mother was the cook—
A prudent dame affectioned of her kin.
They in their innocence and rectitude   ·
Rolled up their sleeves.   Howbeit when they ate
Some of that milk and honey thou hadst said :—
" Both have been stricken by an arrow."   Both
Swooned on the spot and died there in the presence
Of Núshírwán !   The monarch of the world
Beheld, his cheeks like flower of fenugreek,
And gave commandment : " Let them raise in dust
The mansion of Mahbúd, respecting none,
Upon that dust let them cut off his head,
And may he and his cook both cease to be."
    None in the palace of Mahbúd, and few
Among his kindred in the world, survived.
The Sháh gave all his goods, his women, children,
And hoarded wealth, to spoil.   In that affair
Zúrán attained his wish, since Núshírwán
C. 1682   Was quit of that good man, and held the Jew
In high esteem who cloudward raised his head.
Heaven turned awhile with matters in this stay
While from the Sháh right hid its face away.

1 Couplet omitted.

§ 2

*How the Sorcery of Zúrán and the Jew in the Matter of Mahbúd
was discovered, and how both were slain by Command of
Núshírwán*

The Sháh, the world-lord, purposed, as it chanced,
To hunt the wolf and bade that many a steed,
Used in the chase, should pass before his eyes,
Scanned them, and saw the brand-mark of Mahbúd.
His cheeks flamed at those Arab horses, love
Still had a place within him, and he burned.
He wept for pain and with heart sorely seared
Recalled to mind Mahbúd, and thus he said :—
" How much the wicked Div made to transgress
That man of counsel and of high degree !
With that devotion and that rectitude
Why did his spirit seek the path of loss ? [1]
The Master of the world alone can tell
The hidden truth beneath the outward show."
    He thence departed to the hunting-ground,
Seared at his heart and followed by his men.
Upon the route he talked with all and cheered
His heart with words. He took full many a minstrel,
And with their fascinations docked the way.
Now as the Sháh's chief minister and scribes
Were journeying with Zúrán in company
Their converse ran on spells and magic arts,
On witchcraft and pernicious Áhriman.
The king said to the archmages : " Trouble not
Your hearts concerning sorcery, but let
Your talk be all of God and of the Faith ;
Look not for marvels in black arts and magic."
    Zúrán said : " Live for ever, and may wisdom
Feed on thy words. All that they say of witchcraft

[1] Reading with P.

Is true, though this is known but to adepts.
If food have milk therein they by a look
Can from a distance turn it into bane."
    On hearing this a bygone time recurred
To Núshírwán.   He thought upon Mahbúd,
And those two sons of his, and deeply sighed.
He looked upon Zúrán but held his peace,
And quickly urged his prancing charger on.
His mind was in a fume with thought because
Zúrán had been the foeman of Mahbúd.

C. 1683   He said : " I know not what this miscreant
Had done upon the day whereon I slew
Mahbúd, and that great house was overthrown.
Would that almighty God would make all plain,
And give my heart and brain tranquillity,
Because I spy this fellow's marks hereon,
And am fulfilled with sorrow for the past."
    He journeyed on with sad and aching heart,
With lowering visage and with tearful eyes,
And, having reached the ending of the stage,
Set up his camp-enclosure by a stream.
Now when Zúrán had reached the tent they cleared
The place of strangers and the converse ran
Upon the' means of witching milk and honey.
" It is my favourite subject," said Zúrán.
    The Sháh then questioned him about Mahbúd,
And by what means his sons were done to death,
And heard the quaver in Zúrán's reply.
His crime became apparent.   Núshírwán
Addressed him, saying : " Tell to me the truth,
Conceal it not and act not knavishly,
For knavery but causeth evil deeds,
And evil comrades will corrupt good hearts."
    Zúrán told all the truth, revealed the secret,
Threw all the blame upon the Jew, and made
As though he were possessed by grief and anguish.

The great king, having listened, fettered him,
And sent to that enchanter of a Jew,
As swift as smoke, a rider with two steeds.
Whenas the Jew had reached the lofty court
The exalted monarch questioned him with mildness,
And said : " Inform me how the matter went,
And lie not to me touching this affair."
   The Jew asked for protection from the world-lord
If he revealed the mystery of black art,
And then told what Zúrán had said with all
The matter of their secret conference.
The world-lord heard with wonder and convoked
The marchlords, potentates, and archimages,
And in their presence for the second time
Investigated every circumstance.
The evil-minded Jew told everything
Till naught was hidden from the chiefs. The Sháh
Then bade the deathsman rear two lofty gibbets,
From each whereof a twisted lasso hung,
Before the palace-portal in the presence
Of all the host. The executioner
Haled to the gibbets and suspended there
Zúrán on one, the Jew upon the other,
In savage wise. 'Neath showers of stones and arrows
They gave their heads up for bewitching milk.
Tread not the world for evil, for it will,
Past doubt, befall the practiser of ill.
   The Sháh long sought for kindred of Mahbúd,   C. 1684
If so he might find one that had escaped,
And found one damsel of unsullied name,
And three men eminent and excellent.
To these he gave all that Zúrán possessed,
As well as all the fortune of the Jew.
His soul kept burning on Mahbúd's account,
And in the night he wept till it was day,
Would pray to God for pardon and pour forth

His heart's blood on his bosom.   He bestowed
Much largess on the mendicants and made
His tongue moreover prayerful unto God
That He might pardon what was done amiss,
And call him not tyrannic and unjust.
   The worshipper of Gcd, the pure of heart,
Will in no evil doings bear a part,
For though ill actions are not hard to do,
Yet in the end the heart is sure to rue.
Although thy heart shall be a flinty stone,
Yet in the end its secret will be known,
And low soever as thy voice may be
Time also will reveal the mystery,
While, even if the world shall not regard,
Good done in secret is its own reward.
If thou art innocent and pure of rede
A portion in both worlds will be thy meed.

§ 3

*In Praise of the Wisdom of Núshírwán, and how he
built the City of Súrsán*

The matter of Zúrán and of the Jew
Is done, to wisdom now thy praise is due.
Just though thou art here is no tarrying ;
Thy fame will be thy memory, O king !
The unjust sovereign, when all is done,
Will have but sepulchre and malison,
But if in heart thou dealest righteously
Know that the world hath gained new grace by thee ;
So if, O chief ! thou wilt have praise in death
Let wisdom be thy leaf that flourisheth.
Thus, through my words, though Núshírwán is dead,
His justice hath achieved fresh lustihead.

As soon as all the world acknowledged him
He used his greatness only to win praise,
Both great and small reposed in peace while wolf
And sheep were watered at one fount. The mighty
Did service to him and were fain to have
His name upon their diadems, the neck
Had respite from the clasp of habergeon,
The warriors loosed their coats of mail, the shoulder
Had ease from sparth and sword, and naught was heard
But sounds of mirth. None strove against the world-
    lord,
The tribute and the taxes everywhere
Were paid. He took toil easily and loved
The gear of chase and riding-ground. He sat
Within his palace arabesqued with gold,
And uttered counsel even in his cups.
He built a city on the road to Rúm
About two leagues in length. Within were mansions,
And halls and gardens, on one hand a river
And, on the other, heights. He built himself
A palace in the city with a hall
Of audience arabesqued with gold ; the vaulting
Was all in gold and silver, with the gold
Inlaid with divers kinds of precious stones.
He built a cupola of ebony
And ivory with figures of the same
And teak. Artificers from Rúm and Hind,
Whoever was a master in his craft,
And had inherited his master's skill,[1]
With all the illustrious artists of Írán,
As well as from the province of Nímrúz,
He gathered in that city, for it was
At once a great seat and a place of trade.
The prisoners of war brought from Barbar,
From Rúm, and from the parts laid desolate,

C. 168c

---

[1] Perhaps " Or had been recommended by his master."

He furnished with a dwelling-house apiece,
And made the city one of aliens.
The Sháh, the glory of the provinces,
Made of that city an attractive spot,
And, when complete, encircled it with hamlets.
The Sháh provided tracts of arable ;
The soil was fruitful and the trees bore well.
He settled there the hostages from Lúch,
Gilán, and other ravaged provinces,
Assigning occupation to each man,
And gave to each a helper if alone.
He furnished artisans, field-labourers,
And men to measure and survey the land,
Along with traders and with devotees,
With men of station and with underlings.
He decked that city as 'twere Paradise ;
The eye marked no unseemly spot therein.
He called the city by the name Súrsán,
For world-lords take delight in festivals.[1]
His only aim in public and in private
Was justice and the improvement of the world.
Since from the kingship time bare him away,
    And made his crown another's to possess,
'Twill grant not thee an ever-during stay,
    So purge thy heart of deeds of wickedness.
Know that this world is but a tricky show ;
Man keepeth nothing be it high or low.

§ 4

*The Story of the War of the Khán with Ghátkar, the Prince of
the Haitálians, the defeat of Ghátkar, and how they set
Faghánísh[2] upon the Throne*

. 1686   Hear how the Khán and the Haitálians fought,
And since a fight is toward take thy mace.

---

[1] Súr, a feast.   [2] Faghání (Chagháni ?) in original. *Cf.* p. 333.

Thus said the rustic bard, that noble one ;
Keep thou in mind what thou shalt hear from him :—
Of all the chiefs possessed of Grace and justice,
Of men of war, of treasure, and high birth,
Omitting Nushírwán, there was not one
To match the Khán of Chín in all the world.
All people from that realm to the Jíhún
Paid homage to him as their sovereign.
That chief with troops, with treasure, and with crown,
Was camped on the Gulzaryún upon
The further side of Chách.   Reports had spread,
Among the great men and throughout the world,
Of Núshírwán, his manhood, knowledge, Grace,
His greatness and imperial usages.
Then was it that the Khán, that prudent man,
Desired to win the friendship of the king.
He sat awhile with his own counsellors,
And all the men of name were gathered there.
In his desire for amity he sought
The counsel of the nobles and the priests,
Got ready presents that exceeded count—
All keepsakes worthy of a king's acceptance—
Of Rúman chargers and brocade of Chin,
Of thrones and crowns and swords and signet-rings ;
He got him ready five-score camel-loads
Of sundry trinkets that the land produced,
And bade his treasurer provide as largess
A hundred thousand of dínárs of Chín.
He also brought and added to the present
Ten camel-loads of drachms out of his treasures.
He then chose out a man of eloquence
Among his chiefs—a wise and travelled man—
And called a scribe before him with command
To write a letter from the Khán of Chín
On silk, as was the custom of the country,
Profuse in courteous greetings to the Sháh.

The envoy's way lay through the Haitálians' land—
A route beset by shaft and battleax—
Before whose ruler stood a host whose lines
From Sughd extended down to the Jihún.
That people's ruler hight Ghátkar the brave—
The most distinguished of their warriors—
Who when he heard of what the Khán had done,
And of his presents to the Íránian king,
Called from the host his veterans, discoursed
To them at large about the case, and said :—

, 1687   " Ill hath befallen us from the stars. If now
The monarch of Írán and Khán of Chín
Negotiate and thus become good friends,
That friendship will hold menace for ourselves,
And this our state be wasted on two sides.
We needs must make a foray and deprive
The envoy of his life."
               He chose among
The troops a man of name, of rank, and prowess,
Such as befitted, gave up all that wealth,
The camels and the steeds caparisoned,
To plunder and cut off the envoy's head.
One horseman of those warriors of Chín
Escaped. Now when the tidings reached the Khán
His heart was filled with grief, his head with vengeance.
He marched an army from Káchár Báshi ;
No chief was left in Chín or in Khutan.
He let no scion of Afrásiyáb,
Or of Arjásp, partake of rest and sleep.
They all marched forth to the Gulzaryún
With full hearts and with heads set on revenge.
The captain of the army of the Khán
Of Chín was Funj, who made dust reek to heaven.
At Chách the fury of the horsemen flushed
The waters of Gulzaryún rose-red.
Ghátkar heard of the doings of the Khán,

And chose an army from the Haitálians,
An army that obscured the sun, and called
For treasure, money, troops, and arms from Balkh,
Shaknán, Ámwi, the Zam, Khatlán, Tirmid,
And Wísagird ; he gathered troops from all sides ;
From mount and waste, from sands and places bare,
They seethed like ants and locusts. When the Khán
Had passed the mighty river with his host,
With drums and lusty elephants, he massed
His powers round Mái and Margh ; the sun became
As dusky as a falcon's plumes.[1] Bukhárá
Was all fulfilled with mace and ax; for there
The ruler of the Haitálians was encamped.
Ghátkár had come forth with a mighty host,
And gathered all the native chiefs. The troops
Advanced from every quarter to the war,
And left the wind no way. What with the flashing
Of chieftains' swords and play of massive maces,
Thou wouldst have said : " Now iron hath a tongue,
And air a mace for its interpreter ! "
A wind arose, rose too the army's dust,
And light departed from the sun and moon.
Men of Kashán and Sughd were gathered there.
Tears filled the eyes of all—men, women, children—
As to the issue of that battlefield,   C. 1688
And whom the circling sun and moon would favour.
For one whole week those battle-loving hosts
Were opposites. On all sides lay the slain
In heaps, and dust and stones were cercis-like
With blood. So thick were spear, mace, sparth, and
    sword
That thou hadst said : " The clouds are raining
    stones ! "
The sun evanished in the reek ; dust filled
The eyes of eagles as they flew. It veered,

---

[1] Couplet omitted.

Upon the eighth day, 'gainst Ghátkar, the world
Was all bedarkened like night azure-dim,
The Haitálians were o'erthrown, irreparably
For years, the wounded scattered everywhere,
And all the march was full of slain and captives.
The living from their hearts invoked God's name,
And said to one another : " Ne'er have we
Seen such a stubborn fight.   Good sooth ! yon host
Is not of men ; 'tis ill to look on them ; ·
They have the faces of wild beasts and divs,
And heed not right and wrong.   Thou wouldst have
    said :—
' They know not what it is to flee away
From scimitar and spear, from mace and sword.'
They all have dragon-faces and could pierce
A mountain with their spears, they all have claws
Like pards and hearts insatiate of war
And strife, ne'er take the saddle off their steeds,
And think a battle naught.   Their chargers batten
On thorns, their riders sleep not but are watchful ;
They pass the nights in foray and attack,
And hazarding their persons in the flames.
They know not food or sleep.   Would that the Div
Would challenge them to fight !   We cannot strive
Against the Khán, and we must seek Írán.
If now Ghátkar will carry out our wishes
He will submit to Núshírwán, surrender
The Haitálians' land to him, and think no more
Of mace and sparth ; but if not we will choose
Some bold chief of the race of Khúshnawáz,
Some man acceptable to Núshírwán,
One that can make our state renew its youth,
To tell the Khán's proceedings to the Sháh.
The whole world praiseth Núshírwán, for he
Hath Grace, high bearing, destiny, and wisdom,
And wisdom is the cherisher of right.

He hath made Cæsar tributary.   None
Can strive with Núshírwán."
The Haitálians—
Men, women, children—were at one herein.
There was a high-born warrior of Chaghán,   C. 1689
Aspiring, youthful, fortunate, and just—
A man of wisdom, Faghánísh by name,
Possessing troops and treasures of his own :
The chiefs and warriors [1] called him to the throne.

§ 5

*How Núshírwán had Tidings of the Battle of the Khán with
the Haitálians and how he led a Host against the Khán*

Thereafter to the great king tidings came
About the Khán, who was a valiant chief,
The Haitálians and the warriors of that folk,
And how he had o'erthrown them in the fight ;
Moreover of the monarch of Chaghán,
Just seated by new fortune on the throne,
How he had taken that imperial seat,
And, while the brave and glorious warriors
Stood, one and all, before his throne, was ever
Engaged in consultation with his magnates.
The monarch of the world sat full of care
At these his wary emissaries' words,
Then in his palace had a hall prepared
For session, and the warrior-lieges came
With the high priest Ardshír, with Yazdagird,
The scribe, and with Shápúr.   These counsellors,
And sages, all held session at the throne
Of Núshírwán, who said : " Ye archimages
Experienced and ye ministers of state !
I have discomfortable news—accounts

---

[1] Reading with P.

At once unpleasant and injurious—
About the Haitálians and what the Khán
Of Chín and marchlords of Túrán have done.
Troops gathered past all count from Chách, from Chín,
Khutan and Turkistán. They bore their helms
And vengeful scimitars for one whole week,
And never once unsaddled. In the end
The Haitálians were discomfited and most
Were slain or wounded. With renown like theirs—
A folk whose world is mace and partisan—
'Tis wonderful that they were worsted thus :
Defend me from a foolish general !
Had but Ghátkar had prudence and good sense
The sky itself had routed not his host.
The Haitálians, since their land is thus distraught,
Have sought a man descended from Bahrám Gúr,
Have placed him on the throne as their new king,
And done obeisance to him, one and all.
The Khán is posted on this side of Chách
In all his pride with treasure, host, and crown ;
He is descended from Afrásiyáb
And from Arjásp, and dreameth of Irán.
His triumph o'er the army of Ghátkar
Exalteth him in head above the sun.
It is not well for us that we should be
At one in such a story with the Khán.
Kashán, the land wherefrom this folk of Chín
Derive their strength, pertaineth to our realm.
Our subjects are oppressed by them and yield
To them their persons, boundaries, and treasure ;
What are your views herein, and how shall we
Deal with the Turkmans and the Khán of Chin ? "

    The prudent magnates rose and made reply,
First praised the Sháh, and said : " O fortunate
And prescient Sháh ! all the Haitàlian march
Is very Áhriman, the folk thereof

Are double-faced and hostile to our coast.
They merit any ill that they may get,
Although the Shâh is right to speak them fairly.
Had we no grievance, nothing to avenge
In their case save the blood of Shâh Pirúz,
That noble man whom suddenly they slew,
And such a king—the lustre of the world !
May they joy not one day, for right from wrong
Resulteth never. Such is God's requital :
Ill cometh on the heads of all ill-doers.
Now if the Shâh referreth to the Khân
As one vindictive with an ancient grudge,
It may be that he hath ill counsellors—
Some tearful scions of Afrâsiyâb.
Success too may have heartened him : no marvel
If thou dost fear him. As for the Haitálians,
And for Ghátkar's host, neither think nor trouble
Concerning them, but let thy shrewd mind turn
To what the kindred of Afrásiyáb
And of Arjásp, and what the Khán, who now
Is stablished on our bank, are doing. Thou art
The world's exalted king, both soul and wisdom
Derive their light from thee, and he is blest
Whom wisdom nourisheth. Thou art more wise
Than this great concourse and thou hast no need
Of sage or counsellor. The crown and throne
Become thee best of all the world, for thou
Hast Grace divine and might, thou fortunate !
Still if the Shâh shall go to Khurásán
He will have cause to tremble for his realm.
Hosts ever and anon will come from Rúm,
On seeing that our land is left unkinged,
Exact revenge upon the Íránians,
And leave not to Írán or field or fell.
None yet hath set his foot upon our land,
Or meditated evil on this realm,

Yet if the Sháh show fight the crocodiles
Will stir not in the streams for fear of him."

. 1691   On hearing what they said of peace and war
That master of the world agnized full well
The feeling that those sages had at heart—
That none of them had any wish for war,
Preferring rather feasts and pleasuring—
And answered : " God be praised, whom I revere
In both worlds, that Írán through quiet, sleep,
And feasting, hath forgotten how to fight !
Preferring peaceful times and banquet-hall
Ye have become indifferent to war ;
Yet ease should follow toil, the body's travail
Hath treasure for its fruit ; so in God's strength
Will we at this month's end prepare to march.
I will lead forth a host to Khurásán,
Will summon troops from all the provinces—
The men of name and warriors—and bind
The drums upon the lusty elephants.
I will not leave Haitálian or Khán
To call down blessings on Íránian soil,
But I will weed the world of all the wicked,
And by my largess and mine equity
Regenerate the realm."

      The nobles marvelled,
Applauded him, excused themselves, and said :—
" Triumphant Sháh, endowed with Grace and justice !
Oh ! may this age rejoice in thy commands.
We chiefs are all thy thralls and bow our heads
To thy behest and counsel. When the king
Shall bid us fight he will not find us wanting."
 So when the Sháh sat with his counsellors
The conclave held debate a while thereon.
Thus was it till the new moon rose and sat
On its new throne. They saw the moon withal
Upon the Sháh's own face, and acclamations

Rose from his court. Whenas the shining Lamp
O'ertopped the mountains, and the earth resembled
A golden saddle-cover, thou hadst said :—
" They have set a topaz cup upon a robe
Of lapis-lazuli." A shout and blare
Of trump arose. They bound the kettledrums
Upon the elephants, the soldiers trooped
To camp, and with them went the tymbal-players.
Then Yazdagird, the scribe, came to the court
With counselling archmages and Ardshír.
They wrote a letter unto every province,
To every man of name and every chief :—
" The Sháh hath marched forth with the host to war,
So out of loyalty forgo your feastings."
   The Sháh bade send a letter to the Khán,
He offered greetings too to Faghánísh,
And marched an army forth from Madá'in
That covered all the world except the sea ;
Earth was all troops from mountain unto mountain, C. 1692
And at their centre was the world-lord's flag.
The monarch led forth to Gurgán a host
That hid the sun. He rested for a space
O'er mount and meadow to pursue the chase.

§ 6

*How the Khán had Tidings of the Coming of the Host of
Núshírwán to Gurgán and wrote a Letter in the Cause of
Peace*

The Sháh took counsel with his troops what while
The Khán abode at Sughd, which everywhere
Was like a sea with kinsmen of Arjásp
And of Afrásiyáb. The Khán said : " Earth
Will not support this host and throne of mine.
I will lead hence the army to Írán,

And onward to the cities of the brave,
Will bear the very dust away to Chín,
And set the heaven warring with the earth.
I will allow not any to possess
Crown, throne, or kingship, dignity or fortune."
  Such was the language that he held awhile,
Ambitioning the world with troops and fame,
Until the tidings came about the Sháh,
How he had marched forth from Írán in state,
Of his victorious fortune and his might,
And how his army stretched from sea to sea.
The Khán was troubled when he heard the news
That stayed his purposed inroad, and he sat
In anxious conclave with his counsellors.
The great men of the army were assembled,
And he addressed his minister : " We cannot
Afford to blink these tidings. Núshírwán,
I hear, hath reached Gurgán and spread the realm
With troops.   Good sooth, he hath not news of us,
Or hath a witless head.   Mine army stretcheth
From Chín to the Jihún, the world is 'neath
The glory of my crown. I needs must go
And face him in the fight. Delay will shroud
The lustre of my name. Himself he deemeth
The limit and that none is king but he.
Now shall he learn of mine own warriorship,
For I will face him with the cavaliers
Of Chin."
              A wise man thus addressed the Khán :—
" O monarch of the earth ! think not to fight
Against the Sháh, and give not to the winds
Thy realm and host.   None of the kings, unless
His heart and counsel lour, ambitioneth
C. 1693   The Sháh's seat, for none hath his Grace and fortune :
The moon in heaven hath not such a mien.
He claimeth tribute both from Hind and Rúm,

Wherever there is wealth or peopled land.
He is the lord of crown, the ornament
Of throne, the conquering master of the world,
And fortunate."
        The Khán took fitting order,
On hearing this, and asked his shrewd adviser :—
" What aspect hath this matter to the wise ?
Two points confront us which we may not shun,
And cannot readily pass o'er in silence :
If war with him is toil and nothing more
There is no better course than spending treasure.
Dínárs can not be used to purchase raiment,
Or food or carpetings when war is toward,
But can procure peace, provand, fair attire,
And carpetings. Let all afraid of ill
Spurn drachms and be at ease."
        Then from the host
He chose ten fluent speakers apt for parle ;
A learnéd man of Chín too wrote a letter,
All compliments, decked like his idol-houses,
And to the king's court those ten prudent horsemen
Set forth with much to say. Now when men brought
The news to Núshírwán he decked the palace
Of king of kings, then bade to raise the curtain,
And introduce the envoys joyfully.
The ten went in before the king, and took
With them the letter, offerings, and gifts.
The world-lord, when he saw, received them well,
Inquired about the Khán and made them sit.
They bent their heads before him to the ground,
And gave the message of the Khán of Chín.
There was a letter written in that tongue
On silk, and this the envoy laid before
The scribe. When Yazdagird began to read it
The company were filled with wonderment
Thereat. It first of all invoked the blessing

Of God, the All-just, upon the king of earth,
Next manifested forth the eminence,
Wealth, army, arms, and greatness of the Khán,
And thirdly said : " Faghfúr of Chin himself
Acclaimeth me, unasked bestowed upon me
His daughter, and his host is mine to bid.
'Tis for the presents that I sent the Sháh,
Which the Haitálians stopped upon the way,
That I came forth from Chách to take revenge,
To take the crown and treasure from Ghátkar,
So came from the Gulzaryún that all
The waters of Jíhún grew red with blood,
For when in Chin news reached us of the Sháh,
I praised the teller of his victories,
· 1694 His manliness, his wisdom, modesty,
And learning, and in secrecy desired
All friendship with the monarch of the world."
  Now when the Sháh discovered from the letter
The power, the might, and purpose of the Khán,
They made a lodging ready for the envoys,
Praised and made much of them.   Whene'er the board
Was spread for feast and revelry the king
Invited them, and for a month they shared
With him the hall, the banquet, and the chase.
One day he held his court upon the plain,
The air was darkened with the horsemen's dust,
And all the marchlords with their golden girdles,
Men of Balúch and Gil with golden bucklers,
Attended in a body at that court,
Attended to do service to the Sháh,
And brought three hundred steeds caparisoned
With gold, and scimitars with golden scabbards.
Swords, double-headed darts, and javelins glittered :
Thou wouldst have said : " Gold is compact with iron."
Upon one elephant, whose back was all
Housed in brocade, they set a turquoise throne,

Nile-blue, and bruit and stir filled earth and air,
Enough to deafen even the best of ears.
The ambassadors from Barda', Hind, and Rúm,
From every sovereign and peopled realm,
And from the spear-armed horsemen of the desert,
Went in a body to the king who thus
Proved to the men of Chin : " Mine is the sway,
Mine from the sun down to the Fish's back." [1]
Air was all stir and dust of horsemen, earth
All armature of war.   They made mock-battle
Upon the plain whereon there sallied forth
The warlike cavaliers and wheeled awhile
In pride with sparth and arrow, mace and bow.
The plain was full of spear and javelin-men,
And here were foot, there horse.   The envoys, sent
From every clime by every chief and ruler,
Astonied at his host and equipage,
His countenance, his glory, and address,
Held talk with one another, saying thus
In whispers : " This is an exalted Sháh !
He seeketh honour, showeth horsemanship,
Displayeth to the warriors of the host
His spear-point, and the skill that he hath shown us
We ought to lay to heart that on returning,
Each to our king, we may remember it,
And say : ' None, young or old, hath seen one like
Sháh Núshírwán.' "
                        They told to the world's king
The sayings of the ambassadors in private.
He bade his treasurer bring upon the field   C. 1695
His battle-gear, had body-armour brought,
With helm and mail, and bade undo the buckles.[2]
No lusty warrior, though broad of breast,
Could lift the breastplate even from its place !

----

[1] See Vol. i. p. 71.
[2] " les boutons (qui joignaient le casque à la cuirasse) " (Mohl).

The Sháh alone had chest and neck to bear
The body-armour, mace, and morion.
There was no archer in the host like him,
And no such warrior among the nobles.
Like some fierce elephant he sought the field
With ox-head mace in hand and under him
A fiery steed ; his stature 'mazed the throng.
A shout rose and the blast of clarions,
While bells resounded from the elephants' backs,
And drummers with their cymbals led the way ;
Earth was in travail 'neath the horses' hoofs.
The king of kings, helmed on an armoured steed,
Wheeled to the left and right.   The ambassadors
Applauded him and louted to the ground.
The world-lord sought his palace from the plain,
And all the chieftains followed in his train.

§ 7

How Núshírwán answered the Letter of the Khán

The Sháh then bade a scribe come with Ardshír,
The high priest, and the scribe drew up on paper
A royal letter in the olden tongue.
He bathed his pen's two cheeks with ambergris,
And first gave praises to the Judge of all—
The Maker of the sky, height, depth, and love :—
" We all are thralls, He is the King of kings,
And wisdom beareth witness to His might.
No breath can pass, no emmet tread the ground,
Unless by His command.   Him have I prayed
To further, if He will, my benison
Upon the Khán.   Now, first, for what thou saidest
About the Haitálians : ' They have girt up,
As I have told to thee, their loins for ill ;
They have shed blood unjustly, wantonly,

And have been taken in their proper toils : '
The evil-doer, though of lion's strength,
Must not be bold with God. Though these men bare
Themselves like leopards thou hast conquered them.
Again, for what thou said'st about thy treasure,
Host, puissance of Faghfúr, his throne and crown :
The sage is not at one with him that speaketh
Of his own greatness.   Never hast thou seen   C. 1696
The crown and throne of greatness, and the host
And march of Chách to thee are wonderful.
All greatness is a question of degree :
What star is higher than all other stars ?
Such is the language to be held with one
That seeth not treasure, army, march, or travail.
The mighty of the world have seen or heard,
If they have seen not, me, that I account not
The sea of Chín as water, and that mountains
Flee from my wrath.   Earth is my treasury,
My care extendeth over sea and land.
Now, in the third place, thou wouldst be my friend,
And hast at heart to make with me a league.
Since thou art fain to feast I will not fight,
For no one e'er preferreth fight to feast,
And furthermore a wise man never seeketh
To fight against a man of high renown,
Still less with one compact of war, no laggard
Upon the day of battle, used to strife,
In battle-time requiring no instructor,
And one that in the fiercest of the mellay
Is as heart-calm as when enthroned and crowned.
May He that made the world be thine ally,
Thy crown and signet still continue bright."
    They sealed this with the Sháh's seal, gave new
        lustre
To royal crown and throne, prepared a robe
Of honour, as the royal usage is,

And bade the envoys come before the Sháh,
Who gave them verbal messages withal
In further explication of the letter.
The envoys well content then left the palace,
Set forth with acclamations on their way,
And came with tongues all praise before the Khán.
That world-experienced one put all folk forth ;
His minister attended at his throne.
The Khán called in the envoys and inquired
At large of them concerning Núshírwán,
First of his sense, his knowledge, and his counsel,
His mien, his conversation, and his stature ;
And secondly : " How many troops hath he,
And who of them hath crown and signet-ring ? "
Inquired about his rule, if just or not,
About his realm, his treasure, host, and crown.
The spokesman of the envoys loosed his tongue,
And answered touching all that he had seen.
He told the Khán : " Account not Núshírwán,
O king ! as one inferior to thyself.
A hundred ages see but few like him
For leadership, for statesmanship, and favour.
At home, at feast, at war, and at the chase
We never looked on such a sovereign.
In height he is a cypress-tree, in strength
An elephant ; his hand is like the Nile
C. 1697   For bounty ; throned he is a trusty sky,
In battle-tide a baleful crocodile.
When he is wroth he roareth like a cloud ;
The mighty lion quaileth at his voice,
But gentle is it when he revelleth,
And his warm utterances ravish hearts.
In state and throne he is the blest Surúsh ;
He is a royal and fruit-bearing Tree.
The whole folk of Írán compose his host,
And are the adorers of his diadem.

What time he holdeth court upon the plain
The world itself containeth not his troops.
His mace-men all have golden belts and all
His ministers decore and Grace divine.
As for the steps up to his ivory seat,
His elephants, thrones, armlets, torques and crowns,
No one in all the world can estimate
His state except the almighty Judge of all.
Although his foeman were an iron mount
'Twould be a needle's eye before his wrath.
Let him that is aweary of his life
Wax fierce and counter Núshírwán in strife ! ''

§ 8

*How the Khán bethought himself and wrote offering his
Daughter in Marriage to Núshírwán*

On hearing this the Khán turned wan and like
The flower of fenugreek, his heart grew full
Of terror at the words, his brain was rent
By his solicitude. He sat in dudgeon
With his advisers, and he thus addressed
That noble company : " Ye men of wisdom !
What is our rede herein ? Who can be more
Concerned and hurt than I by this mischance ?
He must not conquer in the fight or all
Our fame will turn to infamy."
                                        The sages
Took cognisance of all the affair and spake,
Suggesting divers lines of policy.
Then said the Khán : " Our policy is this—
To send a pledge of good faith to the Sháh,
To take a deeper view and to arrange
That he shall be affined to me. I have
Full many a daughter in my ladies' bower—
All crowns upon the heads of noble dames—

And I will wed one to the king of kings,
And thus cut short my cares in that regard.
If we make blood-relationship with him
None will advise him to our detriment.
On his side it will be a joy and honour,
While war with any other is a jest." [1]

The chiefs approved the counsel of the king,
And cried : " That is the course."

. 1698   He chose three men
Of rank out of the host, men that could speak,
And grasp an answer.   He unlocked his hoards
Of coin and said : " Why should we treasure jewels
Save to win fame, shun shame, or occupy
In largess, feasting, and expedient ? "

He had a gift made ready such as none,
Or great or small, e'er had beheld, and calling
A well experienced scribe declared his mind.
He first of all gave praises to the Maker,
All-wise, all-powerful, and all-sustaining,
The Lord of Saturn and of Sun and Moon,
The Lord of victory and mastery,
Who asketh from his slaves but righteousness,
And brooketh not that justice should be balked :—
" His blessing be upon the Íránian king,
The Lord of scimitar, of mace, and helm,
The Lord of understanding, crown, and throne,
And dowered by the God of victory
With fortune and content.   The king of kings,
Of royal race, wise, weighty, learned, and just,
Is ware that men, albeit great and noble,
Fain would be dear in other men's regard.
Now when my sage ambassadors, the men
That are both mine associates and allies,
Had come back from thy court to mine and told me
At large about the Sháh—his justice, wisdom,

---

[1] Reading with P.

Good fortune, crown, pre-eminence, and throne—
His Grace divine caused to arise in me
A great desire to shadow 'neath his wings.
Now naught is dearer than our own heart's blood,
And prudent children and our hearts are one ;
So let him, if he will, demand of me
One of my stainless daughters—her that is
Most gentle, fair, discreet—and she in sooth
Shall profit him, the marches of Irán
And Chin shall meet, our worship be the more."
    This was all written out on silk of Chín,
And carried with the seal to the wazir.
The Khán selected from among his kin
Three men of noble rank and eloquence,
And they departed from the exalted court
Írán-ward to the exalted Sháh who, when
He heard thereof, prepared his crown and sat
Upon his royal throne of ivory.
So those three men of prudence and high rank
Arrived before the exalted throne. They brought
Three turbans, of dínárs some thirty thousand,
And laid them as a gift before the Sháh.
The gifts of gold and silver, the brocade
Of Chin, made earth more brilliant than the sky.
Now when the envoys duly had been seated
They called down blessings in their native tongue,
And then the Sháh's chief minister prepared   C. 1699
Fit lodging for them. Heaven revolved one night,
And when the bright sun rose above the mountains
The Sháh sat down upon the turquoise throne,
And set a crown of jewels on his head.
He ordered that the archmages and the chiefs
Should sit in conclave with the famous sages,
And said thus : " Bring and lay before the scribe
The letter writ on silk."
                 The nobles all

Sat round while Yazdagird drew near the Sháh,
And read the letter which amazed the throng,
Such good will, fair excuse, and compliment
Were patent in the utterance of the Khán.
All those illustrious and prudent chiefs
Began to praise the king : " Thanks be to God,
With whom our refuge is, that He hath set
Upon the state a Sháh endowed with Grace,
With victory, and majesty, a Sháh
Good, kind, and prudent, one that is in fight
A mighty, raging elephant, in feast
A gallant host. ·All foes are underlings
Of thine, if they be worthy of that title.
We all were fearful of this power from Chách,
And of the Khán, who hath both crown and treasure,
By the imperial Grace is now our friend,
And seeketh with the Sháh affinity.
One that is wise among the warrior-chiefs
Will tender peace and justice. Since the Khán
Is ware that he can not withstand the Sáhh
He seeketh for affinity to him.
There should be no delay in this affair,
For such affinity disgraceth none.
His troops extend from Chin up to Bukhárá,
And all the chiefs are under his protection."
    Now when the Sháh heard what those sages said—
Those magnates and archmages shrewd of heart—
They cleared the hall of strangers and then brought
The ambassadors in haste before the Sháh.
The king of kings received them graciously,
And set them near the throne. Those chosen men
Of Chách beheld the chief in all his pomp
Of troops, wealth, crown, and gave their master's
    message,
Protesting that their words were true. The Sháh,
When he had heard the fervent words thus uttered

In gentle accents by the chiefs of Chin,
Replied : " The Khán is great, wise, worshipful,
Desireth kinship with us through his child,
And illustrateth thus his own good will.
The man whom understanding maketh wise
Will look upon affairs with wisdom's eye ;
We will take order, will advise us well,
And make response to all that he hath said
On this condition—that the Khán of Chín
Shall give our heart the liberty of choice.
I will dispatch a wise man who shall look
On all his women-folk and shall select
The most illustrious and dear to him,
See what her own maternal grandsire was,
And her own quality of royal birth.
When what we name shall have been done the Khán
Will have performed his portion of the pact."
    The envoys called down praises, saying thus :—
" The Khán of Chín rejoiceth in the Sháh,
And were his ladies' bower a cloud of jewels
He would withhold it not from Núshírwán.
Select among the sages one to go
Before the Khán whose ladies shall not fail
In that one's sight their faces to unveil."

C. 1700

§ 9

How Núshírwán answered the Letter, and sent Mihrán Sitád to see and fetch the Daughter, of the Khán

The king of kings heard what they said ; the age,
Outworn, revived for him.   He called a scribe,
Spake of the Khán at large, and bade indite
An answer couched in choice and gracious terms.

He first gave praises to almighty God,
" The World-lord, Conqueror, and Nourisher.
The world is 'stablished by His ordinance ;
He is our Guide to good. He giveth worth
To whom He will and from abasement raiseth
Such to high heaven, the while another man
Is left in luckless case because unfavoured
By Him to Whom I own that thanks are due
For every blessing, and of Whom my heart
Is fearful when I do amiss. I would
That life should cease within my heart if I
E'er should desist from hope and fear in Him.
The worshipful ambassador hath come,
And brought a gracious message from the Khán.
Heard have I what was said about a league,
And of the virtuous daughters of his house :
My heart would joy to be allied to him,
And in especial through his own chaste child.
Lo ! I have sent to thee a prudent man,
A man whose mind esteemeth wisdom dear.
On coming he will tell thee all my views
As touching this alliance first and last.

C. 1701   Mayst thou for ever have a reverent mind,
Be happy-hearted and our warm friend still."
    The writer, when the pen was out of work,
Embellished all the paper, rolled it up,
And, when the last tears of the pen were dry,
Affixed a seal of musk. The Sháh bestowed
A robe of honour on the ambassadors,
Such as amazed the company, and chose
A wise old chief, by name Mihrán Sitád,
And five score famed Íránian cavaliers,
All men renowned, discreet, and eloquent,
And said thus to Mihrán Sitád : " Go forth
Glad and triumphant, and with love and justice.
Be thine the fluent tongue of chiefs, be wisdom

Thy guide, thy heart all lovingkindliness.
Scan well the women's quarters of the Khán,
And throughly search out all their good and ill.
They must not fool thee with a mere display
Of countenance, of grace, and ornament.
The Khán hath many daughters stately, tall,
And crowned, behind his curtains, and of these
The offspring of his slaves are not for me,
Although they have a king to father them ;
Look thou for one that is both meek and good,
Whose mother is descended from the Kháns.
If she hath gifts according to her birth
She will rejoice the world and live in joy."
    Mihrán Sitád, when he had heard, invoked
Much blessing on the crown and throne, and left
The portal of the world-illuming Sháh
At a propitious season on the day
Khurdád. News of his coming reached the Khán,
Who sent out troops to welcome him, and when
He reached the presence of the Khán he kissed
The ground and proffered praise. On seeing him
That world-aspiring king received him well,
Assigning him an honourable room,
But, being much concerned at the affair,
Withdrew to the apartments of the queen,
Declared to her the words of Núshírwán,
Spake of his treasures and his host, and " This
Sháh Núshírwán," he told her, " is still young,
And wary, and his fortune is young also.
Fain am I to bestow on him a daughter
To magnify our worship in his sight.
One such I have, concealed behind the veil—
A Crown upon the head of lady-hood,
The fairest of the fair throughout the world,
And many a chief hath sought her at my hands.
I love her so that never would I cease

To gaze upon her face. I have four others—
The offspring of my slaves, themselves both slaves
And handmaids, clever girls—and one of them
Will I bestow on him, and rest from warfare,
And from dispute."

. 1702　　　　　　　　The queen replied to him :—
" None in the world will oust thee, thou'rt so wise ! "
　In such discourse they passed the night away
Until the sun ascended o'er the mountains,
And then Mihrán Sitád arrived, drew near
The throne, and gave the letter. When the Khán
Had read he smiled upon the union
And goodly choice proposed, gave up the key
That oped his ladies' bower, and said : " Go look
On what is hidden there."

　　　　　　　　　　Four trusty slaves
Came to accompany Mihrán Sitád,
Who, when he heard the Khán, went with the key
And them withal. He oped the doors. They entered,
The slaves protesting to him : " Never star
And sun and moon have seen the sight that thou
Art on thy way to see ! "

　　　　　　　　　　The ladies' bower
Was Paradise adorned—all Suns and Moons
And goodly havings—while upon the throne
Five fay-faced maidens sat crowned and arrayed
In treasures, save the daughter of the queen,
Who wore no crown or bracelet, torque or jewel,
But only had on her a well-worn robe,
And for a crown her musky locks divine.
Her cheeks were made not up : she only wore
What God had given her—a Cypress she,
Surmounted by a new moon that diffused
A lustre o'er the new throne where she sat.
Now when Mihrán Sitád came and beheld
He saw none like to her, and, being shrewd

Of heart and counsel, knew that king and queen
Were fooling him. The damsel used her hands
As kerchief for her eyes. Mihrán Sitád
Grew wroth anew and told the slaves : " The Sháh
Hath many a bracelet, crown, and throne, and I
Choose her that lacketh crown and ornament,
For these will make her still more beautiful.
I came to show discretion in my choice ;
I came not to procure brocade of Chin."
    The queen replied : " Old man ! thou speakest not
One gracious word and art not well advised
If thou preferrest such a child as this
To these princesses who are gracious, fair,
And wise, have reached a marriageable age,
And kindle hearts—girls tall as cypress-trees,
With cheeks like spring and very well aware
Of all the worship that is due to kings."
    Mihrán Sitád said : " If the Khán shall act
Unfairly in this matter let him know
That Núshírwán, the monarch of the world,
Will term me an old knave. The one that sitteth,
All unadorned by bracelet, torque, and crown,
Upon the ivory throne best pleaseth me ;
But, if your Highnesses will not consent,
With your permission I will go my ways."
    The queen observed his words. His policy
And conduct made her muse. The crafty envoy
Then left her, went back to the Khán, and told
All that had passed. The Khán saw him perturbed,
And knew : " This shrewd old man is great and apt
For delicate affairs."
             The prudent king
Sat with his counsellors, put forth the throng,
And, when the place for conclave had been cleared,
The readers of the stars who bore in hand
Their Rúman astrolabes, the mighty men,

C. 1703.

And all the chiefs, attended. Then the Khán
Commanded every loyal liege to mark
The aspect of the sky. The sages scanned
The stars to find out how the Khán should act,
And as to his alliance with the Sháh,
And at the last said thus : " Let not, O king !
Thy heart be vexed by evil any whit,
Because this matter can but end in good,
And time will count thy foemen's counsels ill.
This is the purpose of high heaven herein—
The horoscope and prosperous event—
That from the daughter of the Khán and from
The Sháh's loins a throne-gracing prince will come ;
The country of Írán,[1] the men of name
And worth in Chín, his praises shall proclaim."

§ 10

How the Khán sent his Daughter, escorted by Mihrán,
with a Letter and Treasures to Núshírwán

The Khán, on hearing this, was glad of heart,
Smiled too the sunlike queen. When they had purged
Their hearts of artifice they set the envoy
Before them and told all that he should know
About the queen's child kept secluded thus,
Whom from her sire Mihrán Sitád received
On the victorious king of kings' behalf.
The deputy received, the Khán bestowed,
The only daughter that the queen had borne.
The handmaids came with gifts, came joyfully
Before the king, and afterwards a treasure,
Comprising goods of all sorts, was prepared—
Dínárs, gems, torques, and crowns, a turquoise litter,

---

[1] Reading with P.

An ivory throne, and one of aloe-wood
From Hind, with gold and divers jewelry
Inlaid, and with each throne a royal crown ;
A hundred horses and a hundred camels,
The horses saddled and the camels bearing
Brocade of Chin, and forty tapestries
Of cloth of gold enriched with emeralds.
Of carpets too he laid a hundred loads
On camels, and brought forth three hundred handmaids,
And saw that all were mounted for the journey,
Each with a flag in hand—the use in Chin.
The Khán, victorious of fortune, bade
To set up on an elephant a throne
Embossed with gold and silver all incrusted
With gems unworn, and rear a flaunting flag
That made the ground all viewless with brocade.
It took a hundred men to carry forth,
And raise, that standard skyward from the plain.
A litter tricked out with brocade and gold
Contained the maiden Gem.   Three hundred hand-
      maids,
All blithe of heart and bright of countenance,
Accompanied that moon-faced one.   He sent
His daughter to the Sháh with troops for escort,
And forty eunuchs to precede the slaves,
And march before her with rejoicing hearts.
The preparations over, came the scribe,
And brought with him rose-water, musk, and silk.
The Khán then wrote a letter like the Artang,[1]
All illustration, colour, scent, and beauty,
And first of all gave praises to the Maker,
Lord of the world, all-watchful and all-seeing :—
" He fashioned all things by divine decree
To guide His servants to predestined ends.

C. 1704

---

[1] Arzhang, another form of the same word, in the original. For
Artang, see Vol. ii. p. 19 and *note*.

My crown is the Íránian king of kings.
Not for my daughter's sake have I desired
A league with him, but hearing from the wise,
The great men and the wary-hearted priests,
About his Grace, his majesty, and throne,
I sought for intercourse and league with him
Because so just a ruler girdeth not
His loins in all the world, or one so great
In manhood, victory, and mastery,
In Grace, mien, throne, and crown, while holy God
Sustaineth him with justice and with knowledge,
With Faith and wisdom.   Lo ! we have dispatched,
According to our rites, our very Eye
To Núshírwán the Sháh, commanding her
To serve him as his slave when she shall pass
Behind his curtains.   From his Grace and insight
She will learn wisdom and acquire his ways
And usages.   May wit and fortune guide thee,
Be majesty and knowledge thy supports."
    They set the seal upon that musk of Chin,
And gave the letter to the ambassador
. 1705   With compliments.   The Khán prepared for him
A robe of honour past all precedent
As given by the great ones of the world
In public or in private to an envoy.
The Khán gave presents also to the suite,
And made them happy with dinárs and musk.
He travelled with his daughter and the goods,
The beasts and elephants caparisoned,
Until he reached the bank of the Jíhún,
And poured his heart's blood from his eyes the
    while ;
He thence betook him homeward with full heart
And, in his daughter's stead, had pain for comrade ;
Howbeit he delayed till they had crossed,
And reached dry land upon the further side.

When tidings came about Mihrán Sitád [1]
The folk presented gifts and offerings,
And all with one consent called blessings down
Upon the Sháh and on the chief of Chin.
With hearts rejoiced with largess and with gifts,
And all disposed for hospitality
And amity, the folk decked road and city,
And showered drachms upon the royal bride.
Toward Ámwi and Marv's unwatered ways
All earth was like a pheasant's plumes, and thou
Hadst said of all the journey to Bastám,
And to Gurgán : " The earth saw not the sky
For decorations and triumphal arches
In waste and town wherethrough the progress lay."
Men, women, children, from the palaces,
Met where that Idol brought from Chin would pass,
Showered on her escort drachms from overhead,
And sifted o'er them musk and ambergris.
The scents were mixed on salvers, and the world
Was full of din from trump and kettledrum.
The horses' manes were drenched with musk and
        wine,
And sweets and drachms were scattered under-foot,
While through the din of rebeck, harp, and pipe,
There was no room on earth for rest and sleep.
Now when the Idol reached the royal bower,
And Núshírwán had looked within the litter,
He saw a Cypress with the orbéd moon
Above it and upon the moon a crown
Of ambergris. There was another too
Of musky coils joined chain-wise, link on link,
The links entrammelled, plaited daintily,
And curiously entwined like civet ring-work
Upon a rose's petal, while beneath
The ring-work shone the planet Jupiter.

[1] Reading with P.

Sháh Núshírwán was all astound thereat,
And o'er her oft invoked the name of God,
Assigned her a fit dwelling for her own,
And they made ready for that Moon a throne.

§ 11

*How the Khán withdrew, and how Núshírwán marched
from Gurgán to Taisafún*

C. 1706

When of Írán and of the Íránian king
News reached the Khán of Chín, and of the joy
Wherewith his child had been received, and how
The alliance caused good cheer and happiness,
He gave up Sughd and Samarkand and Chách,
And sent his crown on to Káchár Báshi.
Now when the hosts of Chin had left these states
The Sháh sent marchlords thither. He renewed
The world by equity, and old and young
Could sleep upon their backs. All everywhere
Called blessings down on him with hands upraised
To heaven : " O Ruler over space and time !
Keep in Sháh Núshírwán this justice still,
And turn the ills of fortune from his life,
For by his Grace divine and majesty
Both public ills and private have been banned.
What time he reached Gurgán to hunt none saw
The Khán's face smile ; the cavaliers of Chin
Forwent their food and sleep, and none off-saddled ;
Three hundred thousand Turkman troops dispersed
Instead of striving and of combating ;
There is no need to string the bow, for none
Of Chin, or small or great, remaineth here,
Such were the Grace divine and royal mien
Wherewith the savage Lion sought the chase ;

Such were his reputation and his star
That fortune was the comrade of his throne."
   Then from the regions lying 'twixt Ámwi,
Chách, and Khutan, the nobles met and said :—
"These spacious regions full of pleasances,
Of riding-grounds, of palaces, and halls,
From Chách and the Tarak to Samarkand
And Sughd [1] are wholly waste—the home of owls.
They of Chaghán, Shiknán, Khatlán, and Balkh,
Have all experienced dark and bitter days.
Great are our pain and sorrow when we name
Bukhárá and Kharazm, Ámwi and Zam.
Once none gat rest and sleep, so tyrannous
And cruel was Afrásiyáb ! Howbeit
We found deliverance when Kai Khusrau
Came, and the world had peace from bickering.
Then when Arjásp gained lustihead these marches
Were filled with anguish and calamity,
But when Gushtásp marched from Írán to battle
Arjásp perceived no tarrying-place, and then
The world had quiet from his enterprises.   C. 1707
May heaven ne'er befriend him ! Afterwards,
What time Narsi became the chief, these coasts
Were full of misery, but when Shápúr,
Son of Urmuzd, usurped, and when Narsi
Discerned not hand from foot, the world found justice,
And quiet, and the hand of Áhriman
Was stayed from evil. When the Khán bore off
The world from Yazdagird, and had acquired
Dexterity in ill, there came the world-lord,
Bahrám Gúr, to afflict and trouble him,
To make the states like Paradise with justice,
And scatter the unseemly and the foul.
So Khúshnawáz, what time Pírúz was Sháh,
Filled all the world with bloodshed, heat, and anguish,

---

[1] Reading with P.

And perish Faghánísh that son of his
With all his unjust kith and kin !   And now
The world-lord Núshírwán hath occupied
Our marches and hath made us rich indeed !
For ever may his policy endure,
And may the whole world be at one with him.
Now that the earth beholdeth justice we
Will contemplate no travail, shed no blood." [1]
    Then from the Haitálians, Turkmans, and Khutan
The people met by the Gulzaryún
From every quarter where some shrewd priest lived,
Or other potentate good, learned, and wise,
While all the Turkmans that were well advised
Drew to the Sháh—a mighty company.
It was the policy of all these troops
To come before the Sháh with offerings,
And when they came before him, when they came,
All with one heart and tongue, the monarch's court
Was so fulfilled with people that they barred
The way to ant and gnat !   All louted low,
Called praises down upon the Sháh, and said :—
" O Sháh ! we are thy slaves and live to do
Thy bidding in the world.   We all of us
Are nobles dight for war and rend the hides
Of leopards on the field."
                    The king of kings
Received their gifts, and then they left the presence,
Their leader Faghánísh.   Behind him came
A troop of youthful warriors.   When thus
They had found favour in the monarch's sight
The chamberlain went to the palace-gate
With formal greetings and with compliments,
And lodged them through the city.   Afterwards
The king of kings, that worshipper of God,

---

[1] The historical reminiscences put into the mouths of dwellers beyond
the Oxus and even the Jaxartes are of course valueless.

Passed from the audience-chamber to the dust,
And offered up thanksgivings to the Almighty :—
" O Thou above vicissitudes of fortune !
Thou gav'st me Grace, accomplishment, and counsel,
And art my Guide in all things good and ill,
For all that hear of me seek not thereafter
The crown of majesty, but all submit
To be my lieges.   None hath pluck to fight.
Birds on the mountains, fishes in the water,
Remain awake to watch what time I slumber ;
All the wild creatures are my sentinels,
The mighty of the world mine underlings ;
No abject he whom Thou dost choose who art
The world's sole Lord and giv'st me strength therein
That not an ant may sleep aggrieved by me."
    'Twas thus he spake with many tears to God :
Canst find within the world a king like him ?
Then from his place of prayer he sought his throne,
And they prepared to quit Gurgán.   The blast
Of trumpets and the din of brazen cymbals
Ascended from the court.   He called to horse,
And loaded up, invoking the All-giver.
He took dínárs, brocade, crowns, belts, and treasures
Of drachms and gems, steeds, female slaves, and
        crowns,
The turquoise litter and the ivory throne.
The heart-alluring handmaids and the thralls
Of all descriptions mounted on the saddle.
The Sháh dispatched them all to Taisafún,
Preceded by the women-folk of Chín,
Who fared auspiciously and cheerfully
Surrounded by the eunuchs.   As high priest,
Mihrán Sitád accompanied the queen,
The daughter of the Khán, and thus the treasures
And baggage went toward Taisafún.   A band
Composed of warriors only—all the best

C. 1708

And noblest of the mighty men—approached
Afoot Ázar Ábádagán while troops
Came from each province, soldiers from Gilán
And Dílamán,[1] the mountains of Balúch,
And deserts of Sarúch, and warriors
From Lúch, all came with gifts and offerings
Before the tent-enclosure of the king,
Whereat the famous chiefs rejoiced and thought :—
" The wolf's claws grow too short to reach the sheep ! "
    World without end strife with Balúch had raged,
And filled the cities with distress and anguish,
But by the Grace of Núshírwán the sky
Had changed its use and favour.[2]   Wheresoever
The host was wont to pass it did not use
To harm a crop, to ask for bread and water,
But made its sleeping-quarters on its route.
The Sháh on this wise went about the world,
Surveying every place, both field and waste.
He saw that all the world was full of crops,
While sheep and oxen filled the hills and plains.
A region ne'er before inhabited,
Where none had looked on sowing and on reaping,
He now surveyed and found it bearing fruit,
Found too a family in every house.
The trees were laden through the Grace divine
Of that victorious master of the world.
At one stage of the progress of the Sháh
The ambassador of Cæsar came with presents,
With silver and withal a throne of gold,
And Rúman jewels and brocade—a gift
That covered all the surface of the ground :
So great a tribute ne'er had come from Rúm.
Ten ox-hides had been filled up with dínárs—
The tribute and the taxes of three years—
And with the presents Cæsar had dispatched

‹ 1709

————
[1] =Dilam.   [2] See p. 241 seq.

A letter to the famous king. They set
The envoy in the presence, and the Sháh
Was all attention while they read the letter.
'Twas full of warm expressions of good will
About the gifts that had been sent to him :—
" Hereafter will I send thee greater gifts,
For these are merely meant for largessing."
    The Sháh received them, mounted on his steed,
And sought the temple of Ázargashasp.
When, still afar, he saw the place of worship
His cheeks were hidden by his tears. He lighted
Down from his steed and, sacred twigs [1] in hand,
Made prayer with bated breath ; [2] then drawing near
The Fire he worshipped and adored the Maker.
He gave the temple-bursar all the gold,
And all the many gems that he had brought,
And showered gold and silver on the archmages,
Bestowing on them likewise gems and raiment.
All were enriched by him and sought the Fire
To offer up their thanks in muttered tones, [3]
And blessed withal the righteous judge of earth.
He parted thence for Taisafún ; the host
Made earth a Mount Bistún. That righteous Sháh,
On reaching any city, used to give
Much gold and silver to the mendicants.
Through all the wealth that he disposed of thus
The realm was stuffed with treasure and with drachms.
From Taisafún he drew toward Madá'in,
For there he wont to keep his treasuries' key.
He took the Rose of Chín [4] and forty more
Withal. Mihrán Sitád fared on before.

---

[1] See Vol. i. p. 80, *s.v. Barsam.*
[2] *Id., s.v. Báj.*   [3] *Id.*   [4] Literally " Rose-garden."

§ 12

Discourse on the Justice of Núshírwán and how
Mortals had Peace under his Usages

When Núshírwán ascended to his throne
In pomp, with his good fortune for his mate,
The world was decked like Paradise with justice,
· 1710   With goodliness, and wealth, had rest from strife,
Inequity, and bloodshed, everywhere,
And was renewed by Grace divine. "They have,"
Thou wouldst have said, "bound both the hands of
    evil."
None knew of pillage, raid, or putting forth
The hand to ill ; all came at his behest
From darkness and perverseness to the way.
If any dropped a drachm upon the road
A thief would shun that wealth ! As for brocade
And for dinárs, on land and sea, by daylight,
And in the hours for sleep, the ill-disposed
Would look not to that quarter out of fear,
And through the justice of the Sháh, the world-lord.
The world was pargetted like Paradise,
And dale and desert were fulfilled with wealth.
Dispatches went to all the provinces,
To every man of name and potentate,
While from the Turkman merchants and from Chin,
Sakláb and every province, came such store
Of musk-bags and of silk of Chin, of trinkets
Of Rúm and of the land of Hind, as made
Írán like jocund Paradise ; its dust
Was ambergris, its bricks were gold. The world
Turned toward Írán and rested from distress
And bickering. "The breezes shed rose-water,"
Thou wouldst have said, and men had peace from pain
And leech. The moisture showered upon the rose

In season, and the farmer was not sad
Through lack of rain. The world grew full of herbage
And cattle, plains and valleys were all flowers,
Rooftrees, and dwellings, all the streams seemed seas,
And roses Pleiad-like within the gardens.
Men learned to speak new tongues within Írán,
Illumed their souls with knowledge, and returned
Thanksgiving to their guide, the Sháh, for all
The traffickers that came from every march
And land, from Turkistán, Chin, Hind, and Rúm,
While cattle multiplied amid the herbage.
All learnéd men and ready speakers found
A place at court. The great, the men of lore,
And archimages were esteemed, the wicked
Shook fearful of calamity. What time
The sun adorned the world a proclamation
Would go up from the court : " All ye that are
The servants of the monarch of the world !
Keep not ill hidden, any one of you !
Whoe'er hath toiled at any task shall have
A treasure in proportion to his travail.
Prefer your claims before our chamberlain
That he may seek your recompense from us.
If any creditor shall come and ask
For payment from the poor, my treasurer
Will pay the debt because the destitute
Must not be troubled. Whosoe'er shall look   C. 1711
Upon another's wife, and his accuser
Appeal to us, the offender shall see naught
But pit and gibbet, bondage in the pit,
And arrows on the gibbet. If men find
A horse at large, and any husbandman
Complain thereof at court, let it be slain
Upon that tilth, and he shall have the carcass
Who had the scath, the horseman shall be horseless,
And fare afoot before Ázargashasp

To tender his excuse, the muster-master
Shall strike his name off from the muster-roll,
They shall lay low his dwelling, and the offender,
Whate'er his rank may be, shall be degraded.
The Sháh can not be of one mind with such,
Will have the righteous only at his court,
And at our court God grant there never be
Those that approve not of our policy."

§ 13

How Búzurjmihr counselled Núshírwán and discoursed on good Deeds and Words

One day the world-lord, as he sat rejoicing,
Gave audience to the mighty men of wisdom.
He spake with smiles and open countenance,
And seated Búzurjmihr upon the throne,
Who offered to the king such praise as made
His heart like jocund spring, and thus he said :—
" O righteous judge so fresh of visage ! may
Fault-finders never find a fault in thee.
Blest king of kings, whose fortune prospereth,
The wise, triumphant master of the world !
I erst recorded in the olden tongue
Some thoughts upon a roll of royal paper,
Which I entrusted to thy treasurer
Till there might come a season when the Sháh
Would read it, but I see the mystery
Is one that laggard heaven will disclose not.
What though a man shall quit his seat at feasts,
And take his life within his hands in fight,
Shall sweep the earth of enemies and be
Secure against the toils of Áhrimans,
Shall be the great king over all the world,
And consummate his wishes one by one,

Shall win the wide world by his bravery,
Make rosary and pleasance, park and palace,
Shall lay up wealth, have sons surrounding him,
And reckon many days of happiness,
Shall bring together warriors and wealth,
Shall decorate his palaces and halls,
And, while the poor are toiling for his sake,
Amass on all sides treasure and renown,
Still willy nilly he but gathereth dust ;   C. 1712
His lifetime will not last a century.
He will be dust, his toils will bear no fruit
For him, and all his wealth will be his foe's.
No children, throne or crown or royal hall,
Or treasury or army will be his,
And when he ceaseth to pursue the wind
None in the world will give a thought to him.
Of all his doings when his time is over
A good name will be his memorial.
In this world there are two things that endure,
And only two, the rest will last with none—
Choice sayings and good doings : these will last
Until the world shall end, auspicious Sháh !
Time's course is such that fame and honest speech
Spoil not through sun and water, wind and dust.
The modest man and virtuous is blest.
Avoid, O king ! with all thy might the faults
That shame the soul. Harm not but help ; thus Faith
And precedent prescribe. I leave behind me
Words that, I ween, ne'er will grow obsolete."

He oped the king's shrewd heart who questioned him
On many points : " Who is the glorious man,
Whose heart is glad, who sigheth not ? "

He answered :—
" The innocent, the man whom Áhriman
Hath caused not to transgress."

The Sháh then asked him

Concerning guile, the Div's way, and the way
Of God, the world's Lord. Búzurjmihr replied :—
"To do God's will is best, for in both worlds
The Grace is His. The door of evil leadeth
To Áhriman who is the enemy
Of those that worship God. The high-souled man
Is blesséd in the world, for his adornments
Are holiness and modesty. Since knowledge
Safe-guardeth him his life is one of ease,
He hath nobility and righteousness,
And knocketh not upon the door of guile,
And loss. When he is dead his soul will be
A foe to what pertaineth to the body.
He is not negligent about them both,
But is concerned for either sword or scabbard." [1]

. 1713 Then Núshírwán inquired : "Among the chiefs
What man attaineth to the highest standard ? "
  Said Búzurjmihr : "The man that hath most know-
   ledge,
And most controlment over his desires."
  "Who is the man of knowledge," said the Sháh,
"For knowledge is a matter hid in men ? "
  "The man that neither severeth heart from God,"
He answered, "at the bidding of the Div,
Nor out of wantonness obeyeth one
That is the foe of souls and wisdom's snare.
Ten Áhrimans there are with lion's might,
Who lord it over wisdom and the soul."
  "What then are these ten divs," said Núshírwán,
"Since wisdom hath good reason to bewail them ? "
  He thus made answer, saying : "Greed and Need
Are two o'erweening divs and puissant.[2]
The rest are Anger, Envy, Strife, Revenge,
Backbiting, Treachery, and Faith Impure.
The tenth div is Ingratitude to men

---

[1] Five couplets omitted.   [2] *Cf.* Vol. vi. p. 146.

For benefits and Ignorance of God."
   The Sháh said : " Of these ten divs, ruinous
And black, which Áhriman is lustiest ? "
   He answered Núshírwán thus, saying : " Greed
Is a tyrannic div, the last to go.
Him never wilt thou see content in aught,
But ever labouring for something more.
All those that look on Need behold him blind,
And sallow with anxiety and pain.
The div of Envy is the next, O king !
And is an ailment that no leech can cure.
His soul is pained to see one prosperous.
Strife is another div and passionate,
For ever quick to put his hand to ill ;
Revenge, another, wrathful, turbulent,
And instant to arouse the battle-cry
In men, unloving and ungenerous—
A div malignant and with frowning face ;
Another, Slander, knowing naught but lies,
And doing all his traffic in the dark ;
Another, Treachery, with double face,
Who feareth not the Master of the world,
But flingeth strife and vengeance 'twixt two men,
And toileth to break up alliances :
The last, Ingratitude and Ignorance—
A witless div unconscious of all good,
Contemptuous of rede and modesty,
And in whose sight both good and ill are one."
   The king then asked the sage : "How doth the
     Div
Make war against the heart, and what hath God
Bestowed upon His servants so that they
May counteract the Div ? "
               That man of Faith
Replied : " Wise, glorious Sháh ! against the sword
Of divs the coat of mail is wisdom ; that

Illumineth the sage's heart and mind,

Recordeth what is passed and nourisheth
The soul with knowledge. Oh ! may wisdom be
The guider of thy mind because the way
Is long before thee, and if wisdom prove
A second nature, as the saying is,
So that the heart is fearless of the Div,
The good heart will find pleasure in the world,
And not frequent the portal of desire.
Now will I utter words of hope to guide
The heart to joy : the sage is always hopeful,
And seeth naught but happiness from time,
Not for a moment meditateth ill,
And chooseth not the bow's path but the arrow's.
Moreover one contented doth not stretch
His hand to treasure or fatigue himself ;
He that despiseth drachm and treasury
Will fleet his sum of days in happiness.
Moreover one that is devote to God [1]
In all will turn not from His ordinance
For toil or treasure or the fear of man ;
He hath no strain of evil in his nature,
And by that token he is virtuous too
Because he will sell not God's way for aught."
    Said Núshírwán : " Which is the royal way
Conducting us to good ? "
                              He answered thus :—
" The way of wisdom doubtlessly. surpasseth
All knowledge.   Likewise being well disposed
Will keep a man in honour all his days ;
While of the qualities the mightiest
Is in my view contentment with one's lot ;
The most agreeable, which refresheth most
In travail, and the seemliest, is hope.
In greed I see the weariest of all,

                    [1] Reading with P.

For that is never satiate of wealth."
The Sháh said : "Which accomplishment is best,
The one whereby aspirants win to greatness ? "
He answered : "Knowledge, for the sage is greatest
Among the great as clutching not at treasure,
And holding of himself aloof from travail."
The Sháh then asked him : "How shall we proceed
To overcome the might of enemies ? "
"Ill-doing is the enemy," he answered,
"Alike of wisdom and the soul serene."
The righteous judge then asked the sage and said :—
"Is talent or is application better ? "
The sage made answer, saying : "Application
Is more than natural ability,
For application furnisheth the mind,
While talent only maketh talking easy,
And, when untrained, is wretched, vile, and weak,
But application strengtheneth the soul."
"How can the mind be polished," said the Sháh,
"And what accomplishments commend the body ? "
"Now," said he, "will I make a full reply,   C. 1715
If thou wilt take it from me point by point :
Since wisdom is itself God's robe of honour
No thought can gain it and no evil touch it ;
So one accomplished but withal conceited
Should have no credit for accomplishments,
While no wise man regardeth with disdain
The merest peasant well-disposed by nature,
And though a sage join bounty to high birth,
Join knowledge, conduct, equity, yet will
His greatness, his addition, and uprightness
All suffer if his natural bent be vicious."
Then Núshírwán inquired : "Illustrious scholar !
Doth greatness come from toil or doth the world-lord
Get crown and throne from fortune ? "
He replied :—

" The fortune and accomplishment of men
Are mates allied and joined like soul and body,
The body visible, the soul concealed.
The body is man's instrument for toil,
When wakeful fortune shall bestir itself,
But by his travail ne'er will he attain
To greatness if good fortune guide him not.
Again, the world is all deceit and wind,
Or memory of a dream that vanisheth
When one awaketh, whether he beheld
A pleasant vision or a painful one."
   A question then occurred to Núshírwán ;
He asked the sage : " Who should be praised ? "
                                    He answered :—
" A king that doth adorn the throne and hath
His strength from fortune will, if he doth justly,
And is of fair repute, attain his end
In word and deed."
                  " What man is sorrowful,"
The Shah said, " luckless, and unprofitable ? "
   The sage replied : " The wicked mendicant,
Who loseth both this world and Paradise."
   " Who is the luckless one," rejoined the Shah,
" For whom we must weep always bitterly ? "
   And Búzurjmihr replied : " The man of know-
      ledge,
Whose face is sallow through his evil deeds."
   The Shah asked further : " Who is the contented,
And who is anxious to increase his store ? "
   He made response : " He that regardeth not
The revolutions of the turning sky."
   Then Núshírwán : " What man best suiteth us ? "
And Búzurjmihr replied : " The gentlest man."
   " But who is gentle," asked the Shah, " for why
The hasty give us cause to weep ? "
                                    He answered :—

"Mark him that shunneth converse with fault-
    finders ;
That man hath modesty and gentleness,
With wisdom, counsel, and propriety."
    The famed king asked him : " Who is hopefullest
Of men ? "
                     " The most industrious," he said,   C. 1716
" Whose ears are open unto knowledge most."
    The monarch of the world inquired of him
Of privy rumour as to good and ill.
He thus returned reply : " It is the cause
Of ample chatter but an empty brain.
Say what they will the earth is still in place ;
I know not how the other world doth fare."
    Then Núshírwán : " What land most prospereth,
And how have we contributed therein ? "
    " The justice of the world-lord," he replied,
" Establisheth a land's prosperity."
    Then Núshírwán inquired : " Inform me this :
What man is shrewdest, most approved, and prudent
Within the world because the adept increaseth
One's lustre ? "
                He replied : " An ancient sage
That hath been mindful of experience."
    Said Núshírwán : " Who is the happy man
That liveth upright and right glad ? "
                      He answered :—
" One free from apprehension and possessed
Of gold and silver ? "
                Núshírwán inquired :—
" Which of us best deserveth praise, and who
Is most approved by all ? "
                  He answered thus :—
" He that can hide his need and can suppress
Strife, envy, greed, revenge, and jealousy :
That man will find approval in the world."

The Sháh inquired of the long-suffering,
Whose crown is patience.
                    Búzurjmihr replied :—
" That is the man grown hopeless, with heart dark,
And yet his counsel is sun-bright, or else
The man that hath but little time to live,
And yet hath entered on some vast employ."
    The Sháh said : " Who hath grief so much at heart
That he is weary of his life through care ? "
    And Búzurjmihr made answer thus : " The man
Fall'n from a throne and desperate of fortune."
    The exalted king inquired of him and said :—
" Who of us hath his heart in sorry plight ? "
    The sage replied : " The man that is not wise,
And rich man childless."
                    " Whose heart," asked the Sháh,
" Is sad through trouble and calamity ? "
    He answered thus : "The upright man of know-
    ledge
O'er whom besottedness is sovereign."
    The Sháh said : " Who is fullest of despair
Although possessing power and reputation ? "
    " The man that falleth from a lofty throne,"
He said, " retaining still his pride of birth."
    Sháh Núshírwán inquired of him and said :—
" O man of foresight and of ardent soul !
Whom knowest thou unfamed and lustreless,
And yet deserving both of love and pardon ? "
    He answered thus : " The man of many faults,
The culpable, the mendicant, and needy."
1717   The Sháh inquired and said : " Now tell me truly :
Who is it that repenteth of the past ? "
    He said : " The great king who, when he shall put
The black cap on upon his dying-day,[1]
Repenteth with a heart all terror-stricken

---

[1] *Cf.* Vol. i. p. 109.

Of all his life's ingratitude to God,
And he moreover who hath undergone
Abundant travail for ungrateful men."
    The Sháh inquired : " O sage that dost combine
All excellence ! know'st thou of aught that maketh
.The body profitable and is dear
To all men's hearts withal ? "
                      He made reply :—
" In health the heart will seek but happiness,
But when through suffering the life is failing
The body's one desire is then for health."
    The Sháh rejoined : " Good man ! expound to me
Which is the strongest of the appetites ? "
    Said Búzurjmihr : " The great are not exposed
To such solicitings and, since their bodies,
Which have no wish unsatisfied, fare well,
Have only need to seek their heart's desire."
    The Sháh then asked his guide : " What is the
      heart's
Chief care ? "
            " The sage," he answered, " would inform
His questioner that there are three chief cares—
First, apprehension of the evil day,
Lest ill then should befall the innocent ;
Next, of the practice of a treacherous friend,
Who fain would have brain, life and blood and skin ;
And thirdly, of a great but unjust king,
Who knoweth not the worthless from the good.
How happy is the course of time with him
.That hath a prudent friend and counsellor !
A bright world and a great king who is just—
Thou'lt get from heaven no greater excellence."
    The Sháh next asked of Faith and right—the means
Of banning fraud and falsehood. He replied :—
" Incline, O Sháh ! to one of Faith whose mind
Is filled with thoughts of God—the man averse

From guile and from the Div's way through his awe
Of holy God, the Master of the world,
And hearkening to His law. None such will barter
The Faith."
        The Sháh then asked concerning kings,
Whose rule is o'er the holy : " Which of them
Is of victorious fortune and throne-worthy ? "
  He answered thus : " The just possessed of
    wisdom,
Of counsel,[1] modesty, and excellence.'"
  The Sháh then questioned him about old friends,
Such as are one with us in ear and speech.
He made this answer : " Magnanimity
And generosity are good in them ;
They will wish thee no ill to please another,
But aid and succour thee in thy distress."

. 1718   Said Núshírwán to him : " Who hath most
    friends
That are to him as his own blood and skin ? "
  He thus gave answer : " Save the faithless man
All would be joined to him whose heart is good,
And all the more the kinder that he is,
The more obliging, and conformable."
  The Sháh inquired : " Who hath most enemies
And most antagonistic ? "
             Búzurjmihr
Returned him this reply : " The insolent,
For he incurreth many a malison,
And also any one that speaketh harshly,
Is ever frowning, and is close of fist."
  Then said the Sháh : " Who is the constant
    friend,
One who will weep for pain of severance ? "
  He answered : " 'Tis the friend that faileth not,
Is never vexed, and feareth not to suffer."

               [1] Reading with P.

" What lasteth," said the Sháh, " and doth not
    waste ? "
He made reply : " A benefit conferred
Is ever present to a worthy friend."
    " What hath the chiefest lustre," said the Sháh,
" And is a crown upon the head of all ? "
    He said : " The sage's mind which mastereth
His passions."
                Said the Sháh : " O lord of love !
What is there wider than the turning sky ? "
    He answered : " First, a king with open hand,
And next, the heart of one devote to God."
    The Sháh inquired : " What is the goodliest way
Wherein a wise man may exalt his head ? "
    " O great king ! ne'er bestow," he made reply,
" Thy treasure on unholy men.   For thee
To deal with the unthankful is to fling
Bricks unbaked into water."
                Said the Sháh :—
" What toil diminisheth man's greed for treasure ? "
    Then Búzurjmihr replied : " O king ! for ever
Be thy heart like young spring.   For very travail
The servant of a king of evil nature
Will cease to care for person, life, and wealth."
    The Sháh inquired : " What wonder hast thou seen
Than which a greater cannot be conceived ? "
    And Búzurjmihr made answer to the Sháh :—
" The turning sky is always wonderful.
Thou seest one possessed of mastery,
With crown exalted to the darksome clouds,
Who cannot tell his left hand from his right,
Or fortune's gain from loss discriminate ;
Another man will read the lofty sky,
And tell the why and the wherefore of the stars,
Yet heaven still will lead him into straits,
And evil fortune be his only lot ! "

" What thing know'st thou, as heaviest," asked the
  Sháh ?
He thus returned reply : " The weight of sin."
  The Sháh inquired : " Of matters most unseemly,
Including in the question words and deeds,
· 1719 Which is the greatest cause of shame and blame,
So that all folk pronounce it done amiss ? "
  He thus made answer : " Harshness in a king ;
The persecution of the innocent ;
The nearness practised by the man of wealth
That is a niggard as to dress and food ;
In womankind the loud and strident voice
Of those whose modesty is forfeited ;
The infamy of men that do oppression,
And are high-handed with the indigent ;
While falsehood in a king or in a man
Of no account is ugly, foul, and vile."
  Of all things in the world, apert or secret,
" What is that goodly one," said Núshírwán,
" Whereof the sage will fashion him a breastplate,
And therewithal illuminate his soul ? "
  The sage made answer : " Earnestness of Faith
Will have but approbation from the world,
And secondly thanksgiving unto God
Charactereth a wise and holy man."
  Said Núshírwán : " What is it best for kings
And mighty men to do and to avoid ?
What is there better than to rule, possess,
And look on others as inferiors ?
From what do we do wisely to refrain,
And what is good to seize upon and keep ? "
  The sage replied : " Safeguard thy wrath as
    knowing
That other folk will keep their eyes on thee ;
Next, let thy soul be ever on the watch,
And do thine utmost to abstain from ill.

The soul of him that will forgo revenge,
And hope instead, will shine as doth the sun.
By means of sin thou wilt have many pleasures ;
Reject such pleasures and avoid the sin."
    Thanks to the Master of the moon and sun
The parle of Búzurjmihr and Sháh is done.

PART IV

THE INTRODUCTION OF THE GAME OF CHESS INTO ÍRÁN. THE LEGEND OF THE INVENTION OF THE GAME. THE DISCOVERY OF THE BOOK OF KALÍLA AND DIMNA

ARGUMENT

The Rája of Hind sends an envoy to Núshírwán with the game of chess, proposing certain conditions which the Sháh accepts and, with the help of Búzurjmihr, carries out. Búzurjmihr invents the game of nard, and the Sháh sends him with it to the Rája, proposing similar conditions. The poet then tells the legend of the invention of chess—how two sons of an Indian queen quarrelled about the succession to her throne, how one of them perished and how the other, to console his mother, invented the game. Lastly the poet tells how a prince tributary to Núshírwán was sent at his own request to Hind to find the herb that restores the dead to life, and returned bringing instead the Fables of Bidpai.

NOTE

§§ 1-3. Here, as in the case of the Yátkár-i-Zarírán [1] and the Kárnámak,[2] we are brought into contact with an extant Pahlaví Text—the Tshatrang Námak—which was undoubtedly one of Firdausí's indirect authorities. It was written, probably, about the seventh century A.D., and tells how the king of Hind—Déwasárm—sent an embassy to Núshírwán with gifts and the game of chess which he had invented. The chess-men were one half of emeralds and the other half of rubies. If the Íránians, he writes to Núshírwán, cannot explain the meaning of the game they must pay him tribute or *vice versâ*. None can find the meaning till Búzurjmihr, who has been keeping himself in reserve, appears on the third day, expounds the principle of chess,

---

[1] See Vol. v. p. 24.   [2] *Id.* vi. 195.

and proceeds to win twelve games against Déwasárm's envoy. Búzurjmihr then invents nard, which is a form of backgammon, takes it to *H*ind, puzzles the sages there with it, and returns triumphant with double tribute. The similarity of the Pahlavi Text to the Sháhnáma therefore is obvious. Probably in the original story, no longer extant, the problem set was comparatively a simple one : " What did the board and pieces represent ? " And the answer would be: " A battlefield." The misplaced ingenuity of later redactors, however, has added impossible details. A clever man of the time might guess by what the game had been suggested, but the greatest that ever lived could not have evolved the method of play from his inner consciousness, assuming of course his complete previous ignorance of the game. The Pahlavi Text gives the answer correctly and then proceeds to make Búzurjmihr win twelve games right off! In the Sháhnáma the Indian envoy himself gives away the whole thing by stating what the game represents, and then Búzurjmihr in retirement discovers the powers of the various pieces and the way in which they are manipulated—an impossible achievement. It will be observed that *F*irdausi describes two forms of the game —that introduced into Persia for a board of sixty-four squares, and that, which he considers to be the original, for a board of one hundred squares. The powers of most of the pieces have altered since those days. The tethered minister has changed his sex, become the king's better half, and has acquired as much liberty and preponderance as the most emancipated lady could desire, but the knight's ingenious move has passed unchanged through all vicissitudes.

The Persian word " nard " means a tree-trunk, and it seems not unreasonable to imagine that the game got its name from the resemblance of the pieces on the board to tree-stumps. The author of the Tshatrang-Námak, however, tells us that the game was named after the founder of the Sásánian *D*ynasty, Nau-Ardshír, which became contracted into nard. Like chess it is symbolical and represents human life as swayed or moulded by fate or fortune whose decrees are written in the aspects of the stars and planets. Thus the board represents the earth, the thirty pieces the days of the month, the colour of the pieces the nights and days, &c. Each throw of the dice too had its proper symbolism. The first represented the Unity of Urmuzd, the second the duality of heaven and earth, the third the triad of Good Thoughts, Good Words, and Good *D*eeds, the fourth the four temperaments—dry, damp, warm, and cold, and so forth. Later Arabic writers elaborated the symbolism considerably. The dice were taken to represent the heavens and their motions, and the markings on the dice the seven planets in as much as the numbers on the opposite sides added together always make up the number seven, one being opposite to six, two to five, and three to four. The result of a throw was the decree of fate, &c. Nard may be said therefore to surpass chess in sublimity of conception as much as chess surpasses nard in its demands upon the intellect.

*F*irdausi does not tell us how nard was played, and the introduction of the two kings, apparently on the analogy of those at chess, is quite beside the mark. The poet's whole story of the way in which chess was brought into Írán, and the invention of nard, is quite unhistorical. We have had already in this volume [1] an instance of one king propounding hard questions to another, and in the next volume we shall have the problem of the mysterious box, on the elucidation of which a wager depends as in the present case. According to Mas'údí, nard was invented before chess and before the days of Porus, and chess in the time of one of that king's successors, but he also states that the invention of nard has been attributed to Ardshír Pápakán.[2] Elsewhere Mas'údi tells us that Núshírwán had the book of Kalila and Dimna, chess, and a black hair-dye, brought from Hind.[3]

§ 3. Sháhwí, Firdausí's authority for his story of the invention of chess, perhaps may be identified with the Máhwi who collaborated with four others in the work of putting the Bástán-náma into modern Persian in the tenth century A.D.[4]

§ 4. Shádán, son of Barzin, was, it would seem, another of the five above-mentioned collaborators.[5]

We appear to be here on much firmer historical ground than in the corresponding stories of the introduction of chess and the invention of nard. That the *F*ables of Bidpai were brought from *H*ind to Persia in the reign of Núshírwán, and translated from the Sanscrit into Pahlavi by Barzwí, seems to be admitted generally, though of course we need not accept all the details of Firdausí's version of the transaction. He is not very accurate in what he says with regard to the later literary history of the famous book. It was not translated into Arabic for the first time in the reign of the Khalifa Mámún (A.D. 813–833) but in the

---

[1] See p. 102.   [2] MM, i. 157 *seq.*
[3] *Id.* ii. 203. For the above generally see NPS, II, p. 20 *seq.* ;
HS, ii. 250 *seq.*
[4] See Vol. i. p. 67; NIN, p. 15.   [5] *Id.*

previous century by Ibn Mukaffa.[1] *Firdausí* is correct, however, in stating that the *Fables* were translated into Persian verse by the first great modern Persian poet, Rúdagí, who enjoyed for many years the munificent patronage of the Sámánid prince, Nasr son of Ahmad (A.D. 914–943), and of the minister Abú-l Fazl, and died in A.D. 954. Unfortunately only fragments of Rúdagí's translation survive. The poet is said to have been blind.

To compare small things with great, the *Fables* of Bidpai rival the Romance cycle of Alexander in the extent of their diffusion. They are said to have been translated into thirty-eight languages.[2] It is not possible to enter into the subject here, but one illustration of the way in which the *Fables* passed from one language into another may be given. The earliest English version of them is that of Sir Thomas North—the translator of *Plutarch's Lives*, which Shakespeare put to such good account—and it was published in 1570 under the title of *The Morall Philosophie of Doni.* It comes to us as Sir Walter Blunt came to Henry IV,

"Stain'd with the variation of each soil"

through which it has passed, and its provenance is as follows: "It is the English version of an Italian adaptation of a Spanish translation of a Latin version of a Hebrew translation of an Arabic adaptation of the Pehlevi version of the Indian original."[3] In Sir Thomas North's version, owing, it is said, to a misunderstanding of the letters when the *Fables* were translated from the Hebrew, Núshírwán appears as Anestres Castri.[4] It is interesting to find that the wish expressed to Núshirwán by Barzwí[5] has been gratified. After all the vicissitudes through which the book has passed his name and the story of his discovery of the *Fables* still survive. In the English version he appears as Berozias.[6] We may add that apparently the *Fables* themselves may be traced back to the Indian Játakas or Birth Stories of Buddha,[7] and that the Jewish race, to which the world is indebted for at least three religions, was the chief agent in the wide dissemination of the fables and the scientific study thereof.[8]

---

[1] For whom see Vol. vi. p. 17.   [2] JFB, p. xii.
[3] *Id.* p. xi.   [4] *Id.* p. xxxii.   [5] See p. 429.
[6] JFB, p. 34 *seq.*   [7] *Id.*, pp. xiii., xlix.   [8] *Id.* p. xxv.

§ 1

*How the Rája of Hind sent the Game of Chess to
Núshírwán*

Since this discourse, which so delighted thee,
Hath reached its end let chess our next theme be.
Thus said the archimage : The Sháh one day
Adorned his throne with the brocade of Rúm,
And hung the crown above the ivory throne—
A throne compact of teak and ivory.
The palace seemed all throne, the throne all Sháh,
And all his court an army.   All the palace
Was occupied by marchlords and archmages
From Balkh, Bukhárá, and from every side.
The monarch of the world received these tidings,
Brought by his vigilant intelligencers :—

C. 1720   "The envoy of the king of Hind hath come
With elephants, with parasols, with horsemen
Of Sind and laden camels fifty score,
And seeketh to have access to the king."
    The watchful Sháh, on hearing this, forthwith
Sent certain troops to go and welcome him.
The envoy of that famed and puissant prince,
On coming to the great king's presence, did
Obeisance, as the use of nobles is,
With praises of the Maker of the world,
And gave the Sháh abundant gems as gifts,
With earrings, elephants, and parasols.
These Indian parasols were decked with gold
With many sorts of jewels set therein.
He oped the bales within the court itself,
And brought their whole contents before the Sháh.
There were much gold and silver in the bales
With musk, fresh aloe-wood, and ambergris,
Gems, diamonds, and burnished Indian swords ;

The Rája had amassed from every hand
The products of Kannúj and Mái.   They laid them
Before the throne.   The prince of sleepless fortune
Viewed and dispatched to his own treasury
All that the Rája had so toiled for.   Then
The envoy brought a letter which the Rája
Had written upon silk to Núshírwán,
And also, what had made a treasury void,
A chess-board wrought with cunning workmanship.
The man of Hind thus gave the Rája's message :—
" Mayst thou abide so long as heaven endureth !
Bid those much travailed in the quest for knowledge
To place this board, used in the game of chess,
Before them and set all their wits to work
To find out how that goodly game is played,
To find out what the name is of each piece,
The way to move it and its proper square,
To find out footman, elephant, and host,
Rukh, horse, and how to move wazír and king.
If they discover all this goodly game,
And prove themselves the betters of the wise,
Then, as the Sháh commandeth, I will send
Full tribute to his court with all good will ;
But if the nobles of the Íránian folk
Have not the knowledge to resolve the point,
Then, since their knowledge is no match for ours,
Let them not seek for tax and tribute hence,
But rather pay a tribute unto us,
Since knowledge is of all famed things the best."
    Both heart and ear gave Núshírwán to him
That on this wise discharged his embassage.
They set the board and men before the Sháh,
Who looked upon the pieces for a while.
Half of the set was made of ivory
And bright, the other half of teak.   The Sháh,
Whose fortune never slumbered, then inquired

C. 1721

About the pieces' shapes and that fair board.
The envoy thus replied : " 'Tis all, O king !
An emblem of the art of war, and thou
Wilt see, when thou hast found it out, the tactics,
The plan, and order of a battlefield."
   The Sháh said : " I require a se'nnight's space :
The eighth day we will play right willingly."
   They had a pleasant residence prepared
To lodge the ambassador, and then the chiefs
And archimages that were counsellors
All came before the Sháh and with the chess-board
In front of them considered it at large,
Examined it, tried every device,
And played with one another in all ways.
One spake and questioned, and another heard,
But none discovered how the game was played,
And all departed louring. Búzurjmihr
Came to the Sháh, perceived him vexed and
   troubled,
And saw ere he began the task its end.
" O great king," thus he spake to Núshírwán,
" World-lord and vigilant whose word is law !
I will discover all this goodly game,
Employing wisdom as my guide therein."
   The Sháh replied : " Be this affair thy task,
And thine moreover health and happiness,
Else now the Rája of Kannúj will say :—
' The Sháh hath not a single counsellor,'
Which were a mighty slur upon the archmages,
Court, throne, and men of wisdom."
                        Búzurjmihr
Then took away with him the board and men,
And sat down with his thoughts intent thereon.
He tried to play the game in every way,
And sought to find the place for every piece.
He found the game out in one day and night,

Then hastened from his palace to the Sháh,
And said : " O Sháh whose fortune triumpheth !
These pieces and this goodly board have I
Well studied and I understand it all,
Helped by the fortune of the world's great king.
'Tis fitting that the king of kings should be
The first to see it played.   Thou wilt declare :—
' It is indeed a battlefield ! '   Then call
The Rája's envoy and spectators also."
    The king joyed at his words, saluted him
As prosperous and fortunate, then bade
The archimages, nobles, and famed sages
Attend.   He called the envoy of the Rája,
And seated him before the famous throne.
Said Búzurjmihr, that man of eloquence :—
" Priest of the Rája of the sunlike face !
What were the words thy monarch said to thee
About those pieces ?   Wisdom be thy mate."
    " The illustrious Rája," he replied, " when I
Was quitting him said thus to me : ' Convey
These teak and ivory pieces to the throne
Of him that is the master of the crown,
And say : " Assemble to thee thine archmages
And counsellors, and set before them these.
If they find how to play this clever game
In the approven way, and master it,
We will dispatch unto thee purses, slaves,
And tribute to the utmost of our powers.
The king's worth will arise from knowledge then,
Not from his treasures, men, and lofty throne ;
But if he and his wise men fail herein,
As being dark of counsel, then must he
Demand no tribute from us and no treasure.
His knowing soul then will regret past toils,
Since, realising our shrewd hearts and counsel,
He will dispatch still greater wealth to us." ' "

C. 1722

Then Búzurjmihr brought and set up before
The throne of him whose fortune never slept
The board and men, and said to archimage
And chief : " Ye sages pure of heart and wise !
Heed well his words and his shrewd lord's proposal."
    The sage then fashioned him a battlefield,
Whereon he gave the kings the central place,
And drew their forces up to left and right,
The footmen eager for the fray in front.
Beside the king his prudent minister
Was posted to advise him in the fight.
The warrior-rukhs impetuous on their steeds
Were at the wings and fought on right and left.
Adjoining these the battle-chargers stood,
So that the great king proved the Rája's match,
And then the elephants of war arrayed
On either side both eager for the fight.
When Búzurjmihr had thus disposed the host
The whole assembly stood amazed thereat,
The ambassador of Hind was sorely vexed,
And marvelled at that man of sleepless fortune,
He marvelled at that warlock of a man,
And thus his musings ran while plunged in thought :—
" He never saw the board and game of chess,
Or heard about it from the adepts of Hind !
How hath he learned the fashion of the game ?
None else could take his office."
                        Núshírwán
So treated Búzurjmihr that thou hadst said
That fortune had unveiled its face before him.
The king thereafter gave commands to fill
A cup with royal gems.   This and a purse,
Dínárs and steed with saddle on, gave he
To Búzurjmihr and praised him mightily.

How Búzurjmihr invented Nard, and how Núshírwán
sent it with a Letter to the Rája of Hind

The sage, upon returning to his home, C. 172
Arranged a board and compasses before him,
Selecting first of all a darkened room
To make his wits more keen, then mused on chess
And Indian subtlety, and mustering all
His powers made wisdom wed his ardent heart,
And meditating thus invented nard.
He bade to make two dice of ivory
With dots the colour of teak-wood thereon,
Arrayed a field of battle as in chess,
And drew up the opposing hosts for war,
Arranging them in eight battalions,
All ready for pitch-battles or for sieges.
The ground was dark, the battlefield foursquare,
Two noble, clement kings were in command,
Who had a common movement on the field,
But neither sought the other's injury.
The troops arrayed beneath their leadership
For battle on both sides were keen for fight.
If two friends catch an unsupported foe,
The twain inflict defeat upon the one.
He made the two kings move about the field
In pomp surrounded by their several hosts,
Each wheeling round about upon the other,
And combating by turns on hill and plain.
On this wise till one side was overthrown
The armies of both monarchs kept the field.
'Twas thus that Búzurjmihr, as I have said,
Invented nard, then went and told the Sháh
How from the moves of those imperious kings
Came praise or blame, what powers the pieces had,

And how the armies fought ; these he set forth,
And showed in detail to the Sháh whose heart
Was all astound ; he needed all his wits,
And said : " O man of ardent soul ! mayst thou,
And may thy fortune, still continue young."
He bade the keeper of the camels bring
Two thousand to him and then loaded them
With contributions raised from Rúm and Chín,
The Haitálians, from Makrán, and from Írán,
And from the treasury of the king of kings.
The caravan departed from the court.
Whenas the camel-loads were all arranged,
And that concern was off the monarch's heart,
He called the Rája's envoy unto him,
And of his knowledge uttered many words.
He wrote a letter to the Rája full
Of learning, pleasantry, good sense, and counsel,
And in the first place gave great praise to God,
Who was his refuge from the lusty Div,
Then " Rája, high renowned, of Hind," he said,
" Down from the river of Kannúj ¹ to Sind !
Thy wise ambassador hath come to us
With parasols, with elephants, and escort,
With tribute and with chess, and I have heard
The Rája's embassage. The task is done.
We asked the Indian sage for time, we decked
Our soul with knowledge, and an archimage,
A very prudent sage of holy rede,
Hath sought and found out how the game is played.
Now that wise archimage hath come before
The exalted Rája at Kannúj and brought
Two thousand heavy camel-loads of things ²
Acceptable—a keepsake for thyself—
And we have substituted nard for chess.

C. 1724

What man now will adventure on this game ?
There must be many a Brahman well advised,
Who by his learning can discover it.
The Rája may consign to treasury
The riches that have been the envoy's care,
But if the Rája and his counsellors
Shall try to find out nard, and fail therein,
He must according to our covenant
Load up as many camels as we sent,
And send them back with ours and all their loads ;
Such is our pact and bargain."
                    Búzurjmihr,
What time the sun was radiant in the sky,
Departed from the portal of the Sháh
With baggage,[1] letter, and the game of nard,
His heart absorbed by thoughts of his campaign.
On coming to the Rája from Írán,
The Brahman acting willingly as guide,
He went before the Rája's throne, beheld
His head, his fortunes, and his diadem,
Praised him no little in the olden tongue,
Then gave the royal letter, and repeated
The verbal message of the king of kings.
The Indian Rája's face bloomed like a rose.
The message spake of chess, the Rája's pains,
His tribute, how the game of chess had fared,
The play, the pieces, and the king's right moves,
And those moreover of his counsellors.
It told withal the achievement of the sage,
Who had invented nard in rivalry,
And ended thus : " Now let the Rája read
The letter, act, and swerve not from the right."
    The Rája's face grew pallid at the words,
On hearing that account of chess and nard.
There came a great official and assigned

---

[1] Reading with P.

A fitting lodging to the ambassador.
They had a jocund residence prepared,
And called for wine and harp and minstrelsy.

C. 1725   The Rája asked a space of seven days,
And all the Lights of learning came to him.
He gathered all the elders of the realm,
And laid the game of nard before them there.
For one whole se'nnight all the shrewdest men
Among the nobles, whether old or young,
Sought to discover out of emulation,
For fame and triumph, how the game was played ;
But to the Rája at the se'nnight's end
A sage said : " No one can make aught thereof,
And wisdom must be wedded to his soul,
Who from these pieces can invent a game."
The Rája's heart was troubled at those sages,
His soul was sorrowful, his brow contracted.
Upon the ninth day Búzurjmihr arrived,
With eager heart and furrowed face, and said :—
" The Sháh accorded me no tarriance here,
And he must not be straitened in his heart."
The learnéd magnates went aside and owned
Their ignorance, while Búzurjmihr, on hearing,
Sat down, and all the sages gave good heed
While he set out the board of nard before them,
And told the movements of the various pieces,
Displayed the leader and his warlike troops,
The king's power and the order of the fight.
The Rája and his counsellors were all
Astound, the company in wonderment,
At Búzurjmihr, the chiefs all lauded him,
And hailed him as a holy sage.   The Rája
Interrogated him upon all lore,
And he in each case gave a fit response.
Then from the sages, from the searchers out
Of knowledge, and the scholars rose a cry :—

" Behold an eloquent and learnéd man,
Not merely skilled in games like chess and nard ! "
   The Rája had two thousand camels brought,
And laid on them the tribute of Kannúj,
Gold, camphor, ambergris, and aloe-wood,
As well as raiment, silver, pearls, and gems,
With one year's tribute, and dispatched it all
From his court to the portal of the Sháh.
The Rája had a coronet and robe,
That reached from head to foot, of his own wear
Brought from his treasury and then bestowed them
On Búzurjmihr, gave him much praise withal,
And to his retinue abundant gifts.
So from Kannúj departed Búzurjmihr
With head exalted to the turning sky,
With those two thousand camels brought by him,
And all the gifts and tribute in his charge.
No one had looked on such a caravan
Before, and never had been greater wealth.
He joyed at heart as bearing from the king
Of Hind a script in Indian characters
On silk : " The Rája and his mighty men
Attest for good will, not for fear, that none
Hath looked on any like Sháh Núshírwán,   C. 1726
Or ever heard of one such from the priests,
Or met one wiser than his minister,
The treasurer of whose knowledge is the sky.
The tribute for the year was sent before,
And more shall be if thou demandest it,
While in the matter of the games the stakes
Have been sent likewise as agreed upon."
   Now when the Sháh gat tidings of his sage :—
" He hath arrived well satisfied and glad,"
He was rejoiced at that intelligence,
And bade the chiefs of city and of host,
With elephants and kettledrums and tymbals,

To sally forth to welcome Búzurjmihr.
That honoured sage's entry of the city
Resembled that of some great conquering king,
And when that man of lore approached the throne,
And proffered praise exceedingly, the Sháh,
Lord of the world, embraced him and inquired
About the Rája and the weary way,
While Búzurjmihr told his experiences,
His sleepless fortune and the love of heaven,
Then brought the conquering Rája's letter forth,
And laid it down before the throne. The Sháh
Then gave command for Yazdagird, the scribe,
To come before the knowledge-seeking king,
And when he read the Rája's letter all
The company were in astonishment
Both at the wit and rede of Búzurjmihr,
And at the fortune of his sun-faced Sháh,
Who spake on this wise, saying : " God be praised
That I have such a wise and holy sage.
The great are servants of my crown and throne,
And love of me hath filled their hearts and minds."
    Thanks to the Lord of sun and moon, for He
Bestoweth victory and mastery,
That which I next shall utter will appear
A tale more strange than that of Búzurjmihr,
Whom heaven with such intelligence did bless :
I tell the legend of Talhand and chess.

§ 3

The Story of Gav and Talhand, and the Invention of Chess [1]

Thus spake Sháhwí, the ancient sage, so be
Attentive to the tale of old Sháhwí :—
Once on a time there lived a king in Hind,

[1] This heading is taken from P.

One puissant in treasure, troops, and arms,
And everywhere renowned, Jamhúr by name,
And passing Fúr himself in fame for valour.
Such was this king, of such an ardent spirit,
So vigilant and prudent, that from Bust
And from Kashmír down to the march of Chín   C. 1727
The chieftains homaged him, and all the world
Was in his grasp, so mighty was his prowess.
He had his dwelling-place at Sandali ;
Here was his throne, his treasures, and his troops,
Here were his signet-ring and here his crown.
Jamhúr was worshipful, a man of lore,
Pre-eminent in knowledge and distinction,
And all his lieges, whether of his court
Or of his city, joyed alike in him.
He had a worthy wife, a prudent dame,
Accomplished, learned, and one that injured none.
One night a son was born to him just like
His sire, who when he saw the youthful prince
Bade call him Gav, but soon and suddenly
The monarch sickened, told the queen his will,
And died bequeathing unto Gav a world,
Where justice ruled, though yet he was unfit,
By reason of his infancy, for throne,
For crown and girdle.   All the chieftains' heads
Were full of dust, their hearts were sorrowful
By reason of Jamhúr, and all the world
Still kept in mind the memory of his bounty,
His feasts, and justice.   Troops and citizens—
Men, women, children—met and thus took counsel :—
" This little infant wotteth not of host,
Of justice, rigour, throne, and crown.   The sway
Will suffer if the ruler be not great."
    The monarch had a brother who was wise,
And fitted for the throne : his name was Mái.
The dwelling-place of that idolater

Was at Dambar, and all the veteran chiefs,
In looking for a king, turned to Dambar
Their face from Sandali, while of Kashmir
The potentates up to the march of Chin
Did homage to him as their sovereign.
The exalted Mái came from Dambar and set
His feet upon the throne of majesty,
Placed on his head the crown worn by Jamhúr,
And ruled with justice and with bounteousness.
He took to wife Gav's mother, cherished her,
And held her all as dear as his own life.
The fay-faced dame became with child by Mái,
And that illustrious lady bare a son,
Whom Mái, that mighty monarch, named Talhand,
And loved with all his soul.   Now when the babe
Was two years old and Gav was seven, and grown
A lusty warrior dowered with Grace and stature,
Mái ailed, his glad heart was espoused to care.
He languished for two se'nnights' space, then died,
And passing left the world to other's hands.

C. 1728　All Sandali was sorrowful and wept,
And burned with pain of heart because of him.
They spent a month in mourning for the king,
And at the end thereof the whole host met,
The great men and the warriors of the state—
All that had part in wisdom.   Much talk passed
In that assembly on all points.   At length
A wise man thus addressed the counsellors :—
" This lady, who was once spouse to Jamhúr,
Hath kept herself at all times from ill-doing,
In both her marriages hath sought the right,
And followed after justice all her days.
The lady is of noble lineage,
Just, upright, and inspireth confidence.
'Tis best that she should be our queen, for she
Remaineth—the memorial of two kings."

The assembly all assented thereunto,
And then the sage addressed the wise queen thus :—
" Take thou the throne of thy two sons, for this
Will make for greatness, and there is no choice.
When they grow worthy of the throne resign
To them the majesty, the wealth, and host,
And be from that time forth their counsellor,
Companion, minister, and best of friends."
   The lady—fortune's favourite—at these words
Gave lustre to the crown and graced the throne,
Grew kinder, more considerate, and just,
And all the realm rejoiced in her.   She chose
Two men wise, holy, travelled, and accomplished,
And to their charge entrusted both her sons—
Those princes of high lineage and wise.
Withal she never left them for a day,
And found her happiness in seeing them.
Now as they grew in lustiness and lore,
Becoming mighty men in that regard,
One or the other used to come alone
To his good mother, ever and anon,
And ask : " Which is the fittest of us twain,
Most high of heart, most likely, and most shrewd ? "
   And thus the mother would reply to both :—
" That I may know which is more excellent,
Show prowess, counsel, self-control, and Faith,
Fair speech, and an ambition to be praised ;
For wisdom, modesty, self-governance,
And justice, are required since ye are both
Of royal birth."
                  When one of them would come
Alone at whiles before her and inquire :—
" Which of us twain will have the sovereignty,
Which of us have the treasure, throne, and crown ? "
Then would she answer him : " The throne is thine,
For wisdom, counsel, fortune, are thine own."

She said the same thing to the other also
Until the saying grew inveterate,
And thus she made the heart of each expectant
Of throne, wealth, host, fame, fortune.   They attained,

· 1729 Each with a baleful tutor for his guide,
To man's estate, and through their mutual envy
Both suffered, both were hot for crown and treasure,
The whole realm and the host were rent in twain,
While good men's hearts grew fearful.   Both the sons,
Impassioned by their baleful tutors' talk,
Came to their mother, crying : "Which of us
Is best and meekest under good and ill ? "
    That prudent lady made them this reply :—
"First it is needful for you both to sit
In counsel with the sages pure of heart,
And solve this question in content and peace,
And after do ye and your tutors ask
The great men most renowned throughout the state,
All those possessed of counsel as their portion,
As to your right procedure in this case.
Whoever seeketh crown and throne hath need
Of wisdom, treasure, counsel, and a host,
For when a tyrant hath the sovereignty
He filleth all the world with heat and ruin."
    Shrewd Gav made answer to his mother thus :—
"Seek not to parry so my questioning.
If I am not the lustre of this realm,
Say so, but say not aught that is untrue.
Deliver to Talhand the throne and crown,
And I will be a loyal liege to him,
While if as older, wiser, and by birth
Sprung from Jamhúr, I am to be the king,
Forbid him in his folly to attempt
Strong measures for the sake of crown and throne."
    His mother answered : " Act not hastily :
Thou shouldst push not these matters to extremes.

Whoever sitteth on the throne must have
His two hands open and his girdle girt,
Must keep his pure soul guarded too from evil,
And walk with knowledge in the sage's way,
Must too be wary of the foe in fight,
And heed what maketh for his reputation.
The Master of the sun and moon will judge
His acts just and unjust to state and host,
And if the king oppresseth but a gnat
His spirit will be left to mourn in Hell.
The world is more obscure than night itself,
And hearts must be more subtle than a hair
To keep the soul and body [1] free from evil,
And recognise that guile will profit not.
When one is crowned and sitteth on the throne
Of justice all the world will joy thereat,
Yet is his end a couch of brick and dust,
Or else cremation in the funeral pit.
Of such a stock as this Jamhúr was sprung,
Whose counsels were remote from deeds of ill.
He died before his natural time to die,
And left his younger brother as the heir
To all his world.   Great Mái came from Dambar,   C. 1730
Still young, shrewd-hearted, and a counsellor.
All Sandalí went out to welcome him
With full hearts and all eager for a king.
He came and sat upon the throne of power
With girdle girded and with open hands.
He sought me as his spouse, and we were wedded
That so state-secrets might be secrets still.
Now since thou art the elder of the twain,
The elder both in wisdom and in years,
Strive not to vex thy spirit for the sake
Of eminence, of treasure, and of crown.
If I choose one of you the other one
Will be fulfilled with pain and with revenge

[1] Reading with P.

At me. Shed no blood for the sake of crown
And treasure, for this Wayside Hostelry
Abideth not with any."
                              When Talhand
Had heard his mother's words he liked them not,
And thus replied : "Thy sentence is for Gav,
Because he is the elder, but although
My brother is mine elder as to years
Still every elder is not better too.
Within this host and realm is many a man
As ancient as the vultures of the sky,
And yet such never sought for place or host,
Or diadem or treasure, throne or crown.
My father died when young and did not give
The throne of majesty to any. I see
Thy heart in foolishness disposed toward Gav,
And that thou wilt give him the preference,
Though I could make as good as him from clay !
God grant that ne'er I shame my father's name."

His mother sware a solemn oath and said :—
"May I forgo the azure vault of heaven
If ever I desired of God to make
Gav king or ever set my heart thereon.
Think with all charity concerning this,
And rail not at the process of the sky,
Because it doeth good to whom it will :
So look to God alone and trust none other.
I have advised you to the best I could,
But if my counsel be of no avail
Consider what is better and that do :
Strive and make that the provand of your lives."

The queen thereafter summoned all the wise,
And laid before them all that she proposed.
She brought the keys that oped the treasury
Belonging to those two kings wise and good,
Displayed the wealth therein reposited

Before those men of much experience,
Gave both her sons an equal share and sought
To satisfy the claims of both of them.
Thereafter Gav spake to Talhand and said :—
"Thou, good of heart but bent on novel schemes!
Jamhúr, as thou hast heard, was greater far
Than Mái, alike in counsel and in years.
Thy sire, that virtuous and noble man,
Showed not the least ambition for the crown.
It was no shame to him to be a subject :
He sought no kind of lordship o'er the lords.
Mark if the just Judge will approve that I
Shall gird myself before my younger brother.
Our mother spake but justice, wherefore then
Should thy heart joy in that which is not just ?
Now summon we the leaders of the host,
Wise men and well acquainted with the world,
And having listened to the sages' words,
Assent to their decision and advice ;
We shall learn knowledge from them and illume
Our hearts with understanding."
                              Those two sages—
Men of good counsel—met and much talk passed.
Gav's sage required that Gav should be the king
In Sandali and take the foremost place ;
The other, who was tutor to Talhand,
And wisest of the wise, spoke up for him ;
They wrangled till the princes were at odds.
Within one hall two thrones were set whereon
Those princes of victorious fortune sat,
Each with his lusty sage upon his right,
And covetous of his inheritance.
They summoned all the nobles to the hall,
And seated them to right hand and to left.
Then those two sages loosed their tongues and said :—
"O ye illustrious and famous men !

C. 1731

Of these two chiefs of glorious lineage,
Who keep the customs of their sires in mind,
Which will ye have as ruler over you ?
Which youth do ye esteem the holier ? ''
 The priests, the nobles, and the wise men shrewd
Of heart, were lost in wonderment thereat.
The two young princes sat, each on his throne,
While those ill-omened sages both harangued,
And citizen and soldier knew full well
That only war and strife could come of it,
That all the empire would be rent asunder,
The wise man left in travail and dismay.
Then from the company one raised his head,
Rose to his feet, and said : "How dare we speak
What profiteth before two famous kings ?
Assemble we to-morrow and discuss
The case among ourselves without reserve,
And then announce our sentence to them both :
It may be that they both will be content."
 They left the hall with murmurs and in dudgeon,
Sighs on their lips and sorrow in their souls,
And said : "This business hath grown troublesome
Beyond the handling of experienced men.
We never saw two kings confronted thus,
With two bad ministers upon the dais."
C. 1732 All night their faces had a careworn look,
And when the sun arose above the mountains
The great men of the state, the wise, assembled,
On all sides Sandali was filled with clamour,
And every man spake that which liked him best.
One warrior was the partisan of Gav,
Another for Talhand was advocate.
Tongues tired of talking, there was no accord.
At length that great assembly was dissolved,
And citizens and soldiers went their ways,
One to give in adherence to Talhand,

And utter malisons on Gav, another
To go to Gav with mace and sword, and cry :—
" I will begrudge not life to serve the king."
   Confusion filled the realm of Sandali
Through honest partisanship. Saith the sage :—
" When two command within one house 'twill fall."
Then tidings came to Gav and to Talhand :—
" Each quarter hath a leader of its own,
Who layeth waste the city at his will :
The princes must not suffer it."
                         The news
Filled both of them with fear, and they kept watch
Both night and day, and thus it came to pass,
One day, that both young princes chanced to meet
Without their paladins or any escort.
They set their tongues loose, each against the other,
Frowns on their brows and warlike thoughts within.
The noble Gav was full of lamentation,
The tidings moved him deeply, and he said
Thus to Talhand : " My brother ! act not thus,
Because for us the thing hath passed all bounds,
But be content and follow not mad schemes,
For they have no allurement for the wise.
As thou hast heard, Mái, while Jamhúr still lived,
Was as a slave before him. When he died,
And left me still a miserable babe,
They could give not the throne to one so young.
The world had grown so just beneath his rule
That no one dared to seek to fill his place.
His brother was as body is to soul
To him, and all wished Mái to be their king.
If then I had been fitted for the throne
None ever would have looked at him. Let us
Ensue the precedents of kings of yore,
And hear the wise on points of right and wrong.
I am thy better both by years and father.

Thou sayest : ' I am both the chief and better.'
But say not so. Seek not unworthily
The throne of kingship, or fulfil the realm
With strife."
        Talhand thus answered him : " Enough !
None ever compassed power by subtleties.
This crown and throne received I from my sire,
Received it as the seed that he had sown,
And henceforth I will guard the sovereignty,
The host, and treasure, with the scimitar.
Prate not to me of Mái and of Jamhúr :
If thou wilt have the throne then fight for it."
   They turned away with heads fulfilled with strife,
And went within the city to prepare.
The soldiers and the citizens all keen
For war betook them to the princes' courts.
One faction was in favour of Talhand,
The other favoured Gav.   The battle-cry
Rose at the princes' doors.   No standing-room
Was left within the city for the throng.
Talhand was first to arm him for the fight,
Because his courage would brook no delay.
He oped the portal of his father's hoards,
And served out helm and mail to all his troops.
The state was rent asunder, and the wise
Were full of fear at heart, and thus they said :—
" What is the end that heaven purposeth,
And which of these young men will lose his life ? "
   News of both kings was bruited through the
      realm,
And from all sides hosts gathered troop on troop.
Talhand was first to put his armour on,
And bathe his hands in blood. Gav also donned
His coat of mail and helmet, and invoked
The spirit of his sire.   Embittered thus
They both took action, housed the elephants,

· 1733

And saddled them. Thou wouldst have said : " The
  earth
Is eager for the combat." All the city
Was filled with din of gong and Indian bells,
All ears were charged with blare of clarions.
These two young kings departed to their camps,
And every one took his own life in hand.
That battlefield filled heaven with amaze,
And eyes were darkened by the dust of hosts.
The flourish of the trumpets and the clash
Of brazen cymbals went up from both lines.
The wings were drawn up to the right and left,
And thou hadst said : " Earth is all mountain-like."
The armies' fronts extended o'er two miles.
Those two great kings rode each his elephant.
Their standards waved above their heads. One bore
A tiger, one an eagle, as device.
The footmen were in front equipped with spears
And bucklers, and all ready for the fight.
Gav looked upon the field and saw the air
Streaked like the markings on a savage pard.
Each throat [1] was full of dust, the plain all blood,
And midst the dust the lances led the way.
Gav, though Talhand had angered him, and wisdom
Had stitched not up the lips of his ambition,
Yet chose him out a man of fluent speech—
The chiefest of his nobles—and thus said :—
" Go to Talhand and say to him : ' Ensue not
War with thy brother in this unjust fashion,
Since thou wilt suffer in the other world
For all the blood shed in this strife of ours.
Give ear to Gav's advice and err not thou
Through what an evil counsellor may say.
In this conjuncture ne'er must this reproach
Remain as our [2] memorial—that this realm

C. 1734

---

    [1] Reading with P.   [2] *Id.*

Of Hind is desolate, the lurking-place
Of lions and of pards.   Forbear this war
And strife, and wantonly to shed this blood
Unjustly.   Joy my heart with peace and save
Our necks by making use of wisdom's net.
Stretch out thy rod from this march unto Chin,
And let whate'er thou wilt of earth be thine.
I will esteem thy love as mine own soul,
And set thee as a crown upon my head.
Share we the kingship as we shared the wealth ;
Throne and tiara are not worth such pains ;
But if thus wholly thou art bent on strife,
Injustice, and the scattering of the flock,
Now gathered, in this world thou wilt be blamed,
And judged in that to come.   Incline not, brother !
To wrong ; it cannot stand against the right.' "
    Now when the envoy came before Talhand,
Came with the prudent embassage of Gav,
Talhand returned this answer : " Say to him :—
' Employ not so much subterfuge in warfare.
I call thee neither brother nor a friend ;
Thou art not, brain or skin, akin to me,
And wilt but make the empire desolate
By thus assailing these my gallant troops.
The knaves are with thee and are thine Urmuzd
Upon Bahrám's day.[1]   Thou art guilty too
In God's sight as ill-famed, misgot, and curst.
For all blood shed by thee in fight henceforth
The curses will be thine, the blessings mine.
Thou said'st moreover : " Let us share the realm,
The land, the worship, and the ivory throne,"
But treasure, power, and kingship all are mine,
Mine from the sun down to the Fish's back.[2]
As long as thou dost play the king, dost share

[1] *i.e.* thy leaders on the day of action.   *Cf.* Vol. iii. p. 287.
[2] See Vol. i. p. 71.

The land with me, and wouldest be my mate,
I wish my body and my soul may part
Or ever I shall look on throne and crown.
My host have I arrayed, and even now
The air is like brocade all shot with gold ;
So many are the arrows, darts, and spearheads
That none can tell his stirrups from his reins.
Heads will I scatter on the battlefield,
Will bring a wail of woe from all Gav's troops,
And in such fashion lead my host to fight
That I will sate with war that Warrior-pard.
I will lead Gav himself with bounden hands,
His troops shall see the dust of overthrow,
Their leaders shall be lifeless by my sword,
Their wounded men shall writhe in misery,
For none of them from bondslaves up to prince
Shall don again his breastplate for the fight.'"

C. 1735

The prudent envoy having heard his answer,
Returned and gave it word for word.   Gav's heart
Was sad at hearing it because he saw
No knowledge in Talhand, and full of care
Called his own sage, discoursed of the response
At large, and said : "Suggest a remedy,
Thou seeker after wisdom ! for this case.
The desert is all blood and trunkless heads,
And souls pass to the Judge of all the world.
This battle must not bring, when all is done,
Ill fortune on us."
                              Said the sage : "O king !
Thou needest not a teacher to teach thee,
But if thou wilt have mine advice herein. . . .
In fighting with thy brother be not fierce,
And send him yet another messenger,
A man of high rank, learned, and eloquent,
To give yet one more message.   He still may
Abate hostility.   Resign to him

The treasures gathered by the toil of others,
Preferring thereunto thy brother's life.
Since both the crown and signet-ring are thine
Forbear to wrangle with him as to pelf,
For I have seen from heaven's processes
That his time endeth shortly, and that none
Of all the seven planets favoureth him.
Moreover he will perish on this field
Of strife.   Thou hast no need to press him.   Give him
Whatever he shall ask of steeds and wealth,
So that thou mayst repent not at his death,
The royal signet, crown, and throne excepted,
For fear the troops may call thee faint of heart ;
But thou if king and fortune's favourite
Art versed yet more in heaven's purposes."
    The prince, when he had heard his tutor's words,
Made yet a new endeavour.   With wet face,
Through anguish for his brother's sake, he chose
One favoured by the stars and eloquent,
And said to him :   " Go to Talhand and say :—
' Gav is fulfilled with trouble and with pain
As touching heaven's purpose and this fight,
And prayeth that the almighty Judge of all
Will stir up love and prudence in thy heart,
So that thou mayest yet renounce this strife
Against thy brother.   If 'tis through thy sage,
Who haunteth thee, deceiving thy dark soul,
That thou art grown so fierce and quarrelsome
Still thou canst not escape the course of heaven.
Ask the twelve signs and seven planets how
C. 1736   This unjust work will fare.   Foes compass us,
And all the world is full of wicked men ;
Moreover by the monarch of Kashmír,
And by Faghfúr of Chín, who even now
Are pressing on our realm, we shall be flouted
On two sides, and by other warrior-chiefs.

How they will say : " Why are Talhand and Gav
Contending for the sake of throne and crown ?
Are they not then of common stock by birth,
Not each the offspring of a holy sire ?
And yet when counsellors of evil heart
So prompt them they must put their hands to blood ! "
If thou wilt leave thy host and visit me,
And so illume this darkened soul of mine,
I will bestow on thee dinars, brocade,
Steeds, treasure ; I would have thee all untroubled.
Thou shalt have also jewels, province, signet,
And crown, with armlets and an ivory throne.
These from an elder brother are no shame,
And I desire not battle, but if thou
Wilt hearken not my rede thou wilt repent
At last.' "
        The envoy, speeding torrent-like,
Came to Talhand, the dark of soul, and told
What Gav had said to him and added more
Concerning kingship, wealth, dínárs, and goods.
Whenas Talhand had heard the envoy's speech,
His wisdom, and his prudent policy,
He would assent not to his brother's words,
Because the heaven purposed otherwise,
But made this answer, saying : " Say to Gav :—
' Be thou a schemer still, and may thy tongue
Be severed by the scimitar of ill,
Thy body burnt up in the Magians' fire !
Thy crude proposals have I heard and see
That all thy stock-in-trade is subterfuge.
How wilt thou give to me the royal treasure,
For who art thou amongst this mighty people ?
Good sooth l thy life must be nigh o'er since thou
Displayest such prolonged anxiety !
The armies' ranks extend two miles, the world
Is full of men, of steeds, and elephants.

March forth and set the battle in array :
Thou camest forth to fight ; why dally then ?
Thou'lt see such prowess from me that the stars
Will have to tell the total of thy days.
Thou knowest naught but practice, craft, and lies,
Perceiving that thy downfall is at hand.
Thou art afar from counsel, crown, and throne,
And no wise man will call thee fortunate.' ''
   The envoy came charged with these blustering
     words,
And told the prince's answer. Thus, until
Dark night displayed its face, the envoy fared
Between the twain who, camping on the field,
Dug out a trench before their several hosts.

C. 1737   The outposts went their rounds. Thus passed the
     ` night.
Now when Sol rose in Leo, making earth
As 'twere a sea of splendour, and, all golden,
Enrobed the dome of lapis-lazuli,
From both the camp-enclosures rose the blare
Of clarions and the roar of kettledrums,
The flags of both young princes were displayed,
And both the hosts deployed to right and left,
While at their centres those exalted princes
Were stationed, each with his sage minister.
Gav bade his to proclaim thus to the chiefs :—
" Raise ye your standards, every man of you !
Let every one draw forth his blue steel sword,
But not a warrior advance a step,
Or any of the foot-men quit his post,
For none is sober, wise, and well advised,
That is impetuous on the day of battle :
I would take note of how Talhand deployeth.
The counsel of all-holy God alone
Prevaileth from bright sun to darksome dust,
And I am hopeful that Almighty God

Will grant to us a glorious destiny.
Tried have we counsel and in loving fashion
Have pleaded, but Talhand is still averse.
If now our host shall be victorious,
And if the process of the sun and moon
Afford us fruit, shed ye not blood for spoil,
Because ye shall receive a treasure-hoard ;
And if some famous warrior of our host,
Who chargeth on their centre, shall perchance
Confront Talhand in fight he must not cast
The dust upon him.   Praying as we go,
And with our girdles girt, confront we now
Yon mighty elephants.''
                      The soldiers shouted :—
'' We will perform thy bidding and will make
Thy counsel the adornment of our souls.''
    Upon the other side Talhand harangued
His troops and said : '' Ye warders of the throne
That we may be victorious, and the star
Of our good fortune bring forth fruit for us,
Draw, all of ye, your swords, confide in God,
And slay the foe.   When ye have ta'en Gav captive
Ye must not kill him or address him harshly,
But take him from yon raging elephant,
And bring him to me with his hands in bonds.''
    Thereat the blaring of the clarions
Rose in the court before the royal tent.
At all the neighing of the steeds, the dust
Raised by the chiefs, and whirl of massive maces,
The hills and streams re-echoed.   '' Circling heaven
Recoileth,'' thou hadst said.   At all the shoutings,   C. 1738
And crash of axes, '' No one,'' thou hadst said,
'' Knew head from foot.''   The sun withdrew its
      skirt
From those bright arrow-heads and eagles' plumes.
Earth seemed a sea of blood where heads and hands

Were pebbles in its depths.   The royal princes
Came from the centre, like huge elephants,
And from them both a shout arose : " Avoid
The wind of my two-headed javelin.
O brother ! be not forward in the fight,
And guard thee from my sword."
                                        Thus shouted they,
Each to the other, while the earth seemed all
A sea of blood,   The valiant swordsmen wheeled
About the field, and streams of blood and brains
Ran from the blows of those two warlike princes.
Thus till the sun had left the sky the strife
Surpassed all bounds.   Then from the field a shout
Rose, and the voice of Gav cried : "Combatants,
And youthful warriors l exact not vengeance
On those that would have quarter at our hands.
Know that my brother shrinketh from the fray,
And may abide not, being left unaided."
   Then many chiefs asked quarter, many more
Were slaughtered on the field, Talhand's whole host
Was scattered, and the flock was shepherdless,
The shepherd flockless.   When Talhand was left
Alone upon his elephant, Gav called
To him and said : " Go to thy palace, brother !
And have regard to that and thine own court.
Good sooth ! thou shalt not suffer in thy person
From me or at the hands of this famed host
Of swordsmen.   Know that all good is from God,
And give Him thanks so long as life shall last
That thou hast left this battlefield alive. . . .
But 'tis no time for counsel or delay."
   Now when Talhand had heard his brother's words
He writhed with shame, his face ran tears, he left
The battlefield for Margh.   Troops flocked to him
From every side.   He oped his magazines,
And gave supplies.   His host was well equipped,

Content, and glad.   He gave a robe of honour
To each that in his eyes so merited.
When all the soldiers had received their pay,
And when his warlike heart was freed from dudgeon,
He sent to Gav a message : "Thou that art
To throne as weed to garden ! thou shalt burn
Anon, thy spirit shall be stricken, thine eyes
Sewn up.   Thou deem'st that I can harm thee not,
But girdle not thy heart with self-deceit."
    Gav, when he heard that savage message, washed   C. 1739
Affection for his brother from his soul.
His heart was filled with dudgeon, and he said
Thus to his sage : " Behold this monstrous thing ! "
    The sage replied : " O king ! upon the throne
Thou art the memory of thy sire, more learned
Than seekers after lore, and mightiest
Of kings.   I told my lord the truth, as vouched
By circling sun and shining moon, that till
This famous prince be overthrown, and snake-like
Writhe on the darksome dust, ne'er will he rest,
Or turn away from strife.   In this contention
Thy policy is to affect delay.
Reply not harshly, seek the way for union
And peace with him.   All his endeavouring
Is to work evil.   What is he to do ?
It is God's will.   If he shall fight again,
We too will fight.   He is in haste while we
Can wait."
            King Gav then called the messenger,
Held talk with him at large with courteousness,
And said to him : " Go to, say to my brother :—
' Be not so brutal and so violent,
For violence becometh not a king.
Thy sire was noble ; thou art noble likewise.
I see this clearly that thou dost reject
My counsels and alliance, yet am fain

To have thee fair renowned and well disposed.
Now will I show thee all my heart and tell
The matter that my mind is purposing.
Thine evil minister hath sundered thee
From quiet, good advice, and wisdom's way.
Speak not but what is just because the world,
My brother ! is but mockery and wind.
Incline to peace that I may send thee all
The wealth in full and loyal lieges also
Forthwith, and thy misdoubting soul will see
That there is naught but justice in my heart.
May every one be joyful in thy life !
My purpose is according to my words,
If thou, self-willed one ! wilt attend thereto.
Howbeit if thou art intent on war,
And overtures for peace and pact are vain,
I will array my warriors for battle,
And they suffice to occupy a realm.
Let us go forth beyond these peopled lands,
And lead our two hosts onward to the sea.
Dig we a trench about them there to shut
Our warriors in, then fill it with sea-water,
And urge them to the fray, so that the worsted
May not escape by reason of the trench,

C. 1740   While he of us that is victorious
Shall shed not.blood upon that straitened spot,
But take the foemen captive.   God forbid
That we should use our scimitars and arrows.' "

    The envoy went his way and came like wind.
He told Talhand the words of Gav.   The prince,
When he had listened to that embassage,
Bade summon to his presence all the men
Of leading in his host and seated them,
Each one in due accordance to his rank,
Repeated to them Gav's response, disclosed
The matter, and thus said : " What are your views

On this new-fangled battle by the sea
Proposed by Gav ?   How shall we deal therewith,
And shall we turn his fancy into fact ?
If ye are one with me then not a man
Will draw back for a moment from the fight.
What matter whether it be sea or mountain
When we seek battle in the ranks of war ?
If ye will be my comrades in the strife
The leopard shall fear not the fox's voice.
All those of us that seek for high renown
Shall win their chief ambition from the world.
The aspirant rather should be slain with fame
Than live to grace the triumph of the foe.
Whoe'er shall bear him stoutly in the fight,
His bearing shall not disadvantage him,
For such shall have of me unstinted wealth
With servants and with steeds caparisoned.
Then from Kashmir down to the sea of Chín
The folk in every state will homage us ;
I will bestow their cities on my troops
Or ever kingship, crown, and throne are mine.''
    In answer all the chieftains bowed their faces
Before him till they touched the ground, and said :—
'' Our choice is fame, and thou, who art our king,
Shalt see a turn of fortune.''
                              Then a shout
Rose from the portal of Talhand, and all
The province was astir with troops.   He led
His whole host toward the sea, the troops of Gav
Appeared on their side, and the two kings lighted,
Confronting, for they each would be avenged
Upon the other.   Round the hosts they dug
A trench and, when 'twas deep, let in the water.
Both armies drew up face to face, and foam
Was on the horsemen's lips.   The wings were ranged
To right and left, the baggage was bestowed

Anigh the sea, and those illustrious kings,
All dudgeon and vindictiveness, then saddled
Two elephants, each at his army's centre
Took up his station, and assumed command.
The earth grew pitch-like, heaven azure-dim
With all the spears and silken bannerets,
While air was ebon with the armies' dust.
What with the trumpet's blare and tymbal's din
Thou wouldst have said : "The sea is all a-boil,
The crocodiles therein call out for blood ! "
While at the thud of battle-ax, of mace,
And sword, a red reek went up from the deep,
And as that veil was drawn athwart the sun
The world's face vanished from the eyes of men.
Thou wouldst have said : "The air is raining
    swords,
And planting tulips in the dust ! "   The world
Was heaped so with the fallen that the vulture
Durst fly not overhead.   Some lay within
The trench, which ran with blood, while other some
Were flung down headless on the field.   The sea
Rose with the wind, and still the hosts advanced,
Troop after troop, while all the plain was filled
With livers, brains, and hearts.   The horses' hoofs
Were clogged with gory mire.   Talhand looked forth
Upon his elephant and saw the earth
O'erflowing like the Nile ;   the wind withal
Was in his face, and he had need of meat
And drink, but saw no peace and no escape
From wind and sun and trenchant scimitar,
And, swooning, died upon his golden saddle,
Resigning all the realm of Hind to Gav.

　　When loss betideth one, whose eyes are set
On gain, how great his passion and regret !
And since both gain and loss must pass away
Enjoy, old sage ! the pleasures of to-day,

· 1741

For howsoever much may be thy gains
The world's whole treasure is not worth the pains.
   Gav looking from the centre failed to spy
The prince's flag, so sent a cavalier
To wheel before the elephants, and search
The foemen's front for miles, to find out whither
Had gone the bright red banner that had shadowed
The horsemen's faces, "for the fight is stayed
Unless mine eyes are blinded by the dust."
   The horseman came, looked everywhere but saw
      not
The standard of the chief, howbeit he saw
The foemen's centre all confuséd cries,
And all the horsemen looking for their prince.
Thereat he turned away, came quick as dust,
And told the news to Gav.   That general
Alighted from his elephant and went
Two miles afoot and weeping bitterly.
Whenas he looked upon the dead Talhand,
And saw the soldiers' faces woebegone,
He keenly scanned the corpse from head to foot,
But saw not any wound on breast or skin.
Then that exalted monarch wailed aloud,
Sat grieved and heavy by the corpse, and said :—
"Alack 1 thou youthful warrior ! thou hast gone
Fulfilled with anguish and with wounded soul,
Slain by the process of thine evil star,   C. 1742
Else had the cruel blast not smitten thee.
Thou didst reject the counsel of thy teachers,
Hast gone, and darkened is thy mother's heart.
Much did I warn thee in all kindliness,
But yet my counsel could avail thee naught."
   Now when the sage of Gav arrived and saw
Talhand, the world-aspirant, dead, his brother
Bewailing him on that wide plain with cries
That pierced the sky, he likewise wailed and wallowed

Before Gav, saying : " Woe for thee, young world-
　　lord ! "
　　Addressing then his lips to give advice
He said to Gav : " Exalted king ! what profit
This grief and mourning ?　He hath passed away ;
What was to be hath been.　Thou mayst thank God
In one regard—that thy hand slew him not.
I told my lord all that would be as vouched
By Mars and Saturn, sun and moon : ' This youth
Will bear him so in fight that he will end
His days,' and now his work is as the wind,
And he hath gone through ignorance and haste,
While all this mighty host is full of grief
And anger, and all eyes are fixed on thee.
Content thyself, make us contented too,
And thus contenting do what wisdom would ;
For when the soldiers shall behold their king
Afoot and weeping on the way for grief,
His lustre will be minished in their eyes,
And e'en the basest will wax insolent
Toward him, for the king is like a cup
Filled with rose-water : may the blast not strike him ! "
　　Gav hearkened to that prudent sage's rede.
A proclamation went forth from the host :—
" Ye men of name and warriors of the king !
Let no one tarry on the battlefield,
For yon host is disjoined not now from this ;
Both must be one in act and in acclaim.
Be all 'neath my protection and preserve
For me the memory of my high-souled brother."
　　Then called he all the chiefs, on his eyelashes
Let fall his own heart's blood, made for Talhand
A narrow coffin out of ivory
And gold, of turquoise and teak-wood, and swathed
His brother's face with glossy silk of Chin.
Thus passed away that famous chief of Hind.

They sealed the coffin-lid with gums and pitch,
With musk and camphor. Then Gav marched away
In haste and tarried at no stage for long.
    The princes' mother slept not, rested not,
And fasted after they had chosen their field
Of battle. Ever on the road she kept
A watch and passed each day in bitterness.
So when the host's dust went up from the road   C. 1743
The wakeful watchman saw it from the look-out,
And thence too saw the flag of Gav appear,
While all the realm's face was o'erspread with troops.
He gazed from two miles off in hope to see
The elephant and standard of Talhand,
But failed to recognise them mid the host.
He hurried off a horseman from the look-out
To say : "The army cometh from the mountains,
And Gav is there with all his company,
But I see not Talhand, his elephant,
Or flag, or yet his chiefs with golden boots."
    His mother poured down blood, which drenched her
      breast,
From her eyelashes. When news came : "That Light
Of empire is bedimmed, the atheling,
Talhand, hath died on saddle-back and left
To Gav his seat upon the throne of kingship,"
She hurried to the palace of Talhand,
And ofttimes dashed her head against its walls.
She rent her raiment, tore her cheeks, flung fire
On hall and treasury, and burnt up all
The palace and the throne of majesty.
Thereafter she upreared a mighty pyre
To burn herself, as is the use of Hind,
And by her sorrow illustrate its Faith.
    When tidings of his mother came to Gav
He urged his speedy charger on and came,
Embraced her closely, and entreated her,

With blood upon his eyelids, saying thus :—
" O loving mother ! hearken to my words,
Because we have transgressed not in this fight.
It was not I or my companions,
Or warrior of this noble host, that slew him.
None durst breathe harshly on him : he was slain
Beneath the process of his evil star."
His mother answered him : " Thou wicked man !
On thee will come high heaven's malison ;
Thy brother hast thou slain for crown and throne,
And no good man will call thee fortunate."
" O loving mother ! " thus he answered her,
" Thou oughtest not to think such ill of me,
But be content and I will tell thee all
The case of king and host and battlefield,
For who would dare to go to fight with him ?
Who ever contemplated such dispute ?
Now by the Judge that fashioned sun and moon,
Night, day, and all the process of the sky,
The signet-ring and throne, the steed and mace,
The sword and crown, shall see me never more
Unless I clear this matter up, and turn
Thy heart from harshness into tenderness,
By proving to thy clear soul that the hand
Of none hath put a period to his life.
What man in all the world can 'scape from death,
Though he be clad upon with steel and helm ?
C. 1744   For when the bright lamp faileth none may count
Another breath however brave he be.
If what I prove to thee content thee not,
By God, the Lord of all, my purpose is
To burn my body in the fire and gladden
My foemen's souls."
                              On hearing this, his mother
Had ruth upon his form majestical,
Lest that young hero should consume in fire

His body barely handselled of its soul,
And therefore said to him : " Show me the way
That prince Talhand died on his elephant.
Unless the matter be made clear to me
My fond heart still will burn."

                  Gav sought his palace
In sorrow, summoned his experienced sage,
Told what had passed and how his mother's words
Had angered him until he swore to burn.
They sat down and took counsel by themselves.
The sage spake thus : " My gracious sovereign !
We cannot by ourselves achieve thy wish.
Call we the famed and wise, both old and young,
Among the shrewdest seekers of the way
From every side—Kashmir, Dambar, Margh, Mái."
   Gav sent off cavaliers to every quarter,[1]
Wherever there was any sage of leading.
They all came to the portal of the king,
Came to that famous court.   He held a session
Of wise men and of magnates learned and shrewd.
Gav's sage described the battlefield and how
The prince and host had fought.   They all conversed
With that sharp-witted man about the sea,
About the trench and letting in the water.
That darksome night not one among them slept,
But all held talk together.   When the din
Of kettledrum ascended from the plain
Those men of wisdom called for ebony,
And two of them—ingenious councillors—
Constructed of that wood a board foursquare
To represent the trench and battlefield,
· And with both armies drawn up face to face.
A hundred squares were traced upon the board,
So that the kings and soldiers might manœuvre.
Two hosts were carved of teak and ivory,

                [1] Reading with P.

And two proud kings with crowns and Grace divine.
Both horse and foot were represented there,
And drawn up in two ranks in war-array,
The steeds, the elephants, the ministers,
And warriors charging at the enemy,
All combating as is the use in war,
One in offence, another in defence.
The king was posted at the army's centre,
With at one hand his loyal minister.

C. 1745   Next to the twain were placed two elephants,
Supporting thrones the hue of indigo.
Next to the elephants two camels stood,
Whereon two men of holy counsel sat.
Next to the camels there were placed two steeds,
With riders valiant on the day of battle,
And each wing ended in a warrior-rukh,
His liver's blood a-foam upon his lips.
The footman's move was always to advance,
That he might be of aidance in the fray,
Till, having passed across the battlefield,
He sat—a minister—beside the king ;
The minister might quit not too in battle
His king by more than by a single square,
While o'er three squares the noble elephant
Could move and for two miles survey the field.
The camel likewise moved three squares and raged
And snorted on the field of fight.   The horse
Made too a three squares' move, but in the move
Alighted on a square of diverse hue.
The warrior-rukh might traverse every way,
And charge across the battle at his will.
They all contended in their proper lists,
And each observed the limits of his move.
When one of them beheld the king in fight,
Then would he shout and say : " Avaunt, O king ! "
Whereat the king would change his square till he

Was straitened where he stood. When rukh and horse,
And minister and elephant and troops,
Had blocked the way for him on every side
The king would look forth o'er that field foursquare,
And see his men o'erthrown, their faces lined,
Escape cut off by water and by trench,
With foes to right and left and front and rear,
And being moveless and fordone would die,[1]
For so the process of the heaven decreed.

   King Gav, the great and good, affected much
The game of chess suggested through Talhand ;
His mother studied it. Her heart was filled
With anguish for that prince. Both night and day
She sat possessed by passion and by pain,
With both her eyes intent upon the game.
Her whole desire and purpose centred there ;
Her mind was full of anguish for Talhand.
She kept for ever shedding tears of blood,
With chess to medicine her sufferings,
And thus she fared and neither ate nor stirred
Until her life had reached its period.

   So now my tale is done that I heard told
With other stories of the days of old.

§ 4

How Núshírwán sent Barzwí, the Leech, to Hindústán to fetch a
wondrous Drug, and how Barzwí brought back the Book of
Kalíla and Dimna

Mark what Shádán, son of Barzin, revealed—   C. 1746
A matter that till then had been concealed :—
When Núshírwán was king of kings, and may
His fame endure throughout eternity,
He sought for sages learnéd in all lore

     [1] Sháh mát (check mate).

To give a greater lustre to his court.
The whole world was beneath his sovereign rule—
The great men and the much experienced chiefs,
The doctors, with the eloquent and brave,
The interpreters, proved leaders, and withal [1]
A famous chief, the wearer of a crown.
This was Barzwí, the eloquent physician,
An orator and stricken well in years,
A man proficient in each branch of learning,
And for each branch acclaimed throughout the world.
One day Barzwí at audience-time drew near
The famous king, and said : " O Sháh, the friend
Of knowledge, apt to seek it and retain !
I scanned with heed an Indian scroll to-day,
And there within 'twas written : ' On the mountains
Of Hind there is a herb like Rúman silk,
Which if the expert shall collect, prepare
According unto knowledge, and then strew
Upon the body of one dead, the corpse,
Good sooth, forthwith will speak.'   Now if the king
Permit I will adventure this hard journey,
And, with much lore to guide me on my way,
Achieve perchance this wondrous enterprise.
'Tis fitting that the dead should come to life
When Núshírwán is monarch of the world."
    The Sháh made answer : " Hardly this may be,
But ne'er the less the endeavour should be made.
Convey my letter thither to the Rája,
And look upon the attractions of that land.
Seek for a comrade in the enterprise,
As well as wakeful fortune's comradeship.
Thou wilt reveal some wonder to the world,
Because the words are enigmatical.
Bear to the Rája worthy offerings,
For doubtless he must furnish thee with guides."

<hr>

[1] Reading with P.

Then Núshírwán unlocked his treasury,
And of the havings that are fit for kings [1]—
Dínárs, brocade, silks, beaver-skins, and signets,
Crowns, musk, and spicery, with armlets too,   C. 1747
With royal jewelry, and torques and earrings—
He had three hundred camel-loads made ready.
The envoy left the presence and, on reaching
The Rája, gave the letter, and unpacked
The bales before him, who, when he had read
The letter of the Sháh, said thus : " Good sir !
Hath not my wealth been given by Núshírwán ?
Our persons, troops, and royal treasuries
Are one. 'Twere not strange if the pious world-lord,
By reason of his justice, throne, and Grace,
His splendid fortune and his high achievement,
Should raise the dead. The Brahmans on the moun-
    tains
Are all at thy dispose. My minister,
An idol-worshipper of high degree,
My noble treasurer and hoarded wealth,
With Hindústán and all its good and ill,
And all my power o'er great and small, are thine."
    They lodged the envoy with magnificence
Hard by the Rája as his rank required,
Providing him with provand, tapestries,
With dainty raiment and with carpetings.
All night the Rája held talk with the priests,
The great men of Kannúj and with the sages,
And when the daylight showed above the hills,
And when the world-illuming Lamp appeared,
He called the learned physicians and all those
Best qualified by knowledge to advise,
And bade them wait upon the learned Barzwí
To hear his statement. All the erudite,
Adept in leechcraft, went to him and, when

[1] Reading with P.

He set forth to the mountains, fared with him.
Barzwí roamed all the mountain-tops afoot,
Companioned by his learnéd guides, and culled]
The divers herbs—the dry, the succulent,
The withered, and the flourishing,   He brayed
Herbs succulent and dry of every kind,
And spread them on the dead, but none revived |
For any herb, and verily it seemed
That all the virtue had gone out of them.
The company roamed all the heights afoot,
But had no fruit from travail, and Barzwí
Then understood : " This task is for the King
That liveth and that reigneth evermore."
　　Thoughts of the Sháh, of those illustrious chiefs,
And that long journey, moved his heart to shame.
He thought too of the wealth that he had brought,
And was concerned at all his senseless talk.
He was chagrined about the scroll and said :—
" Why did that ignorant and stupid man
Write in his folly and his levity
That which produceth travail and foul words ? "

C. 1748　　Thereafter he addressed those sages thus :—
" Ye chiefs experienced and worshipful !
Know ye of one more learnéd than yourselves,
One eminent in every company ? "　　　　　`
　　The troop of sages said with one accord :—
" There dwelleth here a very ancient man,[1]
Surpassing us in wisdom and in years,
And in his knowledge besting every chief."
　　Thereat Barzwí said to those men of Hind :—
" Ye men of high renown and ardent soul !
Exert yourselves yet more on my behalf,
And point me out the way to him.   Perchance
That eloquent old sage may succour me
In this affair."
　　　　　They led Barzwí to him,

　　　　　　[1] Reading with P.

Full of solicitude, with much to say.
Now when Barzwí, that man of eloquence,
Approached the sage and told all his own toils,
About the writing that he had discovered,
And of the experts' words, the ancient sage
Replied, informing him at large, and said :—
"We in those writings found the selfsame thing,
We too were instant in the same desire.
Now will I tell thee our discovery :
The noble heart must hear to understand.
The herb then is the sage, the mountain know-
    ledge,
As being ever distant from the throng ;
The corpse the man whose knowledge is to seek,
Because the unwise are kill-joys everywhere.
In sooth 'tis knowledge that doth make men live ;
Blest is the constant toiler for its sake.
When men are stupefied through ignorance [1]
Kalíla [2] is the herb, and understanding
The mountain.   In the monarch's treasury,
On making quest there, thou wilt find a book
Of knowledge that will point thee out the way."
    Barzwí, when he had heard, rejoiced thereat,
And all his travail seemed like wind to him.
He blessed the sage and sped back to the king,
Like fire.   Arrived he praised the Rája, saying :—
"Live thou while Hind shall last.   There is a
    book,
O potent Rája ! that in Indian
Is called Kalíla.[3]   It is under seal,
And fondly treasured in the monarch's hoards—
A guide-book both to knowledge and to counsel.
Kalila is the herb in mystic parlance ;
So now, O king of Hind 1 be thou mine aid,

---

[1] Reading with P.
[2] Being, like the sage, a teacher of knowledge.
[3] Reading with P.

And, if I be not troublesome, command
Thy treasurer to hand the book to me."
   The Rája's soul was sad at that request,
He writhed upon his throne and answered thus
Barzwí : "No one has sought of us this thing
In times of yore or in these latter days.
However if the world-lord Núshírwán
Shall ask of me my body or my soul

C. 1749

I will withhold not from him aught that is
In being whether high or low ; albeit
Thou shalt peruse it not save in my presence,
That spirits ill-disposed to me may say not
Within their hearts : 'Some one hath copied it.'
So read and learn and mark it every way."
   Barzwí made answer thus and said : "O king !
Thou hast expressed my whole intent herein."
   The Rája's minister then brought Kalila ;
Barzwí perused it with a sage's help,
And, as he read each chapter of the book,
He spent the day in learning it by heart,
For, having read as much as he could learn,
He read no further till the morrow came,
But, writing to the monarch of the world,
Sent privily a chapter of Kalila.
The Indians' book by this expedient
Was introduced to royal Núshírwán,
What while Barzwí continued hale and happy,
By laving thus his ardent soul in knowledge,
Until the answer to his letters came :—
"The Sea of Lore hath come to hand for us."
   Then from his palace he approached the Rája
To ask for leave to go.   At that request
The Rája graciously entreated him,
And had prepared an Indian robe of honour—
Two valuable armlets and two earrings,
A torque of jewels worthy of a king,

An Indian turban and an Indian sword,
Whereof the blade was watered steel.   Barzwí
Came from Kannúj, rejoicing, having gained
Much knowledge there.   On his return to court
He went before the Sháh and did obeisance,
Then told about his converse with the Rája,
How knowledge had been found instead of herbs.
The Sháh replied : " O man approved in all !
Kalíla hath restored my soul to life.
Take from my treasurer my treasury's key,
And make thy choice according to thy needs."
    So to the treasury the sage departed,
But gave small trouble to the treasurer.[1]
There drachms and jewels lay to left and right,
And yet he chose him but a royal robe,
Put on that costly raiment and went forth
Back to the court of Núshírwán in haste.
When he approached the throne he did obeisance,
And praised the king, who said : · " O man of toils !
Why hast thou left the treasury and brought
No purses with thee and no royal gems,
For treasure is the meed of them that travail ? "
    Barzwí replied : " O thou whose crown is higher
Than   sun   and   moon !   the   wearer   of   king's
        raiment
Hath access to the crown and throne of might,
And furthermore, when people shall behold   C. 1750
Mine own unworthy self in royal robes,
My foes' hearts will be strait and overcast,
My   friends'   cheeks   keep   their   lustre   and   their
        bloom.
Still there is somewhat I would ask the king
That I may leave my memory in the world—
Let Búzurjmihr, when copying the book,
Show favour to Barzwí's endeavourment,

---

[1] Reading with P.

And give account of me in Chapter One,
By order of the conquering king, that so,
When I am dead, my travailing may be
Forgot not by the sages in the world."
    "A great thing this to ask!" the Sháh replied,
" And one beyond the licence of a liege,
And yet thy labour hath deserved as much,
Although thy standing warranteth it not."
    Then said the Sháh to Búzurjmihr : " This wish
Of his is not to be ignored."
                                        So when
The fashioning of pen from kex was done
The scribe wrote of Barzwí in Chapter One.
    As for the royal book which thus was writ
'Twas in the script of bygone centuries ;
    Among the royal hoards men treasured it,
But 'twas beheld not by unworthy eyes.
    It was perused not, till the people took
To Arabic, save in the ancient tongue ;
But when Mámún had made earth fresh and young
    He dealt in other fashion with the book,
For he had clerkly lore, was politic
    In kingly wise, and learned in every way.
'Twas then translated into Arabic,
    Just as thou mayest hear it read to-day.
In Arabic, till Nasr was king, it stayed ;
    Then noble Abú'l Fazl, his minister
    And, in respect to lore, his treasurer,
Gave orders, which were readily obeyed,[1]
For folk to speak in Persian and Dari.[2]
Thereafter precedent and policy
Conducted Nasr in wisdom's way when he
Was fain by whatsoever means might be
To leave within the world his memory.

---

[1] " mais son pouvoir fut de courte durée " (Mohl).
[2] The more ornate Persian used at court.

They held a session with interpreters,
Who read the whole book out to Rúdagí.[1]
That poet linked the scattered words in verse,
And threaded[2] thus those pregnant pearls, that he
Who is a scholar might new graces find,
And one unlearnéd more facility,
For words in prose escape us, but combined
In metric guise possess the brain and mind.
Life to Mahmúd, the world's great potentate !
May earth and time as slaves before him wait,
How it would joy the heart if but the bad
From Sháh Mahmúd less free allowance had !
Yet be not thou concerned thereat.   Anon,
Since life is far advanced, thou must be gone.
Thou hast thine ups and downs from day to day,   C. 1751
At whiles assistance and at whiles dismay ;
But neither of them will for aye remain
With thee ; the hope of tarriance here is vain.

---

[1] Rúdakí in the original.   [2] Literally " pierced."

INDEX

This Index and the Table of Contents at the beginning of the volume are complementary. References to the latter are in Roman numerals.

Bahrám Gúr, Sháh (Varahran V),
vii *seq.* 3 *seq.*, 160, 164,
165, 170 and *note*, 174, 178,
187, 334, 359
Reign of, 3 *seq.*
Note on, 3 *seq.*
length of, 3
largely legendary, 3
character of, 3
resembles James V of
Scotland, 3
ministers of, 4
his war with Rúm, 4, 5
adventures of, vii *seq.*, 4,
12 *seq.*
his historical defeat of the
Haitálians 4, 5
his alleged reduction of taxa-
tion in consequence, 5
accession of, 7
holds his court for eight
days, 7 *seq.*
summons Jawánwí, 8
holds three days' festivities,
10
rewards Nu'mán and Munzir,
10
honours Khusrau, 10
makes Narsi captain of the
host, 11
burns the registers of taxes,
11
applauded by the folk, 11
restores the nobles exiled by
his father to their honours,
11
makes proclamation to the
people, 12, 79, 82
forbids wine-drinking, 23
allows wine-drinking again,
25
his whip, 47, 54, 63, 64
his equipage for the chase,
48, 76
loses and finds his tughral,
49, 50
his visit to Barzín, 49 *seq.*

Bahrám Gúr, marries Barzín's
daughters, 53
hunting-feats of, 54, 55, 77,
80, 81
visits a jeweller, 56 *seq.*
his course of life bewailed by
Rúzbih, 56
his many wives, 56
asks and obtains Árzú in
marriage, 61 *seq.*
his visit to Farshídward,
68 *seq.*
goes hunting, 76 *seq.*
forbids all plundering, 79
ear-marks and brands ona-
gers, 81
remits the tribute of Barkúh.
and Jaz, 82
visits Baghdád, 83
holds revel at Baghdád, 83
goes to Istakhr, 83, 95
reproaches Rúzbih for parsi-
mony, 83
reported to be given up to
pleasure, 84
reproached by his chiefs, 84
his secret preparations against
the Khán, 85
summons his chiefs, 85
levies a host, 86
makes Narsi regent, 86
goes to Ázar Ábádagán, 86,
94
his march to Marv against
the Khán, 89
defeats the Khán at Kashmi-
han, 90, 170 *note*
marches on Bukhárá, 90
defeats the Turkmans, 91
grants peace to the Turkmans,
91
his boundary-pillar, 92, 160,
161, 164
makes Shahra ruler of Túrán,
92
makes gifts of treasure, 95,
96

M

MADÁ'IN, Ctesiphon (Taisafún), and the neighbouring cities, xi, 201, 244, 266, 272, 337, 363
Núshírwán sends his Rúman captives to, 259
Magi, 171, 184
Magian, Magians, 60
chant, 60
fire, 409
Máh Áfríd, daughter of Barzin, 53
married to Bahrám Gúr, 53
Mahbúd (Mebodes), minister of Kubád, xii, 213, 316 *seq.*
instrumental in making Núshirwán Sháh, 316
fall of, 317, 322
Núshírwán's repentance with regard to, 317, 325
Núshírwán's treasurer, 319
his sons, 319
serve Núshírwán's meals, 319, 321
his wife prepares Núshírwán's food, 321, 222
envied by Zúrán, 319
Máhiyár, Íránian noble, 38
praises Bahrám Gúr, 38
Máhiyár, a jeweller, viii, 55 *seq.*
his daughter. *See* Árzú.
and his daughter entertain Bahrám Gúr, 59 *seq.*
Mahmúd, Sultán, 277, 431
Máhwi (= Sháhwí ?), one of Firdausí's authorities, 382
Mái, city between the Oxus and Bukhárá? 91, 331, 385, 421
Mái, king of Hind, 395, 396, 399, 401, 403, 404
Makrán (Gedrosia, Balúchistán), 390
Malcolm, Sir John, 6
Mámún, Khalifa, 382, 430

Máni, heresiarch, 188
Mansúr, son of Núh, Sámánid, 5
Margh, city between the Oxus and Bukhárá? 91, 331, 412, 421
Mars, planet, 92, 252, 418
Marv, city and district, 88 *seq.*, 174, 357
as rhyme-word, 88 *note*
the Khán reaches, 88
Bahrám Gúr marches on, 89
Azád Sarv finds Búzurjmihr at, 283
Mas'údi, historian, 3, 4, 6, 153, 280
his account of the fortifications at Darband, 215
on the game of nard, 382
chess, 382
Mázandarán, 215
Mazdak, heresiarch, x, 184, 185, 188
his disputation with Núshírwán, 188, 206 *seq.*
account of, 188, 201
becomes chief minister to Kubád, 201
his influence over Kubád, 201
his parable to Kúbad in time of drought, 201
his practical application of Kubád's reply, 202
converts Kubád, 204
his preaching and practice, 204
his attempt to convert Núshirwán, 205
Kubád decides against, 208
and his followers executed by Núshírwán, 208
Mazdakism, 184
Mazdakites, 184
massacre of, 185, 208
great assembly of, 205
Mebodes. *See* Mahbúd.

about 100 miles above, and rejoining it about 100 miles below, Baghdád, 141

Nard, game of, xiii, 5, 389 *seq.*
  invention of, 280, 381, 382, 389
  sent by Núshírwán to the Rája of Hind, 5, 381
  meaning of, 381
  symbolism of, 381
  Mas'údi on, 382
  described, 389

Narsi, brother of Bahrám Gúr, viii, 4, 95, 100
  made captain of the host, 11
  regent, 86
  fails to persuade the Íránians to resist the Khán, 87
  Bahrám Gúr's letter to, 92
  writes to Bahrám Gúr on behalf of the Íránians, 94
  goes with the chiefs to welcome Bahrám Gúr, 96
  made ruler of Khurásán, 99
  welcomes his brother on his return from Hind, 137

Narsi, Sháh, 359

Nasr, son of Ahmad, Sámánid, 383, 430
  patron of Rúdagí, 383

Nau-Ardshír = Nard, 381

Naudar, Sháh, 37, 171

Náztáb, a miller's daughter, 32 and *note*
  taken to wife by Bahrám Gúr, 33

Nero, Emperor, 279

Nestorian Metropolitan, 219
  Patriarch, 219

Nile, river, 48, 250, 344, 416

Nímrúz,[1] 327

Nisá, city in Khurásán, 89

Nöldeke, Professor, 6
  on the Gipsies, 6
  on Súfarai, 171, 185

Nöldeke, on Wisdom-literature, 281

North, Sir Thomas, 383
  his version of the *F*ables of Bidpai, 383

Note on Pronunciation, xviii
  Prefatory, v

Núh, son of Nasr, Sámánid, 5

Nu'mán, prince of Hira, vii, 10
  rewarded by Bahrám Gúr, 10

Núshírwán (Kisrá, Chosroes I), Sháh, x *seq.*, 4, 199, 200, 220, 273 *seq.*, 279 *seq.*, 320, 423 *seq.*
  origin of name, 185, 211 and *note*
  birth of, stories of, 186, 197 *seq.*
  his assistants against Mazdak, 188, 206
  upbringing of, 200
  Mazdak's attempt to convert, 205
  his disputation with Mazdak, 206 *seq.*
  Kubád decides in favour of, 208
  executes Mazdak and his followers, 208
  Kubád's testament in favour of, 210, 316
  Reign of, 212 *seq.*
    Notes on, 212 *seq.*, 279 *seq.*, 316 *seq.*, 380 *seq.*
  Roman Emperors contemporary with, 212
  historical events of his reign in the Sháhnáma, 213
  his marriage with the daughter of the Khán, 213, 317, 347 *seq.*
  his wars with Rúm, 213, 217
    first campaign of, 217, 218, 249

[1] See Vol. i. p. 396 *note.*

Rúmiya (New Antioch), 218
Rúshan Pirúz, city, 160
Rustam, Íránian hero, 151
Rúzbih, Bahrám Gúr's high
   priest, vii, 26 *seq.*, 54, 67
   bewails Bahrám Gúr's course
   of life, 56
   reproached by Bahrám Gúr
   for his parsimony, 83

S

SADA, feast of, 11, 94, 200
Sáda, Íránian noble, 312
Sakláb (Slavonia), 112, 115, 364
Salm, son of Farídún, 101
Sám, Íránian hero, 74
Sámánid, Sámánids, 5, 383
Samarkand (Sughd), city and
   district in Turkistán, 167,
   358, 359
Sandal, Sandali, city in Hind, 140,
   395, 396, 401 *seq.*
   king of, entertained by Bah-
   rám Gúr, 140 *seq.*
Sanscrit, 382
Sapínúd, daughter of Shangul,
   128 *seq.*, 144
   married to Bahrám Gúr, 128
   finds out who her husband
   is, 131
   plans Bahrám Gúr's flight
   from Hind, 132
   reproached by Shangul, 135
   converted to Zoroastrianism,
   139
   visited by Shangul, 142
Sarí, city in Mázandarán, 237
Sar-i-pul-i-Zohab, place, 187
Sarkhán. *See* Súfarai.
Sarúch, desert in Kirmán, 362
Sásánian, Sásánians, 85, 185, 212,
   237, 381
   dynasty, vii, 1 *seq.*
Saturn, planet 92, 151, 252, 267,
   346, 418

Seneca, the younger, Nero's tutor,
   279
Seoses, Persian commander-in-
   chief, 187
Seven, favourite number in Per-
   sian story, 186, 280
   Banquets of Núshírwán, 280
   possible origin of, 280
   planets, 382, 408
   symbolised in the game
   of nard, 382
Shabdíz, Bahrám Gúr's steed, 37,
   80
Shabrang, Bahrám Gúr's steed,
   55
Shádán, one of Firdausí's autho-
   rities, 382, 423
Sháhnáma, 5, 156, 184, 185, 215,
   217, 317, 381
   Wisdom-literature in, 278
   seq.
Shahra, chief, viii, 92
   made king of Túrán by
   Bahrám Gúr, 92
Shahrám-Pirúz. *See* Bádán Pirúz.
Shahrivar, month and day, 76
Sháhwí (= Máhwi?), one of Fir-
   dausí's authorities, 382,
   394
Shakespeare, 383
   quoted, 383
Shambalíd, daughter of Barzin,
   53
   married to Bahrám Gúr, 53
Shammás, Núshzád's general,
   219, 272
Shangul, king of Hind, viii, ix,
   109 *seq.*
   his border-raids, 110
   gives audience to the Íránian
   envoy (Bahrám Gúr), 112
   his state described, 112
   his brother, 113
   his son, 113, 115
   on his own greatness, 114
   his wife the daughter of the
   Faghfúr, 115

Wisdom-literature, Persian, 278 *seq.*
Mohl on, 280
Nöldeke on, 281
Wízagird, city in Túrán, 157, 331
Wizard-land, 120 and *note*
Wolf, viii, 121 *seq.* and *note*
slain by Bahrám Gúr, 123

Y

YAMAN, 262
Yasht XXII, metrical paraphrase of, 318
Yátkár-i-Zarírán, Pahlavi text, 380
Yazdagird, son of Shápúr, (Isdegird I), Sháh, 4, 10, 109, 119, 171, 185, 359
referred to, 74
Yazdagird, son of Bahrám Gúr, (Isdegird II), Sháh, ix, 4, 152, 156, 160, 187
welcomes his father on his return from Hind, 137
appointed by Bahrám Gúr to succeed him, 150
Reign of, 153 *seq.*
Note on, 153
a blank in Sháhnáma, 153
historically important, 153
wars of, 153
fortifies passes in the Caucasus, 153, 187
his title, 153
his sons, 153
appoints Hurmuz to succeed him, 155

Yazdagird, dies, 155
Yazdagird, chief scribe *temp.*
Núshírwán, 304, 307, 312, 333, 337, 339, 394
discourse of, 305
questions Búzurjmihr, 308
Yokel, a, vii
entertains Bahrám Gúr, 43 *seq.*
wife of, her converse with Bahrám Gúr, 45
her presage, 46
rewarded by Bahrám Gúr, 48

Z

ZÁBULISTÁN,[1] 173, 174, 193
Zahhák, Sháh, 185, 199
Zam, river and city (between Tirmid and Ámwi?), 359
Zandavasta, 200, 207, 283, 302
passage from, metrically paraphrased, 318
Zarduhsht (Zarathushtra, Zoroaster), 9, 207, 264, 318
Fire-fane of, 139
high priest of, converts Sapínúd, 139
Zarmihr. *See* Rizmihr.
Zíb-i-Khusrau, city, xi, 259
Zirih, son of Sháh Pirúz, 170
Zoroastrianism, 188, 317
Zúrán, Núshírwán's chamberlain, xii, 319 *seq.*
envies Mahbúd, 319
plots with a Jew against Mahbúd, 320 *seq.*
makes confession to Núshírwán, 324

[1] See Vol. i. p. 396 *note.*

END OF VOL. VII.

Printed by BALLANTYNE, HANSON & Co.
Edinburgh & London

CPSIA information can be obtained
at www.ICGtesting.com
Printed in the USA
LVOW13s0113090917

548119LV00021B/1136/P